Ethical Life in South Asia

Ethical Life in South Asia

Edited by Anand Pandian and Daud Ali

Indiana University Press
Bloomington and Indianapolis

This book is a publication of

Indiana University Press
601 North Morton Street
Bloomington, Indiana 47404-3797 USA

www.iupress.indiana.edu

Telephone orders 800-842-6796
Fax orders 812-855-7931
Orders by e-mail iuporder@indiana.edu

∞ The paper used in this publication meets the minimum requirements of the American National Standard for Information Sciences—Permanence of Paper for Printed Library Materials, ANSI Z39.48-1992.

Manufactured in the United States of America

Library of Congress Cataloging-in-Publication Data

Ethical life in South Asia / Edited by Anand Pandian and Daud Ali.
p. cm.
Includes bibliographical references and index.
ISBN 978-0-253-35528-7 (cloth : alk. paper) — ISBN 978-0-253-22243-5 (pbk. : alk. paper)
1. Social ethics—South Asia. 2. Social values—South Asia. 3. Religion and ethics—South Asia. 4. South Asia—Moral conditions. 5. South Asia—Social conditions. I. Pandian, Anand. II. Ali, Daud.
HN670.3.Z9M647 2010
170.954—dc22

2010009385

1 2 3 4 5 15 14 13 12 11 10

Contents

Acknowledgments

This volume grows out of an international workshop on the subject of South Asian ethical practices, held in Vancouver, Canada, in September 2007. The workshop was funded by the Peter Wall Institute for Advanced Studies (PWIAS) and the Center for India and South Asia Research (CISAR), both at the University of British Columbia (UBC), and we are immensely grateful to these institutions for their generosity and vision in enabling us to organize this event. In particular, we would like to thank PWIAS director Dianne Newell, as well as Jenny MacKay and Markus Pickartz, for facilitating the planning and execution of the workshop. We are equally grateful to CISAR director Ashok Kotwal for his enthusiastic support and encouragement of the venture. We would like to thank the Institute of Asian Research and the Department of Asian Studies at UBC for essential assistance with the event, as well as our colleagues and well-wishers at UBC—Ashok Aklujkar, Mandakranta Bose, Tirthankar Bose, Katherine Hacker, Renisa Mawani, Jisha Menon, Harjot Oberoi, John Roosa, and Adheesh Sathaye—for lending their support and insights to these discussions. We are grateful to Lauren Leve, Rakesh Pandey, and Avril Powell for joining us in Vancouver and sharing their work with workshop participants. The event itself would have come to nothing without the meticulous and indefatigable assistance of our workshop organizer, Noushin

Khushrushahi. We are thankful, too, to Bonar Buffam for his detailed notes concerning the proceedings.

In the months that followed the workshop, as we moved forward to plan an edited volume building on the papers presented, Rebecca Tolen at Indiana University Press proved a crucial supporter and interlocutor. We remain grateful for her editorial guidance, and for the able assistance of Laura MacLeod, Peter Froehlich, and June Silay at the press. Lastly, we would be remiss if we failed to thank our contributors themselves, who have endured with patience and good humor the countless rounds of baiting, nudging, and prodding to which we have submitted them in the last couple of years. More than anything else, for us, this volume attests to all that we have learned from you.

Ethical Life in South Asia

Introduction

Anand Pandian and Daud Ali

Recent years have seen renewed attention in the humanities and social sciences to the subject of ethics and morality. Partly at stake here, perhaps, are the intense moral difficulties of our time: normative injunctions and models proliferate wildly in contemporary life, even as these models seem to fail with implacable persistence. As many both within the academy and without confront the limits of the moral languages and practices at our disposal—and, more troubling and compelling, the violence with which they are nonetheless imposed upon those unable to resist their force—certain challenging questions often resurface in diverse forms and arenas. How else may we conceive what it would mean to live well? Would the neglected moral insights and potentials of the past shed light on the trials of the present? Can the moral foundations of "civilization" and "modernity" be elaborated in new and ethically enabling ways?

To look elsewhere for answers is, of course, to concede to a redoubtable temptation in the midst of crisis. And, indeed, South Asia has long served moral discourse in the West as such an "elsewhere." Venerable writers in the West—figures such as James Mill and G. W. F. Hegel—shored up the moral uncertainties of their own time and milieu by confronting them with the horror of their sheer absence in an imagined India. And, alternatively, many others have sought in the works and lives of the region some abiding religious, philosophical, or cultural ground for an alternative form of moral certitude and exercise. Neither of these orientations, however, is adequate to the moral complexities of the present. This volume seeks, in the ethical thought and practice of South Asia, elements with which to broaden our available languages of moral inquiry. Our approach to these materials is conceptual and heuristic: we examine the moral and ethical traditions of South Asia in their historical diversity, practical vitality, and uneven resonance with the West, with the hope that they may speak to difficult moral problems encountered both here and elsewhere.

Our effort here is oriented toward the investigation of "ethical life" in South Asia. With this phrase, we seek to move away from an understanding of morality as a matter of rules and principles, texts and codes alone: we call attention, instead, to the moral dispositions at work in lived experience, and the embodied practices of ethical engagement through which such dispositions may be cultivated and shared. One durable name for such practices is "virtue," and throughout this volume we seek to open up an engagement with the quotidian pleasures of—and desires for—a virtuous life, as they resonate with diverse traditions of moral thought and exercise. At the same time we also seek to account for the social and historical conditions under which such ethical pleasures and desires arise. We aim to work toward a history of the moral present in South Asia: an accounting of how individual lives and collective forms in the region came to assume their moral valence and tendency. Contributions to this volume are concerned with the traditions that make moral thought and action possible in the region, and also with the conditions under which such forms of ethical life may surface, struggle, and evanesce. Working between history, anthropology, religious studies, and philosophy, we put South Asian traditions of virtuous conduct into conversation with the Aristotelian, Christian, and liberal political traditions that have been so consequential for ethical life in the West.

That said, however, we should also stress at the very outset that many of these framing terms—such as tradition and virtue, for example—are both explored and exceeded by the contributions to this volume. Though many of these essays chart the lineaments of those traditions that sustain durable forms of ethical self-conduct, others tackle disruptive moral "events" whose outcomes remain unknown, whose horizons are uncertain. Although some essays carefully attend to particular moral qualities and dispositions, others investigate moral practices and ethical orientations that resist being named as recognizable virtues. We take these forms of surplus as illuminating and productive. They attest to the ethical itself as a domain of excess, not simply because of the familiar problem of moral failure—the gap between ideals and their realization, between what "is" and what "ought" to be—but also because the ethical might be taken to name the very ground upon which commitments to oneself and to others are made and unmade.

Ultimately, then, we aim not to identify ways of closing the gap between the given and the good more precisely or effectively but rather to explore and nurture the more vital and desirable forms this gap may take: to convey ethical life as a reflexive practice of "freedom," as Foucault argued, from the known and the given.[1] This volume seeks to open consonant analytical and practical horizons with respect to social, cultural, and historical experience in South Asia. A focus on ethical life—on the ways in which people practically engage themselves and their worlds as beings invested with moral potential—provides a supple means of grappling with the complex and variegated moral and political possibilities of the present. We, as editors, have drawn great inspiration in this enterprise from our contributors themselves, but let us first pause for a moment and examine more closely some of the ways in which these matters have been considered thus far.

Questions of Ethics in the Human Sciences

Over many years and in disparate contexts, "ethics" has been specified in divergent ways: as a code of moral duties or a matter of manners and social customs; as a practice of self-conduct or a way of living well with and for others; as a domain of aesthetics, skill, and virtuous exercise, or a claim upon or address to another. One might begin an investigation of these distinctions within the domain of philosophy, where ethics has resurfaced as a subject of great interest in recent years. Bernard Williams makes a useful distinction between "ethics" and "morality" as different strands of moral philosophy. Although these two concepts have complex and intertwined histories in Europe that cannot easily be disentangled, Williams makes the point that over time the term "morality" came to have a quite distinctive meaning in Western modernity—what he calls "a particular development of the ethical."[2] Williams proposes ethics as the answer one might give to the general question, "How ought one to live?" How, in other words, could one most generally and most comprehensively direct one's life in accordance with certain principles through practices of enquiry, reflection, and self-conduct? Morality, on the other hand, for Williams, concerns matters of a far more limited provenance: the choice to obey or disobey commandments and prescriptions, that is, the decision to do good or evil.

This argument for ethics as a domain more expansive than that of morality may be understood as part of a wider endeavor to engage, and in some instances rehabilitate, ethical traditions displaced in the West by the rise of Enlightenment humanism. Consider, for example, Immanuel Kant, who asserted that properly ethical thought was ideal, universal, and rational: it applied to all humans regardless of their social status and in all situations despite any particularity, sanctioned by the a priori presence of universal moral imperatives arising from human rationality itself.[3] For Kant, moral consideration formed an "inner domain" of man's being, standing in opposition to, and ultimately transcending, its "outside": the diverse situations that any human moral agent faced in social life. This must be understood not simply as a neutral demarcation but, instead, as a polemical effort to exclude various traditions of pre-humanistic ethics—often deeply particularistic in the diverse moral orientations they elicited, as we discuss in further detail below—from the ambit of what Kant deemed as the properly ethical. Ethical practices that did not take the form of volitional choice vis-à-vis questions of right and wrong, such as ascetic practices, manners, etiquette, and rhetoric, for example, were problematic from this viewpoint.

The triumph of Kantian humanist and "enlightened" ethics was part of a much wider historical defeat, both institutionally and ideologically, of *anciens régimes* in Europe and the cultural practices associated with them. Indeed, the humanist critique of pre-Enlightenment ethical practices turned on their association with the purported duplicity and tyranny of aristocratic and ecclesiastical institutions. A series of related historical and ideological developments in Europe—the rise of print media, capitalist classes, liberal ideas of enlightened self-interest, and new concepts of political contract—all variously helped to dismantle the religious and sociopolitical institutions that had supported earlier traditions of ethical conduct in the West. The modern triumph of Kant's interiorization of ethical practice, and the apotheosis of altruism as marker of the authentically ethical, occurred at the same time that public institutions were bureaucratically rationalized and the public pursuit of individual self-interest became the ideological cornerstone of liberal society. In other words, the interiorization, universalization, and simplification of ethics in post-Kantian morality must be seen in the context of the realignment of much of human activity—in individual, collective, and institutional life in the modern West—in accordance with principles that might otherwise seem to undercut ethics itself.

For many contemporary philosophers, theorists, and critics struggling with this legacy, the triumph of Kantian ethics has been tantamount to a great diminishment and attenuation of ethical concern, almost to the point of an idealistic irrelevancy. Many have sought, therefore, to reexamine pre-humanistic ethical traditions. Alasdair MacIntyre, for example, has argued that the Aristotelian tradition of the virtues—taken as cultivated dispositions toward the good, and sustained by bodies of moral argumentation, practices of virtuous conduct, and narratives of a potential selfhood—offers hope for a renewed ethics suitable for modern conditions of existence.[4] The later work of Michel Foucault also turned quite significantly to the ethical practices of Greco-Roman antiquity, distinguishing these "technologies" or "care of the self" from code-based moralities founded upon moral rules and their social enforcement.[5] For Foucault, these ethics-oriented moralities were primarily concerned with the types of relationship one could cultivate with himself: the myriad quotidian practices through which individuals took themselves as subjects of ethical self-conduct, and developed a particular embodied stance toward precepts, rules, and other kinds of moral orientations. Classical historian Pierre

Hadot has suggested that this orientation may veer into a kind of modernist "Dandyism"; nevertheless, Hadot also affirms that "modern man can practice the spiritual exercises of antiquity."[6] What emerges from all these disparate positions, in other words, is a more expansive sense of ethics as a practice of remaking oneself as a moral being, reaching far beyond the domain of moral rules and abstract judgments.

Many of the essays in this volume draw upon these philosophical positions to elucidate diverse aspects of ethics in South Asia, such as embodied practices of self-fashioning, durable traditions of moral orientation and exercise, and environments of moral learning and pedagogy. But these essays also suggest that these philosophical concerns may be sharpened by a closer engagement with historical and anthropological work. Consider, for example, the normative and ethical dimensions of historical transformation: the "civilizing process" in the West, for example, as it emerges from the work of Norbert Elias and his many interlocutors,[7] or the "civilizing mission" that European empires have long claimed for themselves in their colonies.[8] At the same time anthropologists have themselves insisted upon the social and cultural specificity of moral traditions and ethical practices, focusing on topics such as moral pedagogy in modern schooling or ideas of moral self-cultivation among practitioners of diverse religious traditions. In our own work on such questions—as a historian of medieval India and a cultural anthropologist of modern India—we have stressed that premodern ethical systems once viewed as determinist justifications for ascriptive social orders may be understood instead as dynamic figurations contributing to ethical sensibilities,[9] and that "the forms of welfare, modes of right conduct, and kinds of living being" at stake in modern moral conduct may also be taken as plural possibilities.[10] In particular, anthropological and historical approaches clarify three essential aspects of ethical practice: their work upon the body; the practical traditions and historical situations that sustain them; and their claims upon collective life.

In their attention to historical and cultural specificity, for example, anthropologists and historians alike have focused attention upon the body as site of ethical engagement. Talal Asad has insisted upon the interweaving of moral argumentation and embodiment: "it always invokes historical bodies, bodies placed within particular traditions, with their potentialities of feeling, of receptivity, and of suspicion."[11] To attend to the ethical body in this manner, as many of the contributors to this volume do, is to provoke a series of essential questions. Upon what aspects of the embodied subject or self—mind, heart, senses, habits, emotions, instincts, desires, or pleasures, for example—are ethics understood to work? Scholars tackling this question have identified diverse domains of moral psychology and physiology subject to ethical work: from the scrutiny of bodily gestures as mirrors of the soul in medieval Europe to the sensory cultivation of an ear for piety in contemporary Cairo.[12] One might also ask whether ethics ought to be understood as always demanding a reflective, deliberative, or rational disposition with respect to practices of moral self-conduct, or whether ethics might also accommodate an engagement with nonvolitional currents of affective and psychic force not as amenable to willful control. Here, certain scholars have emphasized the need for ratiocination in moral and religious practices of embodied self-cultivation, whereas others have focused more closely upon the ethicizing force of feelings such as humiliation and shame.[13]

To reflect upon the ethical status of the body is also to investigate how such ethics may be instantiated in habits, tendencies, and other forms of durable disposition: the "techniques of the body," as Marcel Mauss famously called them, through which bodily capacities for moral action may be cultivated, disciplined, and consolidated.[14] In many pre-humanist contexts, ethical activity was understood to consist in the acquisition and exercise of valued bodily qualities, skills, and dispositions: what might be termed "character traits" or "virtues."[15] This sort of refinement or cultivation of character and disposition has been connected with various forms of explicit bodily and mental transformation in diverse historical circumstances, often with a "technological" or disciplinary orientation. This practical character of the ethical—deeply entwined not only with learned habits and embodied tendencies but also with diverse "vocational" aptitudes in the world and the regimes of practice training them—has sat ill at ease with the "purist" interiority of humanist ethics. In many cases such techniques often took on an explicitly aesthetic dimension, in the sublime beauty of the virtuous body, for instance, or the investiture of practices of beautification and romance with worldly and divine ethical qualities.

The necessary "education" of the body[16] by means of such techniques points toward a second domain of ethical inquiry elucidated by historical and anthropological work: the moral traditions that sustain ethical practices and their diverse historical dimensions. "A living tradition is a historically extended, socially embodied argument" regarding the moral goods proper to a particular community, MacIntyre has argued, an insight borne out in numerous studies that have described the transmission of ethical practices through ongoing dialogue and argumentation over their proper cultivation, effective exercise, and desirable ends.[17] Practices of moral pedagogy—reflective, bodily, and sensory in their nature—are seen to draw forward resources of the past as lessons for the present, not through a recapitulation of the known and familiar—"as though it was the passing on of an unchanging substance," as Asad writes[18]—but rather through an adaptive and generative deployment of moral qualities, aptitudes, and dispositions. The moral learning at stake in many instances of ethical transmission then, as we have both insisted in our own previous work, is a matter of moral "cultivation": moral stories, sermons, verses, proverbs, and manuals do not simply lay down rules to follow, although this may often be the manifest form they assume, but instead put into circulation resources with which to develop a particular mode of existence.

Although such arenas of moral pedagogy may sustain the continuity of a tradition in ethical practice, they may also testify to its transformative development and displacement. Individuals and collectives of diverse sorts have navigated and negotiated transformations in prevailing moral practices and codes in disparate ways: from the English rural aristocracy's transformation of the codes of *civilité* received via the courts of Italian cities to the ways in which Melanesian Christians developed ritual strategies of Christian salvation by mobilizing traditional practices of ecstatic and willful expression.[19] We also find moral traditions transforming and evolving as they intersect and interact with one another: as when instances of conversion, for example, make possible translation of terms and practices across disparate languages, histories, and cultural contexts.[20] Such scholarship shows, in other words—and with an orientation shared by many of the essays in this volume—that the profound displacements of modern existence do not obviate the vitality of moral tradition as such but instead make possible novel and creative forms of ethical conduct.

This observation gestures toward a third domain of ethics elucidated by cultural and historical scholarship: the relation between traditions of ethical practice and particular forms of collective life. Traditions of virtue, for example, often betray an explicitly nonuniversalist tenor: differentiated constellations or scales of virtues in which not all moral subjects are expected to strive toward the same moral ends. Although such constellations may have overlapped in particular social formations, they were often rooted in differing social roles and offices, in constant relation and interaction with one another. So in early medieval Europe, for example, the qualities of the courtier were largely adapted from those of the church, particularly through the figure of the courtier-bishop.[21] The canonical works and foundational narratives of many such traditions may be traced back—as retrospective gestures of authorization often seek to do—to dialogic encounters between individual teachers and pupils and other such face-to-face relations. Subjects of ethics under modern conditions, however, must be understood in relation to more expansive and variegated forms of collective existence. Grappling with the often tense relations between adherents of an Islamic Revival in Egypt and proponents of a nationalist politics of social reform, for example, Hirschkind locates the persistence of a moral tradition of piety in "a contingent and shifting constellation of ideas, practices, and associational forms."[22]

Such scholarship sheds light on how people may come to share a moral world as ethical beings of a certain kind, as well as how the conditions of their collective existence may introduce dissension and disjuncture into their moral and ethical lives. Attending to these rival horizons of possibility, many of our contributors seek to account for the conditions under which particular ethical practices may both flourish and recede as collective orientations. Of particular interest in many of these essays are the modern agencies and institutions—states, laws, sciences, markets, and schools—designed for moral efficacy on the widest scale. How do such authoritative bodies both enable and disable operations within the field of the ethical? To address such concerns is to confront a subject of ethics always and already historical in nature, emerging from a material field of action and interaction.

At the same time, however, many of the contributors to this volume challenge the presumption that forms of collective life fully determine and confine the forms of ethical possibility at stake—the presumption that it is always a coherent subject of particular normative horizons that emerges under given cultural and historical circumstances. Charles Hallisey's essay argues, for example, that there are moral practices within a given tradition that may escape being named and known as particular virtues, and Ajay Skaria reaches toward "unthought" forms in Gandhi's moral writings and engagements foreign to Gandhi's own explicit articulation of them. It is therefore with a commitment to both specificity and openness—and to the lessons that both these perspectives may bring—that the present volume focuses on ethical practices in South Asia. A philosophical return to the ground of classical ethics in the West has mobilized new forms of historical and cultural inquiry working to elucidate the "historical ontology" of Western selfhood: the conditions under which individuals have come to pursue and inhabit the kinds of selfhood they imagine, desire, and exercise for themselves, explored with an eye to making possible other ways of being in the world.[23] Let us turn now to the moral traditions in relation to which such prospects in South Asia may be understood to gain their desirability and intelligibility.

Ethical Life in South Asia

How ought one to live? Well over two millennia of South Asian moral thought and practice have generated diverse ways of answering this question.[24] Early ascetic regimes of practice pursued release from terrestrial suffering. Later scriptures identified *dharma, artha,* and *kāma*—often translated as rectitude, prosperity, and pleasure—as the three ends of worldly existence to be attained by means of knowledge, skill, and moral refinement. Theistic religious orders incorporated these practices into larger ways of life oriented toward submission and devotion to divine lords; medieval court literatures proffered advice on the pursuit of virtue to kings, courtiers, and other men of means. The introduction of Islamic moral traditions that drew on Greek philosophy, West Asian "wisdom" literature, and the moral traditions of the Islamic community further transformed the mosaic of ethical practice in India in early medieval and medieval centuries. Between the eighteenth and the twentieth centuries

European colonialism engaged in a "civilizing" enterprise reliant upon multiple forms of moral and social pedagogy. Currents of anticolonial nationalism and Hindu revivalism in the late nineteenth century put Sanskrit textual legacies and orthodox religious codes in the service of a contrary—and often violently normative—vision of Indian collective life. And, in more recent years, economic and cultural vectors of neoliberal globalization have carried their own pressures for a moral life of civility, flexibility, and technical virtuosity.

In the face of such diverse legacies, on what terms and with what vocabularies ought we to engage the domain of ethics in South Asia? We suggest that broader lessons may be gleaned from the complex character of moral traditions and their inheritance in contemporary South Asia. It is urgent, however, that we develop a more nuanced set of theoretical tools to understand the history and character of these traditions. Prevailing approaches to the subject have been limited for a number of reasons. Many have tried to characterize moral thought in South Asia as the mirror opposite of Western philosophy and social experience, describing the ideal qualities of classical texts and social models in a historical vacuum isolated from everyday life both in the past and the present. Other writings of a revivalist or nationalist orientation have celebrated South Asian moral traditions—whether Hindu, Islamic, or otherwise—as emblems of a more desirable way of being through often naïve and decontextualized appropriations of cultural pasts for dangerous political ends. Furthermore, and for this very reason, critical scholarship by historians, social scientists, and political theorists of the region has often derided these moralities as nothing more than manipulated idioms of religious ideology and social oppression. With such concerns and dangers in mind, this volume is meant to generate a more subtle understanding of moral tradition and ethical practice in South Asia. We trace these histories of thought and conduct with the conviction that they bear a crucial significance for the current difficult struggles in South Asia and beyond.

The conversation on ethics opened by this volume, ranging across large spans of time and space within the subcontinent, is guided by the pursuit of three related aims. First, we seek to recast the history of ethics in South Asia from a prevailing concern with shifting moral rules, codes, and laws toward an attention to changing practices of self-fashioning and collective conduct. Established scholarship has focused widely on the content of normative codes and prescriptions: the historical emergence of doctrines of devotion and nonviolence, for example, or philosophical discourses on morals and ethics in Buddhist and theistic Hindu literatures. Diverse bodies of ethical discourse in South Asia, however—from the *śāstra, nīti,* and *ākhyāyika* genres in Sanskrit to the *tarikh, akhlaqi,* and *malfouz* literatures in Persian, and to the works on *aṟam, nīti* and esoteric medicine in Tamil, the *karanam* literature in Telugu, and wisdom literature and didactic narratives in nearly all regional languages—have sustained varied and shifting means by which moral prescriptions and interdictions have been put into practice. In early historic India, for example, as Vedic sacrificial practices were slowly disarticulated with the rise of ascetic religious orders, displacements were effected not only in the positive content of ethical norms but also in the ways in which individuals were encouraged to relate themselves to such norms. Doctrines of karma and rebirth, intentionality and merit (particularly its accumulation and transfer), encouraged moral subjects to establish entirely new kinds of ethical relationships with moral codes—and, ultimately, with themselves—even as certain kinds of prescriptions had remained in place.

One significant way of charting such shifts in the practice of ethics is to attend to the aspects or qualities of selfhood liable to ethical work in disparate moral traditions. Classical Sanskrit philosophical schools, for example, distinguished variously between the several internal faculties through which the soul was understood to gain experience of the terrestrial world: in Samkhya thought, *buddhi* was understood as the underlying will or disposition, *ahamkāra* as a proud sense of self-awareness, and *manas* as the means of synthesizing and reflecting upon sensory impressions.[25] Mobilized and reworked in later centuries by diverse regimes of ascetic practice, theistic and nontheistic religious orders, and courtly and monastic practices of virtue, this vocabulary has sustained multiple ways of engaging oneself reflexively as a subject of ethics in South Asia. Kings and courtiers were widely exhorted to pay special attention to the *manas* as a means of developing inner discipline in order to exercise ethical mastery at court and beyond. Such grammars of ethical selfhood continue to matter deeply in modern times, as suggested, for example, by Dipesh Chakrabarty's discussion of compassion in nineteenth-century Bengali social reform discourse as an evident gift of exemplary *hriday,* or "heart."[26]

In many South Asian moral, religious, and literary traditions, affective dispositions such as compassion and devotion surface as essential means of negotiating ethical action. One might call attention to the diverse ways in which valorized emotions such as romantic and maternal love, for example, were elaborated within religious spheres into complex devotional templates, serving to ethicize such states in ways that could in turn assume further social valences. Consider the many lives of the Vaisnava devotional saint Mirabai, whose experience of devotional love to the deity may be seen as well as a critique of the conjugal relation on which such notions were putatively based.[27] While elite and courtly traditions tended to celebrate a cultivated indirection and detachment in one's emotional life as a mark of sophistication and moral eminence, often sneering at the village fool who could never know the ways of proper virtue, rural contexts were hardly devoid of their own ethical traditions.[28] Bhavani Raman's work in this volume, for example, shows how institutions such as the *tinnai* schools in the Tamil country of south India circulated modes of affective and ethical self-engagement through the memorization and embodiment of aphorisms—*āṟavatu ciṉam,* for example, or "control your anger," as recommended to young children by the medieval *Ātticūṭi*—in a manner often quite resonant with South Asia's "great traditions." And extending such concerns into the contemporary Tamil countryside, one may find rural people here conceiving "the good and the bad" of their own lives not only in relation to the persistent force of such inherited legacies but also in relation to the moral coordinates of their own practices of agrarian cultivation.[29]

Building upon these regional, social, and cultural variations, this volume is also guided by a second orientation toward ethical traditions in their historical and contextual specificity; these traditions are viewed in relation to social processes such as class and caste formation, political developments like state building, nationalism, and regionalism, and the particular moral horizons formed by legal codes, religious doctrines, and communities of practice. Emma Flatt's essay focuses upon the bodily and spiritual practices of *javānmardī* or "young manliness" desirable for young male members of organized brotherhoods in the medieval Bahmani kingdom in the Deccan, echoing Joseph Alter's work on wrestler practices of self and bodily care in contemporary Banaras.[30] Meanwhile, addressing similar questions from a contemporary vantage point, Craig Jeffrey argues in this volume that the appeal and efficacy of an ethos of *jugār* or pragmatic improvisation in urban north India can only be understood in relation to the circumstances engaged by middle-class and middle-caste young men. Such cases demonstrate that there cannot be a single account of ethics in South Asia and that these traditions must be understood in relation to the specific situations that render them intelligible, desirable, and at least potentially effective. Moral action in courtly traditions of virtue has long been attributed both to the qualities of birth and to the cultivation and training of an ethical sensibility: a tension gesturing toward a deep indeterminacy in South Asian moral tradition between "particularistic and universalist tendencies."[31] The meanings and practices invested in terms such as "dharma" differ notoriously across social classes, with distinctive codes of conduct thought to be relevant for ksatriya, brahmin, sudra, and even thieves.[32]

While discussions of such rectitude or propriety specified particular forms of worldly action appropriate for individual social milieus, castes, and classes, these works also lauded certain virtues—generosity, humility, and valor, for example—as universal moral principles. The broader value attributed to certain moral virtues, practices, and injunctions allowed those of diverse origins to claim them as their own over time, either through individual disciplines of personal practice or through broader movements of collective change such as what sociologist M. N. Srinivas famously identified as "Sanskritization."[33] In attending to the importance of particularity to South Asian moral traditions, then, we may delineate basic forms and locales of ethical practice as well as chart their historical movements and displacements. Diverse environments such as the court, the monastery, the Brahmin domestic *agraharam,* the twice-born or noble household, the marketplace, and the Sufi *kanaqah* have served as distinctive arenas for the articulation of moral orientation and action. But we may also examine the dilemmas and struggles that ensue when such ethical practices cross over between one domain and another: how prosperous Jain merchants, for example, may accommodate their worldly pursuits with the support of ascetic renunciation,[34] or the ways that Hindus and Muslims living side by side in contemporary Delhi find practical means of moral "striving" that cannot be easily identified with one religious tradition or another, as Veena Das describes in her contribution to this volume.

Third, this volume also calls attention to the complex and multiple ties that bind the moral and ethical challenges in South Asia to the legacies, burdens, and expectations of the past. Many influential Western thinkers on the subject of ethics, such as Williams, Foucault, MacIntyre, and Hadot, have engaged sensitively and fruitfully with history—or at least the historicity of ethical ideas and practices—in ways that seem to converge with newer currents of critical scholarship in the context of South Asia. In recent years we have seen a rejection of the kind of historicism that would relegate the ethical concepts and practices of the past to mere museum pieces safely encased in the protective glass of "the history of ideas," on the one hand, but also the universalisms that would consider any such return to history as naïve or irrelevant, on the other. Strands of historical scholarship inspired by postcolonial criticism have insisted upon the significance of diverse remnants of the precolonial past for cultural life in modern times: not only through their deliberate reinvention in nationalist and religious revivalism but also through more diffuse forms of moral inheritance. "Pasts *are* there in taste, in practices of embodiment, in the cultural training the senses have received over generations," writes Dipesh Chakrabarty, for example: "They are there in practices I sometimes do not even know I engage in."[35] From this vantage point, moral traditions may be seen as sustained in the present through dispersed fragments of moral discourse and ethical practice, remnants whose deep historicity may be submerged even as they insist upon vital forms of thought and action.[36]

However differently they may engage history and the contemporary, the essays in this volume are united by a general commitment to link together past and present in the examination of South Asian cultural life. We intend to unravel various ways in which classical, medieval, and colonial pasts continue to shape the moral life of the postcolonial present. One may remain deeply skeptical of both the utility and the historical pedigree of recent political discourse on Ram Raj by political parties in India, or the turn, for example, to ideas of *vāstu* in building techniques. Nevertheless, it is only through a proper historical understanding of precolonial ethical practice that it is possible to understand the potentials and limits of their persistence, recuperation, and utility in contemporary Indian life. Throughout the subcontinent, nationalist resistance to colonialism in the nineteenth and twentieth centuries on the part of Indian writers, reformers, and social ideologues drew from both the moral expectations of colonial public life and the existing ethical vocabularies of Indian literature and philosophy, in order to craft novel and hybridized ideas of a modern yet virtuous selfhood.[37] These multiple forces and currents show that modernity in South Asia has always been two-faced, looking forward to the challenges of contemporary existence only from the standpoint of the inherited traditions that lend meaning and direction to its futures.[38]

If theorists of the present have returned to the past to find such "sources" for the exercise of contemporary selfhood,[39] those with more traditional historical interests have been driven equally toward the present in order to rethink the cultural history of South Asia. In this regard we must acknowledge that the history of ethics in South Asia is overshadowed by the specters of modernity and the need to grapple analytically with their diverse and difficult challenges. Ritu Birla's contribution to this volume, for example, underscores the complexity of identifying the modern subject as a market actor: colonial jurisprudence rendered the mercantile or "bazaar" ethos of indigenous firms illegitimate, even as it took such firms as "universally acknowledged motors of the colonial economy." The growth of modern institutions here such as a capitalist economy, print media, schools, and the constitutional state, however incomplete, hybrid, or fragmentary, saw the gradual erosion and transformation of myriad precolonial cultural practices such as these, including their diverse ethical orientations. The development of modern institutions in South Asia—whether arising through colonial state policy, indigenous reform movements, or critical retrospective writing on Indian traditions—relied widely on certain polemical representations and conceptions of the precolonial past, often involving a condemnation of the amorality of the region's ethical traditions. Though the ideological sharpness of some of these characterizations has perhaps faded with time, their aura still persists in some of our own scholarly interpretive frameworks. Therefore, in order to understand the scope and history of ethics in precolonial India in any effective manner, one cannot help but engage with this interpretive legacy.

We hope that this volume, with its present-sensitive historical work, its close attention to the moral vocabularies of the present, and its concern for the embodiment of ethics in everyday life, will help redraw the terms of reference for the field of the ethical. But part of the project involves a reconsideration of the moral status of the "everyday" itself: from an understanding of the everyday as an arena in which given moral values may be ascribed and enacted toward the idea of a domain in which ethical potential may be actualized, expressed, or redirected in diverse and open ways. Reflecting on the moral sources that both sustain and complicate moral claims and practices in a south Indian pilgrimage town, for example, Leela Prasad describes "labyrinthine relationships between canons that prescribe conduct . . . and complex exigencies of everyday life."[40] Veena Das has insisted upon the value of heeding "the gap between a norm and its actualization," neither to present evidence of a "general rule" nor an exception to it but, instead, "to show how new norms emerge in experiments with life, in spiritual self-creation."[41] And in Lawrence Cohen's essay, such openings are essential to what he calls an "ethical scene," a domain of worldly encounter and address that frames "the possibilities and the limits of an ethical life in relation." Only by attending to such prospects and the circumstances of their realization, we would argue, can we begin to develop the tools with which to determine what living futures might exist for the myriad ethical traditions of South Asia.

An Outline of the Book

Our contributors' approach to the problems and questions outlined here is resolutely interdisciplinary, reflecting multiple lines of conversation between history, anthropology, philosophy, religious studies, and other allied fields of inquiry. These threads of engagement across disparate disciplines, temporal periods, and domains of practical engagement are meant to be sustained as well by the structure of the volume and its four parts.

The first part, "Traditions in Transmission," takes up the dynamic quality of certain major ethical traditions in South Asia, focusing upon the discursive and practical means of their sustenance through ongoing modes of transformation. Daud Ali looks at short sententious and didactic verses in Sanskrit known as *subhâṣitas,* or "well-spoken" sayings, that circulated in vast numbers among elites and were compiled in anthologies and narrative literature. He demonstrates how the preserved literary environments of these verses reveal a "lived" context for this moral knowledge that was at once collectively articulated and highly dialogical. Bhavani Raman's essay examines the ethical force of another tradition of moral pedagogy, exercised in the traditional "verandah school" in Tamil south India. Raman shows how this highly oral learning environment, quite contrary to script-centric colonial stereotypes of rote learning, may be conceived as producing morally virtuous subjects through concrete practices of physical and mental mnemonic discipline. Lastly, James Laidlaw's essay begins with a different kind of problem: the status of an ethical tradition in a contemporary diasporic environment. Focusing on the imbrication of Jain and modern environmentalist ethics in overseas Jain communities, Laidlaw shows that despite apparent convergences on certain issues, vast differences of soteriology, ontology, and attitudes to suffering between these traditions has required a continual articulation and negotiation that has not yet reached closure.

Contributors to the second part of the volume address the subject of ethics and modernity. Each of these essays takes up a different aspect of modern social and intellectual life in South Asia, examining how colonial and postcolonial conjunctures in the region often radically remade the contours of its moral and ethical practices, but also often depended upon these very traditions of practice for their modernizing force. Ritu Birla attends to the ethical stakes of colonial economy, describing proliferating tensions and accommodations between the market models of colonial jurisprudence and the "extensive negotiability" of bazaar commerce and sociality. The ethos embodied in the latter mercantile practices, she suggests, was quarantined in colonial law within the domain of the "ethnic" rather than the ethical. Bernard Bate focuses on the emergence of a Tamil public sphere in colonial south India and Ceylon, arguing that the production of an abstract moral obligation to strangers here was linked to Protestant missionary forms of textual practice, in particular the sermon. Nevertheless, he insists, it was a durable Tamil corpus of ethical texts that provided the "embodied ground" through which these sermons elaborated an ethical universe of strangers. Finally, Dipesh Chakrabarty submits a modern scholarly field to ethical enquiry, examining the pursuit of history as an ascetic "calling" in the historiographic imagination and practice of Jadunath Sarkar. Through a careful reading of Sarkar's colonial conjuncture, Chakrabarty suggests that a larger ethics of history—indeed, one with universal horizons of moral possibility—emerges from this milieu as a "struggle to remain open to someone else's reasoned skepticism."

The third part of the volume, "Practices of the Self," examines diverse modes of cultivating moral selfhood through particular forms of bodily and spiritual practice. Charles Hallisey's essay on Theravâda Buddhist ethics addresses the difficulties of translating virtues such as *satisampajañña* as they emerge from the canon of this tradition's texts. Discussing the importance to these narratives of a nameless yet virtuous practice one might term "moral creativity," Hallisey argues that we, as students of ethical cultures, may find in such "underdetermined" and unspoken elements a way of engaging ethics as both self-relation and life with and for others. Emma Flatt's essay takes up the figure of the wrestler as an ethical paragon of "young manliness" (*javānmardī*) in the Persianate courts of the medieval Deccan. Flatt shows not only how wrestling was invested with spiritual and ethical significance but also how physical training for the young man formed a true occasion for moral instruction, as self-cultivation could lead to errors and excesses if not tempered by moderation. Leela Prasad's contribution focuses on everyday moral experience in the contemporary south Indian pilgrimage town of Sringeri and, in particular, the temporal quality of ethical engagements with mundane space and routine. Examining a pair of retrospective narratives concerning a boat tragedy on the Tunga River in the 1970s, Prasad suggests that differences of "time-consciousness" are essential to the differential exercise of ethical subjectivity. Craig Jeffrey, meanwhile, turns his attention to middle-class Jat student leaders in north India, asking whether practices of "corruption" might themselves be understood to constitute an ethics. Describing a situation of dynamic class inequality, his essay highlights the practice of *jugār*—"the capacity to improvise effectively within particular social situations"—as a controversial mode of self-cultivation in the region, operating in tension with less evidently exploitative notions of morality.

Chapters in the final section of the volume—"Ethical Lives of Others"—each argue in a distinctive way that reflecting upon the relationship between ethical selfhood and alterity allows for a necessary broadening of the moral and ethical field. Ajay Skaria finds in Gandhi's *swarāj* a mode of life contrary to that of modern liberalism, one he describes as "living by dying." In Gandhi's attention to the self-conduct of the warrior, Skaria argues, we find the cultivation of a fearless relationship, even a friendship, with death—an equality with one's own death and therefore, too, an "immeasurable" equality with the other with whom one risks that death. Veena Das asks what it is for a Muslim in post–Independence India to inhabit a world shared with Hindus. Attending to scenes of ordinary life in low-income Delhi neighborhoods, Das identifies a series of experimental practices in ethical conduct—proximate living, bodily engagements, poetic recitation, and others—through which people may "get on with the daily commerce of living together." Lawrence Cohen's essay spans the distance between medieval Sanskrit dream theory and contemporary bioethical scandal, developing a form of moral life he names "ethical publicity." Rather than presuming a "local" morality that might be understood to bridge such a gap, Cohen seeks instead to chart the workings of a publicity of "collective address, participation, and spectatorship" across disparate sites of moral incitement. The "ethical scene of contemporary cosmopolitanism," Cohen suggests, is one in which "I participate in your wound." We, too, would argue that all these essays, taken together, find their ethical force in insisting upon one's own implication in the life and trials of another.

Notes

1. Michel Foucault, "The Ethics of the Concern for the Self as a Practice of Freedom," in *Ethics: Subjectivity and Truth,* ed. Paul Rabinow (New York: New Press, 1997).

2. Bernard Williams, *Ethics and the Limits of Philosophy* (Cambridge, Mass.: Harvard University Press, 1985), 6.

3. Immanuel Kant, *Fundamental Principles of the Metaphysic of Morals* (New York: Prometheus, 1988).

4. See MacIntyre, *After Virtue: A Study in Moral Theory* (Notre Dame, Ind.: University of Notre Dame Press, 1984), and *Whose Justice? Which Rationality?* (Notre Dame, Ind.: University of Notre Dame Press, 1988).

5. See Foucault, *The Use of Pleasure* (New York: Vintage Books, 1988), and *The Care of the Self* (New York: Vintage Books, 1990).

6. Pierre Hadot, *Philosophy as a Way of Life: Spiritual Exercises from Socrates to Foucault* (Oxford: Blackwell, 1995), 211–212.

7. See Norbert Elias, *The Civilizing Process* (Oxford: Blackwell, 1994); Jorge Arditi, *A Genealogy of Manner: Transformations of Social Relations in France and England from the Fourteenth to the Eighteenth Century* (Chicago: University of Chicago Press, 1998); and Anna Bryson, *From Courtesy to Civility: Changing Codes of Conduct in Early Modern England* (New York: Oxford University Press, 1998).

8. See, for example, Harald Fischer-Tine and Michael Mann, *Colonialism as Civilizing Mission: Cultural Ideology in British India* (London: Anthem, 2004).

9. Daud Ali, *Courtly Culture and Political Life in Early Medieval India* (New York: Cambridge University Press, 2004), 91.

10. Anand Pandian, "Pastoral Power in the Postcolony: On the Biopolitics of the Criminal Animal in South India," *Cultural Anthropology* 23 (2008): 85–117.

11. Talal Asad, "The Trouble of Thinking: An Interview with Talal Asad," in *Powers of the Secular Modern: Talal Asad and His Interlocutors,* ed. David Scott and Charles Hirschkind (Stanford, Calif.: Stanford University Press, 2006), 288.

12. See, respectively, Jean-Claude Schmitt, *La Raison des gestes dans l'occident médiéval* (Paris: Gallimard, 1990); and Charles Hirschkind, *The Ethical Soundscape: Cassette Sermons and Islamic Counterpublics* (New York: Columbia University Press, 2006).

13. See, respectively, Saba Mahmood, *Politics of Piety: The Islamic Revival and the Feminist Subject* (Princeton, N.J.: Princeton University Press, 2005); and Joel Robbins, *Becoming Sinners: Christianity and Moral Torment in a Papua New Guinea Society* (Berkeley: University of California Press, 2004).

14. Marcel Mauss, "Techniques of the Body," *Economy and Society* 2 (1973): 70–88.

15. For a discussion, see Greg Pence, "Virtue Theory," in *A Companion to Ethics,* ed. Peter Singer (Oxford: Blackwell, 2001).

16. Mauss, "Techniques of the Body."

17. MacIntyre, *After Virtue,* 222.

18. Talal Asad, *Formations of the Secular: Christianity, Islam, Modernity* (Stanford, Calif.: Stanford University Press, 2003), 222.

19. See Bryson, *From Courtesy to Civility;* and Robbins, *Becoming Sinners,* respectively.

20. See, for example, Webb Keane, *Christian Moderns: Freedom and Fetish in the Mission Encounter* (Berkeley: University of California Press, 2007).

21. Stephen Jaeger, *The Origins of Courtliness: Civilizing Trends and the Formation of Courtly Ideals, 939–1210* (Philadelphia: University of Pennsylvania Press, 1985).

22. Hirschkind, *The Ethical Soundscape,* 207.

23. We borrow this phrase from Michel Foucault, "What Is Enlightenment?" in *Ethics: Subjectivity and Truth,* ed. Paul Rabinow (New York: New Press, 1997).

24. For a discussion of South Asian ethical practice in relation to Kantian and post-Kantian morality in the West, see James Laidlaw, "For an Anthropology of Ethics and Freedom," *Journal of the Royal Anthropological Institute* n.s. 8 (2002): 311–332.

25. See Gerald Larson, *Classical Samkhya: An Interpretation of Its History and Meaning* (Delhi: Motilal Banarsidass, 1979).

26. Chakrabarty, *Provincializing Europe: Postcolonial Thought and Historical Difference* (Princeton, N.J.: Princeton University Press, 2000), 125.

27. See Kumkum Sangari, *Mirabai and the Spiritual Economy of Bhakti* (New Delhi: Nehru Memorial Museum and Library, 1990).

28. On these elite and courtly predilections, see Ali, *Courtly Culture and Political Life,* 183–206.

29. See Anand Pandian, *Crooked Stalks: Cultivating Virtue in South India* (Durham, N.C.: Duke University Press, 2009).

30. Alter, *The Wrestler's Body: Identity and Ideology in North India* (Berkeley: University of California Press, 1992).

31. Ali, *Courtly Culture and Political Life,* 95.

32. The relation between law and ethics in early India also deserves serious reconsideration in light of recent work by Don Davis shedding light on the widespread prevalence of 'intermediate' realms of legal practice, in which local groups, corporations, and even royal agents effectively constituted semiautonomous realms of legal practice. See his "Intermediate Realms of Law: Corporate Groups and Rulers in Medieval India," *Journal of the Economic and Social History of the Orient* 48 (2005): 92–117. Such realms of prescription, particularly palpable from early medieval times, require a reevaluation of the ethical dimensions of apparently universalistic śāstric discourse, on the one hand, and the fragments of "vernacular" and local "customary" practices, on the other.

33. Srinivas, *Social Change in Modern India* (Berkeley: University of California Press, 1966).

34. James Laidlaw, *Riches and Renunciation: Religion, Economy, and Society among the Jains* (New York: Oxford University Press, 1995).

35. Chakrabarty, *Provincializing Europe,* 251.

36. See Anand Pandian, "Tradition in Fragments: Inherited Forms and Fractures in the Ethics of South India," *American Ethnologist* 35 (2008): 466–480.

37. See, for example, Sudipta Kaviraj, *The Unhappy Consciousness: Bankimchandra Chattopadhyay and the Formation of Nationalist Discourse in India* (New York: Oxford University Press, 1995).

38. Ashis Nandy, *Time Warps: Silent and Evasive Pasts in Indian Politics and Religion* (New Brunswick, N.J.: Rutgers University Press, 2002).

39. See Charles Taylor, *Sources of the Self: The Making of the Modern Identity* (Cambridge, Mass.: Harvard University Press, 1989).

40. Leela Prasad, *Poetics of Conduct: Oral Narrative and Moral Being in a South Indian Town* (New York: Columbia University Press, 2007).

41. Das, *Life and Words: Violence and the Descent into the Ordinary* (Berkeley: University of California Press, 2007), 63.

Part 1.

Traditions in Transmission

1.

The *Subhāṣita* as an Artifact of Ethical Life in Medieval India

Daud Ali

> Every day in the evening, after we had taken our meal and finished our excursions, we passed time by reciting *subhāṣitas* and asking each other questions and counter questions.
>
> —Ciranjīvin, *Pañcatantra*

Though early India has left a copious legacy of didactic, proverbial, and wisdom literature in various forms and genres which has been deemed widely influential and important, rarely has this literature been analyzed with the seriousness it deserves. The focus in this essay is a certain species of didactic literature that has particular significance in rethinking the history of ethical practices in the South Asian cultural world during what may be broadly termed its "middle period." That the original contexts of this literature were courtly is clear enough from their content, and provide general clues as to the place of virtue and aesthetics in the ethical world of elite society. More to the point, however, I suggest here that the preserved textual forms and literary contexts of these verses actually tell us as much about the ethical dynamics of the societies in which they were current as their positive topical content. While didactic literature in early India embodied distinctive moral values, its formal aspects help us understand the ways in which these values were assimilated, experienced, and transmitted in different contexts.

A clear focus here is on what Foucault called ethical "subjectivation"—the ways in which individuals cultivated moral sensibilities and developed the capacity to act as ethical subjects.[1] Approaches to ethics in early India have focused on a number of key themes: philosophical discourses on ethical action, concepts of moral duty, and cosmologically sanctioned social values. Despite the obvious contributions of such work, the tendency has been to regard the field of the ethical as an already formed and static entity simply imbibed, imposed, or embodied by the individual or society. Often less clear, and what the didactic literary corpus illuminates, is how ethical subjectivity was formed and experienced. The context for this ethical world was decidedly restricted, to be sure. Early didactic literature suggests a strong courtly and urbane backdrop, a context that has been rather obscured by the dulling paradigm of "classical India" as the predominant interpretive framework for these sources. Yet a substantial amount of didactic material that has survived from the Gupta period and after (c. 350 CE–) was produced in courtly environments. Other types of ethical practice and pedagogy were, of course, current in different social milieus: bodily and mental discipline in monasteries, the esoteric practices in initiated religious lineages, transformative rituals among the twice-born, and the exemplary narratives in Purāṇic recitations, to name the most important. But the didactic literature from the outset reveals a certain porosity with other social locales and a remarkable ability to move across social boundaries over the centuries, both horizontally and vertically, reverberating in "folk," rural, and even modern pedagogic contexts.

Of specific concern here are short, stand-alone verses, generally known in Sanskrit as *subhāṣita* or *sūkti*—meaning 'well-uttered' or 'beautifully said'. These verses, preserved in collections and embedded in narrative literature, are a distinctive feature of precolonial "literary culture" in South Asia which have, until recently, received scant scholarly attention.[2] The breadth of Sanskrit literature echoes with such verses; they seem to have formed part of nearly every conceivable genre of classical Sanskrit literature. Large numbers of such verses are found in the *Mahābhārata,* and some later dharma and particularly courtly didactic texts on *nīti* or policy were composed entirely in these sententious and extractable verses. Indeed, the stanzaic verse as a self-complete whole became a key feature of poetic literature in general, even in its narrative mode, as it developed in the first centuries of the Common Era.[3] What distinguishes the *subhāṣita* from this larger and ubiquitous phenomena is not so much their distinct formal attributes or subject matter but their particular "life-histories," the fact that *subhāṣita*s circulated individually and were extracted, quoted, and collected by others.

The *subhāṣita* as a distinct and recognized literary form, then, presupposed its circulation and collection—and both these processes were in turn linked to new institutional arenas and novel forms of sociability. To wit, the *subhāṣita* anthology presupposed not only the existence of both written and orally exchanged sayings and verses of different kinds but a redactor (and patron) who sought to preserve them and an audience to receive, value, and transmit this knowledge.[4] The turning point seems to have occurred during the social and ideological transformations associated with early historic India (c. 600 BCE–300 CE). The growth of cities, kingdoms, and empires led to the development of institutions such as monasteries, guilds, royal and propertied households, and "associations" (*goṣṭhīs*), all of which would soon take on the character of urban salons and become the spheres of new social being and interaction. These institutions, and the practices they gave rise to, were significant departures from the forms of association typical of the later Vedic world such as the ritual arena or the famed disputational assembly (*brahmodya*), where highly contestual modes of verbal disputation evolved in relation to sacrificial and ritual esoteria.[5] Institutions like the royal assembly and Buddhist monastery were relatively open, both in terms of social access and the types of knowledge and discourse available to their members. The considerable emphasis on values of friendship and enmity in both early political thinking and Buddhist ethics is testament alone to such new forms of sociability, not to mention the phenomenon of conversational speech, which I have more to say about below. These new institutions thus formed a fertile ground not only for new ethical values and orientations, but they also supported the proliferation of a variety of new forms of speech-utterance such as verses (*subhāṣitas*), aphorisms (*sūtras*), and maxims (*nyāyas*). Among these, the most important from the viewpoint of individual ethical self-fashioning, was the *subhāṣita*.[6]

Subhāṣitas are first mentioned in Buddhist teachings, and the earliest extant collections of such poems seem to have been assembled within the early Buddhist *saṁgha*. Anthologies known as the *Theragāthā* (Poems of the early Buddhist monks) and *Therīgāthā* (Poems of the early Buddhist nuns) preserve short musical poems (*gāthā*) that were recited publicly on formal occasions and collected by the monastic community.[7] Single verses and clusters of verses celebrate the spiritual attainment of particular monks, admonish against vices, and exhort adherence to monastic vows. The first courtly anthology of *subhāṣitas*, a collection of Māhārāṣṭri Prakrit *gāthās* known as the *Sattasai* or *Gāhākoso* and attributed to a Sātavāhana king, bears certain similarities to the Buddhist collections, though its verses are finely wrought love poems with bucolic themes.[8]

Though the "well-spoken" verse utterance as a didactic-aesthetic form seems to have circulated in both religious/monastic and royal environments from early times, the collection and circulation of *subhāṣitas* became increasingly linked to the articulation of a specifically courtly ethical culture. Classified within the confines of art poetry, or *kāvya*, the rise of didactic genres as a whole forms one dimension of the larger growth of Sanskrit literary culture in the subcontinent from the fourth century CE.[9] The courtly orientation of surviving didactic literature from this period is explicit. The famous *Pañcatantra*, for example, is said to have been narrated to edify the slow-witted sons of a royal patron. Its moral tales, however, seem to be directed as much to courtiers and the wider community of men aspiring for success at the royal assembly as they are to royal princes. The focus is on *nīti,* a term in Sanskrit denoting 'policy' or prudent and wise behavior in the context of public life. *Subhāṣita* anthologies treat not only the theme of *nīti* but also a vast variety of subjects whose relevance for an educated service class is clear enough.

Ethics in the Courtly Milieu

Three features of ethical practice as it evolved in the courtly scenario provides some context for the *subhāṣita* as a social practice: first, the general emphasis on what might be termed a "virtue-based" ethics in courtly circles; second, the close relationship between moral practice and notions of beauty and aesthetics; and, finally, the associational and "public" underpinnings of ethical life at court. Individually these features were not exclusive to royal courts and urbane assemblies, but together they created a distinctive ethical configuration.

If we are to be guided by courtly sources themselves, we may immediately recognize a significant disjuncture with the assumptions of much modern moral thinking. The prescriptive discourses of the court were concerned neither with identifying a universal moral faculty nor making moral judgments in relation to principles as the sine qua non of ethical life. Instead, it was the acquisition of moral qualities encapsulated in the Sanskrit term *guṇa* or *saṁpad,* literally 'quality', 'virtue', or 'excellence', which was the overweening emphasis of courtly literature and formed the goal of a noble life. This perhaps explains the preponderance in both eulogistic and didactic literature of the enumeration of virtues appropriate to men of different classes, ranks, and functions both within and beyond the nobility. The sources tend to assume that moral qualities (both good and bad) were to some extent inborn and differentiated across the social spectrum. At the same time, however, they emphasize that men could acquire and exhibit these virtues as badges of moral eminence. Though the inclination toward certain qualities was determined by birth, their actualization was owing to individual effort. Courtly discourses stress repeatedly that neither birth nor cultivation was enough. The common metaphor used was that of a gem or precious stone, which, unpolished and unrefined, could hardly shine with virtue.[10] Moreover, even though some moral qualities were thought to be inherent or appropriate to certain classes or both, many overlapped and were to be cultivated by all members at court. Land-grant eulogies present a stock set of virtues to describe a wide range of elites. They included prudent policy (*naya*), humility (*vinaya*), compassion (*dayā*), generosity (*dāna*), politeness (*dākṣiṇya*), valor (*śaurya*), magnanimity (*audārya*), and truthfulness (*satya*).[11]

The key concerns of courtly ethics—and a preponderant focus of ethical practice—were the acquisition and disposition of these moral qualities in the noble person. Equally important was the avoidance of vices, faults, and errors. Numerous *subhāṣitas* and didactic tales dwell on the identification, acquisition, and deployment of different virtues within one's character, as well as guarding against vices or "enemy" qualities.[12] Moral introspection tended to occur over how best to avoid errors and assemble virtues correctly within oneself. Certain virtues were to be linked with others, and many qualities could become vices if cultivated or deployed improperly. Valor, for example, was to be tempered with kindness, and all virtues by that all-important summit of moral attainments, humility. Numerous sources emphasize the skilled deployment of virtues. A seventh-century Pāṇḍuvaṁśin inscription describes the king Tīvaradeva as "greedy" for fame but not other people's wealth, and charming in well-spoken verses (*subhāṣita*) but not in the dalliances of desirous women.[13] A verse from Bhartṛhari's "Centad on Policy" (*nītiśataka*) exemplifies the tenor of such thinking:[14]

dākṣiṇyam svajane dayā parajane śāṭhyaṁ sadā durjane
prītiḥ sādhujane nayo nṛpajane vidvaj jane cārjavam /
śauryaṁ śatrujane kṣamā gurujane kāntajane dhṛṣṭatā
ye caivam puruṣāḥ kalāsu kuśalās teṣveva lokasthitiḥ //

Kindness toward one's own people, generosity to others, deception toward the wicked, affection to the honorable, prudent policy toward kings, sincerity toward the learned, valor toward enemies, patience toward elders, and boldness toward women—men skilled in these arts are the stability of the world.

The aesthetic dimension of this virtue ethics, as of life more generally at court, was extraordinarily complex and operated at a number of levels. Physical, gestural, and verbal beauty had long been deemed outer signs of inner accomplishment since at least the last centuries before the Common Era, but with the rise of elaborate court cultures from Gupta times, they became themselves imbued with a new moral character. In courtly circles personal beauty was at once a mark of moral attainment as well as an attainment in and of itself. The effect of this long sedimentary association and repeated cross-pollination of beauty and virtue was to give forms of moral activity a strong aesthetic dimension. It is thus not surprising that the most common manner in which people of the court imagined the acquisition of virtues was as a "decoration" (*alaṁkāra*) of the "soul." Virtues were "excellences" to be accumulated and, in keeping with the features of virtue-based ethics noted above, arranged in oneself in a judicious and pleasing manner like resplendent ornaments.

Aesthetic activity, on the other hand, often carried a strong ethical valence. All forms of art poetry, or *kāvya,* from the very first theorizations, were seen to be at least partially instructive and edifying for their audiences. Brahmā, for example, in announcing the birth of drama (*nāṭya*) to the Daityas in the *Nāṭyaśāstra,* promises that it would, among other things, demonstrate righteousness to the wicked and provide the world with instruction (*lokopadeśa*).[15] Beyond such generalities, particular genres of literature, most notably stories and single verses (*subhāṣitas*), often had explicitly didactic overtones, particularly in the field of "political policy" (*nīti*). These instructive dimensions made aesthetic enjoyment a morally valued activity itself. Aesthetic sophistication and moral sensitivity were isomorphic, perhaps nowhere more evident than in the idea of the connoisseur, or *sahṛdaya,* a man whose heart empathized with the world.

A final feature of ethics at court important for our discussion here was its public or associative dimension. Two aspects of this element of ethics merit our consideration: the connection of virtue with worldly success and the exterior or collective nature of ethical life. Any review of the evidence from inscriptions and literature suggests immediately that virtues and qualities in this world shaded over into the realm of "skills" or "competencies," and indeed were explicitly conceived as such. Virtues caused a man to prosper in the world.[16] Damanaka, the wily jackal-minister of the *Pañcatantra,* utters a verse (*subhāṣita*) which was to travel widely throughout the medieval world, informing his companion that

> *kalpayati yena vṛttiṁ sadasi ca sadbhiḥ praśasyate yena* /
> *sa guṇas tena guṇavatā vivardhanīyaś ca rakṣyaś ca* //
>
> That virtue (*guṇa*), which helps one earn a livelihood and is praised in the assembly, should be guarded and cultivated by its possessor.[17]

The cultivation and display of good qualities or virtues, then, led to recognition and success in the world of the court, where, sources reiterate, "good people" (*sajjana*) congregated. Indeed, the great concern with virtues in poetry and narrative literature was their display before, and appreciation by, the "society of the good." They were the major constituents of one's reputation and fame—the embodied moral aura that a person possessed in a collective context. Their enumeration among the attributes (*lakṣaṇas*) of particular offices and methods for their detection and examination (*parīkṣā*) formed an important concern in political manuals from Gupta times. The Mithila poet Vidyāpati titled his fifteenth-century book of moral tales, modeled on the *Pañcatantra* but with human rather than animal characters, the "Examination of Man" or *Puruṣaparīkṣā.* The association of virtue-based ethics with skills, competencies, and courtly employment has long made such systems highly dubious in the eyes of modern moral philosophers, who have regarded such achievements as little more than self-aggrandizing behavior. The perennial characterization of moral tales like the *Hitopadeśa* and *Pañcatantra* as "Machiavellian" or "amoral" reveals a serious limitation in perspective. What must be recognized if we are to take the *nīti* literature as a whole with any seriousness is that moral cultivation and pecuniary and political success were not, in the world of court societies, deemed fundamentally opposed to each other.[18]

The public dimension of ethical life meant not only that praise and opprobrium formed important elements of ethical consideration but that association more generally played a crucial role in moral development. Associating with the good and avoiding the wicked is an incessant exhortation in *subhāṣita* literature, so common, in fact, as to appear almost banal. The ubiquitous assumption was that regular contact with the virtuous improved one's character and reputation. It is not surprising, perhaps, that such an association formed a key domain of ethical learning, since the circles of the good were the putative publics where one's moral reputation was established. A verse attributed to Bhartṛhari, once again, makes the point clearly enough: association with the good (*satsaṅgati*) conferred almost every imaginable ethical benefit, from removing dullness in one's intellect and infusing truth in one's speech to avoiding errors and calming the mind.[19]

What did "association with the good" entail? In manuals on polity like the *Arthaśāstra* and *Nītisāra,* it typically meant revering and learning from one's teachers and elders. But it also entailed observing and discussing matters among companions and peers. The career of the seventh-century courtier poet Bāṇa as represented in the opening chapter of his *Harṣacarita* is particularly revealing. As a young man Bāṇa, dejected at the death of his father, leaves home and falls in with men and women of low birth and reputation, bringing his estimation in the eyes of the good (and particularly the royal court) into disrepute. But gradually, we are told, through various new associations, Bāṇa regains a standing suitable to his birth. These associations include, perhaps predictably, the houses of kings and teachers but also "gatherings of the virtuous who were full of worthy discussions" and "circles of the clever whose wealth was naturally deep reflection."[20] The "circle," or *maṇḍala,* and particularly the "gathering," or *goṣṭhī,* denoted comparatively open social congregations, the latter defined by the *Kāmasūtra* as a meeting of men having similar age, wealth, learning, and inclination.[21] These were not formal associations with specific personnel, fixed locales, and preordained hierarchies like the court or teacher's residence but rather shifting groups of like-minded individuals that met in different places. The relations between these gatherings and the world of the court was complex, as sources describe meetings for literary enjoyment both within and beyond the royal assembly,[22] and we hear of *goṣṭhī*s of a less salubrious type as well.[23] But such gatherings, even when outside the confines of the royal assembly, were often attended by men with some connection to the court. And the culture of such gatherings was largely continuous with that of the court, as Bāṇa's "ascent" from disrepute clearly suggests.

"Beautifully Said"

The key element of this new form of sociability, particularly associated with the *goṣṭhī,* was "conversation." Sources from the Gupta period emphasize a new type of verbal interaction distinct from everyday speech, on the one hand, and ritualized and formalized speech, on the other, whose key feature seems to have been that it was a specifically "pleasant" open-ended activity that constituted its own end.[24] The rise to prominence of this sort of verbal intercourse is corroborated across a wide variety of sources. It was anchored in social relationships defined primarily by companionship rather than kinship or ritual. The conversation of the crow Cirañjīvin and his friend, the partridge Kapiñjala, in the *Pañcatantra* cited at the outset of this essay, is described as a "passing of time" (*kālo'tivartate*) together in companionship.

Concomitant with the rise of conversation as a friendly verbal interchange was an explicit care for various dispositional, affective, and gestural aspects of speech. Very common from the Gupta period are general exhortations, widespread in *subhāṣita* and *nīti* literature, to speak to others "sweetly" or "pleasantly."[25] Speaking with cheerful gestures was one of the personal qualities that every king was to possess according to the *Arthaśāstra,*[26] and a Gupta courtier-noble is described in the Junagadh rock inscription as delighting the men of his realm by gifts, honors, and "conversation preceded by smiles" (*pūrvasmitābhāṣaṇa*).[27] Significant here is that the noble's speech in every way, from his facial gestures and the tone of his voice to the import and beauty of his words, was meant to create a sense of happiness, ease, and affection among his listeners. By the second half of the first millennium CE, pleasant verbal exchange had become so much an iconic aspect of lordship that at least one medieval dynasty represented the sovereign in official records as "enjoying pleasant conversation" (*sukhasaṁkathāvinodadiṁ*).[28]

The emphasis on pleasant verbal interchange must be understood against the context not only of new literary genres marshaled under the category of *kāvya* but also of a related oral culture that included many spheres for the exercise of verbal skill and virtuosity. The *Kāmasūtra,* for example, includes among the sixty-four arts of the urbane man not only knowledge of meter, rhetoric, plays, and stories but also skill in riddles, verse-completion games, "tongue twisters," and composing verses ex tempore.[29] Sometimes these game-genres were included in the *subhāṣita* anthologies themselves.[30] Given that these arts were to be enjoyed in the *goṣṭhī,* we may imagine that conversation was interspersed with such displays of linguistic virtuosity.

The *subhāṣita* or *sūkti* formed an integral part of this new configuration. *Subhāṣitas* were short, epigrammatic, and versified sayings that "ornamented" the verbal interchanges and conversation of the virtuous. They were set to memory and orally recalled in everyday discourse among the learned. The story literature of this period, which preserves numerous *subhāṣitas*, indicates how such verses intruded into direct discourse. On the one hand, we have, from the second millennium CE a number of texts like the *Prabandhacintāmaṇi* and the *Bhojaprabandha* in which the great poets of the past are brought together to display their poetic virtuosity. These imagined contests may have some reverberation in contemporary court practice, and perhaps mirror the *kavigoṣṭhī* that theorists like Rājaśekhara have spoken of. On the other hand, a somewhat older tradition in story literature depicts characters reciting morally edifying verses to one another in the course of a discussion to persuade, illustrate, or exemplify an ethical position or recommend a course of action, introducing them with phrases such as "it is said" (*uktaṁ*) or "this puts it well" (*sādhu cedam ucyate*). In the passage from the *Pañcatantra* in the epigraph to this essay, the *subhāṣita* takes its place among the "questions and counter questions" (*praśnapratipraśna*) on various topics exchanged between the crow Cirañjīvin and his friend, the partridge Kapiñjala, to pass the time.[31]

This suggests that the *subhāṣita*, despite its apparent formal autonomy from any given literary or speech context—or perhaps because of it—was a profoundly dialogical utterance. The very nomenclature of the *subhāṣita*, the "well-said utterance," presupposes collective appreciation and invokes the context of verbal exchange. The implications of this fact for our understanding of the social dimensions of literary culture at a number of levels are considerable. Most germane for our purposes, however, is that the *subhāṣita* allows us to see literary practices in a profoundly dialogical manner. Shulman and Narayana Rao have emphasized that these verses, when employed as a form of social communication, evoked a sort of Habermasian "public sphere."[32] Though medieval and early modern associations in India hardly conform to the European bourgeois model, they are right to implicitly question Habermas's exclusion of non-European and pre-bourgeois forms of publicness from the "rational." The communicative potential of premodern forms of association has been vastly underestimated by theorists of modernity.

It is in this connection that we may begin to rethink the role of such verses in the moral formation of their audiences. There can be little doubt as to the edifying intentions of many *subhāṣitas*. If the prefix "su" indicated beautiful speech, it also carried a strong moral valence. Sternbach referred to such verses as a key constituent of the "floating mass of oral tradition" that gave people "ethical advice and guidance, and instruction in practical wisdom."[33] He recognized that *subhāṣitas* as a whole formed an inestimably valuable resource for reconstructing the values of the literate classes in early India. Descriptive verses embody the thematic obsessions of educated and aristocratic life—love, poverty, dependence, service, wealth, war, and the virtues—and also preserve particularly valued aesthetic principles. Didactic verses, on the other hand, present us with the explicitly or indirectly stated "advice" of hundreds of named and nameless intellectuals on diverse topics from the dangers of royal service to the importance of good birth, from the misery of poverty to the virtues of good association.

A notable feature of *subhāṣita* literatures as a whole is that they do not preserve a single set of moral standpoints; in fact, *subhāṣitas* often take contrary positions on particular topics. A verse from the seventeenth-century collection *Sūktimuktāvalī,* for example, extols the fortune of good birth in recommending the worship of Viṣṇu:

> *kulaśīlaśrutācāravatāṁ kila satāṁ kule* /
> *cirād ārādhya jāyante puruṣā. puruṣottamam* //
>
> Men are born into the families of the good, which possess nobility of birth, character, learning, and polite behavior, by worshiping for a long time the best of *puruṣas* (Viṣṇu).[34]

Another verse, however, ascribed to the famous polymath Kṣemendra, takes a darker view:

> *kulasya kamalasyeva mūlam anviṣyate yadi* /
> *doṣapaṅkaprasaktāntas tadāvaśyaṁ prakāśate* //
>
> If an investigation is made into the roots of a noble family, then, like a lotus, it will inevitably come to light that within there clings a blemish of mud.[35]

Such variance is evident in the story literature when characters cite opposing verses to one another in the course of a discussion to illustrate, vindicate, and lend authority to their points. Anthologies, for their part, often include verses on various subjects that have different positions, and some even divide them based on these views; Thus a fourteenth-century south Indian anthology called the *Sūktiratnahāra,* contains consecutive chapters of verses in "praise" and "abuse" of courtesans (*veśyāpraśaṁsā, veśyāninda*).[36] Overall the *subhāṣita* anthologies constitute a sort of repository of ethical consideration on culturally valued topics rather than a set of codes or principles attempting to present a single point of view.

The Content of the Form

The literary dimensions of *subhāṣita* verses, both contextual and internal, tell most about their role in ethical practice. We may begin with the two major preserved contexts of the *subhāṣita:* the anthology (*saṁgraha/kośa*) and the story (*kathā*). As we have seen above, the manner in which verses were "used" typically involved their citation or recitation at courts and *goṣṭhī*s, where they formed part of a highly oral environment. Yet we should not imagine that their provenance was exclusively oral, as Shulman and Narayana Rao have recently done.[37] That such great numbers of these verses are even available to us today stems not from any comprehensive oral transmission but rather from their having been preserved in written verse-anthologies. Known from as early as the Buddhist and courtly collections of *gāthā*s, these anthologies survive in large numbers from the second millennium CE. The relation between orality and literacy in the world of *subhāṣita*s, as with *kāvya* more generally, is complex, as Pollock has demonstrated, and it is impossible to sustain any thorough opposition between the two modes in the realm of literary culture.[38] For our purposes, then, it is necessary to consider both the highly oral and labile dimension of the *subhāṣita* as well as the continual need to "fix" and "record" such verses in anthologies.

Though we possess a number of key collections of anthologies from the second half of the first millennium CE, particularly traditions of moral verses attributed to figures like Bhatṛhari and Cāṇakya, the compilation of independent circulating verses seems to have greatly accelerated from the tenth century, when numerous anthologies of either anonymous or attributed verses were compiled as well as single-authored collections of independent verses. The most important of those that have survived from the period of 1000–1500—many of which are associated with particular royal courts—include Vidyākara's *Subhāṣitaratnakośa* (c. 1150 CE), Halāyudha's *Dharmaviveka* (c. 1179–1206 CE), Śrīdharadāsa's *Saduktikarṇāmṛta* (c. 1205 CE), Jalhaṇa's *Sūktimuktāvalī* (c. 1258 CE), Sūrya's *Sūktiratnahāra* (c. 1300–1350 CE), the *Vyāsasubhāṣitasaṁgraha* (before 1300), Śārṅgadhara's *Śārṅgadharapaddhati* (c. 1363 CE), Sundarapāṇḍya's *Nītidviṣaṣṭikā* (c. 1250 CE?), Kusumadeva's *Dṛṣṭāntaśataka* (c. 1400–1500 CE), Dyā Dviveda's *Nītimañjarī* (c. 1494 CE), and Vallabhadeva's *Subhāṣitāvalī* (c. 1500 CE). The process of verse anthologization continued at an even greater pace in later times. According to Sternbach's survey, vast numbers of anthologies survive from the seventeenth century, and they continued to be compiled well into modern times. From the latter half of the nineteenth century many modern *subhāṣita-saṁgraha*s were compiled and edited as textbooks in Sanskrit to teach the moral thoughts of the "ancients" in modern schools. Of these, the most famous and comprehensive was the celebrated *Subhāṣitasudhāratnabhāṇḍāgara* of Narayana Rama Acharya "Kavyatirtha" and its abridged descendant, the *Subhāṣitaratnabhāṇḍāgāra.* The number of medieval and early modern anthologies that have been published is relatively small and thus any accurate history of anthologies currently remains beyond our reach.

Published anthologies are extremely diverse in their composition. Although some (particularly those attributed to a single author) were organized under the rubric of the four goals of human existence (*puruṣārtha*) or the threefold path of worldly life (*trivarga*), most were divided into numerous topical chapters for easy reference, including various proportions of descriptive, eulogistic, sententious, and even prescriptive verses.[39] The *Śārṅgadharapaddhati* famously includes a chapter on horticulture! Among the sententious and didactic verses, many were devoted to "policy," or *nīti,* perhaps expectedly, given the broadly courtly milieu in which such anthologies circulated. Sternbach demonstrated that the single most important "source" for the *nīti* verses in the *subhāṣita* anthologies was the collection of Cāṇakya's aphorisms known as the *Cāṇakyarājanītiśāstra.*[40]

The more famous and widespread anthologies, moreover, were subject to ongoing imitation and supplementation by later compilers and scribes, resulting in a truly bewildering array of versions, recensions, and imitations.[41] In addition, anthologies often borrowed heavily from one another and often vary considerably in their authorial ascriptions. While this is surely enough to drive the textual critic to the brink, Sternbach recognized that it implied that the authors of these texts had access to a living tradition of *subhāṣita*s with which they freely supplemented their texts. Given this complex intertextuality, it would be erroneous to see the anthology as some kind of direct transcription (or "capture") of a pristine oral environment. The anthologies are far too embedded within a vast skein of written intertextuality. On the other hand, as suggested above, anthologies make little sense without the evanescent orality in which the "well-spoken" verse distinguished itself as an autonomous unit from the sea of literary production. Given this close imbrication of the written and oral dimensions of the *subhāṣita* world, we may plausibly suggest that the anthology functioned as an instrument of fixity which actually helped sustain rather than ossify the continued renewal, transmission, and circulation of this open-ended knowledge. Compilers sought to harness verses for immediate and future use; as verses could be read aloud from the anthology, it formed a source for memory and improvisation. Such works, in other words, facilitated rather than hindered the circulation of wisdom among the elite in an environment at once oral *and* literate.

Hundreds of *subhāṣita*s were also incorporated into the didactic story literature that emerged in courtly circles from the early centuries of the Common Era. They were most frequently simply inserted into the characters' dialogues. In addition, many of the narrative units in these texts are introduced by a verse, uttered by the speaker to his listeners, stating a moral point and alluding to a story. Thus the second book of the *Pañcatantra* is introduced by Viṣṇuśarman with the verse,

asādhanā vittahīnā buddhimantaḥ suhṛn matāḥ /
sādhayanty āśu kāryāṇi kākakūrmamṛgākhuvat //[42]

> Men who are wise and honored by their friends, although they may lack resources and wealth, quickly accomplish their goals, like the crow, turtle, deer, and mouse.

In this case the first three *pāda*s of the verse assert an ethical principle—that friendship is valuable—and the final *pāda* refers cryptically to a story. The princes then ask "How is that?" (*katham etat*), and Viṣṇuśarman begins his tale. The device of introducing narrative units with verses containing a moral principle and story allusion occurs at all levels of the successive story frames in the book. It has been suggested that such verses, partly by virtue of the inherent prestige of poetry itself and partly by capturing the moral essence of the ensuing tales, represent a kind of "truth regime" lending authority to the narratives or, alternatively, as "binding" (shaping and evaluating) narrative events.[43] Though this may explain the role of the verse within a narrated context, it hardly exhausts their role more generally. An unusual series of sculptures depicting scenes from different *Pañcatantra* versions found in Andhra Pradesh, dated between the seventh and tenth centuries, include such verses as "captions" incised below them.[44] In one example, beneath a sculpture depicting a hunter, elephant, and jackal (with a bow piercing its skull), a verse reads,

> *atilobho na kartavyaḥ kartavyañ ca pramāṇataḥ* /
> *atilobhena doṣeṇa jambuko dhanvāpāditaḥ* //[45]

> Do not indulge in excessive greed. Greed should be limited. Due to the fault of excessive greed the jackal died from the bow.

Some version of this verse is found in numerous *Pañcatantra* recensions to introduce the story of the "greedy jackal," a tale told to admonish hoarding.[46] One may imagine that as the literate spectator viewed the image—depicting the jackal's death—he or she was reminded of the ethical purport of the tale by its introductory verse, inscribed beneath it. This suggests that such verses could function outside a fully narrated context (like the image itself in this case, which depicts only the story's climax), as "shorthand" allusions to familiar stories—where a stated moral principle was followed by a brief allusion.

But distinct from these introductory verses are didactic and sententious stanzas taken from a wide variety of sources, appearing throughout the *kathā* literature. Older versions of the *Pañcatantra,* for example, preserve some 537 sententious stanzas, and later versions have approximately twice this number.[47] Nārāyaṇa's *Hitopadeśa,* composed sometime in the ninth or tenth century and drawing heavily on *Pañcatantra* narratives, also incorporated large numbers of sententious verses, as did later *kathā* collections like the *Vetālapañcaviṁśatikā, Vikramacarita,* and *Śukasaptatī.*[48] If anthologies varied greatly from version to version, perhaps it is not surprising that different recensions and versions of key story traditions differed not only in their narrative assemblages but vastly in their stanzaic proportions. Sternbach showed that more recent recensions and versions of a text contained more verses, indicating that copyists and scribes through the generations added further verses as they saw fit.[49] Stories thus accumulated verses in the same way that anthologies were supplemented by their transmitters.

These verses do not necessarily anticipate or lend authority to the moral themes of the wider narrative units in which they occur, but instead are concerned with the situations facing particular characters within the stories. As I have mentioned above, they are often uttered in conversation between characters, typically introduced by phrases like "it is said" (*uktaṁ*), "look" (*paśya*), "for" (*yataḥ*), "in other words" (*tathā hi*), and "moreover" (*aparaṁ ca*). These formulations, in their narrative contexts, suggest two points. First, a presumed body of oral-literate ethical knowledge, in versified form, must have been available to the learned, which was deployed in everyday speech. Sternbach painstakingly traced the origin of these stanzas to a large variety of sources, most notably versified collections on *dharma* and *nīti* such as *Mānavadharmaśāstra,* Kāmandaki's *Nītisāra* and Cāṇakya's aphorisms, but also the *Mahābhārata* and *Purāṇas.*[50] Second, and more generally, they demonstrate the ways in which ethical argumentation as a form of collective and dialogical communication must have actually transpired—through the invocation of literary, gnomic, and śāstric knowledge as encapsulated in verse. The citation of a verse could lend authority on the one hand but could also be countered with another citation. So in the *Pañcatantra* the Jackal Damanaka, having been recited a verse by his companion on the perils of serving kings, retorts, "so it is indeed, but nevertheless" (*evam etat tathāpi*), citing a counter-verse supporting his decision to do so.[51] *Subhāṣita*s, in other words, formed a *communicative* idiom rather than simply a legitimatory discourse. They indicate a deeply dialogical aspect of ethical practice.

A final example of "poetic supplementation" underscores the dialogical dimension in the transmission of ethical verse. As we have seen, some *subhāṣita*s have a two-part structure, with the first part, typically comprising two or three *pāda*s of a verse, expressing a moral maxim, and the second illustrating it. We have seen how this technique was used to introduce narrative units within the story literature, where the maxim was followed by an abbreviated reference to a story of which the narrator and presumably his listeners were aware. This style of ethical verse, however, could also exist independent of any narrative context. The eleventh-century satirist Kṣemendra composed a set of a hundred verses called the *Cārucaryā* in which the first half of each verse took the form of a moral maxim and the second half an illustration (*dṛṣṭānta*) from the epics or Purāṇas. To cite an example, Kṣemendra begins one verse with the observation that "by praising the virtues of the great, one's [own] estimation grows" and illustrates the point in the second half with an example: "through praise, Hanumān was able to take up the work of Rāma."[52] Most notable about this basic structure—which we find more generally in didactic poetry—is that it lent itself to ongoing supplementation and elaboration. So when the Vedic scholar Dyā Dviveda in the fifteenth century composed his *Nītimañjarī,* he borrowed many of the same moral maxims from Kṣemendra but illustrated them with different examples, this time taken from the Vedic hymns.[53]

This process of "intertextual accretion" was current across a wide variety of *subhāṣita* contexts. The existence of large numbers of similar verses in the anthologies is not evidence of a "corrupt" system of textual preservation but rather a continued modulation, remembrance and, improvisation.[54] A notable example, on the theme of the *subhāṣita* itself, may be traced through a string of verses, taken from different anthologies, which all begin with the maxim that anything spoken at an opportune moment becomes "well-uttered" even though it may not, in fact, be so. In each case, however, the poet completes the second half of the verse with a different example:[55]

> *avasarapaṭhitaṁ sarvaṁ subhāṣitatvaṁ prayāty asūktam api* /
> *kṣudhi kadaśanam api nitarāṁ bhoktuḥ saṁpadyate svādu* //
>
> Anything said at the right moment becomes "well-spoken" (*subhāṣita*), though it may not (in fact) be good speech; when hungry, even worthless food will become tasty for the eater.
>
> *avasarapaṭhitaṁ sarvaṁ subhāṣitatvaṁ prayāti yat kiṁcit* /
> *cāṣaḥ prayāṇasamaye kharaninado maṅgalo bhavati* //
>
> Anything said at an opportune moment becomes "well-spoken" (*subhāṣita*); at the start of a journey, [even] the harsh-voiced bluejay is a sign of good fortune.
>
> *avasarapaṭhitā vāṇī guṇagaṇarahitāpi śobhate puṁsām* /
> *ratisamaye ramaṇīnāṁ bhūṣaṇahānis tu bhūṣaṇaṁ bhavati* //
>
> Words recited at an opportune moment, though devoid of any merit, will shine for a man; at the moment of love-making, an absence of ornaments becomes a decoration for a woman!

The first of these verses, composed by the poet Vallabhadeva and included in his own fifteenth-century compilation known as the *Subhāṣitāvalī,* may be the oldest, and the other two versus from more obscure and likely later anthologies, the *Śrīsūktāvalī* and the *Subhāṣitārṇava,* respectively.[56] Each attempts to capture more pithily than the next the spirit of the maxim about the importance of timing in speech. Such poems, of which there are many, dispersed across various anthologies, suggest that poets composed in dialogue with one another and with the tradition itself. Although this series of verses cannot be linked to any single occasion, they are redolent of the sort of improvisational verse-completion contests (*samasyāpūraṇa*) narrated so colorfully in texts like the *Bhojaprabandha*. While the Bhoja narratives tend to portray such verse-swapping as displays of poetic virtuosity, the *kathā* literature makes it clear that sententious verses could also be exchanged to make substantive points in ethical dialogue. The large number of similar verses and accretive supplementation to moral maxims across the vast ocean of *subhāṣita*s are palpable evidence of an ethical culture in which the learned refined their ethical sensibilities in collective environments, *through the well-spoken verse.* The intended point of these three verses, on the other hand, emphasize that the judicious deployment of the *subhāṣita* was as important as its content.[57] Indeed, it would seem that one important aspect of ethical sophistication was not simply knowing *subhāṣita*s but knowing how to use them in everyday conversation, whether in advising friends or explaining one's own ethical views.

I have argued above that the world of the *subhāṣita,* constituted by courtly and semi-courtly associations, presents us with a conception of ethical life largely at odds with our own, where a vast domain of concerns and activities now deemed morally inconsequential or irrelevant were the object of sustained scrutiny and reflection. Many aspects of this moral world have, to date, escaped the attention of historians of ideas. The "well-spoken" verse, in its many contexts, is one of these and has played, or so I have argued, a distinctive role in the formation of ethical and worldly sensibilities in these circles. As beautifully turned poetry, circulating verses embodied the aesthetic preoccupations of the elite classes and linked them closely to concepts of virtue. Furthermore, *subhāṣita*s presented sustained reflection on everyday "policy" (*nīti*) and the cultivation of virtue(s). In this sense they consituted a sort of "floating mass" of practical morality and political wisdom that informed the public orientations and behaviors of "good society."

But more than this, the literary contexts of the *subhāṣita* are both evidence of, and contributed to, a strongly dialogical ethical sensibility within these social realms. The *subhāṣita* is not simply a repository of ethical knowledge but a lived ethical practice. Preserved collections of verses were used for memorization and reference so that "well-spoken" utterances could adorn the everyday conversation of the learned. The story literature preserves many hundreds of verses, placed on tongues of story characters, functioning as exemplars, pithy summations, and narrative abbreviations which together served at once as a sort of ethical "mnemonics" as well as repository of wisdom on *nīti* in the manner of anthologies.

The very nomenclature of the circulating verse—as a "good utterance"—implies not the silent courtroom of the soul but a scenario of collective moral interaction. This is confirmed by the evidence of the story literature which often presents *subhāṣitas* as parts of larger moral arguments between characters. Though the *subhāṣita* took its place among wider forms of "speech-sociability" curent among the elite, it also carried the force of moral persuasion. Considering their use in narrative contexts, and the fact that the anthologies preserve different points of view, what Bisgaard called the "diversity of thought," we may understand the subhāṣita as a form of ratiocinative and dialogical communication. Viewed in this way, the anthologies and to a certain extent the story literature, in their ever increasing verse accretions, may be seen as surviving "traces" of the processes through which individuals came to understand themselves as moral subjects, as agents within an ethical framework.

One issue that has not been explored is the mobility of the sententious verse. *Subhāṣitas* seem to have grown into an oral-literate discursive mass that cut across many different literary genres and social contexts. Though on the one hand it has long been recognized that whole texts such as *Cāṇakyarājanītiśāstra* and the *Pañcatantra* traveled widely in the medieval world, inchoate materials—stray verses, sayings, and narrative cycles—also journeyed, entering what Aziz al-Azmeh felicitously once called, in the West Asian context, "the corpus of universal wisdom."[58] Such processes of circulation and transmission across linguistic boundaries and social classes were also important within South Asia from at least the second millennium CE, when both *subhāṣita* anthologies and story cycles became integral to the rise of "vernacular" literary cultures in India. Beyond this were interactions and articulations of didactic verses with largely non-literate societies and folk traditions. Although some of these processes have now come under the scrutiny of literary historians, their role in the history of ethics still needs to be understood.

Notes

The epigraph is from *Pañcatantra,* ed. and trans. Franklin Edgerton (New Haven, Conn.: American Oriental Society, 1924), book 3, story of Dadhikarṇa.

1. See Michel Foucault, *The Use of Pleasure* (New York: Vintage, 1986), 25–32.

2. The most important work on these verses in their various literary environments was conducted by the great Indologist Ludwik Sternbach. In addition to his many monographs and papers on the *subhāṣita* and its relation to other types of literature, particularly narrative genres, in 1966 Sternbach initiated the monumental text-critical collection and translation of these verses from all their known literary contexts at the Vishveshvaranand Indological Institute in Hoshiarpur, where it is still in progress, published under the title *Mahāsubhāṣitasaṁgraha,* ed. Ludwik Sternbach et al., 7 vols. (Hoshiarpur: Vishveshvaranand Vedic Research Institute, 1974–). Sternbach intended this compilation, currently numbering some thirteen thousand verses, to extend the

collection of von O. Böthlingk (*Indische Sprüche,* 1870–73) published nearly a century earlier. More recently they have been treated, inter alia, in Daniel James Bisgaard, *Social Conscience in Sanskrit Literature* (Delhi: Motilal Banarsidass, 1994), 99–117, and more closely in David Shulman and Velcheru Narayan Rao, *A Poem at the Right Moment: Remembered Verses from Premodern South India* (Berkeley: University of California Press, 1998).

3. See the remarks of Edwin Gerow in Edward C. Dimock Jr. et al., *The Literatures of India: An Introduction* (Chicago: University of Chicago Press, 1974), 126–127.

4. While there may indeed be examples of gnomic and sententious verses in Vedic literature, these cannot be said to constitute formally recognized social practices outside the complex of the sacrificial rites.

5. On the agonism of the *brahmodya,* see Brian Black, *The Character of the Self in Ancient India: Priests, Kings, and Women in the Early Upaniṣads* (Albany: State University of New York Press, 2007), 59ff.

6. Two related but unversified literary/speech forms that often had an ethical character were the *sūtra,* a pithy and often enigmatic aphorism, and the related *lokokti* or *nyāya,* a "proverb" or "maxim" expressing a well-known truth or common sense. The former were often attributed to great sages like Bṛhaspati or Cāṇakya and were sometimes assembled into very influential collections. Maxims and proverbs, as in many other world cultures, formed an important reference point and precedent in legal procedure. See Donald Davis Jr., "Maxims and Precedent in Classical Hindu Law," *Indologica Taurinesia* 33 (2007): 33–55.

7. These are now preserved in the Pali canon. See *Poems of the Early Buddhist Monks (Theragāthā),* trans. K. R. Norman (Oxford: Pali Text Society, 1997); and *Poems of the Early Buddhist Nuns (Therīgāthā),* trans. Rhys Davids and K. R. Norman (Oxford: Pali Text Society, 1997).

8. See *The Prākrit Gāthā-saptaśatī Compiled by Sātavāhana king Hāla,* ed. and trans. Radhagovinda Basak (Calcutta: Asiatic Society 1971). On the relation between the *Sattasai* and Buddhist *gathā*s, see Siegfried Lienhard, "Sur la structure poétique des Theratherīgāthā," *Journal Asiatique* 263 (1975): 375–396.

9. On the wider process, see Sheldon Pollock, *The Language of the Gods in the World of Men: Sanskrit, Culture, and Power in Premodern India* (Berkeley: University of California Press, 2006), pp. 39–222.

10. See the remarks in Kauṭilya's *Arthaśāstra,* ed. and trans. R. P. Kangle (Dehli: Motilal Banarsidass 1988) 1.5.3–4, and the tenth-century manual on *nīti* by Somadevasūri, *Nītivākyāmṛtam,* ed. and trans. S. K. Gupta (Calcutta: Prakrta Bharati Academy, 1987) 5.32, 36. For numerous *subhāṣita*s on this theme, see *Mahāsubhāṣitasaṁgraha,* 10027ff.

11. Ubiquitous in epigraphy and often cited in abbreviation, listing a few qualities followed by "etc." See, for example, the early-eighth-century inscription of the king Bhogaśakti in the Western Deccan, who is praised as *nayavinayadayādānadākṣiṇyādibhir gunaiḥ alaṁkṛtaḥ,* V. V. Mirashi, "Anjaneri Plates (First Set) of Bhogasakti: (Kalachuri) Year 461," *Corpus Inscriptionum Indicarum* 4 (1955): no. 31, 150.

12. Kings were admonished to avoid the sixfold group of enemies (*ṣaḍarivarga*): lust, anger, greed, excitement, pride, and arrogance. The list appears in *Nītisāra,* ed. and trans. Rajendralal Mitra and S. K. Mitra, rev. and repr. ed. (Calcutta: Asiatic Society of Bengal, 1982), 1.57, and in numerous later *subhāṣita*s; see *Mahāsubhāṣitasaṁgraha,* no. 9570ff.

13. See A. M. Shastri, "Rajim Plates of Tīvaradeva, year 7," in *Inscriptions of the Śarabhapurīyas, Pāṇḍuvaṁśins and Somavaṁśins* (Delhi: ICHR, 1995), vol. 2, 3.3, 108.

14. N. R. Acarya and D. D. Kosambi, eds., *Subhāṣitatriśatī* (Delhi: Chowkhamba, 1987), 1.18

15. K. Krishnamoorthy, ed., *Nāṭyaśāstra of Bharatamuni* 4th rev. ed. (Baroda: Oriental Institute, 1992), 1.114–115.

16. So a twelfth-century inscription tells us while eulogizing the career of a successful minister. See F. Kielhorn, "Two Chandella Inscriptions," *Epigraphia Indica* 1 (1892): 211.

17. Literally 'be made to grow' *vivardhanīya*. *Pañcatantra,* 1.26. For the history of this verse, often anthologized in later collections and with West Asian parallels, see *Mahāsubhāṣitasaṁgraha* 9051.

18. There was, of course, criticism of courtly ways, royal service, pretensions to virtue, and the association of beauty and moral eminence (see, for example, Acarya and Kosambi, *Subhāṣitatriśatī,* 1.32). Such criticisms, however, were typically voiced by court intellectuals themselves and do not negate, so much as reflect upon, this general framework.

19. *Subhāṣitatriśatī,* 1.19.

20. "*mahārhālāpagambhīraguṇavadgoṣṭhīḥ... svabhāvagambhīradhīdhanāni vidagdhamaṇḍalāni*"; See P. V. Kane, ed., *The Harṣacarita of Bāṇabhaṭṭa (Text of Ucchvāsas I–VIII)* repr. (Delhi: Motilal Banarsidas, 1997), 19–20.

21. Goswami Damodar Shastri, ed., *Kāmasūtra* (Benares: Jaikrishnadas and Haridas Gupta, 1929), 1.4.34–35.

22. A tenth-century text describes a poet's gathering (*kavigoṣṭhī*) as being held in an assembly hall within the palace and presided over by the king. See C. D. Dalal and R. A. Sastri, eds., *Kāvyamīmāṁsā of Rājaśekhara* (Baroda: Central Library, 1924), 10.21ff.; an entire chapter of Maṅkhaka's twelfth-century *Śrīkaṇṭhacarita* describes the meeting of poets in the assembly hall of the house (*sabhāgṛha*) of the poet's brother, where his work gains acceptance by the men of the assembly (*sabhājana*). See Durgaprasad and Kasinath Pandurang Parab, eds., *Śrīkaṇṭhacarita of Maṅkhaka* 2nd ed. (Bombay: Nirnaya Sagar, 1900) 25.15, 141ff. Despite the fact that Maṅkhaka's meeting transpires outside the court, it is attended by many courtiers, including the host of the gathering, whom the king has appointed the minister of peace and war.

23. Śyāmilaka mentions a "gathering of rogues" (*dhūrtagoṣṭī*) in his *Pādatāḍitakam.* See G. H. Schokker and P. J. Worsley, eds. and trans., *Pādatāḍitakam of Śyamilaka* (Dordercht: Reidel, 1966), verse 4.

24. Typically denoted in sources by the term *ālāpa,* though others were also used. Both the *Kāmasūtra* and *Harṣacarita* mention *ālāpa* as the main activity at the *goṣṭhī.* So strong was the association of the *goṣṭhī* with discussion that the word itself came to denote conversation.

25. See for example Kāmandaki's *Nītisāra,* 3.23–34, esp. 3.23–25.

26. *Arthaśāstra* 6.1.6.

27. R. D. Bhandarkar, "The Junagadh Rock Inscription," *Corpus Inscriptionum Indicarum* 3 (1981): no. 28.

28. Used predominantly in the Kannada (but sometimes also in Sanskrit, as *sukhasaṁkathāvinodena*) inscriptions of the Cāḷukyas of Kalyāṇi and their subordinates. For examples see J. F. Fleet, "Stone Inscription of the Sinda Family at Bhairanmatti," *Epigraphia Indica* 3 (1894–95), no. 33; Lionel Barnett, "Inscriptions at Sudi,"

Epigraphia Indica 15 (1919–20), nos. 6C, 6D, 6E(1), 6H; Barnett, "Two Inscriptions from Kurgod," *Epigraphia Indica* 14 (1917–18), no. 19a. For usage in inscriptions of Cāḷukya subordinates, see Barnett, "Inscriptions from Sudi," no. 6L; "Two Inscriptions from Mutgi," *Epigraphia Indica* 15 (1919–20), no. 3B and B; G. S. Gai, "Nimbal Inscription of Yadava Bhillama," *Epigraphia Indica* 28 (1949–50), no. 18; and V. V. Mirashi, "The Tāḷale Plates of Gaṇḍarāditya: Śaka Year 1032," *Corpus Inscriptionum Indicarum* 6 (1977), no. 45. Fleet (*Dynasties of the Kanarese Districts,* repr. [Madras: AES, 1988], 428 n. 4) understood the phrase to indicate the semi-autonomous status of a feudatory, referring to conversations with the paramount sovereign, an interpretation belied by the fact, noted by Fleet himself, that the phrase is also found in imperial inscriptions. Rather it is more connected to the conception of royal "entertainments" (*vinoda*), detailed at length in the Cāḷukya king Someśvara III's encyclopedic sumptuary manual *Mānasollāsa.*

29. Shastri, *Kāmasūtra,* 1.3.16.

30. See, for example, the fourteenth-century *Śārṅgadharapaddhati,* ed. Peter Peterson, repr. (Chaukhamba Sanskrit Pratishthan, 1987), chaps. 32–35. See also Ludwik Sternbach, *Indian Riddles: A Forgotten Chapter in the History of Sanskrit Literature* (Hoshiarpur: Vishveshvaranand Vedic Research Institute, 1975), 53–55ff.

31. *Pañcatantra,* book 3, story of Dadhikarṇa.

32. Narayana Rao and Shulman, *A Poem at the Right Moment,* 7–8.

33. See Sternbach, *Subhāṣita, Gnomic and Didactic Literature,* 1.

34. Cited in *Mahāsubhāṣitasaṁgraha,* no. 10848, trans. A. A. Ramanathan.

35. *Darpadalana* 1.7 in *Kṣemendralaghukāvyasaṁgraha,* ed. V. V. Raghavacharya and D. G. Padhye (Hyderabad: Osmania Sanskrit Academy, 1961). Also cited in *Mahāsubhāṣitasaṁgraha,* no. 10850.

36. *Sūktiratnahāra,* ed. Sāmbaśiva Śāstrī (Trivandrum: Government Press, 1938). Praise (*praśaṁsā*) and abuse (*nindā*) were common thematic rubrics used by compilers to organize verses. So in the fourteenth-century *Śārṅgadharapaddhati* we have a chapter of verses extolling scholarship under "the praise of the learned" (*paṇḍitapraśaṁsā*) and another with verses on "the censure of bad scholars" (*kupaṇḍitanindā*).

37. Shulman and Narayana Rao, in emphasizing the oral environment of the exchanged verse, have drawn a sharp distinction between what they see as a pristine and dynamic "oral-textual" world of the *subhāṣita* and a wooden, scholastic, text-literate world represented by the anthologies. This distinction, presumably meant to set the stage for their critique of colonial collectors of "proverbial verses," is, unfortunately, not sustainable. A substantial number of "remembered verses" included in their study as examples of pristine text-orality may be traced to written story cycles like the *Prabandhacintāmaṇi* and *Bhojaprabandha* as well as anthologies compiled as early as the thirteenth century. See Narayana Rao and Shulman, *A Poem at the Right Moment,* 6–11; they use the term *cāṭu* 'pleasing utterance', largely a synonym for *subhāṣita.*

38. See the useful discussion in Pollock, *Language of the Gods,* 81ff.

39. Although earlier poetic treatises briefly mention the anthology as a form, the most extensive definition comes from Viśvanātha's *Sāhityadarpaṇa,* glossing the term as a "collection of verses, independent from each other, and arranged according to divisions—this is particularly beautiful" (*koṣaḥ ślokasamūhas tu syād anyonyānapekṣakaḥ / vrajyākrameṇa racitaḥ sa evātimanoramaḥ //*). See *Sāhityadarpaṇa of Viśvanātha,* ed. P. V. Kane, 2nd ed. (Bombay: Nirnaya Sagar, 1923), 6.329.

40. Ludwik Sternbach, *The Subhāṣita-Saṁgrahas as Treasuries of Cāṇakya's Sayings* (Hoshiarpur: Vishveshvaranand Institute, 1966), 3ff.

41. See Sternbach's remarks on the textual history of the *Śārṅgadharapaddhati* and its relation to the *Bṛhacchārṅgadharapaddhati,* and the *Sūktiratnahāra* and its relation to the *Subhāṣitasudhānidhi,* in *Subhāṣita Gnomic and Didactic Literature,* 17ff.

42. *Pañcatantra,* 2.1. Cf *Hitopadeśa,* 1.1.

43. McComas Taylor, *The Fall of Indigo Jackal: The Discourse of Division and Pūrṇabhadra's Pañcatantra* (Albany: State University of New York Press, 2007), 139. See the remarks on the Old Javanese *Tantri Kāmandaka* in A. L. Becker, *Beyond Translation: Essays toward a Modern Philology* (Ann Arbor: University of Michigan Press, 1995), 89–108.

44. See Channabasappa S. Patil, "Pañcatantra Sculptures and Literary Traditions in India and Indonesia: A Comparative Study," in *Narrative Sculpture and Literary Traditions in South and Southeast Asia,* ed. Marijke J. Klokke (Leiden: Brill, 2000), 81–85.

45. *Annual Report on Indian Epigraphy* (1960–61), part B, 67. I have followed Patil's correction of the epigraphic spelling.

46. This verse roughly corresponds with *Tantropākhyānam,* ed. Sāmbaśiva Śāstrī, Trivandrum Sanskrit series 132 (Trivandrum: Government Press, 1938) 68.5, but is also similar in function and purport to the verse beginning *kartavyaḥ saṁcayo nityam* which introduces the tale in Edgerton's edition (2.28).

47. Ludwik Sternbach, *The Kāvya Portions in the Kathā Literature-an Analysis* (Delhi: Meharchand Lacchmandas, 1971), 1:27.

48. For the *Hitopadeśa,* see Sternbach, *Kāvya Portions in the Kathā Literature,* 2:22; for the other texts, see Sternbach, *Kāvya Portions,* vols. 2 and 3.

49. Most notably in the case of the *Pañcatantra.* See Sternbach, *Kāvya Portions in the Kathā Literature,* 1:27ff.,

50. See, in addition to Sternbach's *Kāvya Portions of the Kathā Literature,* his *Juridical Studies in Ancient Indian Law* (Delhi: Motilal Barnarsidass, 1967), 92ff.

51. See *Pañcatantra,* 1.27–28.

52. *guṇastavena kurvīta mahatāṁ mānavardhanam / hanumān abhavat stutyā rāmakāryabharakṣamaḥ //.* See *Cārucaryā* 35, in *Kṣemendralaghukāvyasaṁgraha.*

53. See *Nītimañjarī,* ed. S. J. Joshi (Varanasi: Chowkhamba Sanskrit Series Office, 1998). For verses drawn from Kṣemendra's text, including *Cārucaryā* 35, see xxx–xxxii.

54. Such improvisation is particularly evident in the *Mahāsubhāṣitsaṁgraha,* which organizes verses not in traditional topical order but alphabetically, thereby juxtaposing large numbers of similarly worded verses from different anthologies across time.

55. Taken from *Mahāsubhāṣitasaṁgraha,* 3295–3297.

56. All these verses were anthologized in modern printed collections, and the ascriptions above come from the earliest manuscript material. For the Vallabhadeva verse, see *The Subhāṣitāvalī of Vallabhadeva,* ed. Peter Peterson and Pandit Durgaprasada (Bombay: Education Society, 1886), 150. On the other collections, see Sternbach's introduction and appendix to volume 1 of *Mahāsubhāṣitasaṁgraha.* The last of these verses, inspiration for the title *Poem at the Right Moment* (*avasarapaṭhitā vāṇī*) and cited as an example of the *cāṭu* oral tradition, has, in fact, a longer literate and written ancestry.

57. See the converse maxim, known only from Narayana Rama Acarya's *Subhāṣitasudhābhāṇḍāgara,* that "a *subhāṣita,* which is uttered at a bad time, becomes risible; just like the recitation of the Veda at the time of love sports with passionate women in private!" (*anavasare ca yad uktaṁ subhāṣitaṁ tac ca bhavati hāsyāya / rahasi prauḍhavadhunāṁ ratisamaye vedapāṭha iva //*), cited in *Mahāsubhāṣitasaṁgraha,* no. 1284.

58. Aziz al-Azmeh, *Muslim Kingship: Power and the Sacred in Muslim, Christian, and Pagan Polities* (London: Tauris, 1997), 84–93.

2.

Disciplining the Senses, Schooling the Mind: Inhabiting Virtue in the Tamil Tiṇṇai School

Bhavani Raman

Well before printed textbooks, blackboards, and chalk, Tamil-speaking children learned ethical poems culled from a large corpus of Tamil didactic literature in *tiṇṇaippaḷḷikkūṭam*s (verandah schools). In a typical *tiṇṇai* school, a single master supported by fee-paying parents or the patronage of the settlement's notables taught students, mostly sons of upper- and middle-caste families or daughters of temple women. Students usually attended the school for four or five years where they learned arithmetic, rudimentary writing, and Tamil poetry, before moving on to learn a trade or occupation. So the *tiṇṇai* school, a preeminent site for the inculcation of ethics, was geared to prepare students for apprenticeship, teaching them to learn by doing. Ethical teaching was inseparable from worldly learning.

Among the poems learned in the *tiṇṇai*, compositions attributed to the acerbic legendary poet Auvaiyār, especially the *Ātticūṭi* and the *Koṉṟaivēyntaṉ*, played a pivotal role in its multifaceted curriculum. Her poems simultaneously introduced students to basic vocabulary and computation skills, while teaching them the value of discipline, rectitude, and, most important, the cultivation of virtue, or *aṟam*.[1] Although often taught alongside more sectarian poems, Auvaiyār's compositions were not about deities or liturgical practice.[2] Rather, they addressed a fundamental question of everyday life: How must one live and act toward others? For this reason, placing Auvaiyār's poems in the context of *tiṇṇai* pedagogy allows us to understand the poetics and pedagogics of ethical cultivation in a trans-sectarian but regional context.

Reconstructing *tiṇṇai* pedagogical practices is no easy task, however. The long-standing ubiquity of the *tiṇṇai* school indicates its importance to elementary pedagogic practice and ethical cultivation in the region. Its resemblance to the *tōls*, *pāthshālas*, and *maktabs* of Bengal, or the verandah schools of the Telugu country and the Jaffna peninsula, suggests that *tiṉṉai* techniques were by no means unique.[3] Yet the origins of *tiṉṉai* learning are obscure. Barring a few stray references, the schools only began to be extensively documented in the eighteenth and nineteenth centuries by missionaries and British colonial officers who named them after the front verandahs, or *tiṉṉais*, on which they were held. So much of what we know about *tiṉṉai* learning was generated by colonial and missionary interventions in education that deemed it the pernicious rote-learning double of the modern school while reluctantly accommodating some of its practices. Indeed, it was in this fraught sublation of the *tiṉṉai* that nineteenth-century educational reformers, in search of moral instruction, transposed Auvaiyār's poems about exemplary conduct from the verandahs of the *tiṉṉai* to the modern schoolroom to teach students Tamil literature.

In fact, *tiṉṉai* school pedagogy was driven by the cultivation of memory, in contrast to these reformist efforts that emphasized reading and writing a particular language.[4] It is precisely this quality of *tiṉṉai* pedagogic practice—not reducible to a script-centered notion of learning a Tamil literary corpus—that illuminates *how,* and in what context, *tiṉṉai* schooling produced virtue. The cultivation of memory was not the mere memorization of texts, or the learning of a language or literary culture. It was geared to enhance the mind's capacity to know rather than retain. By providing the fundamental structure for cultivating memory, itself a virtue, Auvaiyār's poems were the exemplary means to know and learn about the world. In turn, the production of virtue did not rest on the mere passive retention of Auvaiyār's poems but encompassed a range of self-disciplining practices oriented toward right action. The cultivation of virtue was closely tied to an understanding of learning by doing.

The pedagogical import of ethical poems like the *Ātticūṭi* and the *Koṉṟaivēyntaṉ* to *tiṉṉai* schooling therefore brings new insights to the textual analyses of subcontinental ethical culture that have tended to rely on commentarial traditions to recover political and ethical thought in the centuries before 1800.[5] In the manuscript-rich performative spaces of shrines, courts, or monastic institutions, specialized commentators and scribal specialists produced erudite arguments that folded ethical visions into a worldly life of governance or aristocratic value.[6] So commentaries, written and performed, offer an embedded vision of the ethical and have provided the mediating ground from which scholars have engaged with the difficulties of translating and contextualizing the plural vocabularies of exemplary conduct. In contrast, this essay takes a different approach to the study of ethics by drawing attention to the place of virtue in *tiṉṉai* practice and the place of learning in the cultivation of virtue. *Tiṉṉai* students were certainly exposed to the commentarial wisdom of their schoolmaster, but the grounds upon which their ethical labor was undertaken can be apprehended only through the juxtaposition of poetic form to pedagogic practice, the milieu of learning. The *tiṇṇai* opens up a new vision of quotidian ethical life—the archetypical village school—to scholarly scrutiny through the palimpsest of records dating to the late eighteenth and early nineteenth centuries. Most *tiṇṇai* boys became practitioners of vocations, lay patrons of temples and monasteries, and the respectable core of the body politic rather than servants or workers, suggesting that the *tiṇṇai* sustained social and skill hierarchies. So the *tiṇṇai* is best understood as a ubiquitous site through which qualities deemed virtuous systematically reproduced dominance in an agrarian society and the dominance of agrarian values of cultivation.

Viewing *aṟam* in the *tiṇṇai* also calls for a re-conceptualization of virtue and ethical life, to follow several contributions to this volume, as a disposition to the world *actively* built rather than an inert reflection of the dominant social order. Consider the Tamil scholar and cultural critic Raj Gautaman's eloquent argument that the precepts of Tamil didactic literature, or virtue texts, have formed an unchanging set of values among Tamil speakers that live in "every breathing human being, determine the codes of the mind, language, and action."[7] Gautaman argues for a close relationship between the cultivation of virtue and durable modes of exercising power and *acting* in the world: *aṟam* (virtue) is *atikāram* or power. In turn, his insight compels us to ask the question, "How is *aṟam* cultivated?" and thereby reevaluate *tiṇṇai* pedagogy as a site of active learning rather than an institution that taught its students to passively learn texts by rote.[8]

Scholarly considerations of moral conduct in South Asia, especially of Islamic *adab,* have convincingly argued that moral or ethical cultivation required techniques of bodily discipline and a self-conscious crafting of dispositions.[9] To these insights we may add more recent work on how ethical dispositions are built through a variety of embodied practices.[10] In this light, *tiṇṇai* learning can be reconceived as somatic practice. Oral and aural recitation, hand copying, computation, and mental repetition then cease to be ways of learning to read texts but, instead, techniques of learning that actively discipline the senses and school the mind.

Ethical verses enabled the somatic techniques of mental cultivation. Ubiquitous in the *tiṇṇai* was the practice of "*vāypāṭam,*" commonly used today to mean multiplication tables or lists that are memorized but that literally means "schooling the mouth," a kind of *nā-payiṟci,* or tongue training.[11] The dual process of inculcating virtue and the skills of memory relied on the sonic patterns of the ethical poems learned in a particular order through mouth practice. The learning of virtue (*aṟam*) in the *tiṇṇai* entailed habituating the body to ethical values through breath control and disciplining the ear and tongue.[12] *Tiṇṇai* schooling thus built ways of seeing and doing, making ethical agents rather than passive followers of moral precepts.[13] In turn, memory was the key to a cultivated and disciplined mind. In this context, learning a text like the *Ātticūṭi* in the *tiṇṇai* school was not just a way of learning Tamil or learning rules of ethics by rote but a means to learn "how to know." These pedagogic practices (the ability to remember, to be disciplined, and to cultivate virtue) formed a mutually reinforcing process of mental or, more correctly, *manasic* (mind/heart, Tamil: *maṉam*) schooling or training. In sum, viewing the learning of these texts in the environment of the *tiṇṇai* school demonstrates how the form, content, and context of learning a poem enabled a student to become the very embodiment of virtue. *Aṟam* was a disposition recursively produced by embodied and disciplined practices.

The Disciplined Production of *Tiṇṇai* Virtue

In the absence of furniture, blackboards, chalk, or even classes, *tiṇṇai* discipline relied on the cane-wielding master, his assistant senior student (*caṭṭāmpiḷḷai*), and pedagogical techniques that emphasized recitation. Students sat in a big group on the floor. Younger students wrote on sand; older ones compiled their own palm-leaf texts (*cuvaṭi*) that accumulated in girth as lessons progressed: with each new lesson learned, a leaf inscribed with writing was added to the *cuvaṭittūkku* (the roped hook that held the palm-leaf texts together in a bundle). The *cuvaṭittūkku* would hang high from the rafters as the air resounded with students repeating the lessons they had learned. The master taught through a style of call and repeat using the cane to keep time and prod students to attention.[14] From all accounts the rod was not spared, suggesting that students were not passive learners but often recalcitrant subjects who tested their master's authority.[15]

Further, *tiṇṇai* learning was heavily circumscribed by considerations of caste, gender, and settlement pattern. Schools were located within circles of kin and associates from known families. Nineteenth-century, early-colonial government surveys indicate that most caste settlements or "*ūr*s"[16] of the region possessed a *tiṇṇai* school and that the children of the working castes were usually completely excluded from attending it.[17] Masters tended to be respectable upper-caste men. They were usually out-of-work scribes, village accountants, or "almanac Brahmans." Attending the *tiṇṇai* was to "belong," marking off those who could properly belong to the *ūr* and the Brahman enclave, the *akirakāram,* from those who served them. Notably these social circumscriptions resonate in Auvaiyār's ethical texts taught in the school. For example, the following verse from *Nalvaḻi* reads:

cāti iraṇṭoḻiya vēṟillai cāṟṟuṅkāl
nīti vaḻuvā neṟimuṟaiyiṉ, mētiṉiyil
iṭṭār periyār iṭātār iḻikulattār
paṭṭāṅkil uḷḷa paṭi[18]
(*Nalvaḻi,* Verse 2)

There only two castes no other,
According to *nīti* [ethics]
Those who give are superior,
Those who don't, are inferior.
So say the great books.

Such verses are usually cited to argue that the social hierarchy of *jāti* rests on right conduct rather than birth. Arguably the earth, if watered and ploughed, yields a rich harvest—the alchemy of cultivation can turn soil to gold.[19] However, these universalistic formulations are undercut when one considers that in the disciplined environment of the *tiṇṇai* the alchemic self-transformative properties of *aṟam* texts was restricted only to those allowed to attend school. Although Auvaiyār's texts may have circulated through other means—they were by no means secret—*aṟam* texts in *tiṇṇai* were a key to disciplined practice, a mark of civility, available to only those allowed to enter the school.

The *tiṇṇai* provided the socially recognized path to rectitude and respectable bearing, and hence its texts and practices were deeply entwined with the social hierarchy of an agrarian world and its transactions. To attend the *tiṇṇai* to discipline oneself was a privilege of resource bearers, those who possessed grain and cash. For example, the ceremonial initiation into the school upheld the virtue of a grain-controlling household and instilled an awareness of a self-disciplined body. The teacher inscribed auspicious letters on the young student's tongue with a finger dipped in honey. Then the teacher would take the student's hand and write the first syllable "A" on a tray of rice.[20] There is a well-known injunction that the child should first write on material owned by the home (*vīṭṭōṭa poruḷ/conta poruḷ*). Hence parents provided the rice for the ceremony and gave it as alms to the *tiṇṇai* teacher. In turn, the child's awareness of the tongue and finger as tactile tools of learning that needed to be disciplined were simultaneous to his awareness of wealth (*poruḷ*) and of an ideal household that endowed resources. Following their initiation, students frequently paid the schoolmaster a small fee for festivals and other ritual occasions, and each time they began a new lesson or text.

Ātticūṭi aphorisms resonate with similar worldly values. It instructs students to "live as your countrymen" (*tēcattōṭu oṭṭi vāḻ*), and to "cherish your wealth and live" (*poruḷ taḷaippōṟṟi vāḻ*). It emphasizes bodily discipline (fasting, alertness, regulated sleep, moderate appetite), the control of emotions (*āṟuvatu ciṉam,* "control your anger"), and the cultivation of good speech (*kaṭivatu maṟa,* "avoid unkind words"), all of which we may take to be prescriptions intended for the good living of resource controllers, unattainable to those on the margins. To be sure, many of these ethical injunctions were polyvalent manuals of action or practice. For example, an injunction such as *neṟpayir viḷaivu cey*—literally, "cultivate rice"—can evoke the idea of the toil involved in the cultivation of paddy, and uphold the virtues of rendering a landscape agrarian, encompassing the idea of toil as self-cultivation.[21] But in the *tiṇṇai,* such injunctions of universal import enabled those rice cultivators and practitioners of vocations deemed artful or skilled to participate in the activities of lay worship by self-transformation, in contrast to those who merely labored. The ethical core of the *tiṇṇai* produced a gendered caste habitus, a habituation and set of dispositions closely tied to the dominance of agrarian values. The children of master-cultivators, weavers, and traders acquired these virtues in a milieu that emphasized discipline over the body and the senses as the key to self-cultivation and resource control.[22]

Cultivating Memory and Virtue in the *Tiṇṇai*

Observers of the *tiṇṇai* school noted that "the schoolmaster first reads and scholars follow in a loud voice. Some don't even look down but repeat by ear what is said by the master."[23] Across the board, most analyses of *tiṇṇai* learning have taken this attentive aural orientation as a sign of learning by rote, generating pupils who could not comprehend the meaning of texts or read at sight texts that were not previously studied. Most nineteenth-century official reports criticized this form of schooling as inept and, worse, morally reprehensible, because students could not absorb the rudiments of grammar or ethics through rote learning. A. D. Campbell, a collector of the East India Company in Bellary, wrote, in 1823, regarding similar schools in Telugu-speaking areas that,

> every schoolboy can repeat verbatim a vast number of verses, the meaning of which he knows no more than the parrot that has been taught to utter certain words . . . and no wonder that with such an education, most natives cannot write a common letter without orthographical errors or grammatical mistakes.[24]

Interpretations of the *tiṇṇai* style that portrayed it as an inept institution of learning began to appear widely in the late eighteenth and early nineteenth centuries with the onset of colonial rule, converging rather felicitously with Protestant missionary interventions and a burgeoning early-colonial office culture that required new kinds of penmanship and recordkeeping skills, skills not produced by *tiṇṇai* schooling. To understand the efficacy of *tiṇṇai* learning, we must look elsewhere. We could turn, for instance, to the theatrical satire, *Paḷḷikkūṭam Vikaṭam* ("A satire on schooling"), part of a larger compilation titled *Palajātikam Vikaṭam* ("The satire of many *jatis*"). The satire was probably performed in the Tanjavur area in the late eighteenth century, and indicates that learning virtue was closely tied to somatic practice and mental discipline.

The text declares:

ucciyilē cuvaṭittūkku ucitamāy māṭṭik koṇṭu
kacciyāy paṭippuyellām kaṉamāka muṟaikaḷaic colli
niccayam teriya vēṇṭum nītikaḷ paṭittuk kaṇṭu
koccaikaḷ tikkuvāykaḷun tīravēṇum[25]

After hanging up the *cuvaṭit tūkku* (the bundle of palm-leaf texts) correctly,
Lessons should be recited appropriately with sobriety and care
The essential *nīti* texts should be learned
[then] slang and stuttering will be corrected.

To learn ethical poems correctly, remembering and reciting them was essential to good speech and was closely tied to enhancing one's mental capacity. U. Ve. Swaminathaiyar, the famous Tamil scholar, describes *muṟai collutal* (repetition/recitation in turn) as recitation from memory in the *tiṇṇai.*[26] *Muṟai* also means "relation," an association suggesting that recitation and repetition involved particular kinds of mental agility. The cultivation of memory was not mere imitation or retention.

Mary Carruthers's well-known study of mnemonic models in medieval Europe suggests that a person with a good memory was not just sagacious but possessed great powers of cognition.[27] The conventional association of mnemonics with rote learning tends to gloss it as a device to aid textual memorization—a pattern of letters, ideas, or images that trigger the retention and recollection of facts—rather than as a technique to refine mental faculties. Properly speaking, mnemonics was widely used in the medieval world as a technique for acquiring the art of memory.[28] In this sense, the cultivation of memory is quite different from the production of historical, social/collective, or personal memory, familiar to historians of South Asia. Carruthers further argues that memory was deeply desired as a representation of learning, but the proof of a good memory was not mere retention. This observation resonates with axioms proffered by Tamil ethical texts. Consider this verse from Auvaiyār's *Mūturai:*

kāṉa mayilāṭak kaṇṭirunta vāṉkōḻi
tāṉum atuvākap pāvittut, tāṉum taṉ
pollāc ciṟakaivirit(tu) āṭiṉāl pōlumē
kallātāṉ kaṟṟa kavi.
(*Mūturai,* Verse 14)

The jungle fowl imitates the peacock
by spreading its plumage and dancing like

an uneducated [*kallātāṉ*] person
reciting a poem committed to memory.

Here *kal* (learning) contrasts with *kallātāṉ* (lack of learning); thus *kallātāṉ kaṟṟ kavi* 'the learned poet who lacked learning' suggests that imitation brought learning without wisdom. In other words, the failure of a jungle fowl to become a peacock through imitation implies that mere retention was not the sign of learning but rather that learning required something else as well.

Who, then, was a learned person? A knowledgeable person did not just recite the palm-leaf text but could cite it appropriately from memory and explain its meaning. The proof of a good memory was the ability to effectively recall elements of learned texts at will and thus demonstrate powerful associative powers.[29] The mind, in a way, worked like a concordance. In order to recollect, the mind had to be agile, capable of quick computation.[30] Mental agility was therefore a kind of virtuosity and also required the cultivation of virtuous qualities.

Philip Lutgendorf's study of Tulasidas's *Ramacharitamanas* in north India argues that learning the epic is a transformative experience in devotional practice. *Charita* experts internalize the *Ramacharitamanas* through repetition, similar to *lectio divina* of medieval Christian monasteries, till the text "is not only memorized but its language, structure and images come to permeate the mental processes so that there is no occurrence, word, or image encountered in life that does not immediately evoke in the devotee some parallel word, phrase or situation from the text."[31] The mnemonic qualities of the *tiṇṇai* curriculum resound with such an interpretation when we consider its ethical texts as a series learned in a particular order. Rather than learning to read at sight, mastering the taxonomy of the sound of the alphabet and learning to cultivate the senses by disciplining the tongue lay at the heart of the learning process. Such orientations upheld learning as a bodily technique.

The Sound of Syllables and the Sound of Virtue

Tiṇṇai methods of learning the Tamil alphabet demonstrate that *tiṇṇai* students were not learning to write letters or do sums on paper but rather were learning phonetic units. Consider, too, that Tamil computation units used the Tamil script, and thus the learning of the alphasyllabary and its taxonomic arrangement was a fundamental skill for the cultivation of memory. The *Aricuvaṭi,* the alphabet book, is a good example to demonstrate how learning the alphabet was associated with disciplining the senses. The *Aricuvaṭi* is a "*vāypāṭu,*"—"mouth practice" or lesson of the mouth—learned like formulaic tables. The *tiṇṇai vāypāṭu* also included the basic units of calculation (*eṉṉilakkam*), computation, and measurements.[32] Computational skills involved learned numerical units and the alphasyllabary, taught in tandem.

Descriptions of *tiṇṇai* methods suggest that learning the *Aricuvaṭi* was comprised of the iterative, the calculative, and the visual, and that it essentially ingrained a sonic taxonomic order into the mind. Thus the students learned the taxonomy of sound by writing the graphemes down repetitively, copying them first on sand so that their fingers would remember, making it a tactile mnemonic technique, while reciting each phonetic unit out loud. Further, the taxonomic organization of Tamil phonology, called the *neṭuṅkaṇakku* (note the suffix *kaṇakku,* or computation) is arranged around the body, particularly the tongue. The sonic order of the Tamil syllables, especially the vowels, is classified according to how the tongue is placed in the mouth and the length of the sound. Each of these was grouped under a name. Soft sounds were called *maḻḻeḻuttu;* hard sounds, *vaḻḻeḻuttu;* and the five short vowels, *āṇpāleḻuttu.* The teaching of the *neṭuṅkaṇakku* was itself a mnemonic device, built into learning the *Aricuvaṭi.*

If the fundamental lesson of early *tiṇṇai* learning was to absorb the basic phonetic units arranged in a taxonomy of sound, it is especially significant that after learning the *Aricuvaṭi* students learned Auvaiyār's best-known compositions, the *Ātticūṭi* and the *Koṉṟaivēyntaṉ.* They are iconic examples of the *varukkam* style characterized by a distinctive structure of verse arrangement. In this arrangement, each of the one-line verses of the two poems begins with a letter of the Tamil alphasyllabary arranged sequentially. After invoking divine blessings, the *Ātticūṭi* begins with the lines:

> *aṟam ceya virumpu*
> Desire to do virtue
> *āṟuvatu ciṉam*
> Control your anger
> *iyalvatu karavēl*
> Don't (unnecessarily) display your capabilities
> *īvatu vilakēl*
> Be generous

Each of these lines begins with a vowel arranged in sequence, "a," "ā," "i," and "ī." The *Ātticūṭi* and the *Koṉṟaivēyntaṉ* represent the taxonomy of the Tamil alphasyllabary.[33] Both have pedagogic intent built into the poetic structure.

The *Ātticūṭi* consisted of memorable ethical aphorisms that reinforced the taxonomic order of sound, helping students retain and recall them easily. As a missionary commentator noted, it fixed the alphabet in memory and "engraft[ed] upon the whole useful concepts."[34] Constantly repeating the *varukkam* order was not only a tool to discipline the mind; the order of the alphasyllabary also became the fundamental units of associative skill and computation. It was a fundamental act of *muṟai collutal,* or associative learning.

Thus the teacher probably taught the students to associate "A" with *aṟam* and, in turn, *aṟam* with the syllable "A."

Computational and Mnemonic Systems in Tamil Poetics

It is widely acknowledged that Tamil poetics privileges the use of tropes infused with a somatic sensibility.[35] In addition, as many students of Tamil poetics may recognize, Tamil poetics rests on predominantly taxonomic, enumerative, and computational skills. The Tamil alphasyllabary, for instance, is conventionally taught as consisting of two types of sound sequences, the *uyir* (vowels or breath) and the *mey* (the body). The twelve *uyir* and sixteen *mey* combine to produce the entire set of Tamil syllables.

The enumerative and associative quality of Tamil language and poetics sits nicely with what A. K. Ramanujan argues is a "prevalence of concentric containments"—a system that displayed a poetics of tropes; an emphasis on context, the concrete; and a concern with taxonomy.[36] It was also, I should emphasize, a mnemonic device. Consider this simple example from the *Koṉṟaivēyntaṉ,*

eṇṇum eḻuttum kaṇ eṉat takum.
(*Koṉṟaivēyntaṉ,* Verse 7)

Numbers and letters are like eyes.

Here the eyes work as a powerful trope (known as *uḷḷuṟai,* or comparison in Tamil poetics) for internalizing the value of numbers and letters. The power of the eyes as a trope derives from the fact that they are enumerative—the hidden *uḷḷuṟai* in this aphorism is the number 2. Thus numbers and letters are likened to two eyes. This submerged device using enumeration renders concrete the knowledge of numbers and letters, or the skill of computation or phonology, by embedding them in the body and directing attention to the relationship between sense (perception, eyes) and the mind. Ramanujan argues that, in this sense of poetics, taxonomy provides the context and structure of relevance, a rule of permissible combinations, and a frame of reference.[37] Tamil ethical traditions suggest that the qualities of persons are learned through enumeration. There are nine emotions and thirty-two virtues, facilitating easy recall and building strong associative powers for paradigmatic thinking also seen in Sanskrit poetical forms. *Aṟam* was associated with the syllable "A" and triggered off the ability to recall that there were thirty-two *aṟams*.

A further elaboration of the mnemonic quality of *tiṇṇai* texts lie in the manner in which the texts nested within one another. Several reports of the *tiṇṇai* in the early nineteenth century observe that, at the end of the day, the *tiṇṇai* master often made students recite long lists of flowers, spices, and so on, before going home. These were not mere lists to be memorized but a catalogue of texts revised at the end of the school day. Consider that many essential *tiṇṇai* texts were associated with a material object: the *Ātticūṭi* with the *Ātti* flower, the *Koṉṟaivēyntaṉ* with the *Koṉṟai* flower, *Tirukaṭukam* with "three seeds or spices," and so on. By reciting this list, *tiṇṇai* students were also recalling a chain of texts by association, each represented by an object or a substance. If the sequence of *tiṇṇai* texts suggests that their purpose was to strengthen the student's minds, and if the *varukkam* style of Auvaiyār's *Ātticūṭi* inculcated taxonomic and sonic order through breath control, a disciplined tongue, and a fingertip, what about the verse form itself?

Virtuous Verses and Memory

The *tiṇṇai* "order of books" began with the *Aricuvaṭi*. Seen from the formal perspective of the verse form, students internalized the taxonomy of the alphasyllabary (the *Aricuvaṭi*). They then developed their skills by learning single verse lines and couplets in the simple alphasyllabic sequence (*varukkam* style of the *Ātticūṭi* and the *Koṉṟaivēyntaṉ*) before finally building on their skills with the *Mūturai*, in the four-line *veṇpā* style.

A well-known Tamil proverb reads: "the sticks of the banyan and pipal tree strengthen the teeth like the four and the two strengthen utterance." In other words, the sticks of the banyan and pipal trees strengthen the teeth like the *veṇpā* (four) and the *kuṟaḷ* (two) deepen knowledge.[38] While to most Tamil speakers, the *veṇpā* immediately brings the *Nālāṭiyār* to mind, as the *kuṟaḷ* immediately references the *Tirukkuṟaḷ*, it is worth emphasizing that all Tamil ethical texts used in the *tiṇṇai*'s mnemonic system were all either couplets or four-line *veṇpā* verses.

How can we understand the way in which "the couplet and the *veṇpā* deepen knowledge?" We might begin by tracing how the role of memory cultivation was built into these two verse forms. The ethical poetry of the *tiṇṇai* provides specific examples of an ideal sonic order that could be detached and cited individually according to context. Through teaching archetypical examples of ideal verse forms, the perfect *kuṟaḷ*, the quintessential *veṇpā*, the *tiṇṇai* not only imprinted and made concrete the rules of permissible combinations of syllables but it also provided a structure of relevance and a frame of reference for cognition.

Consider some basic elements that make up the process of poetic composition in Tamil. Tamil prosody, called *yāppu* ("tying"), uses the alphasyllabary (*eḻuttu*) in basic metrical units (*acai*), metrical feet (*cīr*), and lines (*aṭi*). The rules of *yāppu* denote the rules of combining the elements that make up the verse; the term used for assessing the verse form is called *tūkku*.[39] *Tūkku* represents the process of measuring, analyzing, or "parsing" a verse form. Conventionally *tūkku* is compared to the measuring of gold and silver—a process of discernment divides the meter into feet, lines, and so on, to reveal the difference in sound or rhythm of the verse (*ōcai*) that responds to different meters. Scholars observe that the *kuṟaḷ* and the *veṇpā* verse are distinguished by the declarative sound *ceppal ōcai,* from "*ceppu*" meaning "to proclaim, to state."[40] Now the *ceppal ōcai* is supposed to have the sound and force of a sentence/statement (*vākiyam*) rather than a melody—its didactic tone therefore entailed a recitative function. Even if only advanced scholars learned the skills of *yāppu* and *tūkku* many years after having been schooled in *tiṇṇai,* most young *tiṇṇai* learners were essentially internalizing the form and the sound of the *veṇpā* and the *kuṟaḷ* as frames to know, to recite, and *to act.* Auvaiyār's *Ātticūṭi* always commands the addressee,

aṟam ceya virumpu
Desire to do virtue

In the *Ātticūṭi,* the imperative commanding tone is maintained with specific syllables that ended verbs—the syllables "u" connoting "do" and "ēl" connoting "don't," hence

aṟam ceya virumpu
Desire to do virtue
ōtuvatu oḻiyēl
Don't cease learning

Commanding lends itself to a call-and-repeat style of teaching or constant reiteration. If we consider that *tiṇṇai* school pedagogy emphasized a mode of teaching and learning that we may term "call and repeat," then we can think of the command style as particularly conducive to teaching through question and answer. The verse form of *veṇpā* and *kuṟaḷ* is thus particularly well suited to the pedagogic techniques of cultivating memory.

Somatic Virtues of the Tongue and Ear

Scholars of Tamil textual practice and pedagogy have theorized about the central role of the tongue.[41] This centrality of the tongue is borne out in the famous *Tirukkuṟaḷ* couplet equating the tongue with speech and good speech with virtue.

nānalam eṉṉum nalaṉuṭaimai annalam
yānalattu uḷḷatūm aṉṟu
(*Tirukkuṟaḷ,* Verse 641)

There is no goodness like good speech (tongue)
Among all the known virtues.

Many Tamil poetic compositions relate the mind to the practice of the tongue and mouth, or *nā-payiṟci*. Disciplining the senses schools the mind, and it should come as no surprise, as Sivalingaraja notes, that the poets related these to *paḻakkam,* that practice which through repetition becomes an internalized habit. A stand-alone verse (*taṉip pāṭal*) attributed to Auvaiyār reads,

Cittiramum kaipaḻakkam, ceṉtamiḻ nāpaḻakkam
Vaittavoru kalvi maṉapaḻakkam, mattanaṭaiyum
naṭaipaḻakkam, natpum takaiyum kotaiyum piṟavik kuṇam.[42]

Painting arises from hand-practice, refined Tamil comes from tongue-practice
A physician's knowledge comes from mind-practice, all other great arts come from the practice of styles,
But the qualities of friendship, merit, and gifting come from birth.

In other words, the ability to acquire skills depended on practice, and embedded in this relationship was a relationship of transformation, wherein bodily practice schooled the mind. Here we get important insights into the efficacy of ethical texts. Both the *Ātticūṭi* and the *Koṉṟaivēyntaṉ* are texts about doing, or action. Located within the techniques of somatic discipline inculcated in the *tiṇṇai* school, they articulate the relationship between the mind and bodily senses by emphasizing that disciplined habits and virtuous acts go together. The mind/heart, or *maṉam*, could act and be acted upon. The cultivated person's *maṉam* could judge effectively, absorb good, retain virtue, and appreciate the good qualities of others. Through the skillful use of tropes, the qualities of character (*kuṇam*) assume not just humoral essences but the qualities of matter.

nallār oruvarkkuc ceyta upakāram
kalmēl eḻuttuppōl kāṇumē, allāta
īramilā neñcattārk kīnta upakāram
nīrmēl eḻuttukku nēr.
(*Mūturai,* Verse 2)

To do a good deed for a good person
is like writing on stone,
Unlike a doing good to a dry-hearted person,
which is like writing on water.

This *Mūturai* verse indicates that acting toward others in particular ways—good conduct—cultivates the mind/heart. "Doing good" to others is likened to inscription, that is, inscribing on another's chest. The virtuous person was, as other verses from the *Mūturai* declare, someone who did good to others, who displayed patience and rectitude, who understood that the fruits of labor came with the fullness of time, who associated with the worthy, and who cultivated habits appropriate to his station. The mind/heart, here literally the "chest" (*neñcu*), is a malleable matter, endowed with the material qualities of the earth—retaining imprints, bearing the qualities of compassion (wetness), or cruelty (dryness).

The idea of a malleable chest/heart is especially suggestive when we consider that the common Tamil word for learning texts is *maṉapāṭam* or "schooling the mind/heart." It is now commonly understood as "learning by heart" or "rote learning" or mere retention. In the *tiṇṇai,* disciplining the mouth through *vāypāṭam* and repetition was crucial to *maṉapāṭam* because the mind/heart was malleable. Repetition schooled the heart, and allowed students to ingest virtue and facilitate recollection. On recollecting aphorisms in different contexts, through the exercise of one's trained mental faculties, the power of the recalled words reappeared again and again with new depth, unearthing new levels of understanding.

aṭakkam uṭaiyār aṟivilar eṉṟeṇṇik
kaṭakkak karutavum vēṇṭā—maṭaittalaiyil
ōṭumīṉ ōṭa uṟumīṉ varumaḷavum
vāṭi irukkumām kokku
(*Mūturai,* Verse 16)

Don't think that those with rectitude lack *aṟivu* (intelligence)
The motionless crane waits on the water's edge
To snare the one fish
From the multitude that swim by

Auvaiyār's verse relates self-discipline to intelligence by emphasizing that bodily discipline helps the concentration of the mind and hence discernment. This essay has attempted to demonstrate that the cultivation of virtue rested on techniques of body and sense control, and that these techniques were properly taught only to *tiṇṇai* students, distinguishing them from those who could not enter the precincts of the school. The efficacy of *aṟam* poems appears in new light when viewed in the *tiṇṇai.* The complex relationship between the form and content of these ethical poems emerges only in the context of pedagogic practice, and only when that pedagogy is not reduced by retention or overdetermined by issues of textual materiality—matters of print or palm-leaf. To the extent that the *tiṇṇai* model of teaching was a ubiquitous form of schooling until the advent of the colonial and mission school, learning ethical poems in the context of burgeoning sectarian piety illustrates the close relationship that these texts bore, in both form and content, to the very act of learning itself.

Acknowledgments

Research for this chapter was funded by grants from the Social Science Research Council and the American Institute of Indian Studies. Earlier drafts of this essay were presented at the following conferences: "Genealogies of Virtue" at the University of British Columbia, Vancouver; "Knowledge Production and Pedagogy in Colonial India," School of Oriental and African Studies and the German Institute, London; and to audiences at the University of Michigan, Ann Arbor, and the University of Pennsylvania, Philadelphia. Conversations with the editors of this volume and with D. Senthilbabu, Sumathi Ramaswamy, Francis Cody, and V. Geetha helped greatly in its revision. I thank them all.

Notes

1. At least two poets are believed to bear the name Auvaiyar. One is thought to have lived during the Sangam period in the early centuries of the first millennium. The other is said to have lived in the Chola Empire (ninth to thirteenth century CE) and is credited with the composition of the poems discussed in this essay. Other important ethical poems used in schools and attributed to Auvaiyār or Auvai, as she is affectionately called, are *Nalvaḻi* and *Mūturai*. Other than the Auvaiyār's texts, important ethical compositions, termed *nītinūl* or "books of conduct," include the *Tirukkuṟaḷ*, *Nītiveṇpā, Ulakanīti, Veṟṟivēṟkai, Vivēka cintāmaṇi,* and *Kumarēca catakam*. They date to different centuries but all emphasize ethical conduct and discernment. Norman Cutler notes that the earliest reference to the term "*nītinūl*" occurs in the late thirteenth century in Parimēlaḷagar's commentary on the *Tirukkuṟaḷ*. See Norman Cutler, "Three Moments in the Genealogy of Tamil Literary Culture," in *Literary Cultures in History*, ed. Sheldon Pollock (Berkeley: University of California Press, 2003), 293.

2. See Cutler, "Three Moments in the Genealogy of Tamil Literary Culture," on the difficulties of separating the theological from the nonsectarian and his argument for privileging the literary/ethical rather than the theological moorings of Tamil textual life.

3. On indigenous elementary schooling in the nineteenth century, see P. Radhakrishnan, "Caste Discrimination in the Indian Indigenous Education, Nature and Extent of Education in Early Nineteenth Century British India," *Working Paper* 63 (Chennai: Madras Institute of Development Studies,1986); Paromesh Acharya, "Indigenous Education and Brahmanical Hegemony in Bengal," in *The Transmission of Knowledge in South Asia*, ed. Nigel Crook (Delhi: Oxford University Press, 1996), 98–118; Kazi Shahidullah, "The Purpose and Impact of Government Policy on *Pathsala gurimashays*," in Crook, *The Transmission of Knowledge in South Asia*, 119–134; S. Sivalingaraja and Saraswathi Sivalingaraja, *Pattoṉpatām Nūṟṟāṇṭil Yāḻppāṇattut Tamiḻkkalvi* (Chennai: Kumaran, 2000); D. Senthilbabu, "Memory and Mathematics

in the Tamil *Tiṇṇai* Schools of South India in the Eighteenth and Nineteenth Centuries," *International Journal for the History of Mathematics Education* 2, no.1 (2007): 15–37; and Lisa Mitchell, *Language, Emotion, and Politics in South India: The Making of a Mother Tongue* (Bloomington: Indiana University Press, 2009). For a discussion of *tiṇṇai* schooling's relationship to Tamil literary practice, see Sascha Ebeling, *The Transformation of Tamil Literature in Nineteenth-Century South India* (Albany: State University of New York Press, forthcoming). On the ethical and technical training of Persian *munshi* apprentices in seventeenth-century north India, see Sanjay Subrahmanyam and Muzaffar Alam, "The Making of a Munshi," *Comparative Studies of South Asia, Africa, and the Middle East* 24, no. 2 (2004): 61–72.

4. For similar formulations, see Senthilbabu, "Memory and Mathematics," on the role of memory in mathematical learning. On the issue of memory and Telugu poetic learning, see Mitchell, *Language, Emotion, and Politics in South India.* On contemporary Tamil literacy activists' struggles with the ingrained hegemony of memory-oriented aural pedagogy, see Francis Cody, "Literacy as Enlightenment: Written Language, Activist Mediation, and the State in Rural Tamilnadu, India" (Ph.D. diss., University of Michigan, 2007).

5. Daud Ali, *Courtly Culture and Political Life in Early Medieval India* (Cambridge: Cambridge University Press, 2004); Velcheru Narayana Rao and Sanjay Subrahmanyam, "Notes on Political Thought in Medieval and Early Modern South India," *Modern Asian Studies* 43, no. 1 (2009): 175–210; Muzaffar Alam, *Languages of Political Islam* (Chicago: University of Chicago Press, 2004). Recent work on the *Dharmaśāstra* emphasizes the important of practice or conduct; see Donald Davis, "Dharma in Practice: Ācārā and Authority in Medieval Dharmaśāstra," *Journal of Indian Philosophy* 32 (2004): 813–830, and Leela Prasad, *The Poetics of Conduct: Oral Narrative and Moral Being in a South Indian Town* (New York: Columbia University Press, 2007).

6. Philip Lutgendorf, *The Life of a Text: Performing the Ramcharitramanas of Tulsidas* (Berkeley: University of California Press, 1991); Norman Cutler "Interpreting Tirukkuṟaḷ: The Role of Commentary in the Creation of a Text," *Journal of the American Oriental Society* 112, no. 4 (1992): 549–566; and Cutler, "Three Moments in the Genealogy of Tamil Literary Culture," 312–318.

7. Raj Gautaman, Preface to *Aṟam/Atikāram* (Coimbatore: Viṭiyal, 1997).

8. For a study that emphasizes the epistemic struggle between schooling deemed traditional and schooling deemed modern, and the distinction drawn between rote learning and "real learning" in colonial India, see Sanjay Seth, *Subject Lessons: The Western Education of Colonial India* (Durham, N.C.: Duke University Press, 2007).

9. Barbara Metcalf, ed., *Moral Conduct and Authority: The Place of Adab in South Asian Islam* (Berkeley: University of California Press, 1984).

10. Talal Asad, *Formations of the Secular: Christianity, Islam, Modernity* (Stanford, Calif.: Stanford University Press, 2003); Saba Mahmood, *The Politics of Piety: The Islamic Revival and the Feminist Subject* (Princeton, N.J.: Princeton University Press, 2005); Charles Hirschkind, *The Ethical Soundscape: Cassette Sermons and Islamic Counterpublics* (New York: Columbia University Press, 2006); Ali, *Courtly Culture and Political Life;* and Anand Pandian and Daud Ali, introduction to this volume.

11. J. Bernard Bate, *Tamil Oratory and the Dravidian Aesthetic: Democratic Practice in South India* (New York: Columbia University Press, 2009).

12. J. Bernard Bate, in ibid., and Charles Hirschkind, in *The Ethical Soundscape,* have argued, in very different ways, for the importance of the tongue in political speech

and the ear in receiving sermons as active sites of self-cultivation. *Tiṇṇai* pedagogy, although distinct from the milieus of public oratory and religious sermons, provides an institutional site to analyze how the tongue and the ear (important to the studies of rhetoric) were central to practices of mental cultivation or the art of memory (*ars memorae*).

13. On ethical texts as manuals of self-cultivation in medieval India, see Ali, *Courtly Culture and Political Life.* My formulation builds on this insight.

14. The *tiṇṇai* style also resonated in orthodox sectarian pedagogical practice. The style of teaching through call and repeat resembles what Christopher Fuller's recent ethnographic research on Saivite priestly learning documents as *cantai* and *tiruvai.* See Fuller "Orality, Literacy, and Memorization: Priestly Education in Contemporary South India," *Modern Asian Studies* 35, no. 1 (2001): 1–31.

15. Sivalingaraja and Sivalingaraja, *Pattoṉpatām Nūṟṟāṇṭil Yālppāṇattut Tamiḻkkalvi.*

16. The notion of the *ūr,* or settlement, is embedded in a mutually reinforcing agrarian and caste landscape. It is distinguished from the *kāṭu* (uncultivated waste, or forest), from the *ceri* (settlements of outcaste groups that provided the *ūr* with labor), and the *akirakāram* (enclaves of Brahman residences). *Ūr* settlements were predominantly caste-Hindu but included residences of resource-controlling Muslim and Christian households. Only children from the *akirakāram* and the *ūr* attended *Tiṇṇai* schools. On a recent formulation of the social topography of settlement patterns, see Diane Mines, *Fierce Gods: Inequality, Ritual, and the Politics of Dignity in a South Indian Village* (Bloomington: Indiana University Press, 2005).

17. Radhakrishnan, "Caste Discrimination."

18. These and other verses cited in the chapter are culled from standard editions of Auvaiyār's texts. The translations are my own.

19. On the important relationship between cultivation and virtue in Tamil-speaking south India, see Anand Pandian, *Crooked Stalks: Cultivating Virtue in South India* (Durham, N.C.: Duke University Press, 2009).

20. "A. D. Campbell's Report," in *Papers on Education in Madras Presidency,* ed. A. J. Arbutnoth (Madras: Public Instruction, 1854), Appendix E.

21. I am grateful to Anand Pandian for drawing my attention to this issue and for an engaged discussion of the ideas of work in transforming *kāṭu* (uncultivated waste) into an ordered, settled *nāṭu* in the poems. The trope of cultivation is especially central to dominant caste Vellalar agriculturalist traditions.

22. I draw here on V. Geetha's reading of Raj Gautaman, personal communication and her paper, "Notes Towards a Notion of Tamil Patriarchy," presented at the Southern Regional Seminar on "Women and Regional Histories" held in Hyderabad and organized by the Department of History, Hyderabad Central University and Indian Association of Women's Studies, August–September 1999.

23. "A. D. Campbell's Report on the State of Education in Bellary, Board of Revenue, 17 August, 1823," in Arbutnoth, *Papers on Education in Madras Presidency,* Appendix E; *Mackenzie Papers* 131, no. 3, European mss., Asia Pacific and Africa Collections, British Library, London.

24. "A. D. Campbell's Report" (1854).

25. *Palajātikam-Vikaṭam: Marāṭṭiyar kāla nāṭaka nakaic cuvaik kāṭcita tokuppu,* ed. C. K. Devanayakam (Tanjavur: Tanjavur Saraswati Mahal Publication no. 246, 1986), 4.

26. U. Ve. Swaminathaiyar, *The Story of My Life,* translated in English by Kamil Zvelebil (Chennai: International Institute of Asian Studies, 1994 [1990]), 37.

27. Mary Carruthers, *The Book of Memory: A Study of Memory in Medieval Culture* (New York: Cambridge University Press, 1990).

28. Ibid.

29. Such values resonate closely among poets and scholars with the poetic skill of *avatāṉam.* U. V. Swaminatha Iyer's autobiography is filled with references to *avatāṉam* virtuosos. On *avatāṉam* among Telugu poets, see Mitchell, *Language, Emotion, and Politics in South India.*

30. Carruthers, *The Book of Memory.*

31. Lutgendorf, *The Life of a Text,* 176.

32. Senthilbabu, "Memory and Mathematics."

33. There are multiple reworkings of the *Ātticūṭi* in which the maxims vary but all are in the *varukkam* style. Among the different versions, the poet Subramaniam Bharati's is perhaps the most famous. Other kinds of *varukkam* poems include the *Varukka-k-kōvai,* a verse genre in *kalitturai* meter in which stanzas begin with letters of the alphasyllabary arranged in regular order; and the *Varukkavetukai* (*etukai* rhyming) in which the second letters of the lines of the verse agree. The emphasis is clearly on sound and an aural order.

34. William, Taylor, "Fifth Report of Progress Made in the Examination of the Mackenzie Mss., with an Abstract Account of the Works Examined," *Madras Journal of Literature and Science* 9 (January–June 1839): 329.

35. Sumathi Ramasamy, *Passions of the Tongue: Language Devotion in Tamil India, 1891–1970* (Berkeley: University of California Press, 1997); Indira Peterson, *Poems to Siva: The Hymns of the Tamil Saints* (Princeton, N.J.: Princeton University Press, 1989); Karen Prentiss, *The Embodiment of Bhakti* (New York: Oxford University Press, 1999).

36. A. K. Ramanujan, "Is There an Indian Way of Thinking," in *The Collected Essays of A. K. Ramanujan,* ed. Vinay Dharwadker (Delhi: Oxford University Press, 1999), 44.

37. Ibid., 45.

38. Mu. Varataracan, *A History of Tamil Literature,* trans. E. Sa. Viswanathan (New Delhi: Sahitya Akademi, 1988), 73.

39. V. Rajam, *A Reference Grammar of Classical Tamil Poetry: 150 BC–pre-Fifth/Sixth Century AD* (Philadelphia: American Philosophical Society, 1992), 187.

40. Ibid.

41. Sivalingarajah and Sivalingaraja, *Pattoṉpatām Nūṟṟāṇṭil Yāḻppāṇattut Tamiḻkkalvi;* Gautaman, Preface; and Bate, *Tamil Oratory.*

42. Sivalingaraja and Sivalingaraja, *Pattoṉpatām Nūṟṟāṇṭil Yāḻppāṇattut Tamiḻkkalvi* 39.

3.

Ethical Traditions in Question: Diaspora Jainism and the Environmental and Animal Liberation Movements

James Laidlaw

The Jain tradition originated in north India in the fourth to third centuries BC. Like its close first cousin, Buddhism, it began as one of a number of competing groups of itinerant renouncers pursuing a distinctive project for individuals to refashion themselves radically in the pursuit of enlightenment and liberation. It continues to be distinguished among such traditions by the severity of the ascetic discipline it requires of its renouncers—and recommends to their lay followers—and by the prominence in its teachings and practices of the values of non-attachment (*aparigraha*) and nonviolence (*ahimsa*). Neither the number of Jain renouncers nor of their lay followers ever reached the same scale as Buddhism in India during the first millennium of their history, and until the twentieth century no substantial population of Jains was ever established elsewhere, and yet it did not die out in peninsular India to the extent that Buddhism did. Its small populations of monks and nuns (the latter have always been more numerous than the former) have divided over time into many competing lineages, each enjoying the patronage and veneration of lay communities, mostly rural shopkeepers and traders, and urban merchants, financiers, and professionals. Today Jains form about half of 1 percent of the Indian population but are disproportionately affluent and influential. Lay Jains have for many centuries been concentrated in northwestern India (Gujarat and Rajasthan) and in parts of the south (especially Karnataka), but during the nineteenth century they spread across the subcontinent and during the twentieth overseas, first along British imperial trade routes to east Africa and elsewhere, and subsequently to the same destinations in Europe and the English-speaking countries as has the general diaspora of middle-class Indians.[1]

In recent years many Jains, especially the young and educated and those in the Anglophone countries, have been drawn to the animal liberation and environmentalist movements, maintaining that they are so drawn precisely as Jains. But the nature of the connection or affinity perceived between Jainism and these worldwide social movements is being glossed in a variety of ways. For some, Jainism is the long-established exponent of truths these other movements are only now glimpsing; others see embracing environmentalism and animal liberation as a return to principles from which the tradition has partially strayed; and for still others it requires a more or less radical reinterpretation of those principles. Some, therefore, envisage thoroughgoing reform of established Jain practice, and others imagine the refashioning of environmentalism and animal welfare along Jain lines. Indeed, there are many variations, combinations, and intermediate positions.

The interaction of Jainism with these movements is recent and still developing, and its effects and how it will come to be understood depend on judgments and decisions only now being formulated. A first step in understanding this situation is a description that does not prejudge what the outcome is or should be, and I suggest that this will require thinking in terms of historically embodied traditions rather than employing more common anthropological conceptions of culture.

Problem Situations

The establishment of substantial permanent communities of Jains outside South Asia always made significant religious change likely, not only in countries overseas but also in India. The religious life of lay Jain communities there revolves to a considerable extent around the presence of monks and nuns. In all but the largest cities, the latter's presence is generally intermittent. Renouncers travel from settlement to settlement, generally staying in one place for longer than a few days only during the monsoon. But virtually all forms of lay religious practice are enactments of lay Jains' relationships with them—praising and venerating renouncers, receiving blessings from them, hearing their sermons, being led in meditation or confession, giving alms, undertaking fasts and other austerities by taking vows before them, and so on. Many of these practices may be performed in the absence of renouncers. However, practices that are carried out only in the presence of a symbolic representation of renouncers are thought of as second-best substitutes. In short, a full and rounded lay Jain life may be achieved only in interaction with living renouncers, even if this must be rather infrequent.

Renouncers have no home and no possessions other than those they carry, and in their travels they must maintain a watchful awareness so that they never unnecessarily harm any living thing. The only way to do this, it has always been agreed, is to travel by walking barefoot, gently brushing the ground clear of insects as one goes. Wheeled, mechanical, or motorized transport of any kind is prohibited. Thus overseas Jain communities must do without the expectation of even the most occasional face-to-face interaction with renouncers.[2]

Very few renouncers have attempted to defy these prohibitions, traveling overseas in the hope of spreading Jain life and teachings. These jet-setting dissident monks have each enjoyed a certain celebrity, but they have also lost their authority. They have either been expelled from or deemed to have left their own monastic orders. In almost all cases, they have gone on to break, or radically reinterpret, other vows (such as celibacy), so that the majority of Jains no longer recognize them as sacred exemplars as they do conventional renouncers. One Jain sect, the Svetambar Terapanth, has found a way around the problem; it has created a rank of quasi-renouncers (called *samanis*) who live under monastic authority and are explicitly subordinate to fully ordained renouncers but whose lesser vows allow international travel. Unlike the other Jain orders, the Svetambar Terapanth is a centralized bureaucracy under a single paramount cleric, so although these new quasi-renouncers are not so highly esteemed as a class, their own personal piety and discipline are not put in question by the very fact of their traveling. But there is only a handful of these *samanis*, and their presence, including in overseas Jain communities, remains marginal.

The question remains open, therefore, as to what, if anything, will take the place of the renouncer's pursuit of liberation as the project around which everyday lay religious life for Jains overseas is organized. Of course, this raises another question for Jains in India, as elsewhere, of whether and in what ways the tradition might need to be more generally reformed or redirected. In recent years a chorus of otherwise unconnected or competing Jain voices has suggested that the answer lies in a combination of ecologism and animal welfare. The most influential single statement of what one might call "Eco-Jainism" was issued in London in 1990, as a joint declaration by a number of Jain organizations based in the United Kingdom and India.[3] "The Jain Declaration of Nature," which has since gained virtually scriptural status in certain circles, asserts that the defining principles of environmentalism and animal welfare were anticipated in Jainism from its beginnings, and that Jainism can still point the way forward for these global movements.[4] Thus Jain teachings, the Declaration concludes, "offer the world today a time-tested anchor of moral imperatives and a viable route plan for humanity's common pilgrimage for holistic environmental protection, peace, and harmony in the universe."[5] The Svetambar Terapanth has been characteristically audible. Its leaders have sought to make their brand of Jainism more politically and socially engaged, and environmentalism and animal welfare have become prominent themes, including in the correspondence courses offered by its Jain University. Many other Jain spokespersons, including some of the dissident renouncers mentioned above but also many more orthodox lay community leaders in other traditions, have suggested that Jainism, as a kind of Ur-ecology, represents an urgently needed resource for all humanity, and that its relevance to environmentalism and animal welfare needs to be emphasized and renewed in order to ensure the continuing vitality of the tradition.

The main Jain organizations in the United States, Britain, Canada, Australia, and elsewhere all now include ecology and animal welfare prominently in the programs for their meetings and conferences, in their magazines and Web sites, and in their promotional and educational material. Organizations such as the Young Jains maintain increasingly strong links with other Green and animal-rights organizations. The interest and attraction is mutual to some degree, with animal rights groups and spokespersons for "deep ecology" describing Jainism (though much less frequently than they do Buddhism or "indigenous wisdom") as a prototype of Green sensibility.[6] For many, especially younger Jains in the diaspora, their identity as Jains focuses increasingly on these issues. A considerable number are amending the vegetarianism they have inherited from their families and adopting the vegan diet favored by many of their non-Jain colleagues in these global movements.[7]

Traditional Deliberations

The institutions and practices of Jain renunciation involve the deliberate and self-conscious transmission of a body of religious teaching and ethical practice, and in this process each generation of Jain teachers works *on* as well as *in* that tradition, restating and reemphasizing what they consider central to it and addressing what they perceive to be difficulties and misunderstandings. Its relative coherence and partial systematicity are their ongoing and never completed achievement. The same is obviously true of ecologism and animal liberation. Jains who are currently making judgments and decisions with respect to environmentalism and animal welfare, about whether or how to adjust their own conduct in light of these concerns, have these intellectual and practical resources to draw on. The specific interest of the present situation consists in the fact that at least one of these traditions is now self-consciously open to the other.

Protagonists still have the opportunity and, in their view, the responsibility to decide how to shape their conduct in the light of deliberative reflection on the possibilities that present themselves. There are no positions that endow individuals with the authority to make decisions on behalf of Jainism as a whole or, in most cases, for particular sects or schools, but in these highly self-conscious and reflective traditions people do decide and act on their own account, also self-consciously, as representatives and agents of those traditions, and in their name.

Alasdair MacIntyre provides a valuable account of situations of interaction or dialogue between rival traditions of moral thought. In *Whose Justice? Which Rationality?* he extends the account of moral tradition that he began to develop in *After Virtue*[8] by considering the kinds of deliberation and decision that may be called for when such traditions are brought into genuine interaction. The story MacIntyre tells includes several such episodes, from the dialogue between two rival conceptions of justice in post-Homeric Greek political thought to the emergence of modern liberalism, which MacIntyre sees as the product of a critical engagement between the Scottish Enlightenment and the English legal tradition. The central episodes in his narrative concern the reconciliation of Augustinian Christianity and Aristotelianism that was achieved by Aquinas, and consolidated and institutionalized by Gregory VII, in the great synthesis that was high-medieval Catholicism.

Much in MacIntyre's account is at best irrelevant to anthropological inquiry—including his rather intrusive moral evaluations of these various developments—but as others have noted, there is also much that is of value.[9] Insofar as the common anthropological (and now also real-world political) notion of plural "cultures" gives rise to the problem situation we know as relativism (or multi-culturalism)—cultures imagined as separate, self-enclosed, and fundamentally non-comparable conceptual universes, whose integrity derives from their separateness and distinctiveness, and between which, therefore, interaction must be imagined as disintegration or hybridization—MacIntyre provides not only persuasive exemplification that it is historically unrealistic but also some useful conceptual resources to enable its replacement. He develops an account of historically embodied traditions and something like a formal account of how interactions between them are possible. This he can do because such a conception of tradition is, as Talal Asad notes, "a more mobile, time-sensitive, more open-ended concept than most formulations of culture [and] it looks not just to the past but to the future."[10]

In historically embodied traditions, on MacIntyre's account, conceptions of rational inquiry, human flourishing, and justice are constantly tested and rethought as a result of people's ongoing efforts to live their own particular lives in the light of those conceptions. The change that results is deliberative, and therefore, although it is incremental and uncoordinated, it is not mere directionless drift.[11] "A tradition," he writes, "is an argument extended through time in which certain fundamental agreements are defined and redefined in terms of two kinds of conflict: those with critics and enemies external to the tradition . . . and those internal, interpretive debates . . . by whose progress a tradition is constituted."[12] Thus, in the situations MacIntyre describes, in one tradition, beliefs, values, and practices from another might be seriously entertained as potentially preferable to its own, in the light of its own perceived problems and shortcomings and as judged by its own criteria and standards.[13]

The Jain tradition is fissiparous. Its various schools and sub-traditions are the outcome of many episodes of debate and disagreement, innovation and reform, including vigorous discussions of the merits of inherited ideas and practices compared to those of other religions.[14] This is a tradition that is as used to the active consideration of alternatives as it is to conscientious adherence to precedent. The grounds for current internal questioning have already been mentioned. There is the absence from the diaspora of renouncers who embody its defining project of world renunciation; the apparent anachronism and "unscientific" character of many established beliefs and practices; and its marginality, as critics perceive it, to pressing social and political issues facing the world. To renew the tradition with resources drawn from the animal rights and environmentalist movements, or even to effect a thoroughgoing synthesis with them, seems to some Jain intellectuals to be the basis for a claim that Jainism has something urgently valuable to offer "to society," which, of course, can be conceived on a global as well as a national scale.

MacIntyre describes situations in which internal questioning culminates in critical engagement with a rival tradition as "epistemological crises,"[15] but it is important not to be misled by that term. In some of the cases MacIntyre discusses, a "crisis" leads to a dialogue which comes to be seen, from within the tradition, as an enrichment. Such is the case, for instance, according to MacIntyre, of the challenge presented to medieval Christianity by the rediscovery of Aristotle's major works. In Aquinas's hands, a synthesis was achieved in which "the Augustinian understanding of fallen human nature is used to explain the limitations of Aristotle's arguments, just as the detail of Aristotle often corrects Augustine's generalizations."[16]

MacIntyre himself does not comment on the fact, and perhaps he does not see things this way, but on his own description this is far from being a balanced or symmetrical synthesis: the Augustinian understanding encompasses Aristotelian detail. If what some Jain intellectuals hope to achieve with deep ecology is a synthesis of something such as this, then the question arises regarding which term might turn out to be hierarchically super-ordinate. If we were to suppose that "Eco-Jainism" represents an emergent synthesis of this kind, then one way to understand it might be to chart its genealogy, to identify how its characteristics derive respectively from the Jain tradition and the ecology and animal rights movements, and to consider how these different inheritances have been transformed in the new combination.[17] This, however, would make sense only on the presumption that we are dealing, to speak in genealogical terms, with an offspring that is, as such, distinct from its progenitors. But for the present, at least, imagining what such an offspring might look like would be conjectural. It is still possible that in the long run the encounter will leave both traditions substantially unchanged.

It is also possible that their effects will take the form of what Deleuze calls "double capture"[18] exemplified by the co-evolution of an orchid species whose flowers have come closely to resemble the female of a certain species of wasp, and that wasp species, whose males attempt to mate with the orchid, thereby pollinating it. These two species do not combine in sexual reproduction, and so they are producing no joint offspring, but they do engage in a mutual modification: a becoming-orchid on the part of the wasp and a becoming-wasp by the orchid. They remain separate species, as essentially different as they ever were, yet with an asymmetrical taking up of certain of each other's properties. This self-modification in response to the other is not the same as the creation of a new hybrid entity that will succeed its predecessors, and unlike with the conception of culture as quasi-organic discrete entity, it is an equally plausible outcome of dialogue between traditions.

In what follows I consider a connected series of questions and choices faced by anyone, located within the Jain tradition, taking the claims of the animal rights and Green movements seriously. These questions concern, first of all, the character of moral knowledge and the knowing self; second, the nature of important ethical virtues; and, third, the imputed moral character of "nature." For each I try to identify the kind of challenge that adopting such claims would present both to the core project of Jain ascetic world renunciation and to the accommodations between this and lay life which Jain communities have historically reached.

Forms of Knowledge and Knowing Selves

It is a remarkable fact that, at least in the English-speaking world, a single argument, especially in the form advanced by the philosopher Peter Singer, has become the almost universally accepted central doctrine of the animal liberation movement.[19] Singer claims that it is a prejudice, strictly comparable to racism or sexism, to treat nonhuman animals differently merely because they are not human. In a classic progressivist narrative, Singer predicts the overthrow of this prejudice, just as the abolition of slavery and the liberation and empowerment of women, blacks, gays, and the disabled have successively overcome the illusions and misperceptions that justified their mistreatment. The prejudice of "speciesism," as Singer terms it, is exposed by an avowedly utilitarian ethical argument, according to which the minimization of suffering is the overriding criterion in virtue of which acts and states of affairs may be judged ethically.[20] He argues that animals' capacity to suffer endows them with an interest in its avoidance, and concludes that this endows them with rights to protection from suffering, rights that are strictly equivalent to those enjoyed by humans, since they accrue just in virtue of those interests. And just as rights enjoyed by other humans impose on the rest of us obligations to behave so as to minimize unnecessary suffering, so, too, do animal rights.

Seen from the Jain tradition, one could happily go along with much of this reasoning. Jain scriptures emphasize that all living things wish to continue to live, and, if harmed, they suffer. Jain teachings extend these claims to insects, plants, and aspects of the material world that, at first sight, are not "alive" such as earth, air, water, and fire, all of which are said to be inhabited by tiny, short-lived, single-sensed creatures. A passage in the earliest surviving canonical text describes how trees, in drawing sustenance from the earth, kill earth bodies in the soil around their roots.[21] All living things are classified according to the number of senses they have, and therefore the ways in which they are capable of suffering; they range from five-sensed beings (not only humans and mammals but also gods and hell beings) to those with four, three, and two senses to single-sensed creatures such as the invisible beings who fill up the space around us and are almost invariably referred to in India these days using the English word "germs." Each of these living things has an immortal soul fundamentally like that of a human being. Indeed, virtually every human will have lived many times before as a wild animal, a beast of burden, an insect, plant, and microbe. And the most important factor affecting the next destination of each soul, at each death and rebirth, is the violence and suffering it inflicted on other living things during its previous lives.

These ideas might almost have been invented to give imaginative force to Singer's argument: to make harming other species really seem to be morally equivalent to harming humans. And the image of the world as literally filled with sentient creatures, constantly being born, living, and dying in intricate relations of interdependence, is recognizable to deep ecologists as resembling their own.[22] Furthermore, it is not just that Jain doctrine asserts these beliefs. Much Jain practice is concerned with making them compelling. An important element of what the Jains call the "Right View" (*samyak darshan*) is that individuals should actually learn to experience the space around them as already inhabited. So, for instance, one day a lay teacher interrupted a discourse he was giving me on Jain philosophy and drew my attention to the street outside, which was knee-deep in monsoon rainwater. "You see only rain outside and people rushing to get to work," he said, "but the Jain religion sees much more than that. Today there is much violence being done." All those people wading about were unknowingly killing the creatures in the water. I was expected to reflect on this until, like him, I learned to be imaginatively aware of the living things and therefore the violence and suffering going on all around me. Jain ascetic practices such as prescribed periods of meditation and confession, all involving strict control of physical movement to prevent injury to air-beings, are designed to make the experience of the omnipresence and vulnerability of living things habitual.

Herein, however, is the beginning of two important differences from Singer's argument. These Jain practices are techniques of self-formation that serve as steps on a path of spiritual purification: as with Buddhism, walking a lengthy path is the central organizing image for the acquisition of knowledge. Ascetic practices progressively teach one to control the passions that motivate heedless violence toward other living things, and in so doing are steps toward self-knowledge and the overcoming of desire. Persons progressing along this path—which ultimately may take many lifetimes to complete—will pass through many stages in which the world will be perceived and experienced differently, and they will recognize the most profound truths about the nature of the world only as they approach them on their spiritual journey. Nothing that, even in principle, could be known by an unenlightened person at the outset of this journey could be remotely comparable. Singer's argument purports to provide a very different kind of knowledge, and to provide it, moreover, to any unprejudiced listener. Systematic reasoning from self-evident principles leads to conclusions of such geometric certainty as to command assent from any rational agent, and the conclusions are of such scope and clarity that they may be applied to new situations. They enable the utilitarian to adopt an enlightened stance of impartiality and detachment famously referred to by Henry Sidgwick as "the point of view of the universe."[23] As an ethic of self-formation, Jainism embodies a practical rather than a rationalist conception of knowledge (practical, that is, in something like the Aristotelian sense), and its conclusions are not logically derived from self-evident axioms but need to be learned, experienced, and enacted in practical terms by each person for him- or herself.[24]

Moreover, the self that is envisaged and formed in this tradition is not the bearer of interests and rights presupposed by Singer. The *telos* of Jain asceticism is approached through the progressive renouncing of all the empirical components of the self—one's likes and dislikes, affections and attachments, family ties, and personal identity—so that at the end of this journey one faces one's own death, or even deliberately initiates a fast to bring about death, with equanimity.[25] The point of cultivating experience of the world as teeming with life is to arouse a feeling, which Jains call "disgust" or "revulsion" with the world (*vairagya*), which can motivate self-renunciation of this kind.

What might occur if someone who begins from the understanding of these matters developed within the Jain tradition were then to adopt a version of Singer's argument and reason deductively from it—to attempt, that is, to adopt "the point of view of the universe"? To understand the kind of transformation that might follow, consider the following instance of an enthusiast for Eco-Jainism doing just this.

Sadhvi Shilapi is a member of a small dissident Jain community founded by one of those celebrity monks mentioned above. She holds a doctorate from London University and travels widely as a spokesperson for the group. In an essay on the environmental teachings of Jainism, she tells a famous story concerning Lord Mahavir and his closest disciple, Gautam Swami. Mahavir was an elder contemporary of the Buddha and the founder of the Jain tradition in its historical form, although he is also the last of the twenty-four miraculous Victors (*Jinas*) or Ford-Builders (*Tirthankars*) who, during the long eons of Jain mytho-history, have each re-founded the tradition. Although Gautam was a miraculous guru—all of his disciples had attained enlightenment—he himself had not done so precisely because he had remained so attached to his teacher. Mahavir, knowing that he is approaching his own death, attempts to persuade Gautam to relinquish this attachment. He reveals that in their previous lives, as gods in heaven and humans on earth, they have been bound together by affection. If Gautam will cut these bonds, their souls will be able to join each other but this time forever, in disembodied, omniscient immortality. When this argument proves ineffective, and Gautam's love for his teacher continues to prevent his enlightenment, Mahavir sends him off to prevent a powerful Hindu sage from carrying out a mass animal sacrifice, without telling him that he expects to die while Gautam is gone.

The following is Sadhvi Shilapi's comment on this story.

> When Lord Mahavira sent Gautam to prevent [the Hindu sage's] act of violence, he himself was about to attain *nirvana,* the final death, after which Mahavira would not be able to give any more lessons about perfection to his disciples. Certainly Gautam would not get the chance to sit at the feet of his master. Yet Mahavira preferred to take a step that was more universal, a feeling more concerned about the life of others—nonhuman others—than to work further toward the spiritual benefit of one single individual. Thanks to the efforts of Gautam, the slaughter of animals was stopped, and [the sage] took a vow not to kill animals in the future.[26]

Here the Sadhvi adopts, and attributes to Mahavir, the point of view of the universe, a capacity to transcend his own personal viewpoint and see the situation objectively, putting the interests of all before any particular persons or relationships. The aggregate gain in happiness of all the animals that have been saved from suffering outweighs the pain of a single individual arising from the loss of his teacher. But this involves a distinct transformation of the story, making it different from the form that is commonly told and enacted in Jain temples every year during the autumn festival of Diwali, which marks for Jains the anniversary of these events.[27] In that version the point of sending

Gautam away is to save him from the anguish of watching his friend die, and because Mahavir miraculously knows that when Gautam does learn afterward that he has died, he will reflect again on those final teachings, and this will enable him to achieve enlightenment. This is the significance Jains attribute to the lighting of lamps at Diwali, as Gautam realizes that the illumination of Mahavir's teachings can be continued after the source has gone, and that therefore his death is to be welcomed rather than mourned. Making this last realization, Gautam instantly achieves enlightenment and final release, and is in fact reunited with Mahavir, just as the latter had promised.

In this version of the story there is no need, as envisaged by the Sadhvi, to choose between the interests of the one and those of the many, and no need for Mahavir to apply an abstract principle and take the impersonal decision to save the animals rather than helping his friend, because, in sending him away, Mahavir *was* saving his friend. Moral knowledge is not represented in the traditional version as taking a rational-deductive form; on the contrary, it is approached by practical experience, so that even though enlightenment—the realization of perfect knowledge—takes the form of equanimity and indifference to all formerly personal ties and relationships, this *telos* is necessarily approached through and by means of a teacher-pupil bond, in this case one of legendary closeness. Seen in this light, of course, Mahavir's and Gautam's reluctance to pass through and relinquish their relationship turns this story into a subtle reflection on a necessarily poignant aspect of spiritual progress in a tradition structured by practical knowledge and pedagogical relationships of this kind; whereas a rational-deductive conception of knowledge, as espoused by the Sadhvi, makes especially Gautam's reluctance seem like merely personal partiality, which Mahavir's eventual more systematic application of principle rightly overcomes.

The Nature of Virtues

Many younger Jains in the diaspora have been adopting veganism, as noted earlier, which involves giving up milk and other dairy products traditionally permitted in the vegetarianism practiced by Jains in India. The traditional Jain position on milk products (shared with most other vegetarians in India) has been that, although derived from animals, these foods are not themselves any more alive than other vegetarian foods, and that their extraction need not harm the animals. Thus milk products have been accepted, and indeed highly symbolically valued, components of Jain diets. In recent years the international animal rights group PETA (People for the Ethical Treatment of Animals)[28] has set up stalls at Jain conferences and gatherings, advertised in Jain magazines, and campaigned with student groups, advancing two arguments as to why Jains should join PETA in avoiding dairy products. The first, and the group's fundamental position, is that it is ethically wrong to use animals as a means to human ends rather than respecting the integrity of their lives, that it is wrong to "live off" other sentient beings. Second, they maintain that even if one is not ready to accept the first argument, one should give up dairy products anyway because, in fact, the treatment of animals in commercial farming is inhumane, thus invalidating the assumption that the extraction of milk does not harm the animals. At the very least, PETA asserts, this will put pressure on the commercial dairy-farming industry to improve the treatment of the animals in its care.

The second of these arguments has been taken up by young Jains wishing to participate *as Jains* in animal welfare movements. The first, though attractive to many, is not so straightforward. Traditional Jain teaching is that living things can exist only at the expense of others (recall the textual reference to trees drawing sustenance from creatures in the earth). Short of fasting to death, which is what the truly enlightened may do at the end of their spiritual journey, the ideal has been to limit the burden one places on others, like the bee that gathers pollen from many plants without damaging them or the cow that removes only the top of the grass as it eats. Similarly Jain renouncers collect alms each day in small quantities from several households, so none goes hungry as a result.[29] Milking cows or sheep falls into this pattern, and indeed one may think of them as giving their milk voluntarily (one aspect of the cow's sacredness) and thus consider milk as a harmless food. PETA's special disapproval of the consumption of animals as distinct from vegetable products implies a far more radical moral difference between animals and plants than does the Jain graded hierarchy of five-, four-, three-, two-, and one-sensed creatures, which, by contrast, makes all differences between species merely quantitative. Further, and most crucial, PETA's proposal implies the cultivation in oneself of qualities that are very different from the specific virtues which Jain dietary practices have generally been concerned to nurture.

At first sight compassion for others is an important shared virtue. But in the two traditions compassion is not the same virtue, in character or dynamic importance. For PETA and other animal rights groups, compassion involves empathy or imaginative engagement with the particularity of others' suffering, and the particularity is important because the proper response varies according to qualities and circumstances, including and especially the questions of whether the suffering is innocent (whether the subject's voluntary actions have contributed to it) and whether it is unnecessary. Unmerited and preventable suffering have special moral significance, because compassion motivates a specific duty to take action to prevent such suffering; the more gratuitous and undeserved the suffering, the more urgent the imperative.

The quality of compassion (*karuna*) cultivated by Jain ascetic practice is rather different. First of all, in those who have developed the Right View, *any and all* perceptions of the omnipresence of life around us elicit this compassion, together with a reaction of disgust with the world in which such suffering necessarily occurs. Recall the man who drew my attention to monsoon rain in the street. This was an instance of insight and virtue on his part precisely because what he perceived and responded to was so unremarkable. No gross or deliberate cruelty was being perpetrated. What I was being invited to behold, and to see as "suffering" (*dukh*), was simply the natural consequence of rain. It happens quite routinely, is the fault of no one in particular, and nothing can be done to prevent it. Here it is not the conspicuous injustice or gratuitousness of suffering that makes imaginative engagement with it virtuous and also effective as a spur to action, but rather it is its very generality and ordinariness. That the effects of this violence are invisible to the naked eye only adds to its significance. Perceiving that an attractive but whimpering mammal is suffering takes no special insight or sensitivity. Only when and insofar as we realize that suffering is pervasive throughout the world, right down to the germs in a drop of water, can we be appropriately affected by the enormity of the misery around us.[30] Indeed, on this view, it is a sign of superficiality and lack of insight to place disproportionate emphasis on the sufferings of animals with which it is easy to empathize and to imagine that by not harming them one has found a way to live in harmony with other living things. Thus it is precisely because they are comparatively insignificant, and therefore more difficult to be mindful of, that Jains are enjoined to exercise care with respect to insects and other even smaller living things. As one develops this disposition and becomes more self-disciplined, one's bodily movements, like one's thoughts, become progressively more constrained. In addition to eating less, one does not raise one's voice or wave one's arms about, and one learns not to move while sleeping.[31] This, then, is action to purify and improve the self, which takes the form of the most scrupulous non-action possible with respect to the world around us.

There is much sympathy, especially among younger Jains, for the idea that more admirable than developing this kind of virtue would be a campaign to improve the lives of millions of farm animals, even if it involves raising one's voice and waving one's arms about. In the face of these animals' plight, the threat to the planet, and so on, ascetic self-restraint and withdrawal might even seem not to be virtuous at all. But the choice is not a simple one, because the strict vegetarianism for which Jainism is so well known, and the other ideas and practices which suggest an alliance with environmentalism and animal liberation in the first place, all owe their prominence in the tradition precisely to the thought that these are the highest possible forms of virtue and the most enlightened response to the human condition.

The Virtues of Nature

"The Jain Declaration on Nature" includes the statement that Jainism, "declares unequivocally that waste and creating pollution are acts of violence," and the claim that Jains "must not procreate indiscriminately lest they overburden the universe and its resources."[32] The authors of these statements are referring to certain rules that renouncers (and injunctions that laity) must follow: they should never leave or throw away uneaten food, adhere to traditional procedures for the disposal of bodily waste, and—though renouncers are, of course, entirely celibate—abide by the custom of pious lay Jains of abstaining from sexual activity on holy days. These are all interpreted in the Jain Declaration as self-restraints that have the effect of moderating people's impact on "the environment," of "treading lightly" as the ecologists' slogan has it, and therefore as evidence of a sort of proto-environmentalism. But the nature on which they tread lightly is not the environmentalists' nature.

The ecological movements are centrally concerned with undesirable effects of human action on what is conceptualized as "the environment" or "nature." And, for the purposes of identifying these negative effects, human action is distinguished from nature, even though for other purposes humans are regarded as part of nature; further, that which is to be protected, the environment, intrinsically a relative concept, is operationally identified as everything in the world apart from or prior to the effects of undesirable human action. An important underlying thought in all this is that nature or the environment is intrinsically benign—sometimes even sacralized—and that it is human action, particularly the results of human sins such as greed and pride, that have resulted in the problems or threats presented to us by "the environment." A certain Christian—specifically Augustinian—inheritance is evident in this: the idea, in sharp contrast, for instance, to the view from Greek tragedy, that the world God created is good, and insofar as it presents us with harsh choices or impossible dilemmas, this is not the way God made the world but the way it has become as a result of human wickedness.[33]

The elaborate cosmology inherited by the Jain tradition differs radically from this notion. In it, as in Hindu and Buddhist cosmologies, there are long cyclical eras in which the moral and physical condition of the universe goes through major changes that owe nothing to human agency. In the Jain case the world slowly decays from a state of blissful plenty to one of general misery and squalor, before beginning an equally slow ascent again, and so on ad infinitum. These processes do not apply to a nature that is separate from mankind. Indeed, the stature, longevity, beauty, physical and mental abilities, and virtue of humans in this cosmology all improve and decline in synchronization with everything else. We are currently some way down a descending curve. And, as we saw above, the prevalence and inescapability of violence means that the world we live in is very far from being intrinsically benign.[34]

This means that the practices alluded to in the Jain Declaration, though they do tend to reduce human impact on nature, have a somewhat different valence to apparently related environmentalist measures. The practice of sexual restraint on holy days is partly an element of the general injunction on laity to adopt certain behaviors of renouncers on those days, such as fasting. However, there is also certainly the idea that sexual activity is a kind of violence because of the emotions and physical movements involved, and the passion and attachment it induces, and also because the sexual fluids produced as a result of it contain "germs." Also because of "germs" food must not be left over (renouncers should rinse out the bowls from which they have eaten and then drink the water that was used) and bodily waste should be deposited on open ground and covered with dry earth. These practices are all recommended because they retard the multiplication of "germs." Whereas in ecologism only human fecundity is seen as a threat to nature so that a reduction in human population *in order* that nonhuman life might flourish is seen as a moral imperative (as in Naess's "Basic Principles"),[35] here the imperative is to refrain from anything that will give rise to human *or nonhuman* life. Because the reproduction of "germs," and the insects that might feed on them, the animals that might feed on them, and so on, are all part of the cycle of birth and death and therefore "violence," the impetus is not to nurture natural fecundity in other species but, on the contrary, to render one's surroundings sterile.

But perhaps Jains need not be constrained by this traditional cosmology any more than contemporary Christians are by all of theirs or, indeed, any more than self-described pagan ecologists are by the Christian genealogy of some of their ideas and concerns. Selective quotation and tactical amnesia are necessary to some degree to any assertion of continuity and, together with creative reinterpretation, are bound to be elements in the conscious reform and renewal of a tradition. One can certainly find, in contemporary Eco-Jain writings, attempts to represent "nature" in strikingly benign ways. There is a well-known scriptural passage in which a prince describes his many former lives.[36] A Western scholarly enthusiast for an ecological interpretation of Jainism cites this passage as an example of the capacity Jainism gives its followers to feel the intense suffering of other species and of "the importance and urgency of taking an ecological perspective in thought and action." The passage is cited as follows:

> From clubs and knives, from stakes and maces, from broken limbs,
> have I hopelessly suffered on countless occasions.
> By sharpened razors and knives and spears have I these many times
> been drawn and quartered, torn apart and skinned.
> And as a deer held helpless in snares and traps,
> I have often been bound and fastened and even killed.
> As a helpless fish I have been caught with hooks and nets,
> scaled and scraped, split and gutted, and killed a million times . . .
> Born a tree, I have been felled and stripped, cut with axes and chisels

and sawed into planks innumerable times.
Embodied in iron, I have been subjected to the hammer and tongs
innumerable times, struck and beaten, split and filed . . .
Ever trembling in fear; in pain and suffering always,
I have felt the most excruciating sorrow and agony.[37]

The narrative background to this speech is that the young prince, taking a break one day while spending time with his wives, looks out from the jewel-encrusted balcony of his palace and sees a Jain renouncer. Gazing at him, the prince is granted the miraculous gift of remembering all his former lives. This knowledge produces in him a desire to relinquish his kingdom and become a renouncer. His parents try to dissuade him, stressing the difficulty of a renouncer's life. His reply is that the privations are indeed great, but they are nothing compared to what he now knows he has suffered in his former lives and will have to suffer again, unless he takes the ascetic path: hence the description of life as a deer and a fish and a tree and as iron. However, the impression given in this passage, as quoted, that the prince's former sufferings were all caused by human agency, is sustained only because it omits a number of lines from the original. These concern first his lives in hell, where hairy and dark-skinned demons inflict an inventive range of tortures on the condemned, suspending them over fire, sawing and hacking them to pieces, crushing them in presses, and so on; and, second, sufferings inflicted by other animals, such as when, as a bird, he was caught by birds of prey, and when he was torn to pieces by "black and spotted wild dogs."

Of course, it is not that this author, any more than other environmentalists, is unaware or attempts actually to deny that some animals eat other animals, but unlike in the world-renouncing tradition in Jainism, for which such facts are a morally important aspect of the general vileness of creation, for the ecologist they play no part in the important cosmic moral drama, which concerns the interaction between a fallen but redeemable humankind and "nature" which, if only mankind could be redeemed, could be made good and whole again. Once more, the point, in the Jain tradition, of stressing that suffering occurs simply because of the way the whole world is, is to strengthen the motivation to renounce and escape from it. Exchanging this for the environmentalist's cosmology, as this writer is silently doing, is a non-trivial choice because of the very different calls to action and self-transformation they underwrite.

Although MacIntyre insists that traditions of moral life differ so profoundly in their historical constitution that there can be no purely theoretical analysis of them, distinct from historical exemplifications, he does venture that all such traditions comprise their own distinctive (a) cosmology and metaphysics, (b) conception of the self, and (c) catalogue of virtues.[38] We have seen that as a result of emergent dialogue with environmentalism and animal liberation all three of these components of the tradition are now no longer taken for granted as matters of fact but instead as matters—to borrow a distinction from Latour[39]—of overt questioning and concern.

The reinterpretation of diverse Jain customs as elements of Ur-ecologism are attempts to claim a relevance of apparently arcane Jain practices to urgent concerns in the contemporary world. But the way this is done involves espousing a concept of "nature," and, in particular, a highly positive view of its moral quality, that conflicts with the cosmology that has been elaborated by the tradition's greatest metaphysical philosophers, widely represented in its devotional, decorative, and esoteric arts, and incorporated into everyday life, especially in its didactic narratives. That cosmology presents the whole of the universe and all the lives it contains as a setting so irremediably terrible that it implies and demands a life of ascetic withdrawal; a cosmology that invited intervention with the serious ambition of radically improving all this, rather than changing oneself in order to escape it, would be more than superficially different.

As we have seen, the argument against speciesism could be adopted from the animal liberation movement, but it rests on claims to a rationalistic and abstract form of moral knowledge that contrasts with the practical path toward enlightenment around which the soteriological tradition is organized. It also presupposes a self that is an interest- and rights-bearing entity, quite different from the self that is made up of clusters of acquired and ultimately dispensable attributes.

Proposals for the reform of dietary regulations, such as the adoption of veganism, designed to engage with projects of sociopolitical reform, could be compatible with enthusiastically embracing Jain identity, as is the case for members of burgeoning student Jain organizations, but the projects of self-formation these reformed practices fit into, and the virtues they work to cultivate, are very different and not self-evidently practically combinable with those of nonattachment, equanimity, and "nonviolence" as these have been embodied in Jain monastic orders.

This last point is important because, although lay Jains have never, of course, been able to match the saintly life of a renouncer, they can, to a limited degree, develop those specific virtues in themselves. This has been a precondition for the very possibility of a morally coherent lay Jain life in which ethics as self-formation (the pursuit of enlightenment in a pale imitation of what renouncers do) has been integrated and articulated with ethics as living with and for others (the virtues one practices in human interactions).[40] If these specifically ascetic virtues, which lay Jains share with renouncers, are exchanged by committed laity for the different personal virtues favored by engaged environmental activism, this integration will no longer be possible. What it is to be a Jain, for such activists, would be more or less completely divorced from what renouncers do, unless, of course, the renouncers' project itself were also to be reinterpreted in an activist rather than a world-renouncing direction, so that the ascetic virtues were no longer conditions sine qua non of human excellence in the tradition. That, indeed, would be a profound re-interpretation.

The encounter I have been describing is still in process, and I have not tried to predict the judgments people will come to. Rather, my concern has been to describe the ethical choices that seem to be under active consideration, the contingency of the situation, and the scope for deliberative rationality and imaginative possibility, and also to clarify what could be at stake in these judgments and choices.

Acknowledgments

Earlier versions of this essay were delivered at the seminar "Genealogies of Virtue in South Asia" held at the University of British Columbia in September 2007, and to the Senior Seminar at the Department of Social Anthropology, University of Cambridge, in February 2008. I am grateful to Anand Pandian and Daud Ali for their invitation to the Vancouver gathering, which was a most stimulating event, and to the participants at both seminars for their questions and comments. I am grateful also to Susan Bayly, Matei Candea, Joanna Cook, Jacob Copeman, Caroline Humphrey, Timothy Jenkins, Jonathan Mair, and Joel Robbins, and to the volume editors, for comments on earlier drafts. An earlier attempt to understand some of these issues, though oriented by rather different theoretical questions, appeared as James Laidlaw, "The Intension and Extension of Well-Being: Transformation in Diaspora Jain Understandings of Non-Violence," in *Culture and Well-Being: Anthropological Approaches to Freedom and Political Ethics,* ed. Alberto Corsín Jiménez (London: Pluto, 2007).

Notes

1. For an excellent historical and general introduction to Jainism, see Paul Dundas, *The Jains* (London: Routledge, 2002).

2. See Marcus Banks, *Organizing Jainism in India and England* (Oxford: Clarendon, 1992); and Banks, "Jain Ways of Being," in *Desh Pradesh: The South Asian Presence in Britain,* ed. Roger Ballard (London: Hurst, 1995).

3. L. M. Singhvi, "The Jain Declaration on Nature," in *Jainism and Ecology: Nonviolence in the Web of Life,* ed. Christopher Key Chapple (Cambridge, Mass.: Harvard University Press, 2002).

4. John Cort argues in opposite fashion in "Green Jainism? Notes and Queries toward a Possible Jain Environmental Ethic," in Chapple, *Jainism and Ecology.* While

he himself adopts a "deep ecological" critique of modernity, Cort observes that Jainism is incompatible with some important tenets of "the new episteme of environmentalism" and proposes ways in which Jainism therefore ought to be reformed or rethought.

5. Singhvi, "Jain Declaration," 219–222.

6. For a description of the situation in Canada, and an excellent discussion to which I am much indebted here, see Anne Vallely, "From Liberation to Ecology: Ethical Discourses among Orthodox and Diaspora Jains," in Chapple, *Jainism and Ecology;* abridged version also in Michael Lambek, ed., *Reader in the Anthropology of Religion* (Oxford: Blackwell, 2002).

7. On this, see Anne Vallely, "The Jain Plate: The Semiotics of the Diaspora Diet," in *South Asians in the Diaspora: Histories and Religious Traditions,* ed. Knut A. Jacobsen and P. Pratap Kumar (Leiden: Brill, 2004).

8. Alasdair MacIntyre, *Whose Justice? Which Rationality?* (Notre Dame, Ind.: University of Notra Dame, 1988); MacIntyre, *After Virtue: A Study in Moral Theory* (London: Duckworth, 1981).

9. Examples include Talal Asad, *The Idea of an Anthropology of Islam* (Washington, D.C.: Center for Contemporary Arab Studies, Georgetown University, 1986); Michael Lambek, "The Anthropology of Religion and the Quarrel between Poetry and Philosophy," *Current Anthropology* 41 (2000); and Anand Pandian, "Tradition in Fragments: Inherited Forms and Fractures in the Ethics of South India," *American Ethnologist* 35 (2008).

10. Talal Asad, "Appendix: The Trouble of Thinking," in *Powers of Secular Modern: Talal Asad and his Interlocutors,* ed. David Scott and Charles Hirschkind (Stanford, Calif.: Stanford University Press, 2006), 289.

11. MacIntyre, *Whose Justice?* 355–356.

12. Ibid., 12.

13. Ibid., 365.

14. For a brief summary, see Dundas, *The Jains,* 45–59; 112–149; 246–271.

15. MacIntyre, *Whose Justice?* 361; also MacIntyre, "Epistemological Crises, Dramatic Narrative and the Philosophy of Science," in *The Tasks of Philosophy: Selected Essays, Volume 1* (Cambridge: Cambridge University Press, 2006), 3–23.

16. MacIntyre, *Whose Justice?* 205.

17. On genealogy as a method in these terms, see Michel Foucault, "Nietzsche, Genealogy, History," in *Essential Works of Foucault, 1954–1984,* Vol. 2, *Aesthetics,* ed. James D. Faubion (New York: New Press, 1998 [1971]); and Raymond Geuss, "Nietzsche and Genealogy," in Geuss, *Morality, Culture, and History: Essays on German Philosophy* (Cambridge: Cambridge University Press, 1999).

18. Gilles Deleuze, *Dialogues II* (London: Continuum, 2006), 2–7.

19. Peter Singer, *Animal Liberation* (London: Pimlico, 1997 [1975]). On the history of the animal rights movement, see Harold D. Guither, *Animal Rights: History and Scope of a Radical Social Movement* (Carbondale: Southern Illinois University Press, 1998); Hilda Kean, *Animal Rights: Political and Social Change in Britain since 1800* (London: Reaktion Books, 1998); and Peter Singer, ed., *In Defense of Animals: The Second Wave* (Oxford: Blackwell, 2005 [1985]).

20. The term "animal rights" is used routinely, and a few theorists have formulated their case in strictly rights-based language, e.g., Tom Regan, *The Case for Animal Rights* (Berkeley: University of California Press, 1983). But these arguments provide much weaker claims than activists generally want, and the widespread use of the language of rights is perhaps best described as tactical.

21. See Herman Jacobi, *Jaina Sutras,* pt. 2 (Oxford: Oxford University Press, 1895), 389.

22. See Christopher Key Chapple, *Nonviolence to Animals, Earth, and Self in Asian Traditions* (Albany: State University of New York Press, 1993).

23. Henry Sidgwick, *The Methods of Ethics,* 7th ed. (London: MacMillan, 1907 [1874]), 382, 420. See also the discussion in Bernard Williams, "The Point of View of the Universe," in Williams, *Making Sense of Humanity and Other Philosophical Papers* (Cambridge: Cambridge University Press, 1995).

24. Jainism does feature, very prominently, an idea of the possibility of knowledge "from the point of view of the universe," but this is the idea of omniscience available only to a soul that has reached the end of its last embodied life.

25. James Laidlaw, "A Life Worth Leaving: Fasting to Death as Telos of a Jain Religious Life," *Economy and Society* 34 (2005).

26. Sadhvi Shilapi, "The Environmental and Ecological Teachings of Tirthankara Mahavira," in Chapple, *Jainism and Ecology,* 163.

27. See James Laidlaw, *Riches and Renunciation: Religion, Economy, and Society among the Jains* (Oxford: Clarendon, 1995), 364–387; and John E. Cort, *Jains in the World: Religious Values and Ideology in India* (New York: Oxford University Press, 2001), 164–172.

28. Founded in the United States in 1980, this organization now has branches in India as well as several European countries. For a leading member's own account, see Ingrid Newkirk, *Free the Animals: The Story of the Animal Liberation Front* (Brooklyn, N.Y.: Lantern Books, 2001); for a critical account, see Dave Workman, *PETA Files: The Dark Side of the Animal Rights Movement* (Bellevue, Wash.: Merril, 2003).

29. Laidlaw, *Riches and Renunciation,* 302–323; Cort, *Jains in the World,* 105–108.

30. Padmanabh S. Jaini, *The Jaina Path of Purification* (Berkeley: University of California Press, 1979), 241–243.

31. Laidlaw *Riches and Renunciation,* 153–159.

32. Singhvi, "Jaina Declaration," 223–224.

33. This is true even of overtly "pagan" environmentalists who deify the earth as a sometimes fierce goddess who punishes offences against her. See T. M. Luhrmann, "The Resurgence of Romanticism: Contemporary Neopaganism, Feminist Spirituality, and the Divinity of Nature," in *Environmentalism: The View from Anthropology,* ed. Kay Milton (London: Routledge, 1993).

34. See also Paul Dundas, "The Limits of a Jain Environmental Ethic," in Chapple, *Jainism and Ecology,* 2002).

35. Arne Naess and George Sessions, "Platform Principles of the Deep Ecology Movement," in *The Deep Ecology Movement,* ed. Alan Drengson and Yuichi Inoue (Berkeley, Calif.: North Atlantic Books, 1995), 49–50.

36. *Uttaradhyayana Sutra* 19.61–74. See Jacobi, *Jaina Sutras.*

37. John M. Koller, "Jain Ecological Perspectives," in Chapple, *Jainism and Ecology,* 32.

38. MacIntyre, *Whose Justice?* 349.

39. Bruno Latour, *Reassembling the Social: An Introduction to Actor-Network Theory* (Oxford: University Press, 2005).

40. The institutions, relationships, and practices through which these contrasting ethical orientations can be made combinable in Jain communities is the principal theme of Laidlaw, *Riches and Renunciation.*

Part 2.

Ethics and Modernity

4.

Vernacular Capitalists and the Modern Subject in India: Law, Cultural Politics, and Market Ethics

Ritu Birla

In the global business media India's much celebrated role as emerging capitalist powerhouse inaugurates a story about a transformation in values, both moral and material: a society long associated with a static, anachronistic, and hierarchical social system has reinvented itself as a society of entrepreneurs. The hierarchies of caste, and its logic of incommensurability, seem to have given way to the hierarchies of capitalism and its system of commensurate exchange values. At the same time experts assert that the ethics of entrepreneurship and business have a distinctly *ethnic* flavor in India. Indian management consultants now promote philosophies of corporate governance that claim to employ ancient wisdoms like those found in the *Bhagavad Gita* to learn "self-mastery" for leadership and attracting fortune. Recently management gurus have pronounced the Mahatma himself a model manager; as economist Arindham Chaudhuri asserts, Gandhi was "the perfect case of adopting styles to suit the culture," breaking ground in a "follower-centric" leadership style that took account of existing conditions before setting forth policy.[1] Through a Gandhian ethics of *swaraj,* or self-rule, it seems, business leaders now emphasize forms of self-discipline that are directed not at individuation but rather at the cohesion of the group. In such creative interpretations of the ethics of *dharma,* disciplines of the self (to use the Foucauldian phrase referring to individual subject-formation) structure corporate holism. In other words, ancient concepts of duty and community, rather than a radical individualism, seem to be at the heart of cutting-edge capitalist enterprise in India.

The genealogies of ethics condensed in the marketing of Brand India speak to a long history of discourse on corporate governance in the subcontinent. By this I do not only mean the workings of joint-stock companies, but also the very idea of corporate or group life, of "consociation" as Weber called it, which framed the classic temporizing of *gemeinschaft* and *gesellschaft,* holism and individualism, community and contractually organized society, tradition and modernity, that occupied nineteenth- and early-twentieth-century social and legal theorists. These may seem like old-fashioned distinctions to be bothered with today, but the question of group life and how to modernize it—how to render indigenous forms of kinship-based group association subject to the law and ethics of contractual social relations—structures the story of Indian modernity and its capitalist trajectory. At the heart of this story are indigenous, or what I call "vernacular capitalists," agents of colonial economic relations who operated through informal networks of caste and kinship, negotiated the ethics of the Anglo-Indian legal system, and sought to legitimize themselves as modern subjects. In the modernizing discourse of the late-colonial development regime, vernacular capitalists were universally acknowledged as key economic actors, but their bazaar practices were nevertheless thought to represent an outmoded value-system, one bound by tangled webs of joint family relations and ancient conventions. As vernacular market actors fueled the colonial economy through their vast networks of commerce and credit, policy makers at the turn of the twentieth century, both colonial and nationalist, argued that indigenous businessmen were driven by the narrow-minded and age-old *gemeinschaft* requirements of kinship and clan, rather than a commitment to improving the wealth and material conditions of the colonial public.

In the late nineteenth and early twentieth centuries the ethical parameters of the modern subject were clearly articulated in groundbreaking and unprecedented legal measures governing economic matters. As I will highlight, vernacular capitalist practices did not fit easily within these new parameters, which distinguished between virtuous and productive investment in the public as opposed to the private concerns of family and community. The ways of the bazaar, regulated by local conventions of caste and kinship, were thought to threaten the so-called free circulation of capital and challenge "moral and material progress," the great ethical mantra of the colonial civilizing mission. New, modernizing legal discourses coded indigenous conventions of market exchange and organization as anachronistic *cultural* scripts, thus posing a tension between cultural norms and ethical market practice. Highlighting this tension, I use the figure of the vernacular capitalist to open questions concerning the relationship between the ethics of the modern and the coding of the ethnic.

After 1857 colonial policy in India articulated a double project: economic progress and cultural preservation. While this twin raison d'être has traditionally been understood as a contradiction, a sign of a schizophrenic "official mind," a close look at colonial law on economy requires that we rethink this seeming contradiction in the aims of sovereignty. To do so, it is useful briefly to revisit an established critique of orientalist tropes in historical sociology. This critique, made variously by a wide range of scholars in colonial studies, has argued that the culturalist coding of India as a static, hierarchical society accompanied the emergence of the liberal subject of modernity. What I emphasize here, however, is the production of this modern subject as a *market actor,* that is, the subject of economic, and not just political, liberalism. Two points follow: first, that a key story in the modern genealogy of ethical practice in South Asia is the emergence of new ethico-political discourses on economy; and, second, that any investigation of economy as an ethico-political project requires attention to the discourses on culture that accompany and indeed enable it.

Said differently, my analysis pursues an against-the-grain engagement with Louis Dumont's famed master narrative, *Homo Hierarchicus,* perhaps the most well-known characterization of India as a hierarchical world of *gemeinschaft. Homo Hierarchicus* was followed, we should remember, by Dumont's less discussed but equally significant account of the modern "revolution in values" presented in his *Homo Aequalis: From Mandeville to Marx, the Genesis and Triumph of Economic Ideology. Homo Aequalis,* which informed Dumont's preface to the third edition of Karl Polanyi's *Great Transformation* (itself now a canonical text in the history of market society) began with an interest in "the emergence of a new mode of consideration of human phenomena and the carving out of a separate domain, which is evoked for us by the words *economics, the economy.*"[2] Polanyi's analysis had nostalgically charted what he called the "disembedding" of market exchange from the texture of social life, and the emergence of the market as an abstract mechanism and self-regulating template for social relations. Highlighting a lost preindustrial past in which exchange was characterized by personalized relations of reciprocity and redistribution, Polanyi's narrative had reproduced the classic *gemeinschaft/gesellschaft* distinction even as it challenged its progressive narrative of status to contract.[3] It had inspired Dumont to study, as he put it, the revolution from non-modern to modern, a revolution that "India helps us to grasp and which [was elaborated] in *Homo Aequalis.*"[4] In Dumont, we find a classically orientalist framing of India as a society bound by an ancient culture and hierarchical cosmology, and thus as the Other that throws into relief the great transformation in values that produced the market societies of the West. In contrast, highlighting major shifts in law and jurisprudence directed at standardizing market practice in India, I foreground instead the colonial institutionalization of the market as a model for social relations and a terrain for the making of modern subjects.[5] If, for Dumont, India operates as the origin of a *gemeinschaft* world order, here it becomes a key site for examining the modern production of that everyday abstraction we now call "the market," a supra-local site of governance, and, I argue, a name for the colonial public. I consider some of the ways in which an ethics of utilitarianism, as manifest especially in attempts to standardize market practice and procedure, accompanied the politics of colonial liberalism and so produced the "non-modern" subject of culture as its effect. Again, to do so, I focus on a primary target of these new legal measures, vernacular capitalists, whose kinship and caste-based modes of operation challenged modernizing colonial law, even as they enabled colonial production and extraction.

I begin with two stories from the legal archive that illustrate broadly how colonial governance sought to install relations of *gesellschaft,* the enforcement of written contracts for market exchange and organization, through a public/private ordering. These examples telescope questions about the relationship between market ethics, the making of modern subjects, and the politics of culture. Burdened by Dumont, I also present the problem of indigenous capitalism here as an analytical lever for opening a broader methodological query: How do we map ethical norms and practices without reproducing culturalist discourses?[6] The project at hand, to consider genealogies of virtue and ethical practice in South Asia, requires such a question, for it poses a theoretical agenda—with strong Foucauldian resonances—alongside an area studies inquiry. I address the area studies investigation by detailing some of the ways in which modernizing law challenges aspects of the vernacular mercantile ethos, and elaborate the theoretical agenda by engaging problems of translation across hegemonies, from indigenous capitalist worldviews to a contractually based "modern" market ethics.

To clarify the area studies intervention, I resist charting a nativist voice for capitalism, that is, I resist both uncritical ethnography as well as the trap of celebrating "native agency" in culturalist fashion. Therefore I deploy the term *ethos* as a kind of origin effect: a way of being that can never be fully empirically captured, the traces of which are marked by shifting normative conventions—the ethics that govern the bazaar. I am borrowing here from a robust definition of *ethos* in Foucault's critical reading of Kant on Enlightenment, where he links the Greek term with the idea of an "attitude," or "a mode of relating to contemporary reality; a voluntary choice made by certain people; . . . a way of thinking and feeling; a way too of acting and behaving that at one and the same time marks a relation of belonging and presents itself as a task."[7] As "voluntary choice," *ethos* must be conceived as a theoretical limit, a space where coercion is not at play. As a relation of belonging and a task, *ethos* also bears a relation to the rules and disciplines that sustain normative conventions, regulate practice, and produce identity, thus opening up to the realms of ethics and culture. As an attitude—that which cannot be captured and yet poses a relation of community—the term resists coding as cultural authenticity, thus opening a critical approach to the relationship between ethics, the force of law, and discourses on culture. I address the conventions of indigenous market practice and their regulation by the principles of Anglo-Indian law in this spirit. In closing, returning to Dumont via Foucault on laissez-faire and Weber on economy as a problem of law, I draw particular attention to the culturalist tropes that bring the ethos of bazaar exchange, and vernacular market ethics, into the purview of the rationalizing logics of colonial law.

The *Gesellschaftpolitik* of Colonial Market Governance

A barrage of new statutes directed at the free circulation of capital emerged especially in the two decades succeeding legal codification, from approximately 1880 to 1900, and ranged from law on corporate association and bankruptcy to negotiable instruments to income tax and securities and trusts. Jurisprudence and case law in the period from 1870 to 1930 buttressed principles found in these novel statutory measures and their related amendments. These measures sought to institutionalize forms of group association grounded in contractual relations of individual subjects. The most classic invention of colonial law, the Hindu Undivided Family (HUF), was a key example. The name referred to the shared inheritance and "joint" living arrangements of the extended family, which in practice rigorously defied division into distinct shares; the HUF was a legal translation of these joint arrangements that coded the extended family as a coparcenary, an institution constituted by a contract of a priori shareholders. Colonial law grappled with forms of "embedded" social life, perhaps no more exhaustively than in the discourse on market ethics emerging as colonialism's development regime took shape. Vernacular practitioners of capitalism confronted the establishment of formal legal contract as the universal instrument for market exchange. The confrontation exposes the difficulties in translating vernacular conventions into the ethico-political criteria of capitalist modernity, most pithily and iteratively expressed in new measures as the commitment to "general public utility."

The practices of the bazaar were characterized by what I call an "extensive negotiability" between social capital—that is, the symbolic value of kinship, caste, and lineage—and the arrangements and capital flows of commerce and finance. This extensive negotiability transgressed the distinction between what was considered the "private" world of family, on the one hand, and the arena of "general public utility," or the economy, an abstract site of governance mapped by the circulation of capital, on the other. The extensively negotiable nature of mercantile norms was perhaps most apparent in the basic form of indigenous commercial organization, what was called the "family firm." The vernacular commercial firm sustained porous boundaries between kinship as a symbolic logic and commerce as a material one.[8] Resilient webs of credit operated through unwritten notions of trust, a symbolic currency secured by ties of consanguinity, marriage, and lineage. Marriage secured affinal networks that could bring a firm's activities into new geographic regions. Moreover, the vernacular notion of "family" extended beyond just the household and encompassed a variety of patriarchal relations. The commercial joint family household—father, wife, sons and their wives, and unmarried daughters—existed within a much broader context, the nexus of extended relations harnessed by the firm. These networks were constituted spatially, across villages, bazaars, even global regions, and temporally, through lineage to ancestors. Commercial trust, which bypassed the need for legally binding written contracts, reproduced the value of patrilineal ancestry, for trust could be produced through lineage from a common male ancestor dating back five generations or more. Lines of descent arranged as *gotras,* or exogamous clans within a particular endogamous caste, constituted yet another barometer for degrees of affinity.[9] Women, understood as carriers of the moral substance of their households and patrilineal decent, bound together affinal relations of family, commerce, and finance. The "family firm," then, was not simply a discrete institution tied to a single or perhaps a few households. Its successful operation depended upon extensive networks that were as much "public" in their material import as "private" and "personal" in their selective construction.

In the late nineteenth century, lawmakers sought to regulate this extensive negotiability between social capital and commercial/financial capitalism through the mechanism of written contract and the modern distinction between public and private. The liberal categories of public and private infiltrated commercial and financial law in the late nineteenth century, distinguishing between two general forms of group life, a public of market actors, governed by Anglo-Indian civil and criminal law, and the so-called private arena regulated by personal law, that is, all matters to do with the joint family, caste, and religion—in other words, all that was considered to constitute indigenous culture. Neither reflected the embedded world of the bazaar. Potent examples of the lack of fit between vernacular practice and modernizing visions can be found in ongoing discussions throughout the late nineteenth century about the very nature of the family firm. Lawmakers were thrown into dizzying dilemmas about whether to treat the family firm as a family, or legal partnership, or a firm. If treated as families, vernacular commercial groups would be governed by the Hindu or Muslim personal law. Or could the family firm be understood as a partnership, a joint contract among distinct individuals that would fall under the purview of the civil and criminal law?

In 1907 one such representative discussion emerged over a draft bill in the Imperial Legislative Council that sought the formal registration of family firms as partnerships. A key native opinion on the bill, submitted to the government by the Bombay Native Piece-Goods Merchant's Association, emphasized the flexibility and adaptability of vernacular mercantile conventions, which would be rendered rigid by formalized rules of legal partnership. Though this opinion was submitted by a formal civic association of the modern sort, and not a traditional caste *mahajan* or council, the members of the Native Piece-Goods Merchants Association legitimated customary mercantile practices and their ties to joint family norms. In the majority of Hindu commercial joint families, sons would be considered inheritors of ancestral property at birth, and the birth of a daughter would entitle her to *stridhan*, or her marriage portion, and to maintenance before marriage.[10] Taking a didactic tone, the Association's opinion emphasized the weakness of the proposed legislation, instead highlighting how vernacular market norms challenged written contracts as well as the legal distinction between family (governed by personal law) and partnership (governed by civil law):

> The Committee is of [the] opinion that . . . such legislation . . . which has been under the consideration of Government and [the] mercantile community of India for the last fifty years without any effect, will be met with a general disapproval.
>
> . . . A very considerable part of the native mercantile community of India is composed of firms carried on by joint Hindu families from generations to generations [*sic*] which are called family firms, the members of which are not only males but also females, both adults as well as minors. Every member of the family upon his birth becomes a coparcenor not only in the family property but also in the family concern. Each of the individuals composing a joint Hindu family has an interest in such property and business . . . which varies according to his or her own status; for instance, males ordinarily take specific shares, and in the case of females, daughters are entitled to maintenance and marriage expenses until their marriages, and widows of the deceased members are entitled to maintenance and provision for a suitable residence, and in some cases mothers are entitled to share equally with their son and step-son.
>
> In a family business owned by a large Hindu joint family, there must be deaths and births occurring within short intervals. According to the ordinary law in force as to partnerships, upon the death of a member of the partnership firm, the same stands dissolved. Upon the birth of a child in a joint Hindu family, he becomes interested in the family business. The death in such a case would mean the dissolution of the firm, and the birth would bring about a reconstitution of the firm. . . . If the legislation as to the registration of partnerships were to be enacted, [a] considerable amount of trouble, annoyance and inconvenience would entail upon such family firms to register the constant and successive changes in . . . membership. . . . [Furthermore,] the work of the registra-

> tion department would not only be cumbersome, it would be converted into a regular machinery for noting the births and deaths of a part of the population [i.e., women and children] which is outside the scope and object of the proposed legislation.[11]

The opinion assumed the legitimacy of kinship-based organization for commerce, challenging the government's distinction between publicly relevant forms of contractual association and the bonds of family. In fact, by the time this 1907 draft bill was circulated for discussion, the question of the family firm had been present in legal debates for almost three decades. The 1907 bill for the registration of partnerships ultimately imploded; its failure reflected the ways in which earlier statutes and case law had dealt with, or danced around, vernacular forms of market organization. One early foundational measure that structured the equivocal legal attitude toward the family firm was the Indian Companies Act of 1882, which, by establishing the joint-stock corporation as a *public* legal person with limited liability, exemplified the late-colonial vision of India as a market society. It was a fine-tuning of an earlier statute of 1866, instituted after the boom and bust of the cotton market in western India in the 1870s, following the U.S. Civil War.[12] In this volatile market climate, British merchants launched new companies at an accelerated rate, drew investments from native shareholders, and then defrauded them, absconding with their investments. The public discrediting of British-owned joint-stocks as "huge superstructures of fraud erected to inveigle the unwary and imprudent" resulted in the new 1882 legislation, offering a pumped-up model of the limited liability contract and strict codes for the regulation of bankruptcy.[13] But it is important to note that the 1882 act did not render indigenous firms directly subject to its contractual regulations. Instead, it established the limited liability contract as the model for all commercial organization, throwing the legitimacy of indigenous kinship-based firms into question. The Act regulated indigenous firms via a nod to the official discourse of noninterference in indigenous culture: lawmakers resisted regulating kinship-based commerce through civil law and, instead, left it open for regulation by the Hindu or Muslim personal law, emphasizing that firms were joint families subject to ancient cultural commands. In short, vernacular capitalism was governed, first and foremost, as a cultural rather than an economic mechanism. Colonial governance posed the economy as a public project, and thus ethical, whereas culture, governed as a static and anachronistic system, was "protected" in personal law not on ethical but on political grounds.

If foundational measures such as the Indian Companies Act imposed the legitimacy of what we colloquially refer to today as the corporation (that is, the limited liability joint-stock) over vernacular capitalists' forms of corporate or group life—call it the firm, the family, or both—new law and jurisprudence governing philanthropy and gifts for social welfare confirmed the process by which these vernacular forms of corporate economic organization came to be coded primarily as anachronistic institutions of culture. The legal standardization of charitable endowments law introduced the contractual concept of trust into India and, with it, the legal principle of *mortmain,* which defined the gift for social welfare as a transfer of property in perpetuity. The late-nineteenth-century history of trust and mortmain in India throws light onto the ways in which an ethics of "general public utility" cast the family firm as a legal, though illegitimate, form of economic organization, motivated not primarily by the economic virtues of productivity and investment but rather by the habits of religio-cultural ritual.[14]

In the 1880s charity, or the gift for social welfare, was gradually defined as the transfer of property in perpetuity specifically for the benefit of the public. The first Indian Income Tax Act of 1886 provided exemption for gifts with specifically "*public* charitable purposes." By 1890 the Charitable and Religious Endowments Act had standardized twenty years of case law by coding charity as the advancement of "general public utility."[15] At the same time jurisprudence on indigenous social welfare practices reveals the introduction of a new category—"private" gifting—which referred specifically to family endowments and various practices of social gifting that were highly localized and differed in structure from the more extensively studied large temple complexes abundant especially in south India.[16] Of special significance here are the culturalist implications of coding indigenous firms' gifting as private and so outside the ethics of "general public utility."

Colonial legal measures took particular interest in the social gifting of Hindu commercial groups, which was specifically articulated as an object of new measures and informed the regulation of indigenous gifting in general.[17] The growing capital accumulations of Hindu commercial castes produced a broad range of social welfare institutions in the late nineteenth century. These included gifts such as temples, *dharmshalas* (rest houses), *gaushalas* (shelter for cows), wells, and dispensaries for ayurvedic medicine. These institutions, of course, performed local authority, and rigorously reinforced caste and gender hierarchies, all of which were promoted and sustained by the legal construction of cultural authenticity and its authority in the domain of the private. Vernacular social welfare institutions also defied categorization into public and private, for they represented gifts given for *jagat-hitaya,* for "the benefit of the world." As one prominent scholar of Hindu personal law states, "nowhere do we find the requirement of a 'public element' [in Hindu gifting]. Some gifts . . . [like] shelters and tanks, obviously enure for the benefit of the public. But the conception is that every *act* of dedication is for the benefit of the world (*jagat-hitaya*), since every act of *dharma,* whether obligatory or optional, contributes to the welfare of mankind."[18]

Such vernacular gifts for social welfare were consecrated to deities, dedicated to family members and ancestors, and performed status, producing symbolic capital; a gift for social welfare was good advertising for the family, fueling marriage alliances and credit networks. Income from such properties might support aging members of the family, and simultaneously provide education and relief for local populations. For example, a temple might provide regular free meals to a village population. At the same time, the temple's lands might be rented out and the income from that rent used to support an aging widow in the family. In other words, benefits accrued at once to both the family and the broader population. It is important to note here that precolonial rulers recognized the local authority enacted in such forms of social giving by evaluating the import of these gifts. Sovereigns were not concerned with whether such institutions brought material benefits to the family if they also extended welfare for *jagat-hitaya*. Rulers would affirm the socioeconomic relevance of such gifts by granting merchants autonomy from sovereign regulation—most often, exemptions from customs duties.

In addition, and equally significant, merchant gifting maintained a porous boundary between charitable and profitable endeavors. Income from gifted property—the income from the productive lands of a temple, for example—could be used temporarily to finance commercial enterprises or defray debt. Profits regained in time would be returned and redirected toward the social welfare operations of gifted property. Again, benefits accrued to the business family and the broader community at once. Said differently, in the vernacular ethics of gift giving, we find an extensive negotiability between forms of social capital and the operations of commerce in which market conventions enabled fluidity between the concerns of charity and those of profit, between public welfare and personal interest.

Colonial jurisprudence restructured these customary practices by recoding the indigenous endowment as a legal trust, a contractual relation between donor, beneficiary, and the manager of the trust property. This is a long and detailed history, with many ramifications, but here I only outline basic changes. The recasting of customary social welfare practices through the principles of contract law meant that gifts were no longer classified on their import, as they had been previously, but rather on their intention. Intentionality was the defining criterion of British legal notions of contract. Beginning in the 1880s judges began to ask whether endowments were to be classified as benefiting the public or only serving private interests. They looked for an a priori intention defining the purpose of a gifted transfer of property, and so they turned to the ritual dedications of endowments, which were interpreted as contractual trust deeds. But vernacular endowments were customarily dedicated to family, clan, and ancestors. Though they might offer welfare for the broader community, endowments dedicated in this way—the vast majority of indigenous social gifts—were classified as private, not specifically directed at the public, and thus not charitable at all. By the 1930s case law on private trusts confirmed this characterization of mercantile family endowments as directed at private, rather than public, benefit. For this reason, key cases beginning in the 1920s even revealed that such private trusts would be subject to taxation.

A 1926 suit by the Madras Commissioner of Income Tax against a south Indian business family of the Chettiar commercial caste is a case in point. The family firm had established a *patshala,* an educational institution for religious teaching in Tamil, which was legally coded as a private trust. It had been established because family members had agreed to set aside Rs. 15,000 from their ancestral property in order to found this institution "for teaching Hindu Tamil hymns." The balance on the cost of building the *patshala* was to be invested in land, which would provide income for the maintenance of the *patshala.* But rather than investing this balance in land, the family invested these resources in rice mills, where they had other business investments. The Commissioner of Income tax assessed the family on their return on the investment in the rice mills. The family pleaded tax exemption, emphasizing that the income on the investment in the rice mills had been used for the maintenance of this religious trust property that benefited the local community. However, the Madras High Court held that "the income [derived] not from [trust] property but from business and as such it was liable to income tax, in the name of the manager of the Patshala."[19] Here, the *patshala*'s status as private trust already marked it as a spurious form of social welfare and rendered suspect its status as a nonprofit institution. In the self-affirming and circular logic of colonial jurisprudence, forms of social gifting established by a vernacular business, with its porous boundaries between social welfare and profit, were coded as private trusts. This meant that they benefited the family's particular interests, which in turn meant that such institutions must be tied to the business interests of the firm and were therefore taxable. Colonial law, with its anxieties about distinguishing charity from profit, produced the family firm as a sort of black hole for capital, an institution unable to fully alienate its property in the charitable gift, in much the same way that its kinship-based organization never somehow fully allowed the free circulation of capital. The family firm, in other words, had to be made subject to the disciplines of the invisible hand, which, in Adam Smith's magical account, transformed private vice into public virtue.

In fact, case law focusing on the intention of the gift sought directly to block the porous boundary between profitable and charitable enterprise that characterized vernacular capitalists' social welfare. It did so by casting the endowment as an institution of religio-cultural ritual. This process is encapsulated in a fantastic legal shift: the inauguration of the Hindu "idol"—the deity to which any customary endowment would be consecrated—as the owner of the gifted property and thus as a legal subject. A series of prominent judicial decisions in the Privy Council and Bombay High Court from 1869 to 1887 offer a rich corpus of jurisprudence on the legal status of the deity. These decisions insisted that gifted property was transferred to the deity and that the deity was the owner of gifted property, and that the purpose of the gift, manifest in the "intentions" of "the idol," must exist in perpetuity; that is, income derived from gifted property could only be used for purposes of the gift and could not even temporarily revert to other uses.[20] This rule conveyed the legal principle of *mortmain*—from Latin, meaning the "dead hand" and referring to the perpetual grasp of the testator on the future use of his property. The principle of mortmain insisted that the purpose of the gift was to be fixed in perpetuity. Supplementing the legal institutionalization of the invisible hand with its ghostly cousin, the concept of mortmain had a long history in Britain back to Roman law, and its introduction into India encapsulated two important legal shifts. First, mortmain defined the legitimate gift for charity—that is, philanthropy for general public utility—as the logical complement to modern market ethics: charitable transfers of property for the public, given in perpetuity, became the necessary complement to the capitalist free circulation of property, also in service of the public. Lawmakers restricted the negotiability of symbolic and market values that characterized the gifting of vernacular capitalisms: gifts for social welfare were privatized as family gifts to "idols" and coded as religio-cultural ritual as opposed to profit-oriented market endeavor. To summarize, the legal emphasis on a priori intentionality in the trust contract enabled the coding of indigenous endowments as "private" cultural institutions distinct from the ethics of "general public utility." Indeed, the mercantile relationship with sovereignty had been transformed: to be legitimized as participating in social welfare, gifts had to be given to an abstract public which had legal rights to enforce the perpetual and proper use of gifted property.

To summarize, the legal disembedding of the market, to use Polanyi's term—that is, the abstracting of exchange relations as social relations—relied on *restricting* local systems of negotiability through new disciplines for market practice structured by the public/private distinction. This distinction communicated ethical boundaries between the productive virtues of modern subjects and the constraints of indigenous culture, where culture was not conceived as an *ethos,* as living ground for ethical practice, but rather as an anachronistic system. Standardizing market practice, and installing the mechanism of contract as the instrument for the exchanges of commensurate legal subjects, colonial law grappled with the embeddedness of vernacular capitalism by casting *Homo aequalis* (economic man) as a public actor and *Homo hierarchicus,* his private cultural counterpart, as his effect.

A Genealogy of *Gemeinschaft/Gesellschaft* as a Technique of Governing: Ethics and Culture

Colonial market governance thus produced two kinds of subjects: the modern subject as economic agent and his other, the subject of culture. In colonial India the legal installation of a world of *gesellschaft* relied upon distinguishing proper market ethics from cultural practice, even, and perhaps most significantly, in the case of indigenous capitalists, who were universally acknowledged motors of the colonial economy. Put differently, the very question of ethical practice in South Asia exposes the complicity of discourses on economy with discourses on culture. Our attention to the colonial production of the market as an ethico-political formation, and as ground for subject formation, constructs a genealogy that extends back to Dumont and Polanyi, among others. Such thinkers were interested in the "revolution in values"—the ethical transformations—that marked the move from the hierarchical subjects of *gemeinschaft* holism to the individuated subject of capitalist modernity's *gesellschaft.* I have detailed some major moves of what I term "colonial market governance" as a counterpoint in order to illuminate the naturalizing cultural discourses at the core of such foundational analyses, which seek productively to historicize and denaturalize Western value systems. For example, Dumont's historicizing gesture in *Homo Aequalis*—to chart the "carving out" of the economy—retreats into a distinction between *cultures* of holism and individualism (thus locating individualism synchronically, from Scholasticism to Locke to Smith). Moreover, his critical engagement with the concept of hierarchy and, if we read him generously, with thinking an ethics of situatedness and embeddedness as distinguished from that of commensurability, slips into a culturalist distinction between economic man (*Homo aequalis*) and cultural man (*Homo hierarchicus*).

To extend the genealogy even further, Foucault's 1978–79 lectures at the Collège de France, which are structured by an interest in political economy as a discourse of governing, the themes of which are known mostly in English translation through the essay "Governmentality," are an important source for thinking through the relationship between market ethics, the modern subject, and discourses on culture. Though they make no mention of Dumont, the lectures on liberal and neoliberal governmentality (published in French only recently) open a reading of the *gemeinschaft/gesellschaft* distinction as a technique of governing rather than as a label for cultural difference. We are all familiar with Foucault's famous articulation of the emergence of political economy as a discourse of governing, part of a historical process that "isolates the economy as a specific sector of reality" and, indeed, "the science and the technique of intervention of the government in that field of reality."[21] Here I return briefly to this oft-quoted phrase, which is used in political but not ethical analyses, to bring the "political" Foucault to our questions inspired by the "ethical" Foucault, for governing, of course, is a thread that spans the continuum of politics (forms of domination) and ethics (disciplines of the self/individuation). The lectures on liberal and neoliberal governmentality suffer from a slippage between two meanings of economy—as a practice of governing, as in its Greek root *oikonomia,* and as an object, "the economy"—one unfortunately reproduced by many lazy deployments of the term "governmentality."[22] But they do foreground the problem of the subject of market governance, a modern subject produced and disciplined by an ethics of economy. Foucault's theorizing of the government of laissez-faire is particularly relevant for the study of colonial market governance, for it offers a critique of the autonomous, intending liberal subject.

In Foucault's 1978 lectures at the Collège de France, government is analyzed as direction, arrangement, management (*gérer*), and "*conduite,*" meaning not only "the activity of directing, conducting, if you will, but equally the manner in which one conducts oneself, the manner in which one lets oneself be directed, the manner in which one is directed, and finally how one comports oneself [*on se trouve se comporter*] under the effect of a directing or conducting, which would be the acting out of the direction, or conduct."[23] This slippery relation between agency and instrumentality—to direct, to let oneself be directed, to be directed and comport oneself accordingly in the proper conduct, in sum, the "conduct of conduct"—is pursued in a variety of historical contexts, from the Greek *oikonomia* to laissez-faire's manipulating, facilitating, enabling, and managing.[24] In this vein Foucault contemplates "civil society as an arrangement of economic men," or what he calls "*la technologie de la gouvernementalité libérale* [the technology of liberal governmentality]."[25] The colonial legal anxieties about indigenous capitalism foreground an interest in making such a civil society composed of "economic men," that is, modern subjects whose agency is so directed or managed that there is no distinction between being governed and exercising agency. But the historical context of colonial liberalism, with which Foucault unfortunately does not engage, also charts a different genealogy. Foucault offers a rigorous critique of the a priori, intending individual subject, which is useful for thinking a colonial genealogy of liberal governmentality. At the same time the critique falls short for the Indian context, for here the subjects of colonial market governance were cast legally as both individual contracting actors and collective cultural agents.

The mechanics of colonial governmentality, as David Scott has emphasized, produced a "new game of politics" in which the liberal introduction of public political exchange accompanied disciplines that sought to produce "the automatic regulation of free exchanges" in economic relations. If in liberal colonial political rationalities, "power works not *in spite of* but through the construction of the space of free social exchange, and *through* the construction of a subjectivity normatively experienced as the source of free will and rational, autonomous agency," the details of colonial law on economy also highlight the simultaneous production of this rational subjects' premodern ancestor.[26] Here I have engaged the political rationalities of late colonial India specifically through the legal introduction of a new game of ethics, that of economy, which mapped a tension between two kinds of conduct or practice, located on the public/private legal register: modern market ethics and the customs of culture.

Ethical Practice, Contract, and the Conduct of Bazaar Conduct

In colonial India the legal enforcement of the free circulation of capital, a performance of laissez-faire, posed the ethics of economy as a problem of law. Said differently, the question of ethical practice in South Asia can also be productively seen through tensions between different concepts of law—as formal rules and as customary practice or the conventions of conduct. As colonial legislators sought to conduct bazaar conduct, and they grappled with the relationship between the systematized rules of contract they wished to implement and the vernacular conventions upon which colonial exchange and production relied. The installation of a colonial *gesellschaft* coded local capitalisms as premodern *gemeinschaft,* and bazaar conduct was coded not as ethical practice, but as cultural script. In the making of the colonial subject as modern subject, then, *an ethics of economy buttressed a politics of culture.* In conclusion, weaving this formulation into our critical genealogy of the *gemeinschaft/gesellschaft* distinction, it is useful to revisit Weber, who famously outlines economy as a problem of law, ethics, and conduct in the first two volumes of *Economy and Society.* Reading against the grain of his "status to contract" narrative, we find that Weber draws an important distinction between law as a juridical logic and law as a normative convention, or ethical practice. *Economy and Society* early on poses a distinction between the legal order and the economic order: between the logic of formal law (in my terms, law as *logos* or system making) and the norms that govern conduct (or law as *nomos,* as in *oikonomia*).

For jurists, Weber states, law "aims at the correct meaning of propositions," at a "logically correct" and "logically coherent" meaning. Law as systematized logic is contrasted with "the arena of normative and de facto powers."[27] Economy, a set of ethical disciplines and practices, emerges from this normative arena of what he calls "convention," which is "characterized by the very absence of any coercive apparatus."[28] Remembering his *Protestant Ethic and the Spirit of Capitalism,* we might say that, for Weber, convention reflects a way of being, an attitude or *ethos* manifest in conduct. Under very specific conditions like the Protestant cultural formation, a way of being or *ethos* operates as ethics and channels the force of law. Indeed, in *Economy and Society,* modern market ethics are the crowning example of convention aligned with law's coercive force, aligned so well that legal coercion and self-interest become one: for

Weber, the modern self-interested market actor engages in contractual legal relations exactly because the protection of property and the regularity and predictability of market exchange serves his self-interest, and contracts confirm conventions motivated by self-interest.[29] Law, discipline, and modern subjectivity cohere through the practice of economy. Reading Weber via Foucault's conduct of conduct, and against his own staging of modernity, we can consider the Indian context outside the *gemeinschaft/gesellschaft* logic, drawing attention to the production of a distinction between ethics and culture. We might say that, in India, the *ethos* of commercial life—local mercantile life-worlds—was *not* validated by colonial law as legitimate, that is, as ethical practice. Indeed, the introduction of "modern" market ethics, especially in the enforcement of written contract, and the identification of individual intentionality, classified indigenous market ethics—its normative conventions—as the commands of an ancient Culture, and to use Weber's words, as the "unreflective habituation to a regularity of life that has engraved itself as custom."[30]

Colonial law, then, implementing "modern" market ethics, recognized the indigenous mercantile ethos not as ethical practice but rather in its difference, as *ethnic,* that is, as the expression of a timeless culture. Today, with new corporate philosophies like karma capitalism, Indian capitalists celebrate their ethnic twists on market ethics, making "capitalism" global and legitimizing it through culturalist identity politics. We should think through an ethos-ethics-ethnic relation, so that the project of mapping a genealogy of virtue does not slip into a culturalist classification. Any such mapping that is also an area studies project—a genealogy of ethical life *in South Asia,* for example—must be attentive to the slippages across these categories.

Notes

1. Pete Engardio and Jena MacGregor, "Karma Capitalism," Businessweek.com, October 30, 2006 (accessed July 12, 2007); Priya Ganapathi, "India Inc. Rediscovers Mahatma Gandhi," Rediff.com, April 11, 2003 (accessed July 12, 2007).

2. Dumont, *From Mandeville to Marx* (in French, *Homo Aequalis: From Mandeville to Marx*) (Chicago: University of Chicago Press, 1977), 33.

3. Karl Polanyi, *The Great Transformation* (Boston: Beacon, 1957).

4. Louis Dumont, interview with Christian Delacampagne, "Louis Dumont and the Indian Mirror," *Le Monde,* January 25, 1981, reprinted in RAIN 43 (April 1981): 4–7, http://www.jstor.org (accessed October 25, 2006).

5. For a detailed history of new law and jurisprudence on economy from approximately 1860 to 1940, see Ritu Birla, *Stages of Capital: Law, Culture, and Market Governance in Late Colonial India* (Durham, N.C.: Duke University Press, 2009).

6. Here I draw on Arjun Appadurai's distinctions between culture as a "virtually open-ended archive of differences," as "the subset of those differences that constitutes the diacritics of group identity"; and "culturalism," or the naturalization/politicization of those differences for group mobilization. See Appadurai, *Modernity at Large:*

Cultural Dimensions of Globalization (Minneapolis: University of Minnesota Press, 1996), 11–16.

7. Foucault, "What Is Enlightenment?" in Paul Rabinow, ed., *Essential Works of Foucault,* Vol. 1, *Ethics, Subjectivity, and Truth* (New York: New Press, 1997), 309.

8. See Christopher Bayly, *Rulers, Townsmen, and Bazaars* (Cambridge: Cambridge University Press, 1983), 374–393.

9. For a detailed ethnography of trust and credit networks, see Rudner, "Banker's Trust and the Culture of Banking among the Nattukottai Chettiars of Colonial South India," *Modern Asian Studies* 23, no. 3 (1989): 417–458; also David Rudner, *Caste and Capitalism in Colonial India: The Nattukottai Chettiars* (Berkeley: University of California Press, 1994).

10. This understanding of the joint family was codified in the Hindu law of *Mitakshara,* which governed most Hindu commercial castes. (The other prominent system of Hindu law, the *Dhayabaga,* was predominant among noncommercial groups in eastern India.) Significantly non-Hindu commercial groups, including Jains and Muslims (such as Ismailis of western India), were also regulated through the *Mitakshara,* which became a universal model for all forms of extended family and joint estate. Indeed, Privy Council decisions on inheritance and succession had established as early as the 1860s that "persons who do not profess Hinduism may, nevertheless, adopt Hindu law and usage." See H. D. Cornish, *Handbooks of Hindu Law: Part I, The Hindu Joint Family* (Cambridge: Cambridge University Press, 1915), 18, 22–23.

11. Letter from the Bombay Native Piece-Goods Merchants' Association to the Secretary to the Government of India, Home Department, March 17, 1908, reprinted in Bengal Chamber of Commerce, *Report of the Bengal Chamber of Commerce* (Calcutta, 1908), 123–125.

12. On the debates surrounding the passage of the Indian Companies Act and the legal category of the public person, see Birla, *Stages of Capital,* chap. 1.

13. National Archives of India, Legislative Department, May 1882, Part A, nos. 9–107, K.W. 3, Proc. no. 88, from the Officiating Judge of the Court of Small Causes, Sealdah, to the Undersecretary of the Government of Bengal, November 17, 1881.

14. For a detailed reading of the law of trust in India and its relationship to late-colonial sovereignty, see Birla, *Stages of Capital,* chaps. 2 and 3.

15. For the debates on and original text of the 1886 Indian Income Tax Act, see National Archives of India, Legislative Department, February 1886, Part A, nos. 113–163. For the original text of the Charitable Endowments Act of 1890, see National Archives of India, Home Department, Judicial Branch, November 1888, Part A, nos. 202–254.

16. By the 1920s large temple complexes were considered publicly relevant institutions because of their size and historical relationship with political authority.

17. These trends in the regulation of charitable endowments also affected Muslim commercial groups' *waqfs,* or traditional endowments; their legal history begins to differ in the 1920s.

18. J. D. M. Derrett, *A Critique of Modern Hindu Law* (Bombay: N. M. Tripathi, 1970), 377.

19. Commissioner of Income Tax, *Madras v. The Therava Patshala, by Manager,* Armachalaur Chetty, 51 *Madras Law Journal* 123, cited in B. R. Jain, *Annotated Digest of Income-Tax Cases, 1886–1942* (New Delhi: Income Tax Publishing House, 1942), 137.

20. See Birla, *Stages of Capital,* chap. 2, for a detailed charting of the key Privy Council and High Court decisions and trends in the jurisprudence on mortmain.

21. Foucault, "Governmentality," in *The Foucault Effect,* ed. Graham Burchell, Colin Gordon, and Peter Miller (Chicago: University of Chicago Press, 1991), 102.

22. Foucault, *La Naissance de la Biopolitique: Cours au College de France, 1978–79* (Paris: Seuil/Gallimard, 2004), especially Lecture 4, April 1979; for a summary, see Thomas Lemke, "The Birth of Biopolitics," *Economy and Society* 30, no. 2 (2001): 190–207; and Colin Gordon, "Governmental Rationality: An Introduction," in Burchell, Gordon, and Miller, *The Foucault Effect,* 1–51.

23. My translation. For the definition of conduct, see Foucault, *Sécurité, Territoire, Population: Cours au College de France, 1977–78* (Paris: Seuil/Gallimard, 2004), Lecture 1, March 1978, 196–197: "ce mot 'conduite' se réfère a deux choses. La conduite, c'est bien l'activité qui consiste à conduire, la conduction si vous voulez, mais c'est également la manière dont on se conduit, la manière dont on se laisse conduire, la manière dont on est conduit et dont, finalement, one se trouve se comporter sous l'effet d'une conduite qui serait acte de conduite ou de conduction."

24. See Foucault, *Sécurité, Territoire, Population,* Lecture 5, April 1978, 360–361, on the emergence of political economy and a new governmentality: "Il va falloir manipuler, il va falloir susciter, il va falloir faciliter, il va falloir laisser faire, il va falloir autrement dit, gérer et non plus réglementer." See also Gordon, "Governmental Rationality, 17–20.

25. Colin Gordon, translating Foucault, in "Governmental Rationality," 23; and Michel Foucault, Lecture 1, April 1979, in *La Naissance de la Biopolitique,* 300.

26. David Scott, "Colonial Governmentality," in his *Refashioning Futures: Criticism after Postcoloniality* (Princeton, N.J.: Princeton University Press, 1999), 36.

27. Max Weber, *Economy and Society,* ed. Guenther Roth and Claus Wittich, Vol. 1 (New York: Bedminster, 1968), 311.

28. Weber, *Economy and Society,* 1:312.

29. Ibid., 1:336–337. Weber's relationship to law is most often read as contradictory, as celebrating the noncoercive conventions of capitalist market ethics, even as he emphasizes the coercive force of law. See, for example, Sally Ewing, "Formal Justice and the Spirit of Capitalism: Max Weber's Sociology of Law," *Law and Society Review* 21, no. 3 (1978): 487–512. Instead, I read Weber here via Foucault's mapping of the relationship between the self-interested subject, the "le sujet d'intérêt" of political economy, and the subject of law/rights or "le sujet de droit" of the political theory of sovereignty. See especially *La Naissance de la Biopolitique,* Lecture 28, March 1979, 281–286.

30. Weber, *Economy and Society,* 1:312.

5.

The Ethics of Textuality: The Protestant Sermon and the Tamil Public Sphere

Bernard Bate

Eighteenth- and nineteenth-century Protestant missionaries to the Tamil lands of southern India and Ceylon were appalled by Indian textuality. They encountered a world in which the social relations of the text were highly restricted in terms of person, space, and time, and a world in which the meaningfulness of the text appeared to reside somewhere beyond the word. High-value texts were animated—brought to life in practice—in places and times set aside by persons qualified (by gender, caste, and training) for people qualified to hear them. Literate elites among the Saivites of Jaffna, for instance, deployed Sanskrit Vedas or texts such as the *kandapuranam* written in an archaic Tamil; for the wielders of such texts did not necessarily consider the denotational function of the word *logos* as more important than the aesthetic and spiritual power of *nada,* the "originary form of sound," the source of language, music, and the universe itself.[1] Indic textuality appeared to emphasize the sheer aesthetic experience of linguistic sound over the denotationality of the word, states of being over states of knowing, poetic over prose forms, mood over mind.[2] For the Protestants, on the other hand, *logos* was critically important within the highest-value text, the Bible, for the salvation of peoples' souls depended upon it.[3] They therefore translated the Bible, built schools with the aim of producing literate populations, propagated passages and interpretations of it in tracts to be widely distributed, and—crucially—went out among as many people as they could to preach the vernacular gospel in the marketplaces, mandabams, and bazaars of villages and towns all over the country.

Textuality itself, then, including the social relations of textual animation, was a major site of ethical evaluation for the missionaries, and they waged a campaign against what they judged to be wicked textual ethics that would deny the masses access to the word of God. It was not only what the sermons said that was important in this struggle but also the ethics of the social—or textual—practices themselves. This Protestant turning toward a stranger-audience in tracts and sermons marked a radical departure from existing Indic forms of text—at least among men of higher status.[4] In many ways the Protestants prevailed. Though they only converted a small fraction of the population to Christianity, the wider society was, textually, Protestantized. For, by the mid-nineteenth century, schools, presses, and sermonizing had been widely taken up by non-Christian agents[5] in the formation of entirely new modes of religiosity that we call religion[6] and, some decades later, into new modes of agency and political subjectivity that we call politics. That turning toward everyone, a turning to and calling to all, embodied a new ethic that had a great deal to do with the production of the ethical universe of strangers that we call the modern public sphere.[7]

To illustrate this suggestion I rely on a set of Tamil tracts on Christian preaching in common, public places titled *The Bazaar Book* or *Vernacular Preacher's Companion* (in Tamil, *kiranamalikai,* 1865), one of the very earliest treatises on Tamil homiletic. Written by H. M. Scudder (1822–1895), a Tamil-literate American missionary born of a prominent family of missionaries to the Tamil lands, the text offers a vision of the vernacular preacher delivering a sermon in that space of stranger-mixing, the marketplace or "bazaar," deploying his Tamil Bible along with native texts. "Each address," he writes in the English introduction, "contains, woven into its texture, a few poetical quotations, selected with great care from Hindu works."[8] Prominent among these texts was the *Naladiyar* (*Naladi Naanuuru*), one of Tamil's most famous treatises on ethical being in the world.[9] The *Naladiyar* is especially prominent in discussions on language and the conditions surrounding public sermonizing. The vernacular sermon here involves a conjuncture of European and Tamil notions of text and textual animation along with a conjuncture of moral and political dimensions of being in the world. So, despite the sermon emerging as an alien textual practice in India, something was Indian about these sermons, too, for the texts that were animated in them had ancient lineages in the Tamil world. Although the artifactual (e.g., "books") and interactional (e.g., "sermons") forms of the text were transformed by Protestant textualities, a quintessentially Indic rhetorical framing of being in the world (i.e., the *trivarga,* viz. *dharma, artha, kama*) and the poetics of the expression of that being inhered within the new texts, including sermons. We find these poetics inhering also within a whole series of practices, from worship, to lullabies and dirges, riddles, proverbs, folk songs, games and—as Anand Pandian has discussed—in the myriad, quotidian, and bodily engagements of the cultivator with the soil.[10] In other words, that which appeals to the largest and oldest ideologies and aesthetics of being in the world as structured via mythopoetic and rhetorical forms provided an embodied ground upon which Protestant textual forms would work to transform the world. Indexes of these rhetorics and poetics are the two texts most commonly deployed, even sometimes eclipsing the Bible, in the tracts-of-the-times in mid-century Tamilakam: the sixth- or seventh-century CE Jain masterpieces of being in the world, the *Thirukkural,* and its companion, the *Naladiyar,* texts that are named for the very poetic forms they take: the couplet (*kural*) and the quatrain (*naladi*). For the Christians who wanted to capture souls for Jesus knew that their own texts must first have Tamil souls.

Naladiyar and the Bazaar

The *Bazaar Book* is among the very first texts to provide an outline of Tamil homiletic and models of Tamil sermons (although individual tracts dating back to the 1840s were similarly structured in theme and tone). With the exception of a brief English introduction, the *Bazaar Book* is composed of thirteen "addresses" to a "heathen audience" on topics such as "Guru," "Sin," "God," "Man," "Expiation," "Fate," "Transmigration," "Idolatry Sinful," "Idolatry Ruinous," "Caste," "Brahmanism," and, most important for our purposes, "Shastra" (text, textual precept) and "Mantra" (auspicious and efficacious sound, word, or phrase). The *Bazaar Book* appears to have included a number of tracts that Scudder had been preparing when he took sick leave to return to America, but the tone of the addresses was very much in line with the rather aggressive and offensive style of tract publishing and preaching that characterized the Protestant missionary engagement with south India and Sri Lanka from at least the beginning of the nineteenth century.[11]

The tracts that were joined together in the *Bazaar Book* were clearly meant to be read aloud to a group of people, perhaps memorized and delivered by native assistants or catechists. The addresses are written in an extremely simple Tamil, somewhat more Sanskritic than today's standard in Tamilnadu, but the sentence structure is quite easy to grasp, quick syntactic punches perfect for oral delivery. Other features of the orality of the text include directly addressing the audience as *piriyamanavarkaley* ("Dearly beloved") or simply *janangaley*! ("Oh, people!"). They included a great deal of rhetorical questions designed to engage listeners in situ, and the language was shot through with very simple proverbs, similes, and other appeals to oral literature:

> *piriyamanavarkaley, "nir mel kumizh pol nilaiyila kayam" enkira pazhamozhiyai ninkalellam keddiruppirkal.*[12]
>
> Dearly beloved, you all will have heard the well-known proverb that the "body is as ephemeral as the bubble on the surface of the water."

For complex reasons the *Naladiyar* was highlighted in the *Bazaar Book* at moments involving the animation of the text, the bringing of text to life in the sermonic encounter of missionary or catechist with the stranger-audience in the bazaar itself. Though less prominent today than the *Thirukkural,* its far more famous companion and model, *Naladiyar* was the second Tamil text that we know of to have been printed outside a Christian context by Tamils for Tamils, in Madras in 1812.[13] Its priority in the thinking of Tamil literati (at least) is indexed by its primacy in the order of publication, like the Guttenberg Bible, an index of the *doxa* of textual importance for Tamil people. The nineteenth-century Tamil philologist G. U. Pope writes that the "peculiar terseness and vigor of its style and the fidelity with which it reflects the thoughts and ideas of the great mass of the Tamil people, and indeed of the yeomanry of India," leads it to be called the *Vellalar-Vetham,* "the Bible of the Cultivators." Its import is attested by the fact that U. Ve. Swaminathaiyar, one of the great universalizers of ancient Tamil literature, took it up as his very first lesson upon his appointment to Government College in Kumbakonam in 1880.[14] And by 1893, in G. U. Pope's famous critical edition and translation, the author asserts that it was "taught . . . in every vernacular school in the Tamil country."[15] It was also used among Christians from a very early date, and was included in the formal syllabus of the Americans in Jaffna, for instance, from the foundation of their Seminary there in 1816.[16] Like the *Thirukkural,* the *Naladiyar* in its simple moral counsel was—and remains—immensely attractive to Christians (and everyone else, for that matter). Even Pope, who worked zealously to purge the church of a great deal of indigenous aesthetics in the mid-century,[17] endorsed the texts wholeheartedly and wrote that the two together throw "a flood of light upon the whole ethical and social philosophy of the Tamil people."[18]

The *Naladiyar* contains extraordinarily beautiful verses embodying a timeless ethic with universal appeal. Some of Pope's translations give a taste of their poesy and power.[19] On wealth, *Naladiyar* 28:10 is profound:

> Gathering it together is trouble, and even so the guarding of resplendent wealth is severe trouble. If the guarded heap diminish, it is trouble. If it perish, it is trouble. Wealth is trouble's very dwelling place!

Naladiyar 20:5 would not be out of place in contemporary humanist critiques of caste:

> When men speak of "good caste" and "bad caste" it is a mere form of speech, and has no real meaning. Not even by possessions, made splendid by ancient glories, but by self-denial, learning, and energy is caste determined.

Or who could remain unmoved by the striking observation in *Naladiyar* 3:4 of a funeral procession by some sixth-century century poet who transcended his time and place to capture a chilling truth of the human condition?

> They march and then strike once! A little while they wait, then strike the drum a second time. Behold, how fine! The third stroke sounds. They veil it, take the fire, and go forth—the dying bear the dead.

Although today the *Naladiyar* is not nearly as well known as the *Thirukkural,* its structure is noteworthy for its artifice—and therefore for what might have been important to Tamil speakers for a very, very long time. The origin of the text itself is unknown, though most think it started with the Jains and many felt it to be among the earliest texts of Tamil literature. Traditional scholarly lore has it that prior to the twelfth century the four hundred quatrains were organized in no particular order. It was reorganized by Pathumanar in the twelfth century according to the well-known structure of Indic didactic texts, namely, the three aims of life (*trivarga*): dharma (*aram*), right conduct; artha (*porul*), material gain and rule; and kama (*kamam*), romantic or sexual love. To place the *Naladiyar* in the forefront of sermonic practice, then, is to see it not only as the new use of a native text but one that is organized according to a much earlier, and deeper, pan-Indic aesthetic of human life. It embodies a vernacularization of even earlier meta-structural concerns in the lives of Indian people, concerns that are quite old, indeed, formulated as a paradigm perhaps two thousand years ago. It provides, then, a perfect icon of the ways that preexisting phenomenologies of human action and textualities are taken up in the new newnesses of modern textual forms.

Perhaps the *Naladiyar* was at the forefront in the *Bazaar Book* because it tended to lend itself more easily to the Christian (and, peculiarly, the Tamil modern) exclusion of *kama,* romantic love, from the public world. Visible genres of Indic performance would, in previous ages, emphasize *kama* as an element of life in both oral and scriptural practice—for example, the *kamasutra*—in both the home and the visible world of kingly procession.[20] Entire genres of *prabandham,* for instance, were devoted to outlining the love life of the king (*ula prabandham*),[21] and erotic stories and songs rang out among clutches of women in marriage ceremonies all across the land (to the shock and outrage of the missionaries, of course).[22] Contemporary Tamil public life, however, tends to shunt such expressions either to the most stigmatized forms of theater and street performance (e.g., *karakattam,* or "pot dancing") or to the realm of whisper and gossip regarding the multiple partners or nonstandard sexual practices of the political class. Whereas the *Thirukkural,* for instance, gives almost equal time to *kama*—(330 quatrains out of 1,330 verses), the

Naladiyar devotes only 10 quatrains out of 400 for the subject of bodily desire. Thus the *Naladiyar,* even more than the *Thirukkural,* appears to embody a new kind of sexless publicity that becomes, eventually, the standard for nineteenth- and twentieth-century public discourse.

In taking up the *trivarga* structure, the *Naladiyar* as a textual source for a Protestant ethical sermon emblematizes the overall conjuncture of Indic and European modes of textuality, as it is a Tamil text that will now be cited and discoursed upon just as a Bible verse would be used. This predominance of the denotational (as opposed to, say, poetic) functions of the text, as we shall see, was a key element of the newness in Protestant textuality. At the same time the denotational elements of these texts enabled the deployment of ancient Indic ethics that were timeless, pure, true, and almost all but absent from what the missionaries felt was a wicked and degenerate Hinduism then being practiced. Here was an Indian ethic that the missionaries could wield as Indian—a rhetorical sleight of mind caught as it was within a new ethics of textuality generally.

Protestant Textualities and Their Others

That Scudder cites the use of the *Naladiyar* in the bazaar also provokes rather fruitful conjunctures and contradictions. We imagine that Scudder had in mind a public place where he felt he could address some generalized humanity, some group of "zero-degree individuals," all equal in the sight of God and all deserving of God's good news and salvation. The bazaar may certainly have looked like such a place of stranger-mixing, a site of commerce between people who would normally not interact with one another at all in buying and selling, a place, in other words, of common aims. To be sure, the bazaars of the Tamil lands became the first sites of public meetings and political oratory in the coming decades and the following century. But a bazaar is not a public place in a commonsense understanding of the term for several distinct reasons. Most striking, perhaps, is that it is not opposed to some private realm. Rather, it is the very paradigm of what we have come to understand as one pole of a quintessentially Indic opposition between a ritually enclosed—and therefore semiotically coherent interior as opposed to an exterior essentially defined as a negative space, a non-interior. Rabindranath Tagore's famous opposition, "home and the world" (*ghare/baire*), for instance, is not strictly an opposition between the "home" and the "world"; more precisely, it is an opposition between "inside the house" and "the outside," between a space positively defined by coherent social order and an incoherent negative space defined by its value-contrast in opposition to the interior.[23] The exterior, for which Dipesh Chakrabarty used the bazaar as a paradigm, "has a deeply ambiguous character":

> It is exposed and therefore malevolent. It is not subject to a single set of (enclosing) rules and ritual defining a community. It is where miscegenation occurs. All that do not belong to the "inside" (family/community) lie there, cheek by jowl, in unassorted collection, violating rules of mixing: from feces to prostitutes.[24]

Again, this is where the *Naladiyar* is most prominently deployed in the *Bazaar Book* and provides a sense of just how non-interior, non-ordered these spaces were from the preacher's point of view. Just over half (nine out of sixteen) of the *naladis* (quatrains) cited in the *Bazaar Book* are found in a final section titled "Various Topics," all but two of which are deployed in the subsection titled "Street Opponents, Unfair Disputants, and Cavilers." Reading through the quatrains in this subsection gives us a sense of the general tone that may have greeted these sermons in the altogether non-polis-like atmosphere of the bazaar. Here the vernacular preacher offered *Naladiyar* 26:6 to the "Noisy Disputant":

> No sound comes from the green leaves of the Palmyra tree, but its dry leaves rustle noisily evermore. So learned and wise men, fearing lest they be betrayed into faulty expressions, keep silence; but ignorant men are always jabbering. (*Naladiyar* 26:6)

To the "Abusive Disputant" Scudder suggested the use of three quatrains:

> Senseless as a ladle, which knows not the sweetness of the gruel, empty-headed fools ridicule the words of loving men, who discourse graciously on virtue. The wise, however, accept those words as full of substance. (*Naladiyar* 33:1)

> Words Spoken by an unguarded tongue always scorch the speakers themselves. Hence, men of mature wisdom and intelligence will never hastily give utterance to harsh and angry expressions. (*Naladiyar* 7:3)

> It is the duty of great men not only to forgive abuse cast upon themselves; but also to grieve, because their vilifiers must, as a consequence of their wicked conduct, fall into a fiery hell. (*Naladiyar* 6:8)

And to the "Disputant Who Scorns and Rejects Truth," the vernacular preacher might deploy *Naladiyar* 26:9, which states:

> Base and contemptible souls are like the fly, which, passing by the honey distilled in perfume-breathing flowers, greedily seeks everything that is foul and disgusting. Of what profit to such persons are the clear and sweet words, which drop, nectar-like, from the lips of the great and the wise?

Finally, I think the following suggests, perhaps, the most non-interior-like qualities of the bazaar by offering to the "Obscene Disputant" a universally understood insult:

> When fools, who have failed to profit by instruction, speak detestable words, wise and excellent men feel ashamed, and greatly pity the mother who gave birth to those fools. (*Naladiyar* 32:6)

But the *Naladiyar* and the *Thirukkural* are also cited positively as elements of an ethical universe to which the missionary is bound as much as he is to the Bible. The most famous[25] of all *naladis* (135) offers the following against the use of Indic Shastras:

> Countless are the number of Sastras, but few are the days of those who study them, exposed to a thousand fatalities. Therefore like the Swan, which separating the milk from the water with which it is mingled drinks only the former; let the wise carefully discriminating reject worthless Sastras and study only those which are valuable.

The above translation, by H. M. Scudder's brother, Dr. J. W. Scudder, contains a minor but highly motivated slippage in its translation of the term *kalvi,* 'learning', as 'shastra', a textual form. Pope's 1893 translation gives a better sense of the lovely and famous Tamil line, *kalvi karaiyila karpavar nalcila:*

> Learning hath no bounds, the learner's days are few. If you think calmly diseases many wait around! With clear discrimination learn what is meet for you, like the swan that leaving the water drinks the milk. (*Naladiyar* 135)

Sleight of hand or not, the *Bazaar Book* spent considerable time focusing on what the missionaries felt were evils of textual practice associated with *sastram* and *mantiram* (mantras, auspicious poetic formulas). Among the most heinous elements of Indic textual practice from the Protestant point of view was the restricted social relations of the text. Scudder complains that the "Shastras" pertain only to Brahmins and others invested with the "sacred cord" but excludes women and Sudras who

> are in no case to read or even hear them read. How is this? Can we suppose that God, in giving a Veda, would deny it to Sudras and bestow it only upon those who wear a cord? Is it to these alone that he gives his rain, his wind, and his sun-shine?[26]

Continuing a long-standing theme that Protestants applied equally to Catholic priests and their Latin Bible, they criticized both the restrictions of the texts as well as their semiotic opacity.

> These four Vedas are written in Sanscrit, a language utterly unknown and unintelligible to ordinary people. They are rendered still more difficult by numberless transmutation, augmentation, and elisions. They have been purposely made abstruse and obscure. Not one in a thousand, even among Brahmins, can read and explain them. Such Vedas are utterly useless to the world of mankind. Hence we cannot allow for a moment that these four Vedas have God for their author. Far from being divinely revealed, they are evidently the productions of fraudulent and tricky Brahmins.[27]

In contrast, the missionaries claimed that the Christian Veda, "the true Sastra, is perfectly plain and intelligible. Any one can read it, any one can understand it, any one can meditate on it. Even those, who are not readers, may by the ear easily apprehend its truths, and discover the good way of salvation."[28]

More broadly, the American missionaries understood that they were dealing with minds that processed information darkly. In 1839 one wrote:

> No one who has not had some experience on this point, can understand what is meant by the expression, *the darkness of a heathen's mind,* or know how difficult it is to communicate any correct notions of the Gospel to an uneducated heathen. In order to become intelligent hearers of the Gospel, they must be taught the first principles of Christianity in childhood.[29]

But it was not merely a matter of teaching the principles of the Gospel in childhood; more important was to transform their minds based on rationalized semiotics. Another American missionary with twenty years experience in Jaffna wrote, in 1837,

> Their own false systems blind their understanding. For instance, I call fifty men and women of middle age to hear the following sermon:—
>
> Friends, we are all sinners. We need a Saviour. God has provided a Saviour, Jesus Christ, who will save us from hell and take us to heaven. Repent, therefore, and believe on Jesus Christ!
>
> This sermon if preached to a purely heathen congregation, means either nothing at all, or else these attentive hearers have applied the whole to the most absurd notions of heathenism. *Sinners* means those who are shut up to poverty and suffering through the influence of fate;

> *God* means Siva; *Jesus Christ* is some unknown deity; *Heaven* means Kailaiyam; *Hell* is the suffering of many transmigrations; and *Repentence* is some dictionary word which they cannot understand.[30]

They complained systematically in just this fashion that terms lost their referential grounding, that their denotationality was floating and unstable, that heathens could make words mean precisely what they wanted them to mean. So, in addition to referential fixity, the Protestants were focused on semiotic transparency and the ability to deploy signs in socially universal contexts—just like, or so they imagined, the bazaar.

Thus the Protestants encountered an entirely different phenomenology of textual production and embodiment of textual knowledge. However, for many of the people they encountered, the point was that texts (such as the Tamil Saivite *kandapuranam*), were not necessarily about the transmission of denotational textuality but were more about the embodiment of the text in its recitation by a person qualified to do so via social standing and training. Texts were to be memorized and sung at highly restricted times and only in certain spaces such as a temple, on auspicious dates and times, and by and to people qualified to hear it (mostly upper-caste men). Recitation operated on the logic of textual emblematization, where the animator embodied, became an avatar, of the text. Socially that was the point.

The aesthetics of hearing the text was probably closer to hearing music: although the denotationality of the text (*logos*) was important to the reciter and to some in the audiences, it was the sheer sound of the text (*nada*) that would have beneficial consequences for the vast majority of hearers and, indeed, for the world in which the text had been sung. Ethically Protestant textuality found an Other and a mode of seeing or epistemizing itself: to cultivate the kinds of minds that would be ready to learn the gospel required a transformation of signs, their textual carriers, and their functionality itself. The Protestant missionaries accomplished this through schooling, publishing and distributing tracts and Bibles, and sermonizing. As mentioned at the outset, though only a fraction of the population was converted to Protestantism, the entire society would, over the course of just a few decades, become Protestantized. By the time the *Bazaar Book* was published in 1865, Tamil Saivites had already begun to establish and staff European-style schools, sermonizing broadly, and printing new clear editions of sacred texts that would be simple for all to understand.

The ethics of Protestant textuality lay at the heart of the project to produce a universalizing system of signs. The missionaries recoiled at the restrictions on the animation of the text and sought new institutional means and performative spaces such as schools and bazaars to bring the text to all the people. The ability to universalize texts so that everyone could understand them—to produce vernacular texts written in the language of everyday life—was asserted as ethically superior to the Indian forms of texts which, in the missionaries' view, were ethically unconscionable, for only a qualified few could understand them and comprehend their meaning or, in fact, were even licensed to hear them.

Moreover, in terms of producing the kind of large-scale social imaginary that is the Tamil world today, the Protestant ethic of textuality was also at the center of much of the transformations that we have come to understand as "public" in the most generic—indeed, European—sense of that term. Language came under a peculiar kind of ethical scrutiny, was re-cognized as a new way of knowing and being that came to be used, eventually, to imagine a population that shared a commonality in, and solidarity based on, language. This new understanding enabled language to be used in new ways, to be circulated in new textual forms, particularly in forms designed to interpellate a generalized people, a public, that is, universalized print and universalizing sermons (and, later, political oratory). It was that communicative restructuring of textual practice, that new interpellation, which would eventually speak into being the Tamil people and the Tamil public sphere.

The ethical underpinning of Protestant textuality brought with it transformations in the materiality and ideology of textual artifacts and in the praxis of textual production. These transformations resulted in textual shifts from the poetic to the prosaic, from an aesthetic of the power of sound (*nada*) to an ethic of denotational rationality (*logos*), from a sonocentric to a logocentric universe. In combination with the profound shift from restricted to universalized social relations of textuality, new Protestant forms of textuality utterly transformed the entire project of what one was to do with words and, indeed, the kinds of persons that would be licensed to do those things in new spaces and temporalities. A new kind of agency was born, that of the sermonizer, who would be licensed to speak to and transform the world according to any number of different ethical systems but on a new, mass scale. By the first few decades of the twentieth century, that same agency would come to be applied to various projects such as the human rights of lower castes, women's rights, the labor movement, and eventually independence.

It is worthwhile to recognize, however, at least briefly, that although the Protestants made history, they did not do so just as they pleased. Other textualities were still operating that would be the basis upon which the Tamil public sphere would be experienced. An ancient vernacular aesthetic of textual production—namely, the poetic and rhetorical textual forms carried over from the ancient into the production of the modern—appears to have remained immanent within the transformations of Protestant textuality that yielded a qualitative difference in the nature of the formation of the public. Moreover, it was those poetics and rhetorics that made the experience and disposition of a Tamil public sphere utterly different from the experience of, say, a French one. For texts such as these—and even the ancient ethics of Indian textuality—continued to be deployed by the new agents in their transformative projects of the coming decades and century.

Even in 1893, in his edition of the *Naladiyar,* Pope provided a thorough discussion of the poetic meters of the text so that readers could appreciate its poesy. In both his editions of the *Thirukkural* and the *Naladiyar,* Pope expended a great deal of energy ensuring that readers would be sufficiently familiar with the lovely meter called *Venba,* the [*ven*] 'white, bright, clear' = 'verse'. In essence, readers would be lost—unable to parse the morphemes—were they unable to scan the poem prior to understanding it.[31]

More than that, however readers would be lost aesthetically. Sound itself (*nada*) was important, the sheer sound of words and music as they worked on the hearts of the hearers. Even the missionaries, in their use of Tamil texts such as *Naladiyar,* knew that their sermons—however rational and denotationally explicit—would fail to move the souls of their auditors without a poesy alien to their own ethic. Consider the sense of the sound symbolism between the beating of a funeral drum and the assertion of a callow young man who claims that life is characterized by the bliss of wedded life (*Naladiyar* 3:5).

> *kanankondu cutrattaar kallen ralara*
> *pinankondu kattupparkkandum—manankondin*
> *dundundudunennum unarvinar catrumey*
> *tondondondennum parai*
>
> To him, who, although he sees them bear the corpse to the burning ground, while friends in troops loudly lament, boldly asserts that wedded life is bliss on earth, the funeral drum speaks out, and mocks his vain utterance.[32]

Between the reduplicated echo of the two lines, *undu, undu, undu* (It is, it is, it is) and the onomatopoeic drum beat—*tondondond*—is caught a sense of mocking irony for which the English translation—even at its best in Pope—requires an extra phrase, "*and mocks his vain utterance.*"

The bodily apperception of the sheer sound of language (*nada*), the music of language, and the poetic form remained a key element of the entire project and would come to have fateful political impacts later on in the twentieth-century Tamil nationalist Dravidianist take-up of just such poesy as an index of their own antiquity, of their Tamil cultural authenticity, in the new democratic order of mid-twentieth-century Tamilakam. Examples of this sort are copious in any of the major Dravidianist speakers, such as Kalaiñar Karunanidhi or Ariñar C. N. Annadurai.[33]

Even the embodiment of knowledge through the memorization and recitation of text was resurrected by the Dravidianist politicians who combined the precolonial textual emblematization—indexing and iconically instantiating a consubstantiality of person and text—with the sermonic form in oratorical discourse. To cite the ancient text was to embody it, to become an avatar of the text itself and all its properties: grammatical refinement, antiquity, and civilizational authenticity. This kind of emblematization became a key element of the very character of the interpellation of the Tamil public sphere, of its leaders and its people.

This is a strikingly clear example—among many we could enumerate—of how deep vernacular aesthetics track the manner in which the new newnesses of modernity would be laid down in south Asia (and elsewhere). In this case, it was these ancient, broad, and deep Indic rhetorical and mythopoetic structures that provided an embodied ground for the infrastructural transformation of the Tamil public sphere based on the ethical prescriptions of textuality and textual practice associated with the Protestant Reformation and the European Enlightenment.

Acknowledgments

Research for this chapter was made possible by a research grant from the American Institute of Sri Lankan Studies (2005) and by generous support from the Department of Anthropology and the MacMillan Center for International and Area Studies, Yale University. Earlier drafts of the chapter were presented at "Vernacular Public Spheres/South Asia," April 6, 2007, Yale University; "Vernacular Social Imaginaries: Public Spheres, Modernities, Nations," CASCA/AES, May 8–12, 2007, Toronto, Canada; and at the conference that inaugurated this volume, "Genealogies of Virtue," September 2007, University of Vancouver, Canada. Thanks to all the members of those meetings for constructive interventions. For very helpful comments on earlier drafts and general encouragement, I thank Anand Pandian and Daud Ali. Thanks also to Rebecca Tolen of Indiana University Press and one outside reader for their helpful suggestions. All errors and infelicities are my own. Very special thanks to M. S. S. Pandian who originally brought the *Bazaar Book* to my attention in 2003.

Notes

1. Sudipta Kaviraj, "Writing, Speaking, Being: Language and the Historical Formation of Identities in India." In *Nationalstaat und Sprachkonflickt in Sud—und Sudostasien,* ed. Dagmar Hellmann-Rajanayagam and Dietmar Rothermund (Stuttgart:

Steiner, 1992), 27–28. Cf. also Robert A. Yelle, *Explaining Mantras: Ritual, Rhetoric, and the Dream of a Natural Language in Hindu Tantra* (New York: Routledge, 2003).

2. E. Valentine Daniel, *Charred Lullabies: Chapters in an Anthropography of Violence* (Princeton, N.J.: Princeton University Press), 1996.

3. Sababathy Kulendran, *kristhava tamil vethagamaththin varalaru (History of the Tamil Bible)* (Bangalore: Bible Society of India, 1967).

4. Whereas high-status textual practice did not appear to deploy sermonic forms, lower classes/castes engaged in a number of different genres of generalized interpellation. See, for instance, Isabelle Clarke-Deces, *No One Cries for the Dead: Tamil Dirges, Rowdy Songs, and Graveyard Petitions* (Berkeley: University of California Press, 2005).

5. Hugald Grafe, "Hindu Apologetics at the Beginning of the Protestant Mission Era in India," in *Missionsberichet aus Indien im 18. Jahrhundert,* ed. Michael Bergunder (Halle: Verlag der Franckeschen Stiftungen zu Halle, 1999), 69–93; Dennis Hudson, "Tamil Hindu Responses to Protestants: Nineteenth-Century Literati in Jaffna and Tinnevelly," in *Indigenous Responses to Western Christianity,* ed. Steven Kaplan (New York: New York University Press, 1995), 95, 123; Richard F. Young and S. Jebanesan, *The Bible Trembled: The Hindu-Christian Controversies of Nineteenth-Century Ceylon* (Vienna: Samlung De Nobili, 1995).

6. E. Valentine Daniel, "The Arrogation of Being and the Blindspot of Religion," in *Discrimination and Toleration,* ed. K. Hastrup and G. Ulrich (Great Britain: Kluwer Law International, 2002); Richard King. *Orientalism and Religion: Postcolonial Theory, India, and Mythic East* (London: Routledge, 1999).

7. Benedict Anderson, *Imagined Communities: Reflections on the Origin and Spread of Nationalism* (New York: Verso, 1991); Charles Taylor, *Modern Social Imaginaries* (Durham, N.C.: Duke University Press, 2004), and *A Secular Age* (Cambridge, Mass.: Harvard University Press, 2007); Michael Warner, *Publics and Counterpublics* (New York: Zone Books, 2002).

8. Rev. H. M. Scudder, D.D., *Bazaar Book or Vernacular Preacher's Companion* (in Tamil, *kiranamaligai*) (Madras: American Arcot Mission Press, 1865), vi.

9. It is actually the third most prominent Indic text: the *Thirukkural* is by far the first with thirty-two citations, the Telegu *Vemanar* is the second with twenty-three citations; and the *Naladiyar* is third with sixteen.

10. Anand Pandian, *Crooked Stalks: Cultivating Virtue in South India* (Durham, N.C.: Duke University Press, 2009).

11. Hugald Grafe, *History of Christianity in India,* Vol. 3, *South India* (Bangalore: Church History Association of India/Theological Publications in India, 1992), 140–141. For a startling example of the vitriol with which the Christians attacked Indic religiosity, cf. Winslow and Vedanayaka Sastri's notorious tract *kuruththuvazhi* (The blind way), Jaffna Tract Society, c. 1845.

12. Scudder, *Bazaar Book or Vernacular Preacher's Companion,* 5.

13. Stuart Blackburn, *Print, Folklore, and Nationalism in Colonial South India* (New Delhi: Permanent Black, 2003), 82; Kamil Zvelebil, *Companion Studies to the History of Tamil Literature* (Leiden: Brill, 1992), 219.

14. Zvelebil, *Companion Studies to the History of Tamil Literature,* 189.

15. G. U. Pope, ed., *The Naladiyar or Four Hundred Quatrains in Tamil* (Oxford: Clarendon, 1893), viii.

16. *The Second Triennial Report of the American Mission Seminary: Jaffna, Ceylon* (Nellore: Church Mission Press, 1830). The report was signed by B. C. Meigs, D. Poor, M. Winslow, L. Spaulding, H. Woodward, and J. Scudder.

17. Indira Peterson, "Between Print and Performance: The Tamil Christian Poems of Vedanayaka Sastri and the Literary Cultures of Nineteenth-century South India," in *India's Literary History: Essays on the Nineteenth Century*, ed. Stuart Blackburn and Vasudha Dalmia (Delhi: Permanent Black, 2004), 49–51.

18. Pope, *The Naladiyar or Four Hundred Quatrains in Tamil*, vii.

19. The following three verses are taken from Pope, *The Naladiyar or Four Hundred Quatrains in Tamil*, 181, 125, 18.

20. Sumanta Bannerjee, "Marginalization of Women's Popular Culture in Nineteenth Century Bengal," in *Recasting Women: Essays in Indian Colonial History*, ed. Kumkum Sangari and Sudesh Vaid (New Brunswick, N.J.: Rutgers University Press, 1990), 127–179; Velcheru Narayana Rao, David Shulman, and Sanjay Subrahmanyam, *Symbols of Substance: Coutr and State in Nayaka Period Tamilnadu* (New York: Oxford University Press, 1992).

21. Daud Ali, *Courtly Culture and Political Life in Early Medieval India* (Cambridge: University of Cambridge Press, 2004); Blake Wentworth, "Yearning for a Dreamed Real: The Procession of the Lord in the Tamil Ulaa" (Ph.D. diss., University of Chicago, 2009).

22. Gloria Raheja and Anne Gold, *Listen to the Heron's Words: Reimagining Gender and Kinship in North India* (Berkeley: University of California Press, 1994).

23. Sudipta Kaviraj, "Filth and the Public Sphere: Concepts and Practices about Space in Calcutta," *Public Culture* 10 (1997): 93.

24. Dipesh Chakrabarty, "Open Space/Public Place: Garbage, Modernity, and India," *South Asia* 14 (1991): 25.

25. That it was famous even in the mid-nineteenth century is suggested by the fact that it is the only *naladi* left unnumbered in the original Tamil edition as well as in the English translation of 1869.

26. Scudder, *The Bazaar Book or Vernacular Preacher's Companion*, trans. Rev. J. W. Scudder, M.D. (Madras: Graves, Cookson, 1869), 19.

27. Ibid.

28. Ibid., 25.

29. *The Fifth Triennial Report of the American Mission Seminary, Jaffna, Ceylon*, includes an appendix (Jaffna: Press of the American Mission, 1839), 24.

30. Ibid., 25–36.

31. Pope, *The Naladiyar or Four Hundred Quatrains in Tamil*, xxviii, xxix.

32. Ibid., 18.

33. For a fuller discussion of the Dravidianist paradigm of political oratory, see Bernard Bate, *Tamil Oratory and the Dravidian Aesthetic: Democratic Practice in South India* (New York: Columbia University Press, 2009).

6.

Empire, Ethics, and the Calling of History

Dipesh Chakrabarty

What I offer here is a critique, though by no means a rejection, of those strands in postcolonial criticism that have left a legacy of unquestioned suspicion of any idea of "universal history." To explain why I do so, I must begin where I actually end this paper, with the current crisis of climate change. That crisis, I believe, has produced a predicament for human beings beyond the differences of history or cultural practices. Scientists often describe this crisis as one *for* the human species; other informed aesthetic responses to the crisis express anxieties *about* the species. It seems important to me, in this context, to review the history of the idea of "universal history," see why and when the idea lost ground, and determine whether anything remains of that history as a useful legacy for the present. I should also clarify that versions of "universal history" that originated long before the nineteenth century, Christian and Islamic ones, for example, do not concern me here.

I

Over the nineteenth century history became an important academic discipline in the West. One of the most salient aspects of that story was how, in spite of all the contestation that Ranke's idea of "scientific history" was subjected to—sometimes by his own students such as Jacob Burkhardt—the rubric (for the expression was not always expressive of the same idea) of "universal history" held sway for most of the nineteenth century and for the first half of the twentieth. After the end of the Second World War, however, the conception of "universal history" steadily declined and has never recovered.

Consider, for instance, two landmark books, Marc Bloch's *The Historian's Craft* (1941) and E. H. Carr's *What Is History?* (1961). In writing *The Historian's Craft,* Bloch thought he was writing for the future, the next generation, for his book was framed as a response to the question a young man had put to him: "Tell me, Daddy. What is the use of history?"[1] Indeed, in his "Notes on the Manuscript" of the book, Lucien Febvre also pointed to his and Bloch's shared desire "to give our younger generation a kind of a new Langlois and Seigbonos [the authors of the popular text *Introduction aux Études Historiques*], to be the manifesto of another generation and the embodiment of an entirely different spirit."[2] Bloch's answer to this question from the young boy began with this statement:

> As far back as I can remember, it [history] has been for me a constant source of pleasure. As for all historians, I think. If not, why have they chosen this occupation? To anyone who is not a blockhead, all the sciences are interesting; yet each scholar finds but one that absorbs him. Finding it, in order to further devote himself to it, he terms it his "vocation," his "calling."[3]

Writing more than a hundred years ago before Bloch, Leopold von Ranke, in a letter dated November 1829 to his brother Heinrich, expressed sentiments that were not all that different from Bloch's:

> I have been here in Rome for a long time . . . There is something invigorating and refreshing in this searching and finding, in the uninterrupted pursuit of a greater universal purpose, . . . You are always on a venture. . . . In the end, you must say: I was called to this, for this is why I was born, for this I exist: in this I find my joys and sorrow; my life and my destiny are included in it.[4]

"Calling" was a word with theological resonance. As Ranke's student Meinecke said of the teacher, "Ranke was always anxious to show 'what things really had been like.' . . . A serious and priestly approach lay concealed in this desire, and Ranke was indeed filled with something of the priest's exaltation."[5]

Between Ranke and Bloch, then, in spite of the years that separated them and in spite of all the criticism that the Rankean approach had faced by the end of the nineteenth century and all the differences between French and German historiography, there was still this shared idea that history was a vocation, a calling.[6] Along with the idea of the calling went the ideal of "universal truth" or "universal history." As we know, this ideal is easily traced in the case of Ranke. Bloch also, in his turn, understood each science, including history, as representing "but a fragment of the universal march toward knowledge."[7] Later in the book, he would repeat the point: "We simply ask to bear in mind that historical research will tolerate no autarchy. Isolated, each will understand only halves, even within his own field of study; for the only *true history*, which can be advanced only through mutual aid, is *universal* history."[8]

What, one might ask, was the relation between the idea of calling and that of universal history or true history? Connecting them, it seems to me, was the idea of a practice of asceticism that followed from the idea of calling. Meinecke remarked that there was something "priest-like" in Ranke's method. Bloch expressed the idea in his own way when he said that what characterized the scholar (and the judge) was "their honest submission to truth."[9] What would it mean to honestly submit to truth? It meant, first of all, cultivating an ethic of renunciation with regard to one's own attachments, that which connected the historian to his or her present. The present, Bloch would happily grant, always tended to influence our sense of the past, but he was also sure that "misunderstanding of the present is an inevitable consequence of ignorance of the past."[10] It took a great amount of mental strength for the historian to be able to "submit to truth" in an honest manner. That there was something approaching the religious in such submission is suggested also by the close parallel that this thought bears to what William James, for instance, said about "evidence" in his essay, "The Will to Believe." James spoke there of "patience and postponement," of the "choking down of preferences," "the submission to the icy laws of outer fact," and the thousand of "disinterested moral lives" that went into the making of the "absolutely impersonal" edifice of "the physical sciences" which made "every little sentimentalist" who pretended "to decide things out of his private dream" seem "besotted and contemptible."[11]

"In truth," wrote Bloch, "whoever lacks the strength, while seated at his desk, to rid the mind of the virus of the present may readily permit its poison to infiltrate even a commentary on the *Iliad* or the *Ramayana*."[12] This "strength" shows itself in the historian's developed capacity for what Bloch called "historical criticism"—his "method of doubt." This entailed the historian being able to interrogate evidence, right from dates to the detection of forgery. "I have before me a batch of medieval charters. Some are dated; others are not. Wherever a date appears, it must be verified, for experience proves that it may be false," wrote Bloch.[13] "Incorrect evidence" was not "the only stimulus to the first efforts for a technique of the truth" but, for Bloch, "it continues to be the first starting-point from which that technique must necessarily proceed in order to develop its analysis."[14]

The twenty years that separated Marc Bloch's *The Historian's Craft* and E. H. Carr's George Macaulay Trevelyan lectures of 1961 that were published in the same year under the title *What Is History?* saw a sea change in our idea of historical truth and objectivity. I say "sea change," but I do not deny the opposition Carr's lectures received from several other stalwarts of the time:

Sir Isaiah Berlin, Hugh Trevor-Roper, Geoffrey Elton, to name a few. But the influence of *What Is History?* is reflected in the fact that even today it is among the best-sellers on history and had sold a quarter of a million copies by the time Jonathan Haslam published his biography of Carr.[15] What Bloch called historical criticism with the help of which the historian was able to question and correct documents now belonged, in Carr's judgment, to the "prehistory" of history. The relevant passage occurs in the first chapter of the book: "The Historian and His Facts." Carr, as you know, was never an absolute relativist. But nor would he subscribe to what he saw as the nineteenth-century fetish of facts. There were, of course, according to him, "certain basic facts which are the same for all historians and which form, so to speak, the backbone of history . . . The historian must not get these things [the basic facts] wrong." But "accuracy," he went on to quote the classical scholar and poet A. E. Housman, "is a duty, not a virtue." The labor that goes into the production of "basic facts"—historical dates or names, for instance, whose accuracy is generally accepted by historians—fell, in Carr's point of view, outside the labor specific to the historian. It came prior to the historian's work in the same way as the brick maker's labor came prior to that of a builder; in that sense, it belonged to the prehistory of the historian's activity. As Carr put it: "To praise a historian for his accuracy [with dates, etc.] is like praising an architect for using well-seasoned timber or properly mixed concrete in his building. It is a necessary condition of his work but not his essential function." And, as if contradicting Bloch, he added:

> The historian is not required to have the special skills which enable the expert to determine the origin and period of a fragment of pottery or marble, to decipher an obscure inscription, or make the elaborate astronomical calculations necessary to establish a precise date. These so-called basic facts, which are the same for all historians, commonly belong to the category of the raw materials of the historian rather than of history itself.[16]

Not only did the status of "facts" and "historical criticism" change in the years intervening between Bloch's and Carr's books. More significant, it seems to me, is that the idea of "universal" history or truth lost ground in proportion to the importance that the idea of perspective or point of view gained in historians' thinking. Carr's book provides us with some arresting "internal evidence" of the chronology of this shift. Lord Acton's October 1896 report to the Syndics of the Cambridge University Press on the forthcoming *Cambridge Modern History,* in which the venerable historian extolled the aim of producing "ultimate history," works as a milestone for Carr. Acton had written: "Ultimate history we cannot have in this generation; but we can dispose of conventional history, and show the point we have reached on the road from one to the other."[17] Some kind of "universal history" clearly formed the horizon of Lord Acton's vision. In stark contrast stood the general introduction Sir George Clark wrote to *The New Cambridge Modern History* of 1957. Writing some sixty years after Lord Acton, Sir George regarded the idea of a universal or ultimate history as a failed ideal. Its place had been taken by a triumphant perspectivalism: "since all historical judgments involve persons and points of view, one is as good as the other and there is no 'objective historical truth.'"[18]

Documenting such ascendancy of the importance given to different points of view in the twentieth century, Carr cites Collingwood from his *The Idea of History* (1946) as one of the earliest contemporary sources of perspectivalism—this particular quote comes from a letter that Collingwood (who in turn was a disciple of Croce) wrote to T. H. Knox, the British Hegel scholar who also edited *The Idea of History* after Collingwood's death. Collingwood's letter read:

> St Augustine looked at history from the point of view of the early Christian; Tillamont, from that of a seventeenth-century Frenchman; Gibbon, from that of an eighteenth-century Englishman; Mommsen, from that of a nineteenth-century German. There is no point asking which was the right point of view. Each was the only one possible for the man who adopted it.[19]

Carr, of course, would not approve of such absolute glorification of points of view and would eventually proceed to spell out his own understanding of objectivity in the work of a historian. "What do we mean when we praise a historian for being objective?" he asked and answered: "When we call a historian objective, we mean I think two things. First . . . that he has a capacity to rise above the limited vision of his own situation in society and history—a capacity . . . partly dependent on his capacity . . . to recognize the impossibility of total objectivity."[20]

Carr thus effected an important shift in the historian's relation to objectivity and the horizon of "universal histories." He gives us a paradoxical formulation regarding objectivity—we become objective only to the extent that we realize the impossibility of being totally objective. He thus replaced universal historical truths with a non-historical universal: "the impossibility of total objectivity." Carr did not reject the idea of "universal truth" as such—how else would he speak of "the impossibility of total objectivity" or "the nature of man"? What he rejected was the idea, popular into the days of Marc Bloch, that the historian was capable of adjudicating universal truths. Deciding questions like "the impossibility of total objectivity" or "the nature of man" was clearly a task that fell outside the domain of the historian's labor. Hence the interesting point here, it seems to me, is not whether or not "universal truths" actually exist, but that Carr himself documents a point in the history of the discipline of history when the discipline abandoned the idea that the methods of history entailed a practice of self-cultivation on the part of the historian: the "choking down" of one's preferences in order to prepare to face "the truth."

What Carr both documents and elaborates for us is precisely the demise of the idea of history as a vocation, of the spirit that the well-known imperial historian Sir Keith Hancock borrowing deliberately from his father's priestly vocabulary, once etched into the very title of the first volume of his autobiography, *Country and Calling.*[21] To repeat, then: for a Ranke or a Bloch, approaching historical truth required some amount of ethical preparation on the part of the historian, something like the utopian work that Ranke thought would help him realize his impossible wish to "extinguish" himself so that he could be open to the truth about the past.[22] I should clarify here that what I am speaking of is the history of the aspirations of historians of the past. I am not discussing whether they actually succeeded in realizing those aspirations. If Ranke or Bloch, or my case in point, Jadunath Sarkar, actually failed to write histories that genuinely succeeded in rising above clashing points of view, this fact would not alter my argument. My focus remains on their methodological ambitions, however unsuccessful they may have been.

The pursuit of historical truth today does not, as a rule, require such ethical relation to one's own self, for, as Peter Novick rightly comments, the historian's sense of "objectivity" now is grounded "more in social mechanisms of criticism and evaluation, and *less in the quality of individuals.*"[23] The ethics of history writing, as we shall see, now seem to lie more in what is perceived as the "politics" of such writing. For the demise of a sense of vocation also released the historian from any obligation to be bound to an ethical, nonpartisan relation to historical truth. The rise of perspectivalism signaled the coming of an era in which historical truth came to be widely recognized as necessarily partisan. I return to this point in my concluding remarks.

How do we understand this change? I say, very broadly, democracy. A certain kind of democratization of the subject—a turn toward the history of "the common people"—played a role in pushing history toward the social sciences by promoting the importance of such subfields as social and economic history. One can see some evidence of this in G. D. H. Cole and Raymond Postgate's 1938 book, *The Common People,* which pioneered a trend toward making the non-elite the subject of history by turning to economic and social statistics. And by the time Carr gave his lectures, history had been largely claimed by the social sciences triumphant, globally, over the humanities in the 1960s.[24]

And a certain understanding of democracy also impacted on the idea of "calling." You will recall that Max Weber, in the famous speech on science that he gave to the Bavarian Free Students' Association in 1917, defined calling—the institution of vocation as opposed to profession (though the German word *beruf* can mean both "profession" and "vocation")—as a kind of "intellectual aristocracy" that he felt was under threat because "German university life" and "German life in general" was being generally "Americanized."[25] To the idea of vocation, an "inward" sense of science as a calling, he opposed the idea of the "large, capitalist, university enterprises" promoting mass education.[26] That was his sense of Americanization. "I have a deep distrust," wrote Weber, "of courses that draw crowds, however unavoidable they may be." "Democracy," he continued, "should be used only where it is in place. Scientific training, as we are held to practice it in accordance with the tradition of German universities, is the affair of an intellectual aristocracy, and we should not hide it from ourselves."[27] This was not sour grapes, not the case of a Schopenhauer grudging Hegel his crowded classes while his own ran empty. Weber's lectures in Vienna were a "sensational success," writes Wolfgang Schluchter—"he landed in the largest auditorium where an irreverent curiosity kept the doors in perpetual motion"! Theodor Heuss, who attended these lectures and saw how the curious crowds pained Weber, records Weber's response to them: "it certainly is not possible to roar the word 'asceticism' into such a room."[28] We do not need to fetishize Weber's lectures into any absolute chronology for the beginning of the end for the idea of "calling," for the lecture evoked resistance among several of Weber's contemporaries and juniors, including Erich von Kahler and Ernst Troeltsch, the latter mobilizing the writings of Croce in his favor.[29] But I do think that Weber's lectures mark a shift in the history of how we practice the human sciences.

Weber's essay suggests a second figuration of democratization of society that may have threatened the idea of calling: that of mass education. But I want to argue, with the help of Indian history, that there was yet another global figure of democracy at work here transforming the nature of the discipline, and that was decolonization, a process whose beginnings may be glimpsed in the 1920s but which really unfolded in the succeeding decades achieving its climax in the era of Bandung and what followed that historic gathering.

II

It seems clear that the assumed ethical relation between the historian and the truths of history was related to a perception that such truths were "universal" and constituted a kind of public good that was underwritten by some universalist institution—the Roman Empire or the Prussian state in Ranke's case or French republicanism in Bloch's. The decline of the historian's ethical agency, and the consequent decline in the status of historical truth, has something to do with the decline of this idea of history as a public good bolstered by some institution of universal significance. It is this part of my unfolding hypothesis that I illustrate with an Indian story.

The protagonist of my story is Sir Jadunath Sarkar who lived between 1870 and 1958. Usually regarded as "the doyen of modern history" in India, he is also seen as someone superseded by later research. During most of his working life his official duties had to do with the teaching of literature (and history in the last few years of his career) at undergraduate institutions such as the Ripon College in Calcutta, Patna College in Bihar, and the Ravenshaw College in Cuttak, Orissa. He retired in 1926 when he was appointed Vice-Chancellor of the University of Calcutta for two years. Sarkar became a self-taught historian with a strong interest in the last phase of the history of the Mughal Empire. He wrote a five-volume history of the last great Mughal, Aurangzeb, published between 1912 and 1924. Between 1932 and 1950 he published four volumes of *Fall of the Mughal Empire.*[30] He wrote numerous other books and essays besides these. Sarkar would be a retired person, an independent scholar, from 1929 on. He was knighted in 1929 and is, until now, the only Indian historian to have ever been elected—as he was in 1952—an Honorary Fellow of the American Historical Association.

Most interesting to me in studying Sarkar was his role in pioneering a Rankean spirit of historiography, however vulgate and vulgar its Indian incarnation. Though Ranke's name was popular among history enthusiasts and collectors of documents in nineteenth-century India, Sarkar was one of the few who cultivated systematically the spirit of "scientific history" and for that reason was also one of the first to articulate the need for institutions that would make the writing of such history possible. Thus in 1915, speaking at a nationalist conference in Bengal as the president of the History Branch, Sarkar made it quite clear that the way forward in historical research of the Mughal times was through European historiography. And his use of the expression "scientific history" had a distinctly German ring to it:

> The best method for writing history is the scientific one. This method does not vary with time and place because it is equally effective in all departments of knowledge and is inherent in all that is truthful. If, intoxicated by the passion of nationalism, we happen to ignore this method on the ground that Europeans have adopted it, then we will only harm our own cause. . . . The histories we write will be imperfect because they will be unscientific.[31]

What Meinecke wrote about Ranke finds an echo in what Sarkar said throughout his life on the question of historical truth. As many of Sarkar's biographers have noted, he looked upon history as some kind of a calling, a call to truth, its objective method as something to be practiced as a matter of personal virtue. The historical truth he looked for was indeed the "universal truth" that many European savants spoke of even in the early part of the twentieth century.

"Our history of India," he wrote in 1937, "in order to find acceptance in the wide world of scholarship, must appeal to universal reason by transcending the narrow limits of national prejudices and beliefs, it must be scientific in its method, and science knows no barriers of country or race and owes no homage except to truth."[32] In speaking of himself in a radio broadcast in 1948, he spoke of the "eternal vitality" that was always there in honest efforts and true words. He thought it impossible that someone could be a historian without "the right mental attitude." Historical research, he said, called for *sadhana,* a pursuit that had a distinctly ascetic and religious quality about it, perhaps not far from what Meinecke may have meant by the word "priestly" with reference to Ranke.[33]

Bloch's observation about the importance of the historian being able to question and correct his or her sources is also reminiscent of Sarkar's practices. "Incorrect evidence," wrote Bloch, was not "the only stimulus to the first efforts for a technique of the truth," but "it continues to be the first starting-point from which that technique must necessarily proceed in order to develop its analysis."[34] Sarkar, too, spent many of his hours correcting errors in primary sources. A typical letter of his (from 1937) reads: "I spent a couple of days correcting the dates in Dongre's volume and Maheshwar D['s] *Batani Patrén* which also I corrected laboriously."[35]

A Rankean spirit drove his institutional ambitions as well. When the government of India set up the Indian Historical Research Commission in 1919 and made Sarkar a founding member of the body, his efforts remained focused on publishing selections of documents—in the model of Mommsen, he said in one of his letters—and on holding academic sessions where he could impart to aspiring Indian historians the art of *quellenkritik,* or source criticism.[36] In the 1930s, when many universities in India started up departments for postgraduate studies and research in history and younger historians took the initiative for establishing the first professional association called the Indian History Congress in 1935, Sarkar stayed away and thought the whole thing—the very idea of a conference—a "vulgar tamasha" (public entertainment).[37] In response, he and Sardesai held an annual seminar for a few years at Sardesai's home in Kamshet near Poona, modeled pretty much on the Rankean ideal of the research seminar where a master craftsman, in this case Sarkar, would spend time with disciples discussing sources and their uses.[38]

Sarkar's Rankeanism, the seeds of which lay in a nineteenth-century understanding of—and a sense of loyalty to—the British Empire, interests me here for its untimeliness in twentieth-century India when mass nationalism became the mainstay of politics in the subcontinent. In other words, it was untimely precisely because of the rise of anticolonial mass movements. It is well known that from time to time many illustrious Indians who grew up in the nineteenth century, from Gandhi to Nirad Chaudhuri, declared themselves to be proud subjects of the British Empire. Like Rome to Ranke or Neibuhr or Gibbon, the British Empire signaled to them the possibility of a universal, a state that stood above all particular conflicts in society and upheld principles that were good for all. The great Indologist Sir R. G. Bhandarkar (1837–1925), for example—older than Sarkar by a few decades—pronounced it "an act of Divine Providence that the English alone of all the candidates who appeared about the same time for the empire of India should have succeeded."[39] Like Sarkar, Bhandarkar connected the very issue of "critical methods" in Indology to the question of learning from European scholars. "It is no use ignoring the fact that Europe is far ahead of us in all that constitutes civilization. And knowledge is one of the elements of civilization," he declared in 1888 in a lecture titled, significantly, "The Critical, Comparative, and Historical Method of Inquiry."[40] Bhandarkar has often been described as an early Rankean in India and has been compared to Sarkar: "Sir Ramakrishna Bhandarkar was the father of scientific historical scholarship in the ancient period of Indian history as Sir Jadunath Sarkar was in medieval and early British period. . . . He could have easily passed master as a historian in the view of Ranke."[41]

Bhandarkar did not like the identity politics of nationalism in so far as it impinged on questions of knowledge. Much like Sarkar, he was a patriot and not an anticolonial nationalist. He held that the "true patriot" considered it his duty to "fearlessly expose" the faults in "the character of his people," and he criticized the nationalists of "Bengal and our part of the country" for their "false race-pride."[42] But the difference was that Bhandarkar died in 1925, just as nationalism was beginning to assume a mass form. Sarkar, a younger person, lived on till 1957, preaching and practicing his untimely faith in the empire when younger historians—and the question of Indian history itself—were caught up in the vortex of anti-imperial nationalism. Sarkar (and, to some degree, his friend Sardesai) never had any sympathy for the street politics of *satyagraha* and strikes that, in combination with limited franchise, were to become the language of mass politics in the 1930s and 1940s. As official funds for their project for bringing out selections of Marathi documents seemed to run dry around 1930, Sardesai complained to Sarkar about the British Commissioner in Poona: "He is altogether pre-occupied with Civil-Disobedience-wallas and has no room in his brain for anything else."[43] Sarkar, in turn, complained in 1940: "I am sick of this cat and mouse game which the blind Congress is trying to play with Pax Britannica under the 'whip' of a demented Gujarati bania's son, who believes himself *buwa* [original Nagari] or *avatar* [original Nagari; incarnation]."[44] This is the age of democracy and demagogy," Sardesai said in 1934, expressing feelings of frustration and resignation, having failed to move the Vice Chancellor of the University of Bombay into taking an active interest in his selection of Peshwa documents.[45]

I have described elsewhere the conflicts that erupted between Sarkar (and Sardesai) and a group of historians mostly based in Poona (such as Rajwade or the younger Potdar, but there was the Bengali S. N. Sen among them as well) who worked out of a strong sense of regional identity.[46] As the nationalist movement picked up momentum, the country saw a surge of caste- or religion-based historical consciousness. The Maratha region was especially consumed by conflicts between Brahmins and the so-called non-Brahmins that in the 1920s assumed party-political forms when the Bombay legislature had, for the first time, elected non-Brahmin ministers. The Poona historians and the non-Brahmin political leaders were unhappy when, at the instance of Sarkar, Sardesai, a Brahmin, was picked by the Bombay government in 1929 to edit and publish collections of papers from the office of the Peshwas, the eighteenth-century rulers of the region. Sardesai's appointment was hotly debated in the Bombay Legislative Council at the beginning of 1931, when non-Brahmin legislators raised questions that today would be clearly seen as identity politics. They asked, in effect, if it were ever possible for a Brahmin to write the history of non-Brahmins, and if the non-Brahmins—the Marathas, for instance—would not find histories written by Brahmins injurious to their pride.[47]

Sarkar fumed—both in public and private—at the aspersion that the identity politicians cast on the quality of his scholarship or on Sardesai's financial and scholarly integrity. Yet he did not see the writing on the wall: that the days of "scientific" and "universal" historical truths were numbered. Nationalist politics gave rise to "identities" of different kinds—from national to caste to community identities—and the demand would be for what we might term, to distinguish it from "universal" histories, "point-of-view" histories. The colonial bureaucracy was, willingly or unwillingly, complicit in this process, for that was the only way they could share power, at least for the time being, with increasingly politicized Indians. The empire, in decline, was a hollow and receding utopia of the universal. On the rise, from the 1940s on, was the demand for "nationalist" histories, those written by Indians from Indian points of view. K M Munshi, who was to later edit a series of nationalist volumes on Indian history, wrote to Sardesai in November 1943, saying, "I am most anxious that the world is presented with a history of India written by Indians at the end of the war."[48] When the nationalist historian Tarachand of Allahabad University approached Sarkar just after Independence inviting him to chair a History of India Board, Sarkar could only fulminate against the poor standards of Indian scholarship and of Indian English:

> I know that a debating club—especially one composed of educated Indians—cannot bring any work to completion. In case Allahabad agrees to have me, they must endow me with full powers, exactly as . . . Cambridge University [of India] did to Sir W. Haig . . . If I have to

> correct and rewrite the rubbish which our Indian professors of history write—as I found to my bitter experience when editing the second volume of Dacca University's *History of Bengal*—I must be paid an extra fee for this *dhobi* [washerman's] work.[49]

The reference to Cambridge University points to the Europe that Sarkar idealized as the home of scholarship. Unlike Bhandarkar, however, Sarkar had never personally been to Europe. Nor was he in conversation with European scholars, as Bhandarkar had been. His mentors, if any, were the scholars that the Raj produced from within the ranks of its colonial administrators. Yet an imaginary Europe worked for him as a constant reference of the ultimate and universal measure of scholarly standards. And because he believed that reason was something that belonged to everybody, even if the Europeans had been the first to deploy it in the writing of history, he did not see his own position as a demeaning one. He was a proud and private man. He would not have voiced this respect for Europe in his letters to Sardesai if such opinions hurt his sense of self-respect. For reasons of space, only a few examples will have to suffice. When, for instance, in 1931, Sarkar drafted a foreword to *Selections from Peshwa Daftar,* a volume edited by Sardesai, the latter did not like the draft: "Your mention of Khare, Parasnis, Gulgule Daftar and . . . your omission of Rajwade [historians belonging to the Bharat Itihas Samshodhan Mandal in Poona] will again give rise to dying embers now happily subsiding." He went on to ask, without irony, "Probably you mean this foreword for European readers outside India."[50] The earnest tone of Sarkar's reply shows, perhaps, how indifferent he was to nationalist pride and how seriously he took his assumption about the intellectual superiority of Europe. "Literary grace," he wrote, "is the sine qua non for my foreword, as for an essay in the *Edinburgh Review* . . . Rajwade's letters may be mentioned with praise in my foreword by adding a line . . . But I do not consider any further change desirable to placate the howling mob of Puna. My foreword is intended for readers in Europe, where they require such a comprehensible readable survey and not an official report."[51]

Or take this instance from 1932. When Sardesai suggested to him that he apply for the position of the editor of the Poona Residency Records even when the Commissioner of the Central Division wanted an English person (like Professor H. G. Rawlinson, the retired principal of Ferguson College in Poona) to do the job and was actively contemplating appointing a local English woman simply because the documents were in English, Sarkar did not immediately want to jump into the fray. He was by then a well-known scholar who had been the Vice-Chancellor of Calcutta University. At fifty-two years of age, he was no longer a young person. And yet he still wanted to wait and prove himself to the English. He wrote back to Sardesai defending the Commissioner:

> You see he is justified in holding that this . . . cannot be done by your staff, as it requires a special and deep knowledge of the English diplomatic history of the 18th century . . . If I can after a week's work convince Rawlinson by *actual* demonstration . . . that a scholar of the highest university distinction and experience of history in *European* languages can do the work not a whit worse—probably better (by reason of my historical information, in which the lady lacks)—than any English man or woman—that will be the stage at which I can require the work to be entrusted to me. I don't care to court a rebuff . . . [now].[52]

Even more explicit was what Sarkar wrote to comfort Sardesai when the latter's edition of documents selected from the Peshwa Daftar were criticized by Poona scholars. "My dear Nana," wrote Sarkar: "In Europe, your work as editor of the Peshwa's Dafter records would have been promptly recognised by your own university and every university where Maratha history is taught by conferring on you the honorary degree of D. Litt. In England, Mr Loeb, a mere rich man probably innocent of the classics, was created a Doctor by the Cambridge University because he financed the issue of a new edition of the Greek and Latin classics. True scholars are there honoured even more surely and quickly. But here, half the Senate (and Board of History) are blissfully ignorant of the present state of research . . ., and the other half are consumed by jealousy of your achievements."[53] "This has been my experience," he continued:

> but I don't care, as I have secured recognition in Europe in no small measure. Here, on the other hand, one man takes the opportunity of his visit to any provincial University as an external examiner, to whisper what he represents as mistakes in my work—and his professor audience, ignorant of Portuguese and Marathi (at least, of that particular history) swallow his lies without questions. But as you see, I survive these tactics.[54]

Sarkar's letter actually suggests that it was the colonial bureaucracy—and not an abstract or actual "universal Europe"—that was the key to his success with officialdom: "Governments and Vice-Chancellors have sought and accepted my recommendations in selecting men for high history professorships."[55] It was the European administrator-scholar *in India,* a Beveridge or an Irvine, who was his real patron. In an earlier letter he had, in fact, advised Sardesai to send a set of the volumes of the Peshwa Daftar to one of these former administrator scholars, Sir Edward Gait, who had retired to England. His advice itself spoke a peculiar ethnography possible only in a colonial relationship of which he himself may not have been aware: "Mr Hudson will soon issue orders for sending out one set of your selections to Sir Edward Gait in London. Please see that only the soon-to-be-issued *bound* volumes are sent and *not loose parts,* as Englishmen (unlike Frenchmen and [the] Portuguese) care to handle only bound books and dislike brochures in paper cover."[56] It was these colonial administrator scholars who both practiced exclusivism—after all, they managed the 1920s *Cambridge History of India* project without asking any single Indian scholar to contribute—and played mentors to scholars such as Sarkar.

If there was a tragedy to Sarkar's life, it lay in his constantly mistaking the very particular and pragmatic British colonial bureaucracy in India for the universal figure of the empire. He could not see that the colony/empire was an internally fissured formation. The empire spoke of principles; the colonial officials were ruthlessly pragmatic. By the time Sarkar lost out to younger historians—such as S. N. Sen and D. V. Potdar—in his battle to control the future of historical research in India, colonial officials had silently made room for nationalists to take control of the educational bureaucracy. The Department of Imperial Records, renamed the National Archives after Independence, came to be controlled by Sen in the years immediately preceding the transfer of power. Sen and his cohorts pursued a politics of ensuring greater access to official documents for Indian scholars and moved away from Sarkar's emphasis on source criticism.[57] They dropped Sarkar quite unceremoniously from important committees in 1940. The research seminar at Kamshet that Sarkar had started in collaboration with Sardesai to help young researchers resist the temptations of the Indian History Congress (1935) languished and died. In the last fifteen years of his life, Sarkar lived the life of a solitary researcher, respected for his erudition and knowledge but bypassed by the new schools of Mughal history that were to take shape at the Universities of Aligarh and Allahabad.[58] The rise of a Marxist and avowedly secular school of Mughal history at Aligarh in the 1950s would eventually be proof that the time of partisan—and not universal—history had come.

Sarkar's project of creating a discipline in which historians sought to renounce their political and other affiliations with flourish did not succeed in India. One could say that the project, in its innate aspiration toward making history into a public good for citizens, was too identified with the ideology of the empire. Yet the project did not die immediately. In the first decade after Independence, Prime Minister Nehru presided over the transition from colonial to postcolonial nationhood and assumed that the nation could effectively take over and even improve on the imperial project of creating history as a public good. He and his colleagues dreamed of achieving liberalism without the empire. It was remarkable that when the time came for the Government of India to sponsor an official history celebrating the centenary of the so-called

Mutiny of 1857, Maulana Abul Kalam Azad, the then education minister, directed the official historian, Dr. S. N. Sen (once Sir Jadunath's adversary), to write an "objective" piece of history that would oppose any a priori nationalist narrative of the event. "Some Indians," he said, "have written on the [nationalist] struggle in the early years of this century. If the truth is to be told . . . the books they have written are not history but mere propaganda."[59] Quite a remarkable statement: clearly Azad was asking for a history that would not be propaganda even for the nation.

Indian democracy today is an interesting case where all nostalgia for historical truth, born of the historian seeking to renounce his or her political passion, has evaporated. A spirit of partisanship reigns supreme. The blurring of the line between perspective and knowledge can be seen, for instance, even in the statements of some of the most respected historians. In a recent essay Romila Thapar, who has been engaged in a series of debates against "Hindu" views of the past, put her argument about history and political partisanship in the following form. Acknowledging that "there is a link between the social sciences and political ideologies," she cautioned against "invoking history to support political agendas," as that distorted historical knowledge; and yet she went on to claim that her own defense of history "as an exploration of knowledge . . . is also a part of the defense of the idea of a democratic, secular society," as though supporting a political agenda was not "invoking history" (it does not matter for my argument that I actually support her agenda)![60] But let me not appear to be picking on Thapar alone in Indian debates on history. We in Subaltern Studies began by fundamentally defining Indian history as a battleground for some particular points of view: nationalist-Marxist views, the views of the so-called and (in our eyes) imperialist Cambridge school, and our own. We espoused a Maoist view in propounding the thesis that peasant rebellions invariably began with the act of inverting the codes of social honor, and that the best way to read the archives of the elite was by inverting their perspective: when the landlord says "bandit," hear "rebel."[61] It is not surprising, then, that the current and serious Maoist violence in India today is justified by a similar view. As Ganapathi, the General Secretary of the Communist Party of India (Maoist), wrote in the well-known Indian publication *Economic and Political Weekly* in January 2007: "The truth of the oppressed is different from the truth of the oppressor. . . . if Bhagat Singh [a revolutionary nationalist] was a hero for the Indian people, he was the greatest terrorist and villain for the British colonialists."[62] If debates on history are any indication of the democratic culture of a country, one may say that the democratization of Indian society has led to an increasing chasm between liberalism and democracy.[63] Perhaps Uday Singh Mehta is right to say that the liberal imagination of the world was underwritten by the fact of the empire.[64]

III

The decline of universal history that I have sought to describe was not—as must be clear by now—a uniquely Indian story. To me the story seems to belong to a global conjuncture. Historians stand in a different relationship to truth today. They do not talk so much about "historical truth" as about "objectivity." Why have we moved from the idea of truth to that of objectivity? I have tried to suggest the role of different figurations of democracy: the rise in importance of the idea of "the history of the common people," the rise of mass education in the West and elsewhere, and the global process of decolonization after the War. One could also add the roles that nationalism and the modern media have played in the process.

Objectivity is not the same as what nineteenth-century historians may have meant by the word "truth." You will remember Novick's remark quoted earlier that "objectivity" is no longer seen as something that depends on "the qualities of the individual." It does not, in that sense, refer to any ethical struggles on the part of the historian. David Hollinger, for instance, contends that the basis for historical objectivity now lies "in the wide degree of inter-subjective agreement among professional historians as to the criteria for a successful historical scholarship."[65] So it is, ultimately, a matter of opinion, albeit the collective opinion of one's peers. Allan Megill has recently written in robust defense of historical objectivity. He also requires, minimally, "a measure of detachment" on the historian's part from his or her "own commitments" in the interest of objectivity.[66] But it is not clear today if this detachment is something the historian consciously cultivates—in the manner of a Sarkar—or if it is to be detected by peer review! Arnaldo Momigliano, in a 1954 essay titled "A Hundred Years after Ranke," left us some fascinating thoughts on what is left of Ranke's methods: it is mainly the idea of source criticism bereft of any ethical or theological connotation.[67]

No inherent conflict exists between objectivity and perspectives. Maps we use, for example, are both perspectival and objective in that they help us navigate the world. Similarly there has been much committed and commendable history writing by Marxist, feminist, indigenous, or subaltern scholars that might be described as objective. "Objectivity" can allow for perspectives or points of view—in short, for "presentism," the urge to make history useful for present struggles. I suggest, however, that the older questions about historical truth as a value remains encrypted in the talk about objectivity. Otherwise, if objectivity were as wide of the mark as any subjective procedures, why would we bother to be objective at all? The very practice of historical objectivity, one might say, gains traction from the tension that exists between the two horizons that delimit it: that of perspective and the horizon of truth. This is the tension between the presentism that goes with the emphasis on perspectives and the idea that in order to approach the truth about the past one has to, as Leo Strauss once put it in a stringent critique of Collingwood, "leave the shores of the present."[68] The pursuit of historical truth—it was assumed by Ranke, Bloch, and others—involved some profoundly ascetic techniques of the self. And we have seen that in spite of the general decline of the Rankean methods of writing history, this particular idea persisted well into the twentieth century. Truth was necessarily anti-presentism, while objectivity has no necessary hostility to historical findings being anchored in the concerns of the present. However, consider this thought experiment: absent this tension between the idea of truth and that of perspectives, objectivity would give ground to partisanship in history, converting the subject into a mere clash of perspectives. In other words, to the degree that the present understanding of "objectivity" carries within itself an encrypted and barely recognizable idea of historical truth, it also carries a residual desire for some lost universal, for the ethical nature of historical truth, as we have seen, was tied to the historian's faith in some universal institution undergirding ideas about public good. I have used the case of Sir Jadunath Sarkar to suggest that his own ascetic ideal of historical truth was dependent on a political co-relate—what might be called an "imperial liberalism," the assumption that the British Empire embodied a universal political institution in the interest of all, a universal that made historical truth into a "public good."

Why raise the ghost of historical truth? I do so from certain concerns of the present. In what is being called "climate change" or "global warming," we are now faced with a crisis of planetary proportions. "Will human beings survive as a species and, if they do, for how long?"—is a question that circulates insistently in the anxious imaginations of our times.[69] Climate scientists have already given us a narrative of human/natural history through their anthropogenic theories of global warming. The imminent crisis in the availability of fresh water and food emphasizes the case for partial global governance at least in some areas of our lives. The need of the hour, it seems, is for shared and general histories of human beings—in other words, for some kind of universalist thinking that bears on questions of "global good." History—the story that human beings tell themselves about themselves—needs to be part of that global good.

But what kind of universalist thinking can it be? It should be clear at the outset that the case for global governance cannot be a case for the reinvention of empires. Niall Ferguson's work, for example, will not show us the way forward; pro-imperial histories only recycle universals that have already been discredited by histories of colonial and racial domination.[70] Nor is there is any question of merely repeating or reviving the gestures of a Ranke, a Sarkar, or even a Bloch. Empires and states have indeed used universal languages for pushing partisan ends. We now write history out of a consciousness that can only be described as post-imperial and democratic (though not always or necessarily liberal). If the craft of history today—in India, but perhaps elsewhere as well—were to find an ethical dimension internal to its practice, historians would have to work out in what sense, and under what conditions, history could still be seen as a public good over and above the clash of perspectives and experiences. But this would mean moving our democratic struggles beyond the politics of representation and toward new forms of sovereignty and correspondingly new sets of universals. The "universals" we think about can no longer be Hegelian entities that render all particulars into particular instances of a general. There lies the history of domination. Here I find postcolonial suspicions of "universals" just and valid.

But such suspicions are not adequate to the current crisis that calls us to all that is general and shared between human beings and even other life forms. History will once again reclaim its ground as a form of knowledge. Motivated by shared and similar concerns, scholars are reaching out in different directions. The historian Daniel Lord Smail has made a beginning in the direction of "the natural history of man" in his book, *On Deep History and the Brain*.[71] Antonio Y. Vazquez-Arroyo, a literary critic who has written illuminatingly on Adorno's concept of the negative dialectic and on his debates with Benjamin, has developed the idea of a "negative universal"—a contingent and catastrophic event (such as climate change) that brings us all together.[72] I myself have begun to examine whether the idea of "species history" offers historical thought any possibilities when we work with the idea of a "negative universal."[73] Today we cannot revive the somewhat theological and mystic nature of "truth" with which a Ranke or Sarkar worked. Nor need we argue for the existence of "hard" truths in history. But for history to claim its place as a form of knowledge, a form of reasoning, it will not be enough for its practitioners to flaunt their political passions. The crucial question will be: Do they struggle to remain open to someone else's reasoned skepticism? In that question lies the legacy of Bloch, Ranke, and others. It is the seriously unfinished nature of this task that marks the historiographical struggles of our times, the struggle to conceptualize shared and general accounts of the human being's place and history among those of other life forms on the planet. Out of this struggle new ethics will emerge for the writing of history.

Acknowledgments

I am grateful for comments received from various audiences at the University of British Columbia, the University of Chicago, the University of Wisconsin, the University of Michigan, the University of Cambridge, and the University of Heidelberg.

Notes

1. Marc Bloch, *The Historian's Craft,* trans. Peter Putnam (Manchester, England: Manchester University Press, 1984 [1954]), 3.

2. Lucien Febvre, "A Note on the Manuscript of the Present Book," in Bloch, *Craft,* vii. The Langlois-Seigbonos text was "long used in courses in methodology both in France and the United States" (ibid.).

3. Bloch, *Craft,* 7.

4. Ranke's letter cited in Theodore H. Von Laue, *Leopold Ranke: The Formative Years* (Princeton, N.J.: Princeton University Press, 1950), 40.

5. Friedrich Meinecke, *Historism: The Rise of a New Historical Outlook,* trans. J. E. Anderson (London: Routledge and Kegan Paul, 1972), 498.

6. For a discussion of some of the overlaps and clashes between German and French historiographical traditions, see Carole Fink, *Marc Bloch: A Life in History* (Cambridge: Cambridge University Press, 1991), chaps. 2 and 3.

7. Bloch, *Craft,* 18.

8. Ibid., 47 (emphasis added).

9. Ibid., 138.

10. Ibid., 43.

11. William James, *The Will to Believe, and Other Essays in Popular Philosophy* (Cambridge, Mass.: Harvard University Press, 1979), 17; cited in Charles Taylor, *Varieties of Religion Today: William James Revisited* (Cambridge, Mass.: Harvard University Press, 2003), 44–45.

12. Bloch, *Craft,* 38.

13. Ibid., 89.

14. Ibid., 90.

15. See Jonathan Haslam, *The Vices of Integrity: E. H. Carr, 1892–1982* (London: Verso, 2000), 191–205, 217.

16. E. H. Carr, *What Is History?* (Harmondsworth: Penguin, 1970 [1961]), 10–11.

17. Ibid., 7.

18. Both cited in ibid., 7–8.

19. R. Collingwood, *The Idea of History* (1946); cited in Carr, *What Is History?* 26. I say a "contemporary source" for perspectivalist thinking because, as Susanne Rau has claimed in a review of Costantin Fasolt's *The Limits of History* (Chicago: University of Chicago Press, 2004), the recognition of the problem of perspectives in historical writing goes back at least to "the beginning of the German Enlightenment . . . , [to] Johann Martin Chladenius, a Lutheran theologian and historian" who spoke of "sehepunckt" or "point of view or perspective." Susanne Rau, review of Constatin Fasolt, *The Limits of History* in H-German, December 2006.

20. Carr, *What Is History?* 123.

21. See the discussion in Sandra Stanley Holton, "'History is about Chaps': Professional, National and Gender Identities in Hancock's autobiographies," in *Keith Hancock: The Legacies of an Historian,* ed. D. A. Low (Melbourne: Melbourne University Press, 2001) 269–286.

22. Cited in Peter Novick, *That Noble Dream: The "Objectivity Question" and the American Historical Profession* (Cambridge: Cambridge University Press, 1993 [1988]), 28.

23. Ibid., 2.

24. Haslam discusses this development in his chapter "What Is History?"

25. Max Weber, "Science as a Vocation," in *From Max Weber: Essays in Sociology,* ed. H. H. Gerth and C. Wright Mills (London: Routledge and Kegan Paul, 1974 [1948]), 133, 134.

26. Ibid., 131, 134.

27. Ibid., 133–134.

28. Wolfgand Schluchter, *Paradoxes of Modernity: Culture and Conduct in the Theory of Max Weber,* trans. Neil Solomon (Stanford, Calif.: Stanford University Press, 1996), 18–19. I am grateful to Thomas Kemple for directing me to this reference.

29. See Peter Lassman, Irving Velody, and Herminio Martins, *Max Weber's "Science as a Vocation"* (London: Unwin Hyman, 1989), 35–45, 58–69. I owe this reference to Professor Kemple.

30. H. R. Gupta, ed., *Life and Letters of Sir Jadunath Sarkar* (Hoshiarpur: Punjab University, 1957), 108–109; Anil Chandra Banerjee, *Jadunath Sarkar* (Delhi: Sahitya Akademi, 1989), 6–7; Moni Bagchi, *Acharya Jadunath: jibon o shadhona* (Calcutta: Jijnasha, 1975), 47–49.

31. This speech, first made in 1915, was later reprinted in Jadunath Sarkar, "Itihash rachanar pronali o itihasher gurutta" [in Bengali], in the Bengali magazine *shonibarer chthi,* Aswin [Bengali month] 1355 [Bengali year] [1949], 513. See also *ashtam bangiya shahitya shammelan, itihash shakha* [Proceedings of the Eighth Bengal Literary Conference, History Branch] (1915), address by the president of the History Branch, 1. Thanks to Gautam Bhadra for this reference but my copy does not have a printer's line.

32. Sarkar's speech at the Indian Academy of History, proceedings of the inaugural session at Banaras, December 30–31, 1937, 20–23; cited in Raghuvir Singh, "Jadunath Sarkar as a Historian of the Marathas," in *History in Practice: Historians and Sources of Medieval Deccan—Marathas,* ed. A. R. Kulkarni (New Delhi: Books and Books, 1993), 66.

33. See Moni Bagchi, *Acharya Jadunath: jibon o shadhona* [in Bengali] (Calcutta: Jijnasha, 1975), 3.

34. Bloch, *Craft,* 90.

35. Jadunath Sarkar Papers (hereafter, JP), National Library, Calcutta (hereafter, NL), Letter No. 458, from Sarkar to Sardesai, Darjiling, April 15, 1937.

36. I elaborate on this in my unpublished essay "Towards a History of the National Archives."

37. JP, NL, Letter No. 586, from Sarkar to Sardesai, Calcutta, September 8, 1939: "I always avoid the Indian History Congress and shall do so even when I am here during its sitting. It is a vulgar tamasha started by a drunkard [a reference, probably, to Shafaat Ahmad Khan]" (ibid.).

38. See *Report on the Meeting of Workers in Indian History at Kamshet (Poona District), 2nd–6th October 1938* (Bombay: S. R. Tikekar, 1938?). I owe this reference to Gautam Bhadra.

39. See A. D. Pusalkar, "R. G. Bhandarkar," in *Historians and Historiography in Modern India,* ed. S. P. Sen (Calcutta: Institute of Historical Research, 1973), 42.

40. R. G. Bhandarkar, "The Critical, Comparative, and Historical Method of Inquiry, as applied to Sanskrit Scholarship and Philology and Indian Archaeology," in *Collected Works of Sir R. G. Bhandarkar,* ed. Bapuji Utgikar and Vasudev Gopal Paranjpe (Poona: Bhandarkar Oriental Research Institute, 1933), 1:390.

41. Pusalkar, "Bhandarkar," 44–45. See also R. N. Dandekar, "Ramakrishna Gopl Bhandarkar and the Academic Renaissance in Maharashtra," in *Writers, Editors, and Reformers: Social and Political Transformations in Maharashtra, 1830–1930,* ed. N. K. Wagle (Delhi: Manohar, 1999), 138.

42. Pusalkar, "Bhandarkar," 45.

43. JP, NL, Letter No. 136, from G. S. Sardesai to Sarkar, Kamshet, September 21, 1930.

44. JP, NL, Letter No. 657, from Sarkar to Sardesai, Calcutta, November 16, 1940.

45. JP, NL, Letter No. 315, from Sardesai to Sarkar, Bombay, August 14, 1934.

46. See my essay, "The Public Life of History: An Argument out of India," *Public Culture* 20, no. 1 (February 2008), special issue: *The Public Life of History,* ed. Bain Attwood, Dipesh Chakrabarty, and Claudio Lomnitz.

47. I discuss these developments in some detail in "The Public Life of History."

48. JP, NL, Munshi's letter attached to Letter No. 757 from Sardesai to Sarkar, Kamshet, November 19, 1943.

49. JP, NL, Letter No. 989, from Sarkar to Sardesai, Calcutta, January 5, 1949.

50. JP, NL, Letter No. 166, from Sardesai to Sarkar, Kamshet, September 30, 1931.

51. JP, NL, Letter No. 168, from Sarkar to Sardesai, Darling, October [?] 14, 1931.

52. JP, NL, Letter No. 240, from Sarkar to Sardesai, Darling, November 28, 1932.

53. JP, NL. Letter No. 306, from Sarkar to Sardesai, Darjiling, May 1, 1934.

54. Ibid.

55. Ibid.

56. JP, NL, Letter No. 159, from Sarkar to Sardesai, Darjiling, July 1, 1931.

57. I tell this story in my unpublished essay "Towards a History of the National Archives in India."

58. Satish Chandra tells part of this story in the introduction to his *Essays on Medieval Indian History* (Delhi: Oxford University Press, 2003), pp. 1–20.

59. Azad cited in Rochona Majumdar and Dipesh Chakrabarty, "*Mangal Pandey:* Film and History," *Economic and Political Weekly* 42, no. 19 (May 12, 2007): 1776.

60. Romila Thapar, "Secularism, History, and Contemporary Politics in India," in *The Crisis of Secularism in India,* ed. Anuradha Dingwaney Needham and Rajeswari Sundar Rajan (Durham, N.C.: Duke University Press, 2007), 191.

61. Ranajit Guha's brilliant essay "The Prose of Counter-Insurgency" in Gayatri Chakravorty Spivak and Ranajit Guha ed. *Selected Subaltern Studies* (New York: Oxford University Press, 1988) was the *locus classicus* of this position.

62. Ganapathi, "Open Reply to Independent Citizens' Initiative," *Economic and Political Weekly* 42, no. 1 (January 6–12, 2007): 67–71.

63. See my essays "The Public Life of History: An Argument out of India"; and "History and the Politics of Recognition," in *Manifestos for History,* ed. Keith Jenkins, Alan Munslow, and Sue Morgan (London: Routledge, 2007).

64. Mehta, *Liberalism and Empire.*

65. Hollinger cited in Allan Megill, "Introduction: Four Senses of Objectivity," in *Rethinking Objectivity,* ed. Allan Megill (Durham, N.C.: Duke University Press, 1994), 7.

66. Allan Megill, *Historical Knowledge, Historical Error: A Contemporary Guide to Practice* (Chicago: University of Chicago Press, 2007), 109.

67. Arnaldo Momigliano, "A Hundred Years after Ranke," in his *Studies in Historiography* (New York: Harper, 1966), 105–111.

68. Leo Strauss, "On Collingwood's Philosophy of History," *Review of Metaphysics* 5, no. 4 (1952): 559–586.

69. See Alan Weisman, *The World Without Us* (New York: St. Martin's, 2007.

70. Niall Ferguson, *Empire: The Rise and Demise of the British World Order and the Lessons for Global Power* (New York: Basic Books, 2003).

71. Daniel Lord Smail, *On Deep History and the Brain* (Berkeley: University of California Press, 2008).

72. Antonio Y. Vasquez-Arroyo, "Universal History Disavowed: On Critical Theory and Postcolonialism" (unpublished essay).

73. "Debating Presentism: From Species-Autonomy to Species-Finitude," paper presented at the conference "Critical Theory Today," a Hannah Arendt/Reiner Schürmann Symposium in Political Philosophy, New School for Social Research, November 30–December 1, 2007.

Part 3.

Practices of the Self

7.

Between Intuition and Judgment: Moral Creativity in Theravada Buddhist Ethics

Charles Hallisey

The scope of this brief essay is meant to exceed its focus in significant ways. In one sense this is because the essay considers a quite restricted body of evidence—only two small examples, really—with the intent of illuminating a large-scale challenge that inflects all investigations of the diverse moral cultures and ethical traditions of South Asia. This discrepancy between scope and focus in this essay is not only one of scale, however. The focus of the essay is more contained and, to that extent, of course, more easily specified—what is called *satisampajañña* in Pali (which can be provisionally translated as "moral discernment" or "prudence") and moral creativity as virtues and their respective places in the moral life. The essay is also concerned with how the activity of reading was included among the practices that Theravada Buddhists used to cultivate these two virtues. The scope of the essay is not only more general, encouraging us to take the essay's focus as an example of something beyond itself, but it is also more reticulating and, to that extent, less capable of being adequately specified in any stable and definitive way. Provisionally we can say that the scope of the essay concerns how our investigations of ethics in South Asia generally take us beyond what we might comfortably and conventionally want to call ethics or morality, whether in terms of the inherited vocabularies of South Asia or the vocabularies of European traditions; indeed, they do so to such an extent that we may even have doubts about whether the interpretive choices we have made and that have brought us to some particular material and issues at hand have actually brought us to anything that truly merits consideration as ethics. My hope is that it will be clear by the end of this essay that by letting such doubts be and not resisting them, either categorically or descriptively, we can arrive at better accounts of the moral cultures and ethical traditions of South Asia. Here at the outset, however, I simply want to emphasize that this discrepancy between focus and scope is, crucially and usefully, between "their" practices and "our" practices. Thus the essay's focus turns our attention to a few moral virtues and practices of men and women as they are depicted in some particular Theravada Buddhist narratives, while its scope draws our attention to some constitutive interpretive practices of students of moral cultures and ethical traditions in South Asia. And, finally, it should be acknowledged that the reflection entailed in what I am calling the scope of the essay frames its focus hermeneutically in so far as the interpretive practices considered here encourage a perception of the ethical in culture and history as open-ended and connected, transformative as well as transformable; the scope of the essay also frames its focus hermeneutically in so far as these interpretive practices are presented here normatively.

Keeping in mind this normative perception of the open-endedness of the ethical in culture and history, we may want to avoid beginning any investigation of the diverse moral cultures and ethical traditions of South Asia with a particular answer to the question of what is "ethical," whether in general or with respect to a particular context, as tempting as that might be in terms of being aware of what we are looking to describe and account for. More helpful heuristically is to set in play more than one conceptions of ethics, to see what each might bring to light in the material available to us and to make some of it into evidence for our considerations. Equally necessary heuristically is to ask how these different conceptions of ethics might continually be kept in tension as well as brought into connection with one another as our investigation progresses. As a way of illustrating the interpretive practice that I have in mind, albeit perhaps somewhat arbitrarily, I set in play here two conceptions of ethics from contemporary discussions that draw on the ethical vocabularies of the modern West. The first conception is represented by Paul Ricoeur when he reminds us that answering that ancient question of "How ought one to live?" involves thinking about how one aims to live well with and for others.[1] The second is represented by Michel Foucault when he reminds us that answering that same question of "How ought one to live?" involves thinking about the self's relationship to the self.[2] It is the latter conception, of course, that commonly turns our attention to investigating the place of concrete practices of self-fashioning—what Foucault named "technologies of the self"—in the moral life, but even when we might have a primary interest in such moral practices we want to be cautious about setting aside the first conception of ethics too quickly, if only because the desire to live well with and for others frequently provides both motive and guidance to those undertaking a wide range of practices of self-fashioning in any particular moral culture or ethical tradition. This is especially the case whenever these practices of self-fashioning presume and entail a critique of the self and a desire to become other than what one discovers oneself to be. Often—and for my own tastes, too often—we may find ourselves inclined to keep these two conceptions of ethics apart, to investigate either one or the other, whether because of habits of definition and naming (for example, we may reduce the first conception of ethics about how we aim to live well with and for others to issues of agency and thus see it as quite distinct from the second conception of ethics as the self's relation to the self when it is reduced to issues of subjectivity or subjection or both) or because of entrenched habits of reading and reflection (that is, to stick to the same examples, do students of moral cultures and ethical traditions read both Ricoeur and Foucault, much less read one in the light of the other?) Uprooting such unreflective habits of interpretation is particularly difficult, I think, because they themselves are reinforced by certain received patterns in the diverse moral cultures and ethical traditions of the now globalized modern West in which academics generally participate in their ordinary lives.

The notion of "virtues" is centrally visible in both conceptions of ethics, which can help us connect the two even if their basic orientations are clearly in tension with each other. "Virtue" is a helpful category whether one is thinking about how one lives well with and for others or about the self's relation to the self. In other words, we can ask two important questions: What are the virtues of a person who is capable of living well with and for others? And what are the virtues of a person who undertakes practices of self-fashioning for the sake of becoming someone who is capable of living well with and for others?

When we ask these questions, however, two other issues immediately present themselves for consideration, and they cannot be postponed interpretively. The first is about whether a particular virtue changes in its contours when it is associated with ethics construed as concerning how one lives with others and when it is associated with ethics construed with the self's relation to the self. The second issue concerns whether a particular virtue is linked with different "associated" virtues depending on whether it is tied to the first conception of ethics or the second. The heuristic point I want to emphasize here is that such issues encourage us to look for connections and reticulations, expecting them to be shifting even as we are aware that they will be key to describing a particular virtue.

For example, let us consider the virtue of *satisampajañña* as found in Theravada Buddhism, the religious and civilizational tradition of Buddhism found historically in South India, Sri Lanka, and Southeast Asia. This illustration is also colored by one of the local cultures of the Theravada Buddhist world, since it is taken from an ethical work, the *Gatilok,* composed by a Cambodian monk in the early twentieth century.[3] The term *satisampajañña* is found frequently in authoritative texts in the Pali language and can be translated as "mindfulness and awareness of the way things are." This translation, however, drawing as it does on familiar Buddhist soteriological categories and associated with meditational practices, may not prepare us for the way that Ind, our Cambodian monk, treats it as a virtue necessary to the moral life. Ind tells a tale, drawn perhaps from oral tradition and thus already familiar to his audience, about a basket weaver who climbs a tree to cut leaves. When he finds an excellent bunch of leaves, he begins to imagine his profits and then, in turn, to imagine what he will do after he has these profits, all in considerable and humorous detail, including kicking a servant who will be working for his family. So caught up is he in his fantasy that he actually kicks out his foot, loses his balance, and begins to fall from the tree. Hanging onto a branch, he sees an elephant driver and begs for help. Because he is so high up, the *mahout* has to stand up to reach him, but he, too, is careless in his movements and gives a signal unintentionally for the elephant to run. The elephant races off and the mahout ends up holding the foot of the man he was to save. They both shout and blame each other. They then see four bald men approaching with a fishing net and beg them for help. The fishermen stretch out the net but tie it to their necks. When the basket weaver and the elephant driver jump into the net they are saved, but, inevitably, the four men supporting the net are killed. Ind thus presents *satisampajañña* as a kind of necessary self-critique one must cultivate to protect oneself from one's own carelessness as well as a kind of prudence one must have because one must live with others, indeed depend on them for one's well-being, but still be prudent enough to protect oneself from their carelessness. Thus Ind not only changes the category of *satsampajañña* when he "translates" it from a meditative and soteriological context to a moral one; it also seems that something shifts in the notion of *satisampajañña* as Ind uses it, depending on whether it names a realistic self-appraisal (as in Foucault's sense of the ethical) or a prudence based on one's realistic appraisal of others (as in Ricoeur's sense of the ethical). The person who somehow does not cultivate this virtue is truly an innocent abroad in the ordinary world, as Ind makes clear:

> The knowledge possessed by newborn babies and little children is like very shallow water; *satisampajañña* has not yet arisen to any great extent. Young children can be deceived by adults, who say, "Don't cry or the scarecrow will come and bite you" or "Ta Breng [a local spirit of god] will pour rice water on your head." Babies lack . . . *satisampajañña* . . . and are thus ignorant of adult's deceptions.[4]

Also apparent in Ind's discussion of *satisampajañña* is that its contours as either realistic self-appraisal or prudence about others actually takes shape through different forms of cultivation. A striking irony, too, is that the cultivation of prudence toward others, necessary not only to live well in the world but just to survive, is learned from others. This knowledge, of course, can be gotten from bad experiences—the school of hard knocks, so to speak—as well as from intentional programs of moral education, such as Ind himself is providing his readers in the narratives he includes in his *Gatilok* about the foibles of others against which one must always be on guard. This last point about reading is worth considering carefully, and I will return below to the manner in which reading is a practice sometimes used in the cultivation of particular moral virtues.[5]

It is possible that Ind has fashioned from the meditative category *satisampajañña* an ethical category that is useful not only for learning about the moral cultures and ethical traditions of Theravada Buddhism but one that students of ethics more generally might learn from, deploying the insights it affords in the interpretation of moral cultures and ethical traditions far from those of Theravada Buddhism. Indeed, the implications of Ind's category are such that he helps us to see that understanding the moral life entails a quality of self-discernment that can enhance our understanding of the practices of self-fashioning as they have been described by Michel Foucault, for example.

In introducing the example of *satisampajañña* I pointed out that the term originally comes from soteriological discourse and the practice of meditation, but here, in Ind's use, *satisampajañña* has become a moral necessity, and in his translation of the term from the soteriological to the moral, the practices of self-fashioning associated with this virtue have also changed, from meditation to life experience and reading.

Acknowledging Ind's translation of *satisampajañña* from the soteriological to the ethical is to identify something significant about the genealogy of this moral virtue, and indeed this genealogy is hardly remarkable in the ethical traditions of Theravada Buddhism. An overlap between the soteriological and the moral is ubiquitous in the Theravada, as is obvious from the inclusion of morality (*sila*) in the classical triad of the soteriology—morality, meditation, and wisdom—that structures the *Visuddhimagga,* the encyclopedic manual of doctrine and practice by the greatest thinker of Theravada Buddhism, the fifth-century commentator Buddhaghosa.[6] Hardly remarkable, too, is the change of meaning of the term *satisampajañña,* as any historical account of the moral cultures and ethical traditions of South Asia will include numerous examples of the changing meanings of basic moral categories in different times and contexts.

A historical concern with the genealogies of virtues in a moral culture or ethical tradition, however, must also anticipate the possibility of the "namelessness" of some key virtues in that culture or tradition, and when such nameless virtues are encountered it is necessary to somehow bring them into visibility as moral categories, whether through tracing their genealogy or by overriding their genealogy through the creation of "nontraditional" terminology. What

I called "moral creativity" at the outset of this essay is one such virtue, but before exploring that further, let us first look at the phenomenon of the relative namelessness of virtues in a culture or tradition.

With Ind's use of the term *satisampajannña,* we saw that it would be wrong to assume that if the name of a virtue is the same as another, then the virtues themselves are the same. Equally wrong would be to assume that if the name of a virtue is lacking in an ethical tradition, then that virtue itself is lacking. Aristotle knew this. In his *Rhetoric* and *Nichmachean Ethics,* Aristotle discussed certain patterns of virtuous conduct that he could clearly describe and exemplify from his culture but that had no single, adequate term in his language either to define it or specify it in the world.[7] His resourcefulness in pointing to what he was forced to call "mildness" or "calmness" is important to keep in mind when we set out to describe the range of virtues in the different lifeworlds of South Asia. It reminds us that although language, and the conceptual categories that language produces, may shape moral life in key ways, the necessity of language for the practice of the moral life can be overestimated, and relying exclusively on conceptual categories to describe the workings of moral cultures may similarly be misleading.

Because the virtue I now want to discuss does not have a stable name in the ethical traditions of Theravada Buddhism, I illustrate it here with a story that comes from a nested tale within the *Maha-ummagga Jataka,* the next to last story in the collection of accounts of the Buddha's previous lives. The *Jatakas* historically were the site for considerable moral reflection in the Theravada world and were the vehicles for the transmission of ethical ideals and values.[8] Like the *Vessantara Jataka,* the account of the future Buddha's last life in which he gave away his wife and children as a final necessary step in his accomplishment of Buddhahood, the *Maha-ummagga Jataka* circulated independently of the larger *Jataka* collection. It was translated from Pali into various local languages, and its Sinhala translation has a special prestige and visibility in the Buddhist traditions of Sri Lanka.[9] The *Maha-ummagga* also left a marked imprint on other texts such as the medieval Pali moral compendium, the *Lokaneyyapakarana.*[10] Unlike the *Vessantara jataka,* however, the *Maha-ummagga* seems to have hardly any soteriological relevance beyond a vague and general reference that could be made to wisdom as a structuring theme in the narrative; wisdom is, of course, one of the constitutive features of a Buddha, but beyond this observation there is little that helps us see how the practical wisdom exemplified in the *Maha-ummagga* should be connected to the transcendent insight of a Buddha. The *Maha-ummagga* is very much a text of this world, and it frequently resonates with what in South Asian ethical traditions is known as *niti* literature. It tells the account of how the future Buddha, as an adviser to a king, repeatedly bested his jealous rivals through his intelligence and cunning. Ostensibly the *Maha-ummagga* is about the future

Buddha's perfection of wisdom, but the wisdom in this story is very much of the practical sort. The answer it often seems to give to the question "How ought one to live?" is disconcerting: "better outsmart them."

Like the moral cultures and ethical traditions of Theravada Buddhism itself, the *Maha-ummagga* defies any easy summary of its moral view, if indeed it has one. Even its effect on readers cannot be conveyed by an account of its plot, which also defies a ready summation because of its narrative device of nesting stories within stories. As noted, my example is from one of these nested stories, and I selected it because it concerns a nameless virtue that seems necessary for one to live well *for* others, not because it is a major episode in the *Maha-ummagga.* The story is nested within a commentary on a verse that is the canonical part of the *Maha-ummagga Jataka,* explaining why a king's mother is included in his council of advisers; in fact, the story is unconnected, except as background, to the story around it:

> It is said that the mother of the king was wiser (*atirekatarapañña*) than those wise men (*panditehi*); she, having become the eleventh (in the council of advisers), encouraged and advised the army of Pancala. One day, it is said, a certain man took a measure of husked rice, some cooked rice in a leaf, and a thousand coins and went down to the river with the thought of crossing it. Having reached the middle of the river, he was unable to go further. He called to some men who were standing on the shore: "Hey, mates, there is in my hand one measure of husked rice, some cooked rice in a leaf, and a thousand coins. What is pleasing to me from these things, I will give to whoever is capable of rescuing me." One strong man, tying his clothes tightly, plunged into the river and, taking the man by the hand, pulled him out. "Give me what you said would be given," he said. "Take the measure of husked rice or the cooked rice in the leaf," the man replied. "I risked my life and pulled you out. There is no value in those for me. Give me the coins." "I said, 'What is pleasing to me from these things, I will give," and now I give what [ever] is pleasing to me; if you want it, take it." The rescuer told the whole exchange to someone standing close by, but that one said, "He said that he would give whatever was his own pleasure to you, so you better take it." "I will not take it," and, taking the rescued man [with him], he brought him to a court and repeated the whole story to the justices of the court. They, having heard everything, came to the same conclusion. The rescuer was not happy with their judgment, so he appealed to the king. The king summoned the justices and listened to both sides of the story in their presence. Not really knowing how to decide the case, he decided, as the previous justices had, against the one who had plunged into the river risking his own life to save the other.

> Now at that moment Talatadevi, the mother of the king, was seated nearby, and knowing that it was a bad decision she asked the king whether the case had been decided properly. The king said, "Mother, I decided as best as I am able; if you know how to do any better, then bring a judgment yourself." "I will then," she said. She summoned that man, and said, "Dear one, please place in order on the ground those three things you have in your hand." Then she asked, "Now when you were in the water, what did you say to this one?" And when he had said what he had said (i.e., "What is pleasing to me from these things, I will give"), she said, "Then now take what is pleasing to you." The man took the thousand coins, and as he started to move away, she called him back, and asked, "Dear one, is it the thousand coins that please you?" When he answered yes, that they were what pleased him, she asked, "Dear one, did you or did you not say to this one, "What is pleasing to me from these things, I will give." "That's what was said, Queen." "Because of that," she said, "give the thousand coins to this one." He gave them, crying and weeping. Then the king and the justices were delighted and shouted out praise, and from then on her wise nature (*panditabhavo*) was known everywhere.[11]

This brief story begins with an incident concerning a moral vision of the world that would have been familiar to our twentieth-century Cambodian monk Ind, a world where one finds oneself needing and giving help, but also where the people with whom one enters into relationships are just as liable to take advantage of you as aid you, even when you help them. It is a world in which *satisampajañña* is a moral necessity. It is worth pausing over the beginning of the story, where a man risks his life to help another man in danger of drowning, with the latter promising a reward. The moral and social world depicted here simply accepts the reality of self-interest. There is nothing to suggest that the rescuer would have or should have come to the other's aid had no reward been promised.

Key to the plot of the story is the exploitation of what linguists call "relevance," the need to connect a statement to facts from the surrounding world in order to understand the meaning of that statement. The combination of our knowledge of what is and our competence in determining relevance allows us to decide whether the statement "I am going to marry a Swede" means "I don't know who I am going to marry, but all I know is that it will be a Swede," or "I know who I am going to marry and that person is a Swede."[12] In the story the rescued man tries to swindle his rescuer by playing on what he knows his rescuer will understand and his ability to escape the implications of that understanding by subsequently invoking another relevance to his original words. This plot device drives a wedge between what the reader knows to be the spirit of the law and what the reader must acknowledge, along with the characters in the story, that the letter of the law is determined by the later determined relevance.

The *Jataka* stories, as a body of literature, are commonly dismissed by modern academic students of Buddhism as mere folktales, but it is a profound mistake to do so. The above narrative reveals why. The story is sophisticated in its manipulation of the reader's experience. We know—and how we know is important but for now let's say by intuition—that the rescuer is in the right, but, like all the characters in the story, we may not see how we can make results in the world cohere with what we intuit to be what is right. Everything seems to be on the side of the swindler. The rescuer refuses to accept this injustice, but his appeals are futile since the rule of law—here the laws of language as well as the law of the court—seems to be against him. A significant point about ethics, indeed a theoretical point, is implied by this gap between what we intuit about what should be done and what is actually done in the story, namely, that the moral cannot be reduced to language and, consequently, cannot be reduced to any naïve account of culture structured around a schema of conceptual categories. This important point of ethical theory may deserve to be reflected in the practices that we use in interpreting moral cultures themselves, as I suggested at the outset of this essay.

A crucial turning point in the story comes with the exchange between the king and his mother, which itself reveals many ambiguities in the social world both within the text and outside it. The king, of course, is institutionally the highest authority in this world, but it is his mother who comes to occupy a place of moral, if not legal, authority above him. We might assume that, like us, the king sees what is wrong in the unfolding of the case, but, also like us, he sees no way to prevent it, and, again like us, is only able to repeat the previous judgments made by others in the story. The implied theme here, known by characters and readers alike, is that living well for others entails not only knowing what is good and right but also seeing how to realize that goodness in a world that has among its inhabitants cheats and swindlers. It is not a question of making the rich man see what is right; we know that his rescuer has done that from the start. What is necessary is getting the rich man to accept what must be when he does not want it to be so and is seeking a way to avoid doing what is right. The wisdom required here is to outsmart him, and, in this, this particular little story resonates with many of the other stories in the *Maha-ummagga Jataka*.

Outsmarting the rescued man is precisely what the king's mother accomplishes, and she achieves her aim by engaging in the same sort of manipulation of linguistic relevance that the rescued man himself had done earlier. Key in all this is the role of time, and the gap between what was heard and what was intended to be said. The king's mother gets the would-be swindler to reveal that what was in his mind at the time of his original statement was different from what he was saying was in his mind. Within some pandit cultures of South Asia, the queen's actions might be described as an example of *pratyutpannamati,* a term that brings together, in a relatively amoral fashion, quick-wittedness, confidence, and boldness,[13] all of which are exhibited by the king's mother, but this category is not invoked in the story itself nor does it seem centrally visible in Theravadin scholastic culture; indeed, the story employs only an ad hoc term about the queen being "excessively wise" (*atirekatarapañña*) compared to the other advisers. But even the broad category of *pratyutpannamati* does not adequately convey the moral character of this trait as it is depicted in this story. In other words, whether we describe the mother's quality in the story as excessive wisdom or as cleverness, we see that this generic quality of intellect is made into something "sub-ethical" in the story.[14] Deserving of emphasis is that key to the story is a nameless virtue which we might describe as a moral creativity necessary to achieve a desired ethical end when one is living with and for others. Moreover, the story makes clear that this desired end seems to be known by everyone immediately, readers and characters alike, by intuition rather than abstract reasoning, but what sets the king's mother apart is her practical skill in devising a plan that will make the world cohere with what we want it to be.

Let us return to the exchange between the king and his mother and note the king's retort when his mother rebukes him for his legal decision: "do better if you can." Evident here is a practical depiction of another necessary virtue for the functioning of the moral life as it is commonly depicted in the Theravadin ethical tradition, a recognition of the need to depend on others for advice and correction if one is to become, and eventually remain, a moral person.[15] Many of the ethical subjects in the story are profoundly dependent on others, for better or worse, and are not good examples of the autonomous agent so typically assumed in much of modern Western ethics. The king, most notably, is portrayed as knowing no better decision than what was previously made by the justices. As readers, we may find ourselves identifying with the aggrieved rescuer, convinced that justice is not being served in the judgments against him, and we may also identify with the king, in that we, too, do not know how to produce a better judgment than that which the bystander and justices have pronounced; in this respect, the act of identifying with characters in a story, so basic to the practices of reading, becomes part of a larger set of practices of moral self-fashioning. The construction of the narrative reminds us that we, as readers, were also incapable of seeing the strategy that allows the king's mother to accomplish what we ourselves knew to be the right action; we then discover that our own road to moral capability, the practices we ourselves will have to engage in to become capable of living well for others as well as living well with others, can only begin with our own personal recognition that we are incapable of doing what is necessary and will need help from others in order to become competent moral subjects. In this sense, then, the practices of reading and the transformations that reading effects on us as subjects become embedded in larger complexes of moral self-fashioning.

For us, in the context of the scope of this essay, the important lesson is not about how to become a competent moral subject but rather how to become a competent student of the moral cultures and ethical traditions of South Asia. However, as this essay demonstrated, our practices of reading cultivate in us certain expectations that will shape future investigations of moral lives, whether Buddhist or something else. Above all, we will expect to see as moral those creative practices that encourage men and women to take full advantage of the contextual under-determination of moral situations as a part of striving to realize the Good.

Acknowledgments

Earlier versions of this essay were presented at the "Geneologies of Virtue: Ethical Practice in South Asia" workshop that was the origin of this volume; the Harvard Buddhist Studies Forum; and the Princeton University Buddhist Studies Workshop. I thank the participants in each for their questions, comments, and objections. I also would like to acknowledge the particularly helpful comments that were received on earlier versions from Anand Pandian and Daud Ali, as well as from Herman Tull, Paul Dundas, Preeti Chopra, Kenneth George, and Janet Gyatso.

Notes

1. See, for example, Paul Ricoeur, *Oneself as Another* (Chicago: University of Chicago Press, 1994), 172. It is important to note, to do justice to Ricoeur, that there is a final clause in Ricoeur's statement as found in *Oneself as Another:* "one aims to live well with and for others, in just institutions."

2. For instance, Michel Foucault, "Polemics, Politics, and Problematizations," in *Ethics: Subjectivity and Truth,* ed. Paul Rabinow (New York: New Press, 1997), 116–117.

3. This example and my discussion of it here draws on and depends on Anne Hansen, *How to Behave: Buddhism and Modernity in Colonial Cambodia 1860–1930* (Honolulu: University of Hawai'i Press, 2007), 164.

4. Ibid., 166.

5. For a discussion of the place in moral formation of reading narratives, in particular, see Charles Hallisey and Anne Hansen, "Narrative, Sub-ethics, and the Moral Life: Some Evidence from Theravada Buddhism," *Journal of Religious Ethics* 24, no. 2 (1996): 305–328.

6. See Buddhaghosa, *Path of Purification,* trans. Bhikkhu Nanamoli (Seattle: BPS Pariyatti Editions, 1999).

7. See A. G. Nikolaides, "Aristotle's Treatment of the Concept of *Praotes,*" *Hermes* 110 (1982): 414–422. Martha Nussbaum has also noted this observation by Aristotle: "This 'namelessness' probably has some significance. For example, the fact that there was no name for a moderate disposition of character with regard to anger and retaliation (Aristotle has to co-opt the concededly imperfect term "mildness" [*praotes*]) probably reflects the fact that his culture placed an unusually high value on retributive conduct, and spoke about it far more than about mild conduct." See Martha Nussbaum, *The Upheaval of Thought: The Intelligence of Emotions* (Cambridge: Cambridge University Press, 2001), 155.

8. On the *Jatakas* as vehicles of ethical reflection, see Gananath Obeyesekere, "Buddhism and Conscience: An Exploratory Essay," *Daedalus* 120 (1991): 219–239. The *Jatakas* in the Theravada Buddhist tradition give excellent examples of Ricoeur's observation that "the actions refigured by narrative fictions are complex ones, rich in anticipations of an ethical nature. Telling a story . . . is deploying an imaginary space for thought experiments in which moral judgement operates in a hypothetical mode" (*Oneself as Another,* 170).

9. For translations of the Sinhala version, see T. B. Yatawara, *Ummagga Jataka: The Story of the Tunnel* (London: Luzac, 1898); and David Karunaratne, *Ummagga Jataka: The Story of the Tunnel* (Colombo: Gunasena, 1962). The Sinhala translation from Pali was completed in about the fourteenth century, and linguistic evidence suggests that the translator was a native speaker of Tamil or Malayalam.

10. See P. S. Jain, ed., *Lokaneyyapakarana* (Oxford: Pali Text Society, 1986).

11. *Jataka, together with its Commentary,* ed. V. Fausboll (London: Trubner, 1877–1896), 6:397–398.

12. On the linguistic phenomenon of relevance, see Dan Sperber and Diedre Wilson, *Relevance: Communication and Cognition* (London: Wiley-Blackwell, 1996).

13. See Monier Monier-Williams, *A Sanskrit-English Dictionary* (Oxford: Clarendon, 1970), s.v. pratyutpanna. I would like to thank Paul Dundas for bringing this category to my attention.

14. On the notion of sub-ethics in Theravada Buddhist ethics, see Hallisey and Hansen, "Narrative, Sub-ethics, and the Moral Life," 305–328.

15. For a classical Theravada Buddhist account of such depictions, see Charles Hallisey, "Auspicious Things," in *Buddhism in Practice,* ed. Donald Lopez (Princeton, N.J.: Princeton University Press, 1995), 412–426.

8.

Young Manliness: Ethical Culture in the Gymnasiums of the Medieval Deccan

Emma Flatt

A careful look at a map of the town of Bidar, once the capital city of the Bahmani kingdom, reveals a curious phenomenon: the urban space is divided according to four schools of physical training, located in the four cardinal quarters of the city. From the mid-fifteenth century until the beginning of the twentieth these schools, known locally as *ta'līm k̲h̲āna* (house of instruction, abbreviated as *ta'līm*) provided the young men of the four quarters of the city with moral and physical education, including wrestling, club exercises, and fencing, which they would display in mock fights during Muharram.[1] In the Muharram processions of the early twentieth century the members of each *ta'līm* carried an emblematic wooden lion symbolizing their institutional affiliation to 'Ali.

This essay investigates the ethic of *javānmardī,* or young manliness, which was taught in these *ta'līms* of Bidar and the *zūrk̲h̲ānas* (gymnasiums) of Iran. By focusing on the continuum between an intensive exercise regime with the aim of constant bodily refinement and the cultural understanding of character as a malleable matter to be refined through habitual physical and mental exercises, the essay approaches ethics as a daily process of self-fashioning rather than adherence to a set of laws laid out in a foundational text. In its focus on the medieval Deccan region, moreover, the essay also explores how certain cultural ideas about character, body, and ethics widely shared across the Persian-speaking world were translated into practice in specific local contexts in South Asia.

Although this investigation is largely based on textual sources, it is worth noting that, as demonstrated by the physical location of the *ta'līms* of Bidar on the axial roads of the Bahmani capital, carving up the city into four zones of influence, the ethic discussed here had a significant spatial and temporal dimension. That is to say, the location of the four *ta'līms,* which instructed students in a particular physical and moral ethic, in a particular locality of the city; the affiliation of the young men of a particular locality to their own *ta'līm;* and the rooting of this affiliation in the sacred season of Muharram structured both the spatial and temporal landscapes of the capital city of the Bahmani kingdom according to the institution and practices of the *ta'līms.* The temporal and spatial aspect of the ethic propounded by the *ta'līms* serves as a reminder that although *javānmardī* was intended as a particularist way of living one's life restricted to initiated members, at another level the ethic demonstrated a universalizing tendency, reaching beyond the membership of each *ta'līm* to frame the quotidian experience of all inhabitants of the city.

This essay describes the lineaments of the ethic of *javānmardī* as depicted in normative texts circulating in the medieval Persianate world, and then considers how this particular ethic was both lived and contested in the Bahmani kingdom and its successor states in the medieval Deccan. First, however, I begin with a brief discussion of the anxieties surrounding the ideas of youth, education, and character development that percolated into normative literature of the "Persian Cosmopolis."

Youth, Education, and Character

The question of how best to ensure the perpetuation of social rank and prestige for succeeding generations of one's own kinsmen was a perennial preoccupation among the ruling classes at a time when personal property was not yet inviolable and rank and power depended largely on proximity to the throne. In the medieval Persian-speaking world the anxiety generated over the issue of the correct education of children and young adults found voice in a wide range of literary genres including mirrors for princes texts, moralistic stories like the *Gūlistān,* ethical treatises *(akẖlāq),* letter writing *(inshā')* manuals, poetic works, and historical chronicles.

Underlying the concern for education was a deeper-rooted anxiety about youth itself. A newly born infant was described as an "uncut jewel devoid of any form or carving" which was so highly susceptible to perverse influences that it had to be disciplined and trained from the moment of weaning lest "destructive dispositions gain[ed] a hold."[2] The anxiety surrounding the volatile nature of youth is clearly reflected in the opening lines of the *Qābūsnāma*'s chapter on age and youth, which bristle with awareness of the dichotomies of ages:

> Although you are young my son, be old in understanding. I do not demand that you shall not behave as a young man, but be a young man governed by self-restraint. Yet neither be a lackluster young man; it is well for a young man to be spirited for as Aristotle says, "Youth is a species of madness." Be not foolhardy; no harm can come out of high spirits, but misfortune can come from foolhardy conduct. To the full extent of your powers enjoy the period of your youth for when you reach old age you will be unable to achieve much.[3]

Youth was also a time of dangerous liminality and ambiguity when the defining characteristics of male and female bodies were less starkly distinguished than in adults. The beard had long been fetishized in both hadith literature and popular culture as a symbol of masculinity and virility, and its absence made a pretty boy both disturbing and terribly tempting.[4] Normative literature urged measures to encourage manliness and virility, including wearing rough clothes and undertaking habitual physical exercise such as hunting, polo, swimming, sword fighting, and horseback riding.[5] These activities, which can be seen as early training in skills that would later stand boys in good stead for employment at court, also reflect an attempt to erase the dichotomies between youth and adulthood, and to impose an early "virilization" on youths as yet unmarked by the physical signs of virility.[6] Even the common words used to describe the desirable qualities in a human reinforce the elision between correct behavior and the attributes of a man; *murūwat*—literally, "manliness" or "virility"—is used to mean humanity, generosity, politeness, and courtesy.

At the base of these conceptions was an idea of character that reflected a profound engagement with Greek philosophy. Although admitting that some people were born superior to others, philosophers like Ibn Miskawayh, al-Ghazali, and Nasir al-din Tusi conceived of character as mutable, meaning that true virtue could be obtained regardless of one's station in life.[7] Drawing heavily on medical understandings of the four bodily humors, Ghazali posited the idea that the four cardinal virtues—wisdom, courage, temperance, and justice—should be maintained in equilibrium since imbalance, either through defect or excess, would produce a sickness in the soul.

So how was one's character to be refined? Ghazali's answer was that the correct equilibrium of virtues could be acquired through habituation and constantly acting contrary to one's desires. Thus an avaricious man could become generous by constantly forcing himself to give money away until generosity became habitual to his character. Here the key techniques were *riyāẓa* (rigorous discipline or training) and *muḥāsaba* (self-examination), techniques derived from both ancient Greece and Islamic mysticism.[8] They were also rooted in the daily carnal reality of Muslims, most particularly through the ritual of *ṭahārat,* or bodily purification. Theologically the original purity of man is affected through mere existence, because whatever the body eliminates is impure, tarnishes the body, and invalidates the pillars of Islam.[9] Precise and rigorous purificatory techniques involving constant attention to the body must be learned to achieve the state of purity. Hence there developed an attitude of continuous self-observance of the slightest details of physiological life, "lying in wait for" or "spying on one's own body," which required strict training in will and self-control, without falling into excess.[10] In Ghazali's theology and in the ethic of *javānmardī,* the techniques of *ṭahārat* were not only transposed onto character refinement, but *ṭahārat* itself became a precondition of refinement, which was in turn a precondition of progress toward the fulfillment of man's aim in life: meeting God. Consequently, as the daily control of the body became essential to the control of character and the soul, a continuum between the carnal and spiritual parts of man was clearly laid out.

Javānmardī and *Futūvat*

Epitomizing this anxiety over youth, masculinity, bodily control, and character refinement was the ethic of *javānmardī*—literally, "young manliness." The Arabic word *futūvat* (young manliness) was frequently used as a synonym in Persian writings on the subject.[11] Rather than a single virtue, *javānmardī* should be seen as a constellation of praiseworthy qualities that make up a distinctive ethical system, encapsulating both an ideal and a historically embodied practice.[12] From at least the time of Firdausi's epic *Shāhnāma* (1010) to the present day, *javānmardī* has been used in literature written throughout the Persian-speaking world to describe a man who possessed the aggregate of manly virtues, including courage, integrity, honesty, hospitality, and generosity.[13]

The ideal of *javānmardī* drew initially on both Sassanian and pre-Islamic Arab warrior traditions of the champion (*pahlavān*) whose duty consisted in protecting the kingdom by his selfless acts of valor. Early in the Islamic period this figure coalesced with the character of the religious warrior (*g͟hāzī*), fighting to expand the dominion of Islam.[14] Over time the ideas of manly behavior inherited from both *g͟hāzīs* and mercenary soldiers were adopted by guilds of professionals and craftsmen and institutionalized into organized *futūvat* brotherhoods, which provided a socioeconomic support network for their members.[15] In the thirteenth century, under the influence of the Abbasid caliph Nasir-li Din Allah and the powerful Sufi Sheikh, Umar Suhrawardi, *futūvat,* which had already been strongly influenced by Islamic mysticism, became more fully absorbed into Sufism.[16] In Sufic terms, *javānmardī* enjoined externally ethical behavior toward others, necessitating the acquisition of the virtues of wisdom, justice, chastity, and magnanimity. Simultaneously a *javānmard* was expected to internalize these values in order to restore man's nature to its original purity. The meaning of spiritual *javānmardī* thus modified the values originally associated with warriors to signify the attitude required in the greater *jihād* against the desires of the carnal soul (*nafs*).[17]

Despite its absorption into Sufic theology, in practice *javānmardī* institutions seem to have preserved a distinction from the various Sufi *silsila* (lineages). Medieval *futūvat* texts describe the *javānmardī* brotherhoods as formal institutions with an initiation ceremony, a uniform, a hierarchy of authority, and codes of conduct (*adab*).[18] Although the hierarchies of *futūvat* organizations may have varied, one distinction emphasized by all treatises is that between the student (*shāgird* or *murīd*) and the teacher or master (*ustād*, *ṣāḥib* or *pīr*), reflecting the pedagogical thrust of this ethic.[19] The highly particularized codes of proper conduct focus especially on the acquisition of proper conduct by both the teacher and the initiate.

The pedagogical drive of the ethic of *javānmardī* aimed not merely at the character but, intrinsically, also at the external body of the *javānmard* (young man). This defining aspect was preserved at the level of physical space: the most distinctive feature of the buildings of *javānmardī* associations was that, unlike the Sufi hospices (*k̲h̲ānaqa*), they generally included a space for physical exercise known as a *zūrk̲h̲āna* (gymnasium, house of force) or a *varzish-k̲h̲āna* (house of exercise). Moreover, unlike the *k̲h̲ānaqas*, which were open to the public, access to the *zūrk̲h̲āna* was usually restricted to members of the brotherhood only. In medieval Iran, merchants involved in lucrative long-distance trade would send their children to *zūrk̲h̲ānas* for both physical and moral training, and the *zūrk̲h̲āna* has endured as a central institution in Iran until the present day.[20] Here, under the guidance of a teacher (*ustād*), the *javānmards* would build up their physical strength and prowess through wrestling, club twirling, sword fighting, archery, and spear throwing.

Lineaments of the Ethic

By medieval times the historical trajectory described above had endowed the concept and institution of *javānmardī* with a multilayered sedimentation of meanings, so that *javānmardī* stood for a constellation of virtues, a way of behaving and a particular lifestyle. Although there are no historical descriptions of the activities of *javānmardī* associations in India, it is possible to reconstruct a picture, from various other sources relating to Khorasan and Iran, of the normative way of life recommended in textual sources, although the extent to which this reflects historical reality is naturally a matter for further research. A *javānmard*'s lifestyle would commence with his initiation ceremony and subsequent membership in a brotherhood attached to a particular *zūrk̲h̲āna*.[21] Having undergone the initiation ceremony, a *javānmard* would then have particular duties toward his fellow members or brotherhood (*birādarīyat*) and could expect the same support in return.[22] Under the critical guidance of a teacher, the *javānmard* would subject himself to a disciplined daily routine of physical exercise, including use of the *kabāda* (practice bow), the *nāls* (weights), and clubs, as well as *ḍanḍ*s (jack-knife push-ups) and *baiṭhak* (squats).[23] Exercises would often be undertaken communally while repeating the name of ʻAli as *ẕikr,* under the watchful eye of the teacher and, in modern-day Iran at least, to the accompaniment of percussion instruments.[24] Wrestling moves should also be practiced repeatedly and analyzed critically by both the teacher and the practitioner with a constant vigilance toward refining the practitioner's bodily technique. A similar watchfulness should be directed toward all aspects of his behavior both inside and outside the *zūrḵẖāna,* including in donning or removing his leather breaches before wrestling or in making special wrestler's food known as *bughra.*[25] Outside the *zūrḵẖāna,* a *javānmard* would be expected to conceive of his routine daily work as an opportunity for *ẕikr,* that is, to focus the mind and as a step on the path toward an attitude of constant attention to one's character and its refinement.

One may object that what I define as the "ethic" of *javānmardī* is actually no more than a collection of skills. The problem with this objection is that it ignores the diverse nature of pre-humanist ethics. As discussed in the introduction to this volume, ethics in premodern times had a very different aspect to contemporary post-Kantian understandings of ethics as ideal, universal, and rational. Medieval Islamic ethics can be more profitably analyzed through Foucault's influential conception of "ethics-based moralities," wherein a person establishes a particular kind of relationship with himself that perceives his own body as malleable matter to be subjected to techniques of formation and refinement—what Foucault termed "subjectivation."[26] It has long been recognized that Aristotelian philosophy, partly at the basis of Foucault's discussion, was absorbed into and reworked in medieval Islamic philosophy, particularly by thinkers like Nasir al-Din Tusi and al-Ghazali. In some aspects of medieval Islamic thought, as in pre-humanist European thought, "a collection of skills" is therefore in no way counterposed to ethics; rather, the refinement of a particular collection of skills is integral to an ethical life. Frequent, repetitive practice of particular mundane skills that focus on refining the physical or external aspect of an individual is understood to be the tool by which a person works upon his own interior: his character or his heart (*dil*). As Mahmood argues, both the specificity of a bodily practice and the kind of relationship it presupposes between the body and its actions should be objects of analysis, since the particular form the body takes can transform our understanding of its actions.[27] In this sense, then, the importance of these practices is, above all, the work they do on the body, enabling it to become a necessary tool for constituting the individual.

The techniques of bodily refinement advocated by the *javānmardī* ethic were expected to create an identical attitude of vigilance and identical habits of repetitive practice in order to develop a range of moral qualities. These qualities were summarized in a hadith attributed to 'Ali in response to a question from his son, Hassan: "*futūvat* is mastery of the self when one has power; courtesy when one has strength; it is being generous when one is poor; it is giving without ever expecting a return."[28] The fourteenth-century treatise by 'Abd al-Razzaq Kashani, *Tuhfat al-Ikhwān fi khasāis al fityān,* gives a more expansive list of eight moral qualities expected of a *javānmard,* as follows: *tauba* (repentance or internal conversion), *sakhā* (generosity), *tavāẓu'* (courtesy),[29] *amān* (confidence and serenity), *ṣidq* (sincerity), *hidāyat* (guidance), *naṣīḥat* (advising others), and *vafā* (fidelity). Above all, Kashani stressed, a *javānmard* must avoid vanity, rivalry with others, and self-admiration, because the ethic of *javānmardī* requires that one should refine one's character from all profane ambition. Nevertheless, a *javānmard* had to walk a fine line between eliminating profane ambition and involving himself in worldly affairs, particularly in defense of his brotherhood, in line with the Naqshbandi Sufi strictures against hermetic seclusion; as the vizier of the Deccani state of Golconda advised his son:

> Don't avert your face from involvement in affairs,
> Show great compassion like the *javānmards.*[30]

Wrestling and *Javānmardī*

In pre-Islamic Iran wrestling rather than skill in weaponry was the test of superior strength, and the epics are full of legendary wrestling matches between heroes, paramount among whom was Rustom, and sometimes even between men and dangerous beasts such as lions or elephants.[31] Early in the Islamic period, the figure of Rustom became fused with that of 'Ali, whom tradition still recognizes as the founder of the guild of wrestlers, the true master of the wrestling pit and the founder of the path of *pahlavāni* and *futūvat.*[32] Though a variety of physical activities were practiced in the *zūrkhāna* of the futūvat associations, one of the preeminent models of *javānmardī* was the wrestler (*kushtī-gīr*) based on two factors: first, the sharp contrast between the physical force of his occupation and the self-control required by the *javānmardī* ethic; and, second, the comparison between the rigorous and continuous discipline to which a wrestler was expected to submit his body in order to become a champion and the discipline that a *javānmard* was expected to apply to his character. Kashifi describes wrestling as a metaphor for each individual's battle against the carnal soul (*nafs*):

> [Wrestling is] that which a man does in altering his character and the truth of this word is that a struggle will [always] happen between praiseworthy qualities and a reprehensible character [. . .] [and] through the power of disciplined exercise (*riyāẓa*) bad natures will be subdued.[33]

A wrestler in medieval Persianate societies is a good example of what the philosopher MacIntyre calls a "character." In MacIntyre's definition, certain social roles specific to particular cultures

> furnish recognizable characters, and the ability to recognize them is socially crucial because a knowledge of the character provides an interpretation of the actions of those individuals who have assumed the character. It does so precisely because those individuals have used the very same knowledge to guide and to structure their behavior.[34]

These characters effectively become the moral representatives of their culture, because they give moral and metaphysical ideas and theories an embodied existence in the social world. Although MacIntyre applied his conception of "character" to Western societies, the shared Aristotelian inheritance of medieval Islamic ethics suggests that this usage could be a helpful way of considering how an ethic was lived out. The Persian word *akẖlāq,* usually translated as "ethics," also refers to human character or nature and indeed the genre of *Akẖlāqi* literature focuses on the development and training of one's *khalq,* or nature. Nasir al-Din Tusi's seminal text, the *Akẖlāq-i Nasiri,* explains that every kind of every type of thing—animal, mineral, and vegetable—has a certain function it is meant to perform and that the aim of each thing should be to perfect itself either through nature or through discipline in the performance of that function in order to be termed good.[35] Thus the function of a sword is to penetrate and cut smoothly, and the best sword is one that cuts smoothly and penetrates well, but if it cuts with difficulty it will be used as a mere iron tool which represents a "decline in its rank."[36] Tusi's highly influential quadripartite social model, drawing on both Sassanian social ideals and Platonic ideas, divided men into four groups: men of the pen, of the sword, of transactions, and of agriculture.[37] This model, based on the understanding that men's intellectual and spiritual aptitudes qualified them for different degrees of political and spiritual authority within the community, allowed Tusi to argue that the best men of each class must strive to perform their own particular social function to the best of their ability, through acquiring the habit of discipline. It is easy to see how this philosophical background, which emphasized the perfectibility of each class, would have been receptive to the development of particular exemplary "characters," in MacIntyre's sense of social roles which embodied specific moral and metaphysical ideals that were attached to the quadripartite division of society. It is in this situation that the wrestler emerged as a character in courtly society, which relied so heavily on the martial skills and service of its members.

In medieval Persianate societies, literature and the ethic of *javānmardī* had imbued the character of the wrestler with certain immediately recognizable traits and functions, some of which related to his behavior in the arena (*ma'raka*) and still more to his daily behavior. Thus, when the wrestler makes an appearance in a text, the well-educated reader is expected to understand immediately from certain established traits that he is a wrestler, even before the author confirms the fact. Moreover, having understood that a certain figure is a wrestler, the reader would then assume that this figure would possess a particular and recognizable set of qualities, visible both in his physical and moral characteristics and lived out in his life, both inside and outside the arena. The wrestler thus becomes a sign for a particular way of living one's life, a shorthand for the ethic of *javānmardī*. Indeed, drawing on recent arguments made by Hallisey concerning the existence of "nameless ethics," it may be that the sign itself can become so well known that there is no longer any need of overtly naming the ethic for which it stands.[38]

Javānmardī in the Deccan

Although there has been significant interest in *javānmardī* and *futūvat* among scholars writing on Iran, Turkey, and Central Asia, it has been almost totally ignored by scholars working in South Asia, even those working on Sufism.[39] This can be attributed partly to the lack of extant Indian treatises on either *futūvat* or *javānmardī*. Nevertheless treatises written elsewhere would have been well known in India, given the streams of courtiers who moved between Iran, Central Asia, and the subcontinent and the constellations of transcontinental contacts established by powerful viziers, merchants, and scholars.[40] That *javānmardī* was a living ethic in the Deccan is also confirmed by the presence of *zūrkẖānas,* or gymnasiums, both in literary descriptions of the cities of Ahmadnagar and Bidar, and in physical form, in the shape of the four ruined *ta'līms* that sit at the four corners of the city of Bidar.[41]

However, one of the clearest indications that the ethic of *javānmardī* was current in the Deccan is the account of the rise to prominence of Yusuf 'Adil Shah in the *Taẕkirat al-Mulūk,* a sixteenth-century chronicle of Bijapur by Rafi'al-din Shirazi.[42] An analysis of this account may also help illustrate some of the qualities inherent in the "character" of the wrestler as disseminated by contemporary literature. In brief, Shirazi's story is as follows: Yusuf, a young Iranian noble, is exiled by a rebellion and advised in a dream to seek his fortune in the Deccan. He obtains passage on a slave ship, arrives at the Bahmani court, and is given a position in the kitchen. To vent his frustration at his un-heroic life, he establishes a *zūrkẖāna* where he instructs his fellow cooks and entertains the townspeople. A champion wrestler from Delhi comes to town, vanquishes the court wrestlers, and leaves the king's reputation in tatters. Yusuf comes to the rescue, beats the rival champion, and is promoted up through the ranks, eventually becoming a leading noble of the Bahmani kingdom. The following paragraphs extricate some of the lineaments of the wrestler's "character" and consider how the ethic of *javānmardī* is illuminated by Shirazi's tale.

Physical Beauty

One of the key aspects of the wrestler was the perfection of his physical appearance. Persian chronicles frequently described how spectators at a wrestling match would be bewitched by the wrestler's beauty.[43] Writers of *futūvat* treatises like Amuli saw physical perfection as a sign of the true *fatan* (young man).[44] This drew from wider understandings of the equivalence between beauty of external form and internal perfection of character based on theories of the continuum between the microcosm and the macrocosm. In Persian poetry physical beauty reflects nobility of character, because outward beauty is a reflection of the soul's inner light.[45] The first clue in Shirazi's narrative that Yusuf might be a wrestler comes while he is searching for a ship going to India. Some Turkish and Ethiopian slaves who had been purchased by a merchant in the pay of the Bahmani emperor are so struck by his youthful appearance, his sweet face, his strong body, and his Turkish disposition that they convince their master to include him among them.[46] The true meaning of Yusuf's beauty is rapidly revealed to the reader when Shirazi describes how he passes the voyage wrestling with the slaves: he is a wrestler.

The Importance of Work

Yusuf's job as cook at the Bahmani court is a lowly one, but when he tires of it and returns to Iran, he has another dream in which he is reproached for impatience and urged to return to his humble occupation in the Deccan "because his lamp will be lighted in that place."[47] This he does, subsuming his frustration by establishing a gymnasium in the kitchen and teaching the other cooks to wrestle. The implication here is the importance of mundane work to character development, which had become a crucial part of the *javānmardī* ethic under the influence of the politically powerful Naqshbandi Sufi *silsila* which dominated the intellectual and ruling classes of fifteenth-century Herat. Known for their rejection of flamboyant displays of spirituality such as ecstatic dancing, vocal *ẕikr* or isolationist asceticism, the Naqshbandis advocated the path of *k̲h̲alwat dar anjuman,* or "solitude in society."[48] This meant that an initiate should pursue his daily life and work but should consider the repetitive tasks of his mundane life as both an opportunity and a means of prayer, or *ẕikr.* Work was therefore understood to exert a transformative and refining impact on one's character. These ideas were incorporated into the *javānmardī* ethic through the treatise on *futūvat* by the prolific writer Husain Va'iz Kashifi who dedicated two detailed sections of his book to the *futūvat* requirements of the members of various professions, including wrestlers, orators, porters, basket carriers, jugglers, stone carriers, plasterers, and swordsmen.[49]

The Initiation Ceremony

Having established the gymnasium and collected fifty students from among his fellow cooks, Yusuf then presents them all with leather breeches, underwear, and knee bands. With the mention of leather breeches, the implication is clear: Yusuf has conducted an initiation ritual, which was one of the central features of the *javānmardī* organizations, and one whose elements remained remarkably stable over time and space.[50] Like earlier *futūvat* organizations that had ritualized and fetishized the presentation and the wearing of the trousers (*zīr-jāma*) as a symbol of *javānmardī,* the distinguishing item of a wrestler were his leather breeches (*tumbān*), which were presented at an initiation ceremony and made the subject of precise regulations for putting them on, removing them, and storing them.[51] Like the *zīr-jāma,* the breeches symbolized the prerequisite of *futūvat:* the moral chastity of the *javānmard* and the rupture with the inferior regions of man.[52] Binding the loins and waist have long been associated with chastity, virility, and readiness in a warrior; the loins were both the locus of male procreative power and the site of constant strict control through the medium of *ṭahārat,* or ritual purification, the precondition for character refinement.[53] Accordingly, in Kashifi's enumeration of the rules for the wearing of the leather breeches, concern is shown for the wrestler's bodily and ritual purity while wearing them as well as for his modesty and chastity at the vulnerable moment of undress.[54] Shirazi's description of Yusuf and his students preparing for the match against the Delhi wrestler dwells at length on the details of the rituals the heroes follow when putting on their breeches, reflecting their central importance in the *javānmardī* ethic.

The Centrality of Teaching

The didactic strand of the *javānmardī* ethic and the teacher's role within *javānmardī* organizations are clearly highlighted in Shirazi's description of Yusuf's *zūrkhāna.* Rather than turning to an individualistic attempt to refine his own body and character, Yusuf establishes a *zūrkhāna* and teaches his fellow cooks how to wrestle according to the Khorasani style. Every morning he submits them to rigorous exercise, including the use of the *kabāda* (millstone) and various wrestling moves, under his own guidance.[55]

The anxiety surrounding the teacher's role (*ustād*) penetrated to the core of the *javānmardī* ethic and reflected wider concerns about education in *Akhlāqi* literature. In his section on the *futūvat* of wrestlers, Kashifi identifies twelve rules of conduct for the teacher, which together summarize the whole ethical attitude of *javānmardī.*[56] Recalling the importance of ritual and bodily cleanliness as a prerequisite for character refinement, the first rules concern the ritual purity and bodily health of the teacher, and the importance of teaching those rules to the student (*shāgird*). The next rules concern his character traits, which again reflect the stock characteristics associated with *javānmardī:* a teacher should be generous and kind, not covetous, hypocritical, nor desirous of evil for his students. The importance of pedagogy not only as a technique for propagating the skills and underlying ethic of *javānmardī* but also as a way of behaving, which itself should be constantly subjected to refinement, is reflected in the next set of rules. A teacher should be gentle in correcting a student if he makes mistakes in wrestling, discreet when advising a student who is fighting in the arena, and punctilious in remembering his own teachers.[57] Finally, his own knowledge is stressed: he should be up-to-date in the science of wrestling, which Kashifi defines as knowledge of 1,080 moves and countermoves. Moreover, a perfect teacher should also be skilled in medicine, astrology, geomancy, magic, and physiognomy.[58]

The King and the Wrestler

Kingly patronage for wrestlers was widespread throughout the Persianate world.[59] The Mughal Emperor Akbar maintained a large number of Persian and Turani wrestlers and athletes from Hindustan and watched them fight daily. The wrestlers were paid a salary and given presents when they fought.[60] Kashifi notes that "wrestling is a skill which is acceptable and pleasing to kings and sultans, and the strongest of those occupied in this work are those who possess purity and rectitude."[61] By merging strength with perfect knowledge and justice, a wrestler represented not only the king but, by extension, the whole kingdom in his body. As Kashifi argues:

> Force (*qūvat*) without knowledge (*dānish*) is like an emperor without justice, and knowledge without force is like a just emperor without an army, but when knowledge and force are in harmony, together they bring affairs to their desired end.[62]

The arrival at Bidar of a wrestler from Delhi who had vanquished all the wrestlers of every town of Hindustan and Gujarat was therefore an implicit challenge to the Bahmani kingdom, and the defeat of the Bidar court wrestlers brought disgrace and severe loss of reputation to the Bahmani king. In this context, Yusuf's actions were of fundamental importance to the king and his kingdom, and yet, aware that his defeat would worsen the situation, Yusuf pleads for permission to challenge the Delhi champion, framing his request in terms of his current lowly social position:

> If I fall, it will become known that Yusuf the friend of the kitchen fell and if I throw him it will expel the vexation from the heart of the *pādshāh* [king] and I will be set free from my adversities.[63]

The awareness, inherent in this speech, of the likely rewards that would meet his success in the wrestling match remind us that, despite all efforts by the *futūvat* writers to spiritualize the *javānmardī* ethic, it remained a route to social mobility in a court society, where heroic deeds were liberally rewarded by the gifts of gold, jewels, and horses and the award of an office and rank. Indeed, Yusuf's reward for defeating the Delhi wrestler is an immediate promotion from cook to *kotwāl* (magistrate), followed by an expedition against highway robbers in Telingana to test his prowess on the real battlefield.[64]

The connection between Yusuf's final triumph as king of Bijapur and his early career as a wrestler is also significant. Kings themselves sometimes indulged in wrestling: feats of prodigious strength are attributed to the Mughal Emperor Akbar who wrestled and threw an older prince onto his back when he was only two, and in the Deccan to Mujahid Bahmani who challenged his father's spice bearer to a wrestling match while still a child and threw him so forcefully that he died.[65] Portuguese writers attest to the daily wrestling practice of Krishnaraya of Vijayanagar.[66] Even today success in the wrestling arena can lead to a political career, as the example of the former chief minister of Uttar Pradesh, Mulayum Singh Yadav, attests.[67]

The Match

The climax of Shirazi's narrative is of course, the wrestling match between Yusuf and the Delhi champion.[68] As a literary device, the account of the match encompasses and reiterates the characteristics of the wrestler in terms of a struggle between good and evil, a true *javānmard* and a false *javānmard,* with Yusuf's superiority to the Delhi wrestler demonstrated at every turn. First, in the preparations for the match, while the Delhi wrestler struts around arrogantly boasting of his prowess, Yusuf and his students arrive, salute the king, rub their bodies with powder, dress according to the ritual stipulations, and prostrate themselves before Mecca. Second, as a teacher, the sight of Yusuf and his students doing their limbering up exercises in the previously unseen Khorasani style fascinates the audience, draws fulsome praise from the sultan, and terrifies the Delhi wrestler to such an extent that his arms are left "dangling with fear."[69] Third, regarding the challenge, the arrogant Delhi wrestler, when confronted by Yusuf, claims that he is tired and tells Yusuf to fight one of his students instead. Rejecting a challenge was both unmanly and a breach of *adab,* and the Delhi wrestler does it not once but twice.[70] Yusuf then humiliates him with a direct attack on his knowledge of proper conduct (*adab*) and pretensions to be a true *javānmard,* saying:

> Following the order of the sultan is the conduct of a Turk, [and] according to the desire of the sultan it is now necessary to wrestle, so exert yourself in this affair.[71]

O'Hanlon has suggested that in the Mughal courts of North India, manliness was partly constructed in opposition to the effeminacy of the Deccan courts and the nobles from Transoxania.[72] Yusuf's provocative rebuke to the Delhi wrestler, which implies that the wrestler's refusal to fight must be attributed to the Delhi wrestler's unmanly race, and Shirazi's repeated emphasis on Yusuf's supremacy being the result of the *Khorasani* custom of wrestling suggest a reverse tendency in the Deccan. Shirazi's chronicle was written against the background of the Mughal threat to the Deccan, so the slur on the northerner's manliness would also have held a politically relevant message.

Finally, Yusuf proves his superiority in the arena, vanquishing the Delhi wrestler by a move that Kashifi refers to as the "mother of wrestling holds," carrying him on his thighs and throwing him down in front of the king with such force that he was no longer able to rise; a classic description of a victorious climax in a wrestling match, which mirrors the ideal moves recommended by Kashifi's *futūvat* treatise.[73]

The above discussion demonstrates how some of the lineaments of the "character" of the medieval Persian wrestler function in the construction of a moral exemplar embodying the ethic of *javānmardī.* Bodily beauty, disciplined participation in mundane work, submission to the regulations of an organized brotherhood, thoughtful engagement in pedagogy, devoted service to others, humility, and strict adherence to proper conduct, or *adab,* together form part of the character and the way of life of a true *javānmard.* In Shirazi's account, the detailed description of Yusuf's rise to prominence by following the ethic of a wrestler successfully presents him as a moral exemplar worthy of kingship. Both this account and the establishment of the *ta'līm k̲h̲āna* structuring the urban space of Bidar, suggest that wrestlers and gymnasiums, and the ethic of *javānmardī* they embodied, constituted one of the concrete answers to the Socratic question, "How should one live?" in the medieval Deccan.

The Historian as Ethical Critic

Shirazi's description of Yusuf Adil Shah's rise to prominence suggests that the ethic of *javānmardī* had gained support at the state level. Nevertheless not everyone approved of this way of life. Shirazi's colleague, the historian Firishta who had lived and worked in the courts of both Ahmadnagar and Bijapur, used his chronicle, *Tarīk̲h̲-i Firishta,* to express his opposition to the official sponsorship of a martial ethic. The ethical nature of the genre of historical chronicles in Persian is still frequently overlooked by modern scholars, yet, as Meisami has argued, the medieval historian's primary interest lay less in recording facts of history than in the construction of a meaningful narrative and, I would add, in the construction of an ethical reader.[74] By interspersing accounts of events with pithy versified aphorisms and recasting moral anecdotes drawn from a large store of classical literature, historians were able to build up a picture of an ideal man. It is against the background of this generic characteristic, then, that Firishta's account of the gymnasiums of Ahmadnagar should be viewed.[75]

Firishta attributes the Deccani custom of *yekung*, a kind of sword fighting, to the establishment of gymnasiums (*varzish-k̲h̲āna*) by Ahmad Nizam Shah in every street of Ahmadnagar "in place of the schoolhouses which are usually found in Islamic cities." The king's passion for this sport sparked a similar craze among both young and old men of the city. A culture of one-upmanship broke out among the youth, who would eventually resort to the king to arbitrate their *yekung* battles at court. The craze reached such proportions that two or three people were killed every day in the *dīvān-k̲h̲āna*. Eventually even the king wearied of the daily slaughter and refused to adjudicate any longer. Still the withdrawal of royal patronage did not stem the practice; rather, in Firishta's words:

> This depraved heresy (*bid'at*) of the Muslims of the Deccan passed from Ahmadnagar by means of the sultans of India and infected all the cities of the Deccan becoming excessively diffuse and lucrative (*rābiḥ*), and the victory of that odious practice so obliterated the hearts that at present the seekers of knowledge and the sheikhs and lords and amirs and the khans of the realm of the Deccan practice *yekung* and they give it such status and great skill and if their sons do not practice *yekung* they do not reckon them courageous and they rebuke them.[76]

Firishta then continues his narrative by citing a case he himself had witnessed in which six respectable men of noble descent—two of whom were "white beards," that is, old and wise—became embroiled in a *yekung* duel after a trivial incident in the bazaar and massacred each other in only a few minutes. In a challenge to accepted ideas of martial skills, courage and manliness, Firishta argued:

> It is abundantly clear that the Muslims of the Deccan are unrivaled in swordplay and *yekung* and no one can slight this art. One cannot oppose them with swords, [but] the end is that since men of the Deccan practice the exercise of swordplay on the surface of the earth, they are ignorant and useless at riding horses and throwing arrows and playing with spears and playing polo. Consequently in war the soldiers, particularly if the enemy is not Deccani [. . .] will be inadequate. In every battle they are the weakest but in domestic quarrels (*jang-i k̲h̲āna*) and narrow lanes and bazaars they are as fierce as lions and manly (*mardāna*).[77]

He concludes by making a plea for the other sultans of the Deccan to follow the examples of his patron, Ibrahim 'Adil Shah II, and of Muhammad Quli Qutb Shah, both of whom had prohibited *yekung*.

Firishta's attack on the practice of *yekung* could be explained by a mere dislike of a martial practice that had resulted in excessive bloodshed, rather than a criticism of the *javānmardī* ethic that motivated it. However, the implicit disapproval in his statement that the gymnasiums had replaced schools and that parents were imposing *yekung* on their children, as well as his use of the term "heresy" (*bid'at*), usually reserved for innovation in religion, imply a stronger criticism than simply distaste for bloodshed. In counterposing the real valor of the battlefield to the laughable valor of domestic quarrels and bazaar tiffs, Firishta is attacking the ethic of manliness created by such a practice and the excesses which that ethic produced.[78]

As a physician who had studied Indian medicine systems in depth, Firishta argues in a way that reflects a concern with moderation, balance, and equilibrium that informed both the medical and ethical thinking of his day.[79] By criticizing these examples of excess, Firishta may have been arguing for a reformed ethic of *javānmardī* or perhaps, more radically, for an ethic of daily living that was not so susceptible to excesses as one that fetishized both youth and manliness. Nevertheless his attack on this ethic should not be seen as a refutation of the underlying idea that physical discipline had a transformative effect on character. Unlike the writers of other chronicles such as the fourteenth-century Delhi Sultanate noble, Zia al-Din Barani, who clearly refuted the very principle that each man could transform his own character, Firishta clearly conceived of a universe where even external conditions such as climate and geography had the potential to transform the character of humans.[80] Indeed, it is precisely because physical discipline has the potential for such a transformative effect on character that it must be strictly controlled, if such perversions and excesses were to be avoided.

This essay has considered the ethic of *javānmardī* in both its theoretical underpinnings and in some of the ways in which it was lived out and negotiated in the daily experiences of the medieval Deccan. It has been argued that even though there is no overt textual evidence—for example, in the form of a treatise on *futūvat*—of the existence of this ethic in the Deccan, by looking more closely both at the physical environment, including the ruins of the *ta'līm k͟hānas,* and at episodes recounted in the Persian chronicles, we can see how this ethic was lived out in practice. By considering how an ethic was sometimes reduced to a "character," as in the case of the wrestler, or embodied in a physical structure, this essay suggests some strategies for exploring the diverse genealogies of ethics in premodern India. The absence of obvious sources forces us to investigate textual signifiers more carefully and to think more broadly about the complex socio-cultural worlds in which certain texts were being composed. Only in this way will the study of ethics in premodern India move beyond analyses of the classical ethical traditions embodied in foundational religious texts to concentrate, instead, on the daily experiences and practices of an ethical life, a life frequently lived in a land strikingly distant from the cultural world of that foundational text.

Notes

This essay owes its genesis to a brief footnote describing the *ta'līm ḵẖāna* in H. K. Sherwani, *The Bahmanis of the Deccan* (Delhi: Manoharlal, 1985), 136 n. 1. Although the idea, propounded in this essay, of wrestlers as ethical subjects bears some similarity to the findings of Joseph Alter's classic work, *The Wrestler's Body: Identity and Ideology in North India* (Berkeley: University of California Press, 1992), further work needs to be done on the historical intersections and divergences between the Indic and Islamicate traditions of wrestling in South Asia and the varying processes and theoretical understandings of formulating an ethical subject in each tradition. This issue merits a separate investigation and therefore has not been discussed here.

1. In the early twentieth century each *ta'līm ḵẖāna* included an *ashur ḵẖāna* (a place that houses copies of the standards carried by Imam Husain in the battle of Karbala) and an uncovered hall or arena for physical exercises. At least two of the *ta'līms* were located in close proximity to a mosque or a tomb. Each school is named after its founder; Siddiq Shah, Nur Khan, Maniyar, and Pansal. The *Ta'līm* Pansal contains the grave of a former teacher, Ustad Yār Muhammad. See G. Yazdani, *Bidar: Its History and Monuments* (Delhi: Motilal Banarsidas, 1995), 103–110.

2. Al-Ghazali, *On Disciplining the Soul, Kītāb riyāḍat al-nafs* and *On Breaking the Two Desires, Kitāb kasr al-shahwatayn,* books 22 and 23 of the *Revival of the Religious Sciences, Iḥyā' 'ulūm al-Dīn,* trans. and ed. T. J. Winter (Cambridge: Islamic Texts Society, 1995), 75. Nasir al-Dīn Tusi, *The Nasirean Ethics by Nasir ad-Din Tusi,* trans. and ed. G. M. Wickens (London: Allen and Unwin, 1964).

3. Kai Kā'ūs ibn Iskandar, *A Mirror for Princes: The Qabūsnāma by Kai Kā'ūs ibn Iskandar, Prince of Gurgān,* trans. and ed. Reuben Levy (London: Cresset, 1951), 49.

4. Abdelwahab Bouhdiba, *Sexuality in Islam,* trans. Alan Sheridan (London: Routledge and Kegan Paul, 1985), 34; Rosalind O'Hanlon, "Kingdom, Household and Body: History, Gender and Imperial Service under Akbar," *Modern Asian Studies* 41, no. 5 (2007): 26–27, discusses the popular belief in Mughal India that the beard drew its nourishment from semen. Bouhdiba quotes Al Hassan Ibn Dhakwam on the danger young boys can bring (*Sexuality,* 32).

5. Al-Ghazali, *Disciplining,* 77–79; Tusi, *Ethics,* 166ff.

6. Norbert Elias, "The Civilising of Parents," in *The Norbert Elias Reader: A Biographical Selection,* ed. Jouhan Goudsblom and Stephen Mennell (Oxford: Blackwell, 1998), 189–211.

7. Winter, *Disciplining,* xlv–lviii.

8. Ibid., xxvi–iii.

9. Bouhdiba, *Sexuality,* chap. 5.

10. Ibid., *Sexuality,* 49.

11. On the Arabic term *fatan* (young man; pl., *fityan,* abstract noun, *futūvat*), see Arley Loewen, "The Concept of *Jawānmardī* (manliness) in Persian Literature and Society" (Ph.D. diss., University of Toronto, 2001).

12. In the eleventh century *Qābūsnāma, javānmardī* is defined as both a series of professions and the constellation of virtues associated with each one. Four kinds of *javānmard* were distinguished: first, mercenaries, soldiers, and artisans; second, religious lawyers and Sufis; third, saints; and fourth, prophets (Kai Ka'us ibn Iskandar, *Qabūsnāma,* 239–263).

13. Instances from Unsuri, Firdausi, and Sa'di are cited in Muhammad Ja'far Mahjub, "Chivalry and Early Persian Sufism," in *The Heritage of Sufism, Classical Persian Sufism from Its Origins to Rumi (700–1300),* Vol. 1, ed. Leonard Lewisohn (Oxford: Oneworld, 1999), 549–582.

14. Loewen, "Concept," chap. 1.

15. Ibn Battuta described the competitive displays of skills and hospitality among the various urban *futūvat* brotherhoods in Anatolia. See G. G. Arnakis, "Futuwwa Traditions in the Ottoman Empire: Akhis, Bektashi Dervishes, and Craftsmen," *Journal of Near Eastern Studies* 12, no. 4 (1953): 232–247.

16. Loewen, "Concept," 13, argues that by the time of Uthman Hujwiri (d 1072), the first author of a Persian treatise on Sufism, the terms *javānmardī, futūvat, 'ayyari,* and *tasavuf* (Sufism) were interrelated.

17. Henry Corbin, Introduction to *Traités des compagnons-chevaliers (Rasa'il-e Jawanmardān): Recueil de sept "Fotowwat-nameh,* ed. Morteza Sarraf (Tehran/Paris: Département d'Iranologie de l'institut Franco-Iranien de Recherche/Librairie d'Amérique et d'Orient Adrien-Maisonneuve, 1973); henceforth, *RJ.*

18. Muhammad Riyaz, *Aḥwāl wa āsār wa ashā 'r-i Mir Sayyid al-Hamadānī* (Islamabad: n.p., 1991), 328–334, lists thirty medieval works on *futūvat.* See Arley Loewen, "Proper Conduct (*Adab*) is Everything: The *Futuwwat-nāmah-i Sulṭāni of Husain Vaiz-i Kashifi,*" *Iranian Studies* 36, no. 4 (2003): 543–570 n. 3. See also Sarraf, ed., *RJ* and Husain Vaiz Kashifi, *Futuwwat-nāmah-i Sulṭāni ta'līf-i Ḥusayn Vā'iẓ Kāshifi Sabzavārī,* ed. Muḥammad Ja'far Maḥjūb (Tehran: Intisharat-i Bunyad-i Farhang-i Iran, 1350/1971); henceforth, *FNS.* On *adab,* see Barbara Metcalfe, ed., *Moral Conduct and Authority: The Place of Adab in South Asian Islam* (Berkeley: University of California Press, 1984).

19. Corbin, Introduction to Amuli, in Sarraf, *RJ.* Detailed gradations of hierarchy between teacher and initiates are suggested in Amuli's *Futūvat-nama* (ca. 14th century), which lists twenty-five technical terms used by *futūvat* associations.

20. Jean Calmard, "The Iranian Merchants: Formation and Rise of a Pressure Group between the Sixteenth and Nineteenth Centuries," in *Asian Merchants and Businessmen in the Indian Ocean and the China Sea,* ed. Denys Lombard and Jean Aubin (New Delhi: Oxford University Press, 2000).

21. For the initiation ceremony, see the *Futūvat-nāmas* of Kashani, Amuli, and Tabrizi in Sarraf, *RJ.*

22. See the *Futūvat-nāma* of Amuli in Sarraf, *RJ.*

23. A *kabāda,* or *lezam,* is a practice bow with an iron chain rather than a bowstring and is used to increase upper-body strength. See D. C. Majumdar, *Encyclopaedia of Indian Physical Culture* (Baroda: Good Companions, 1950), 19–20.

24. Husayn Partaw Bayẕā'ī Kāshānī, *Ṯārīkẖ-i varzish-i bāstānī-i Īrānī zūrkhānah* (Tihrān: Intishārāt-i Zavvār, 1382 [2003 or 2004]).

25. Kashifi, *FNS,* 310–311.

26. Michel Foucault, *The History of Sexuality: The Use of Pleasure,* Vol. 2 (London: Penguin Books, 1992), 1–32.

27. Saba Mahmood, *Politics of Piety: the Islamic Revival and the Feminist Subject* (Princeton, N.J.: Princeton University Press, 2005).

28. Corbin, Introduction to Kashani, in Sarraf, *RJ.*

29. Corbin notes that in Kashani the literal meaning of *tawāẓu'* is modesty or humility but that it also has a more precise nuance: everything that is comprehended by *muruvat* (manliness)—courtesy, civility, willingness, attentiveness, and a sense of hospitality (Introduction to Kashani, in Sarraf, *RJ.*

30. Ruh al-Amin, *Falak al-Burūj* Khuda Bhaksh Oriental Public Library, Patna, Ms. No. 302, fol. 73v.

31. *Pahlavān,* the word used in the epics for hero, later became synonymous with the more precise word for wrestlers, *kushtī-gīr* (literally, belt seizer). See Loewen, "Concept," chap. 4.

32. Ibid.

33. Kashifi, *FNS,* 307–308.

34. Alasdair MacIntyre, *After Virtue: a Study in Moral Theory* (Notre Dame, Ind.: University of Notre Dame Press, 2007), 27ff. Roland Barthes's seminal essay on wrestling in France makes a similar point when he argues that the highly dramatized theatrical displays in the wrestling arena are a result of the wrestlers assuming certain character roles immediately recognizable to both the spectators and their adversary ("The World of Wrestling," in *Mythologies,* trans. Annette Lavers [New York: Hill and Wang, 1984]).

35. Tusi, *Ethics,* 108ff.

36. Ibid., 48ff.

37. Ibid., 230; Louise Marlow, *Hierarchy and Egalitarianism in Islamic Thought* (Cambridge: Cambridge University Press, 1997); A. K. S. Lambton, "Justice in the Medieval Persian Theory of Kingship," *Studia Islamica* 17 (1962): 91–119; E. I. J. Rosenthal, *Political Thought in Medieval Islam* (Cambridge: Cambridge University Press, 1962).

38. Charles Hallisey, "Relevance and Moral Action in Theravada Buddhism," paper presented at the conference "Genealogies of Virtues: Ethical Practice in South Asia," University of British Columbia, Canada, September 6–8, 2007.

39. The only exception to this is Rosalind O'Hanlon who has written a series of groundbreaking articles on martial practices in India, including "Military Sports and the History of the Martial Body in India," *Journal of the Economic and Social History of the Orient (JESHO)* 50, no. 4 (2007): 490–523; and "Kingdom, Household, and Body," and "Manliness and Imperial Service in Mughal North India," *JESHO* 42, no. 1 (1999): 47–93. O'Hanlon approaches *javānmardī* as a philosophical idea underpinning particular constructions of gender among the Mughals, whereas the present essay attempts to consider *javānmardī* as a lived ethical system.

40. It seems likely, for example, given the Bahmani vizier Mahmud Gawan's frequent correspondence with the poet Jami, that he may have come into contact with the work of Jami's son-in-law, Husain Va'iz Kashifi, whose voluminous *Futūvat Nāma-i Sulṯāni* incorporated much of the earlier work on *futūvat* and *javānmardī.* See H. K.

Sherwani, *Mahmud Gawan, the Great Bahmani Wazir* (Allahabad: Allahabad Law Journal Press, 1942). On the polymathic Kashifi, see Maria E. Subtelny, ed., *Iranian Studies* 36, no. 4 (2003) (special issue).

41. Yazdani, *Bidar,* 102–110.

42. Rafi' al-din Shirazi, *Tazkirat al-Mulūk,* Ethe No. 2838, Ms. I.O. Islamic 3541 (esp. ff. 17–20b); hereafter, *TM.* I also compared this manuscript to Rieu, Vol. 1, British Museum, Additional Mss., 23,883. All references hereafter refer to the Ethe Ms.

43. Loewen, "Concept," chap. 4.

44. Amuli, in Sarraf, *RJ.*

45. Julie Scott Meisami, *Medieval Persian Court Poetry* (Princeton, N.J.: Princeton University Press, 1987), esp. chap. 3.

46. *TM* f. 18v.

47. Ibid.

48. Lowen, "Proper Conduct," 547.

49. Ibid., 564.

50. Remarkable similarities are found in the initiation ceremony of the *Khalsa panth,* for example.

51. For the rules on wearing or removing the breeches, see Kashifi, *FNS,* 310.

52. Corbin, Introduction to *RJ,* in Sarraf, 19.

53. O'Hanlon, "Manliness," 64, points out that the Persian phrases "*kamar band*" or "*kamar basta*"—literally, "waist bound up"—signified a man ready for service, bravery, and heroism, whereas "*susti-yi kamar,*" or "feeble-waisted," signified both physical and sexual impotence. As she further remarks, a strong waist was essential for wielding heavy weapons on horseback, a vital skill in a warrior culture.

54. Kashifi, *FNS,* 310.

55. *TM,* f. 18r.

56. Kashifi, *FNS,* 308.

57. These rules reflect the ideal relationship between teacher and student in akhlāqi literature and in the earlier *futūvat* treatises. See Corbin, Introduction to *RJ,* in Sarraf, on Suhrawardi's second treatise, and compare Tusi, *Ethics,* on the regulation of children, 166–177.

58. Kashifi, *FNS,* 309.

59. See Abul Fazl-i-'Allami, *'Ain-i Akbarī,* trans. H. Blochman (Delhi: Low Price, 2006), 1:262–263.

60. Ibid., 263.

61. Kashifi, *FNS,* 306.

62. Ibid., 308.

63. *TM,* f. 25b.

64. *TM,* f. 20r and following.

65. H. Beveridge, trans. and ed., *The Akbarnama of Abul Fazl* (Calcutta: Asiatic Society, 2000), 1:455–456; and Briggs, *Rise of the Mahomedan Power,* 1:203–204.

66. Majumdar, *Physical Culture,* introduction.

67. Sutapa Mukherjee, "'Kushti Evolved Here, It Flows in Our Blood': Interview with Mulayam Singh Yadav," *Outlook India,* May 22, 2000. Available at http://www.outlookindia.com/full.asp?fodname=20000522&fname=wrestling&sid=2 (accessed September 17, 2008).

68. *TM,* ff. 19r–20r.

69. *TM,* f. 20v.

70. Loewen, "Concept," 243, gives an account of the fight between Pahlawan Muhammad and Pahlawan Muhammad Malani.

71. *TM,* f. 20v.

72. O'Hanlon, "Kingdom, Household, and Body," 5, 22.

73. Kashifi, *FNS,* 311–312.

74. Julie Scott Meisami, *Persian Historiography to the End of the Twelfth Century* (Edinburgh: Edinburgh University Press, 1999).

75. Muhammad Qasim Hindu Shah Firishta, *Tarīkẖ-i Firishta,* ed. John Briggs and Mir Khairat Ali Khan (Kanpur: Naval Kishore, 1884), 1:101–102; Briggs, *Mahomedan Power,* 2:127–128.

76. That the practice of *yekung* was common at the court of Bijapur is confirmed by the description in 'Ali Adil Shah's encyclopaedic work, *Nujūm al-'Ulum,* of how to draw two kinds of astrological tables to predict the outcome of a *yekung* battle. Since these tables could predict not only the victor but also the places on the body that each fighter would be injured and with which part of the stick, they may have been used in conjunction with gambling—hence Firishta's description of *yekung* as lucrative. See *Nujūm al 'Ulum,* Wellcome Library, Persian Mss. 373, f. 67.

77. Firishta, *Tarīkẖ-i Firishta,* 102.

78. Firishta's earlier account of Mujahid Bahmani who had the epithet Balwant, or strong, similarly detailed how this king, while still a prince, had challenged his father's spice bearer to a wrestling match and, lacking moderation or self-control, killed him. After a short tyrannical reign, Mujahid was killed by the son of the murdered spice bearer. See Briggs, *Mahomedan Power,* 1:203–204.

79. Firishta was also the author of a *materia medica* based on Sanskrit sources. See *Dastūr al-ạṭibbā,* Ethe No. 2318, Ms. I. O. Islamic 2364.

80. Compare Zia al Din Barani, in Afsar Afzal ud din, "The Fatawa-i Jahandari of Zia al-Din Barani" (Ph.D. diss., SOAS, 1955), 412–429, to Firishta, *Dastūr al-ạṭibbā,* ff. 223r–224v.

9.

Ethical Subjects: Time, Timing, and Tellability

Leela Prasad

"The things above the sky, the things below the earth, and the things between the earth and the sky, as well as all those things people here refer to past, present and future—on what, Yāgnavalkya, are all these woven back and forth?" asks Gargi, the daughter of Vācaknāvi, in a well-known *Upaniṣadic* dialogue on the nature of existence.[1] Yāgnavalkya, the sage, replies that all forms and time itself are woven on space, and space is ultimately woven on that which is imperishable. The Sanskrit term for imperishable is *akṣara,* which also means "syllable" and implies "word" or "speech," making time-consciousness and temporal movements (the back and forth on the warp of space) simultaneous with the act of expression. This ancient metaphor of weaving teases out one of the most important insights of the *Upaniṣads*—that a fabric of connectedness binds time, space, and expression in ethical relationships—and leads me in this essay to reflect on how time and ethical praxis are interwoven in oral narrative.[2] I situate this exploration in the more immediate ethnographic locale of Sringeri in the Malnad ghats of south India through two narrations that were shared with me of a boat accident that occurred on the river Tunga in the 1970s. Analyzing these narrations in the contexts of the lives and reflections of narrators, I show how narrative works to make ethical connections between "the past" and "the present." How could the timing of gestures become layered with moral significance? How is the tellability of an experience conditioned by the tacit understanding that the temporal is a moral phenomenon? In attending to the poetics of temporality embedded in these recollections (that include my participation), I hope to evoke the particular commentary they make on how ethical subjectivities create, are intertwined with, and are shaped by imaginations of time. I end with a reflection on what indeed might remain "imperishable" in the experience of narrative. Ultimately the essay is an attempt to understand empathy—a gestalt of timing, gestures, memories, and retellings—which is fundamental to the intersubjective relationships that shape the ethical self and its expression.

The Context of Sringeri

Sringeri has been historically connected to a monastic institution (*maṭha*) that, since its establishment in the eighth century CE by Śaṅkara, has traditionally specialized in interpreting Hindu codes of conduct known collectively as the *Dharmaśāstras* (or the "*śāstras*" in daily usage). Compiled by different authors approximately between 500 BCE and 400 CE, the Dharmaśāstras discuss, in impressive diversity and detail, a wide variety of topics relating to social and religious conduct, law, and righteousness. For twelve hundred years the *maṭha* has counseled its followers on a broad range of ethical subjects including royal diplomacy, property disputes, marriage alliances, travel and business propositions, and worship. Over the centuries, as records of the *maṭha* as well as other inscriptional sources tell us, the *maṭha* grew into a powerful monastic institution with significant political leverage, evident in its relationships and negotiations with rulers such as Vijayanagara emperors, the Mysore Wodeyars, the local Keladi kings, Muslim and Maratha rulers, or even the colonial British administration. Without going into details here, I will simply note that the tax-exempt (*sarvamānya*) gift of nine villages in 1346 by the Vijayanagara rulers Harihara and Bukka to the guru Bharati Tīrtha began a six-century tradition of land gifting and other endowments to the *maṭha*. I have argued in my longer work on Sringeri that this tradition carefully charts moral and material reciprocities that evolved between patronage and counsellorship, on the one hand, and landowner and tenants, on the other.[3] Until the 1960s and the 1970s, when land-reform legislation altered its economic status, the *maṭha* owned and governed Sringeri as an independent land-grant state (*jāgirdāri*) through an intimate web of tenancy relationships with local populations.[4] Sringeri's history, from one perspective, is intertwined with the history of the *maṭha*—its sociopolitical networks, its spiritual lineages, its adherents and dissidents, and its temples. This ethos of interrelationships that has made Sringeri a significant sacred center is enriched by the region's reputation for the performance of *upacāra*, specifically understood as traditions of hospitality (in which both the *maṭha* as a local host and the townspeople participate) but, more broadly, concerns appropriateness in conduct.

Yet, from another perspective, it is crucial to note that a *maṭha*-centered configuration of the "historical record" of Sringeri does not call up the many ways in which oral histories of Sringeri tell the story of how Sringeri came to be *experienced* as a geocultural location and how it is remembered. These histories trace particular inter-family dynamics, or family-*maṭha* negotiations, recount the emergence of new agrarian or tourist markets, chart the successes and failures of local businesses, narrate the dramas surrounding municipal elections, and describe the vivid traditions of dance dramas and fairs. The *maṭha* itself is hardly a faceless monolithic institution exuding nothing but some generic version of "brahminical dominance," as those outside Sringeri tend to perceive it; rather, for locals, it is a *peopled* place with relationships that have always accommodated contestations and cooperations, distance and affiliations. In its varied contexts of usage, "the *maṭha*" could index a guiding institution, metonymically refer to the Sharada temple, and stand for a symbol of a particular period of history or as a voice in contemporary politics. Generally people associate with one or two specific gurus of the *maṭha* (which follows the lineage system) whom they regard as their personal guru, and such reverence informs their routines and ideals, and their assessments of the *maṭha*'s current practices.

This essay seeks to extend my previous research in Sringeri, in which I have argued that stories heard and told in conversation, stylized performance traditions, and the multitude of seeing-and-doing orientations that characterize everyday life (often displaced in studies of Hindu ethics) reveal in profound ways how individuals and communities engage in moral theorization and practice.[5] Everyday life, full of refractions, demands that notions which inform the ethical self—notions of the normative, of "text," of moral authority, or of propriety, for example—need to be kept in flux as they critically involve the agency of imagination.[6] In Sringeri the shelling of harvested arecanut, the practice of Malnad cooking, the thatching of roofs with areca fronds, or the performing of hospitality reflect distinctive literacies which recognize that particular practices and moral orientations are embedded in each other and are reflected in the routines of everyday life.[7] A study of the histories of specific practices (such as, in Sringeri, the co-ownership of one's home and lands with a deity, the temporary assumption of secular power by renunciants who enact erstwhile courtly rituals, and the narration of place stories) delineates interlinked contours of intangible but influential conceptions of "ethos." Jürgen Habermas rightly observes, "As long as moral philosophy concerns itself with clarifying the everyday intuitions into which we are socialized, it must be able to adopt at least virtually the attitude of someone who participates in the communicative practice of everyday life."[8] However, his "discourse ethics" remains rooted in a search for universal norms that are arrived at through intersubjective recognition by "free" individuals bound to one another by tacit solidarities. Ultimately, therefore, I find that discourse ethics, with its predetermined commitment to the discovery of universal moral imperatives, misses the lived vivacity and debates of "everyday moral intuitions." The promise of the "phenomenology of the moral," which Habermas draws from the British moral philosopher Peter Strawson, cannot be realized by the program he specifies for it.[9]

With the broad contexts of Sringeri in mind, I now turn to the two narrations of the boat tragedy. I heard the first complete recounting of this episode from Dodda Murthy (whose official name is N. S. Lakshminarasimha Murthy), who is in his late-eighties as I write this in 2008. My association with him and his wife, Chayamma, goes back to my childhood when my parents and I would visit Sringeri's temples, and we would not pass up the opportunity to enjoy Chayamma's delectable meals which she lovingly cooked for us. Nor would I, even though I had only a limited understanding of Kannada then, pass up the opportunity to listen to my father and Dodda Murthy trade stories of Sringeri, and of the days when my grandfather lived there in the 1950s. Although in the years after these early visits we remained sporadically in touch with the Murthy family, during the last fifteen years that began with my doctoral research I have became close to many people in Sringeri, and especially to Dodda Murthy and Chayamma as well as the extended family that lives in the same house, a two-hundred-year-old house rich with the character of Malnad architecture. Dodda Murthy retired as a schoolteacher, never quite having taken to farming, leaving the cultivation of the family's lands to his brother's family. Deeply influenced by Gandhi and the time he spent in Gandhi's ashram in Sevagram in the early 1940s, Dodda Murthy brought alive for me a lived experience of the independence struggle through a description of the speeches he had thronged to hear, the protest marches he had joined, and local negotiations between Sringeri's residents and British administrators over property and surveillance.

Dodda Murthy's stories about incidents that had taken place decades ago (some of which I recorded twice with an intervening gap of ten years) were nearly the same in emphasis and detail. These were not the rehearsed performances of an accomplished storyteller; rather, they came from his unshakeable conviction, as he said, to "stick to facts," a conviction that also has to do with how he has preserved, through his life, documents, clippings of news items, invitations, old books, photographs, almanacs, and a journal (that he has now discontinued to write). History, especially the documented past, fascinates him. Our conversations were anchored in stories that came from his rich archives of memory and documents. One evening, in 1995, Dodda Murthy visited my apartment (I lived down the street from him). I mentioned in conversation that I had been chatting that afternoon with Giridhara Shastry, a college lecturer and social worker in Sringeri (formerly the administrator of the *maṭha*). Dodda Murthy had often encouraged me to consult Giridhara Shastry, as he felt his knowledge in various subjects—philosophy, culture, and the *maṭha*'s history—would be of help to me. On this day Dodda Murthy asked if I had heard how Giridhara Shastry's father had met a tragic death many years ago. I told him I had heard that it had been an accident but was unaware of the details, and asked how it happened.[10] The following is my translation of the taped original which was in Kannada.

DM: The family was big into Kannada literature and that kind of thing.

When scholars came to the maṭha, *they would invite them home and arrange lectures. They would invite luminaries for lectures.*

Every *week they would host an hour-long lecture.*

Even in the maṭha, *he was very involved in all the programs, making the arrangements, running around.*

He was this way . . . and then, what a tragic end (duranta) *he had, you know.*

It was during the monsoon, a very heavy monsoon that year. He went across the river to see the guru—apparently it had been a while since he had had the guru's darśan *("seeing" for obtaining blessings). The husband and wife both went for the darśan of the guru. So they went, and there used to be the* dōṇi *(boat)—*

L: Yes, there was no bridge then . . .

DM: No bridge, the dōṇi would ferry people across the river. And the river was full then.

As soon as they went, they had the darśan of the guru . . .

L: Oh, they did *reach the other side!*

DM: Yes, yes, they reached the other side.

(DM pauses for some time to drink the milk I had offered him)

Let me finish this and then tell you the rest of it.

It isn't right to drink milk immediately after recounting a tragic incident.

L: Oh.

DM: He was a very good person.

L: It's hard to know what is written, isn't it? (i.e, "hard to know what is destined")

DM: The older son too—also very erudite. Now I've forgotten his name . . . he lived here for many years. I used to know him well.

(referring to the younger son) *A very honest person.*

L: True . . . when one talks to him, one feels that right away. A very sattvic (virtuous, good) person.

DM: A very sattvic man, yes.

. . .

I like the milk when it is this hot! Coffee, too.

(I have omitted here a brief discussion that follows: DM tells me of how hot or cold he likes his food; I mention my own preferences)

(Sound of cup being set down.)

So, to get back.

It was a very heavy monsoon season.

It was pouring.

Rain and wind, the month of āśāḍha.

So he went (to the bank where the gurus reside).

As soon as he went, the guru met him.

He had to report something to the guru, must have been something to do with the maṭha.

It was 10 in the morning.

On seeing him, the guru said, "What is this, you've come in the cold in just a pance *(more commonly known as* dhoti, *a cloth wrap worn by men)! It's so cold and windy and all you've worn is this* pance.

Couldn't you have draped a shawl?"

Calling out to one of the disciples, the guru said, "Bring him a shawl!"

The shawl was brought, a new shawl.

"Cover yourself warmly and go. It's cold."

So after their meeting, they left.

As soon as they reached the riverbank, there was this dōṇi—making trips back and forth—that was about to leave. There were many people on it, though.

His wife said, "Let this ferry go, let's take the next one."

But he said, "I have a lot of work. I have to go to the bank, and there are many errands to do. Let's take it."

So they got in.

L: Both of them?

DM: Yes, husband and wife, both.

They were almost here, on this side.

Just as they reached the bank on this side, the boat hit the bank with some force.

The impact was such that it overturned.

L: Ayyo.

DM: All of them fell out.

Those who could swim came out of the water.

His wife somehow managed to come out of the water.

L: Was it deep?

DM: No, but the current was strong and the river was flowing fast.

Two-three were drowned.

L: Ayyo.

DM: There was one woman too.

They pulled her body out.

I saw this (the body) *with my own eyes.*

They pulled her body out immediately, but his body, they didn't find it.
L: Oh no, they never found it?
DM: It was swept away in the current.
Then, the son came.
But what could he do? (in a low tone)
He took his mother home.
The body was found three days later.

Embedded in Dodda Murthy's recollection are several temporalities that point to the ethical orientations of the narrative. Images from the past string themselves in a way as to remind one of how Giridhara Shastry's father is remembered in the collective imagination of Sringeri: this was a man who had been committed to learning and to social service, whose voluntary and energetic involvement in the *maṭha*'s literary and religious activities had established his, and indeed his family's, respect in the community. Dodda Murthy's recognition, "He was a very good person" is grounded in his tracing of the daily and periodic activities of the elder Shastry, but it is this very dailyness of his selfless living that makes it harder for us to reconcile the manner of his death. This obscurity of destiny is indexed by my remark, "Who can predict . . ."

As I thought about the incident later on, I was struck by how well-known Hindu frameworks resonated sadly and ironically in the episode: Sringeri was a greatly desired *tīrtha*—literally, "crossing place"—the Sanskrit term for a place of pilgrimage. As Diana Eck notes, "The river, the crossing, and the far shore have formed an important symbolic complex in the Indian imaging of transition and transcendence. While the word employed in speaking of such passages may not always derive from the *tīr* root ["to cross over"], the specific image of fording the river flood to the far shore remains a key image and is utilized in a variety of contexts."[11] In a *tīrtha,* pilgrims can experience an immersion in a place made potent by the descent and presence of divine beings. Usually located on the banks of a sacred river, a *tīrtha* is a spiritual ford, the crossing of which ensures a pilgrim an unhindered transition to the "far shore" where one is liberated from the cycle of birth and death. Worldliness, birth, and death are things of the "near shore." Pilgrimages are therefore considered transformative. Crucially, "it is a crossing which must be made with the aid of a guide, a guru, and by means of the knowledge he imparts."[12] While Dodda Murthy did not allude to any of these frameworks, it was common knowledge in Sringeri that a few families, including the elder Shastry's, had relocated to Sringeri to live in this *tīrtha,* especially to live in the vicinity of their guru.

Aside from this metaphysical temporality that links life and afterlife, a reading I develop as I reflect on the tragedy in the context of the family's reasons for moving to Sringeri from Mysore, another kind of temporality is at work in the physical realities Dodda Murthy describes. First, anyone familiar with Sringeri immediately registers the visual transformation that occurs in Sringeri's landscape during an unusually heavy monsoon. Though ordinarily the Tunga has a fecund place in Sringeri's folklore and folklife, the monsoon season brings out the *might* of the fast-flowing Tunga, whose water level is popularly measured by the number of steps on the bank that the waters have covered.[13] This is not the same summer river into which tourists wade to feed puffed rice to fish. Second, the tragedy pivots a crucial change that took place in the geography of Sringeri: a bridge was soon built over the river replacing the age-old ferry system. Now connecting the temple complex on the town side with the guru's residence in the secluded Narasimha gardens, the bridge makes both sites more accessible to residents and visitors than ever before. These temporalities—indexed by the monsoon season and the new construction (which suggests the "before" and "after" of the tragedy)—are intertwined with the "actual" sequence of events Dodda Murthy recounts as having taken place on that tragic morning. Through this sequential narrative, practices that are deeply familiar to Sringeri residents, such as crossing the Tunga or visiting the guru for *darśan,* keep the episode proximal, not in chronological time but in quotidian practice and time. Similarly "everyday" conversations like that between Giridhara Shastry's father and the guru about the shawl, or that between the couple about errands that needed to be done, bring the experience into a familiar temporality. But beyond this familiarity of specific routines is the temporality of *everydayness* itself that makes a powerful moral formulation. In other words, our recognition of the disquieting implications of a sudden truncation of routine—the ordinary experience of time—closes the gaps between the then and the now, the them and the us, and contributes to the formation of ethical relationships between actors in the narrative, narrators, and listeners.

Dodda Murthy's deliberate drinking of the milk before resuming his narration of the episode singularly impressed me with how oral narration is itself an ethical act. What work does the digression into "hot and cold food" do? Is it even a digression at all? Although the tragedy has become absorbed into Sringeri tellings of its history, for Dodda Murthy *this* instance of narration charted an ethical continuum between two prominent time frames: the tragic time he describes (time in the narrative) and the time when he narrated this episode to me (time of the narrative). An unremarkable gesture of hospitality—my offering him a glass of milk—created an ethico-temporal continuum in which the past witnesses the present, making it inappropriate (*anaucitya*) to speak of the death of somebody one has known and respected and to *simultaneously* perform actions that contribute to a feeling of satisfaction, however mundane these actions may be.[14] Indeed, the mundane *is* the space for moral articulations, and it is in the mundane that "speech" and "doing" are ethically germane to each other. By this understanding, the full import of which I grasped over the years when I began to notice what else I was doing when speaking about death, "tragedy" and "satisfaction" are tacitly identified as morally incompatible. This incompatibility had circumscribed the tellability of the episode, and spontaneously heeding this, Dodda Murthy created a gap in time between the act of drinking milk and the act of narrating the episode. The digression was a necessary deferral of narration so that the life being spoken about could continue to occupy the place of respect it had earned in its lifetime.

Ten years later I heard this episode recounted again, this time by Giridhara Shastry's mother, whom everyone in Sringeri knows as Ajji ("Grandmother"). Now in her late eighties, Ajji lives in the town of Sringeri with Giridhara Shastry, where the latter teaches English at the local college. When I first met them they lived in Vidyaranyapura, a brisk fifteen-minute walk from Sringeri. Wherever they have lived their house was always bustling with neighborhood children, college youth, and other visitors. Outside of his teaching duties at the college and his own writing projects, Giridhara Shastry conducts many volunteer services such as providing Sanskrit and yoga lessons, running a homeopathy clinic, and teaching recitation. Ajji participates in many of these activities, but most characteristic is her daily visit to the temple, sometimes a good thirty-minute walk. Ajji had been raised in Mysore in a large joint family and married at a young age into the extended family. She once told me that she never worried about whether something was scripturally right; her yardstick was always what she had learned from her grandmother and her uncle, a professor of Kannada at Mysore University. She told me, "I never had any doubts and as such have not consulted anyone." On one occasion, we had been talking about the meaning of "*śāstra*" in everyday usage, and I asked her what she thought about the preponderance of shastric discourse on how one ought to live. Ajji responded that, while she observed certain ritual activity as legislated by relevant *śāstras,* ethics, in her view, eventually came down to family traditions, a sense of fulfillment (*manas trupti*), and, above all, consideration for others.

In the particular context of the narrative I now explore, we had been talking about how she and her husband had moved to Sringeri in the early 1970s after his retirement from a government position in Mysore. She described how he spent his retirement editing works of philosophy, teaching neighborhood children the *Bhagavad Gīta* and school lessons, and helping with *maṭha* -related events. "Not for money or anything," she added. "He used to think, '*They* [children] are the *devatas* [gods].' He didn't feel 'Oh that child or this child shouldn't be allowed [to the place of worship, for example],' and he didn't tell them 'You can't touch this or that.'" I had not anticipated that the conversation, which I recorded on tape, would start on the subject of her current daily routines and drift into a recollection of her husband's retired life and the life-changing loss she had experienced. Her reminiscences reminded me that routines are filled with traces of the past.[15]

AJJI: He would go to the samādhi *side of the river only when he wanted the guru's* darśan.[16]

He'd finish his pūja *(prayers) at home, eat some food, and then go for* darśan. *He would stay with children out there and teach them* stōtras *(sacred verses) and so on. He wasn't accustomed to just sitting in front of the guru or at the* samādhi.

L: In those days I suppose one had to take the dōṇi *to get to the other side.*

AJJI: Yes, one had to take the dōṇi. *When he went on the* dōṇi, *he did not worry about* mailige *(pollution).*

L: The bridge came later.

AJJI: Yes, later. When the boat overturned and he drowned, the guru immediately had the bridge built.

L: How did he fall in? Was he alone? I heard . . .

AJJI: No . . . I too had gone with him that day.

L: Oh yes, you were with him (remembering this detail from conversations of many years ago).

AJJI: We had gone for the guru's darśan *and had received the* tīrtha *(sanctified water). He had been translating a* stōtra *of Shankara.*

The guru remarked, "That's enough. You don't have to write any more. It will be a strain on you at your age."

My son had gone on the earlier dōṇi.

A police dignitary (she names him) *was visiting Sringeri, and he spent some time chatting with him.*

Fourteen of us took the next dōṇi. (The dignitary did not go on the boat, I gathered).

L: Hanh.

AJJI: He even chatted with the dōṇi *boy, "Which school do you go to?" "What class are you in?" That kind of thing. He talked with the boy all through the ride.*

L: Hanh.

AJJI: The dōṇi *reached the other bank and stopped.*

The person behind us stepped off the dōṇi *onto the bank's steps, and—it overturned.*

L: Ayyo.

AJJI: The dōṇi *boy, he [her husband], and one woman, all three were drowned.*

L: The river was full, wasn't it?

AJJI: . . .?

L: So where were you waiting?

AJJI: What can we do? (ignores L's question).

L: So where had you been waiting?

AJJI: I too fell out of the dōṇi *but they pulled me out of the water.*

My karma *was still unspent, right?*

L: hmm, yes.

AJJI: Right? (with some emphasis).

L: I suppose so.

AJJI: Then they came and asked, the police.

They wanted a statement.

I refused to give it.

I said, "It was our fault. Our stepping out of the boat turned it over."

That was all that happened.

Why should we bring hardship on others? (referring perhaps to the dōṇi owners).

L: I suppose one must think that that was all the life span (āyuś) *he had. . . .*

AJJI: Yes. That's it.

L: Then everybody came?

AJJI: He was found after three days.

L: Oh.

AJJI: Somewhere it is said in our śāstras *that when a woman gets married and goes to her husband's home, she desires all the pleasures of life—isn't that correct?*

Jewelry, nice saris, a comfortable life, and so on.

When the object of all pleasure itself is lost, what do we need all this for?

I had got made all the jewelry I wanted, but that day I gave away anything anybody asked for.

L: Really?

AJJI: I didn't keep anything.

I had no desire for those things.

Desire, *that is what needs to be given up.*

L: So you gave away everything? Everything?

AJJI: Yes. The woman who pulled me out of the river, she said, "Amma, give me your bangles" (a key symbol of a woman's marital status).

I gave them to her.

I had many silk saris.

She asked for a sari.

I gave it.

L: Who asked for this? (aghast).

(Ajji continues to say something but L insists on an answer.)

I mean, Ajji, who asked? Why, I mean they saw you fall into the water and still asked for your things. . . .?

AJJI: The woman who pulled me out, the boatman's daughter, asked me.

L: But why *did she ask?*

AJJI: Ask what?

L: For your bangles.

AJJI: Why should I ask anybody when I want to give away my things?

L (realizing she has been unclear in her question): *No, no, I meant, why did that woman ask you?*

AJJI: "Amma, will you give me your bangles?" she said, and I said, "Okay, take them." I've never asked anybody's permission to give away things.

The more you keep things, the more desires are born. Isn't this true?

L: That's true, Ajji.

AJJI: I had a lot of silver vessels.
I gave them away to my daughter-in-law.
They do all the vratas *and* pūjas *I used to do.*
"You use them now," I told her.

In Ajji's narration, too, time is marked in complex ways that intertwine, mingle, and jolt conventional demarcations of past, present, and future. The visit to see the guru, Sri Abhinava Vidyatīrtha, the *maṭha*'s spiritual head from 1954 to 1989, was much like other visits that were occasioned by the desire to seek *darśan,* or advice. In this instance, the impetus was provided by a translation he had been working on. The guru's instruction that he halt the work alludes to foreknowledge he may have had, a visionary awareness of a borderless temporal order. The significance of the compassionate advice is that it provides a formal closure to the project (so that it is then not left "incomplete" because of the elder Shastry's death) and, more important, through that closure, a guru's blessing is bestowed on the work. Might we understand this gesture as part of the guidance that a guru provides to a disciple during the "crossing"? Why then did the guru not articulate the course of forthcoming events? The answer to this question may be that foreknowledge comes with an additional responsibility: to engage in appropriate communication navigating the tellable and the silential.

From the point in Ajji's narration when the boat overturns, I struggle to gather the physical sequence of events (Was the river full? Where was Ajji waiting?), but Ajji is not so much interested in the sequence as she is in accepting a metaphysical causality ("What can we do?" "My karma was still unspent, right?"), one that would explain why she survived the accident and her husband did not. This divergence between her time-consciousness and mine explains why we talk at cross-purposes—until I synchronize my time frame with hers, agreeing with her that, ultimately, one's life span is a matter of one's karma. Yet Ajji does acknowledge cause and consequence in physical time when she ascribes the boat's overturning to passengers stepping improperly from the boat. Tellingly, although we both were concerned with physical time, I wanted to find out what had led to what whereas her concern reflected her ethics of consideration (Why bring hardship on the boat owners who could be charged by the police?).

Perhaps the most layered temporality in this narration concerns the giving away of the bangles and sari to the "boatman's daughter." I was appalled and disturbed by what seemed to me a mercenary claim for compensation by the woman who had rescued Ajji and, more so, by the timing of that claim. Why had this woman asked for Ajji's bangles—as I noted earlier, bangles are traditionally considered symbolic of a woman's auspicious married state—in the bleakest moment of Ajji's life? Why had Ajji not seen this demand as callous and exploitative, or even indicative of the woman's dire economic straits—all of which I express through my incredulity and intense focus on mapping physical time? As I later attempted to understand the transaction on the riverbank, I was struck with questions such as whether Ajji had known of a custom in which it is obligatory to monetarily repay such a debt.[17] Yet Ajji had not been appalled nor had she registered any of my shock. For her, giving away her bangles and other possessions was part of a new process of reconstituting her life in which possessions of her marital life are emptied of the meaning they earlier held. The larger question, for her, is how to do the deeper work of freeing herself from desire, which is fed by possessing and clinging to things. My questions, which were stuck in unraveling temporal specificities—Who asked her for the bangles? When? Why?—are all irrelevant when the very concept of ownership has changed for Ajji, and the process of imbuing objects with meaning has ended. Thus she gently rebukes my questions: "Why should I ask anybody? . . . I've never asked anybody's permission to give away things." Rather than track the precise sequence of events, Ajji telescopes to her act of giving away her bangles, as this one act embodies her passage to another shore.[18]

Recently (some years after I recorded this story), I shared the transcript of the conversation and a draft of my tentative reflections on it with Giridhara Shastry, who discussed it with his mother. A significant misunderstanding on my part came to light. I had assumed that "the boatman's daughter" had pressed for compensation *immediately* after the rescue. Giridhara Shastry informed me, however, that the bangles had been given to the woman a *few days after* the rescue and, moreover, that Ajji's family had sought out the woman, whose name was Pushpa, and given her the bangles and sari to express their gratitude (I am still unclear about whether the family had decided on the particular gifts or whether Pushpa herself had specified them). One reading of Ajji's sequencing of events may be to recognize that trauma induces ellipsis in memory, but this explanation overlooks Ajji's agency as a narrator, her experience of that time, and the work she has put into refiguring her life subsequent to the episode. Veena Das, in arguing for the presence of subtle relationships between temporality and subjectivity, says, "The point is not that there are moment-to-moment beliefs and then there are stable temporal maps, but rather that the particular mode in which the subject is immersed in the temporal shapes the contours of the event."[19] Though this is true of Ajji whose experience and memory of that time determine her telling, Pushpa's actions remind us that there is at least one more side to this story. How the temporal is conceptualized influences our understanding of the ethical subject: whereas, in Ajji's narration (or, more correctly, in my understanding of it), Pushpa's act appears opportunistic as she seems to insist on "immediate repayment" for the rescue, in Giridhara Shastry's clarification her act becomes part of a reciprocal gesture by Ajji's family.

Indeed, this essay, in a sense, has attempted to explore Ricoeur's question: "In what way is the ordinary experience of time, borne by daily acting and suffering [enduring], refashioned by its passage through the grid of narrative?"[20] The answer, for Ricoeur, is provided in the concept of mimesis as articulated within the Aristotelian tradition. Ricoeur posits that a pre-narrative structure of experience undergoes interrelated mimetic transformations that could eventually result in transforming our perception of the world. "Prefiguration" is an understanding of the world—"what human action is, its semantics, its symbolism, its temporality"—that precedes the narrative phase of mimesis. This pre-understanding becomes *configured* into a narrative order, in which the narrator, through emplotment, weaves multiple conceptions of time (for example, "lasted an eternity," "the other day," "a long, long time ago," or "in the past") into an interpretation of experience and action. Emplotment itself is an imaginative experiment that seeks to reconstruct temporality through, for example, as Gerard Genette notes, order (sequencing of events), duration (tempo that maps time spans of real life), and frequency (the relationship between a "happening" and the number of times it is narrated).[21] The narrative world, now emplotted, bears a complex relationship with "tradition," and this emplotted "world of text" encounters the "world of the reader."[22] Through this encounter, individuals refigure the narrated world into their lived experiences, making narrated time part of their "ordinary experience of time." Crucial to refiguration is sympathetic emoting and imagination. Ricoeur's formulation is helpful because, although it appears linear in its "stages" of mimesis, it understands moral experience as an eddy, rippling out of the narrator's experience into the experience of the reader/listener. But the oral narrative experience, with its "back and forth" movements in which starting and end points are diffuse, is far more complex than can be accommodated in Ricoeur's framework. Temporal logic in the narratives I have presented, and frequently in all conversationally shared stories, is co-constructed, and unevenly so. In this kind of dialogic environment prefiguration, configuration, and refiguration are open to contestation and refashioning; they can occur simultaneously, be blurred, and often be present one in the other. For example, Ajji's configuration of "that episode" emerges in response to my contribution to that configuration in the dialogue. Another possibility would be to see my attempt to elicit the story from her as an attempt to piece the contours of my configuration that is itself in the process. Indeed, we can also say that Giridhara Shastry's clarification on the question of timing works to unsettle my developing (re)configuration of Ajji's story. That the world of gestures, practices, and non-narrative actions shapes the very scope of the narrative experience is evident from Dodda Murthy's temporal adjustments when I interrupt his recounting of the episode with a glass of milk. Time-consciousness, in the plural, is thus instrumental in the ethical subject formation that occurs in conversational narratives.

If the profound reflections on time contained in the *Upaniṣads* rest the question of temporality in the time-transcendent imperishable *akṣara* or *Brahman,* is there an analogous form of the imperishable in the experience of narrative? In other words, what has made the times of those events and the times of those tellings endure the passage of time? Why am I as a listener moved, and moved enough, to want to emulate something I have gleaned from these stories and their tellings? Rasa poetics, developed first in Sanskrit and then later through various regional languages of India, provides one of the most searching explorations of similar questions in the area of artistic representation. The concept of "rasa," which literally means "flavor" but denotes "emotional mood" in poetry, was introduced in Bharata's panoramic treatise on stagecraft, the *Nāṭyaśāstra* (dated sometime between the second century BCE and the second century CE), but it is in the theories of literary critics such as Anandavardhana (early ninth century) and Abhinavagupta (eleventh century) that rasa poetics blossomed. Rasa, the goal of all poetic effort, is distilled aesthetic emotion that arises when "feelings" are depersonalized and transcend their historical contexts. Sanskrit literary critics singled out eight stable feelings from the multitude of feelings (love, joy, grief, anger, fear, energy, disgust, and wonder) for the dramatic representation of life. The aim of poetic representation is to evoke the specific rasa, which can only come from a successful metamorphosis of "feelings" into a corresponding dominant mood or emotion (rasa), namely, the erotic, the comic, the tragic, the furious, the fearsome, the heroic, the disgusting, or the wondrous.[23]

I continue to look for ways in which the insights of rasa poetics could shed light on our largely off-stage, everyday lives, for, after all, rasa critics in seeking to distinguish the world of art from the everyday world did not do so without a situated knowledge of the everyday, its languages, its life forms, its preoccupations. To return to the questions posed earlier: Can we abstract a metaphysics of time from the structure underlying the production of rasa to understand what makes us be present—Dodda Murthy's or Ajji's narration? Even though the elicitation of rasa depends on temporal and other alignments, rasa is itself atemporal and transcends time. As A. K. Ramanujan notes, "Rasa comes into being with the experiencing."[24] The everyday routines and talk, gestures that embody respect for a life, the crossing of bangles from one set of hands to another all work intangibly to create a tragic mood that overcomes the temporality peculiar to those lives and those contexts. Thus unbound from particularities, empathy generates a moral resonance that endures. If "duration" is, as Das rightly puts it, not an aspect but the "very condition of subjectivity,"[25] then the goal of rasa is the transcendence of duration. Through the experience of being moved by the intimation of possibility—that this experience could be mine—we enter a realm of non-duration, where Ajji's story or Dodda Murthy's gesture become our story, our gesture, and thus "timeless." In duration, we are beyond it.

Notes

1. *Brihadāraṇyaka Upaniṣad* 3.8, in *Upaniṣads,* trans. Patrick Olivelle (Oxford: Oxford University Press, 1996).

2. For a succinct analytical overview of notions of time in Hindu philosophical traditions and early Indian narrative literature, see Randy Kloetzli and Alf Hiltebeitel, "Kāla," in *The Hindu World,* ed. Sushil Mittal and Gene Thursby (New York: Routledge, 2004), 553–586. Also in the same vein, but with a focus on philosophical discourses across Indian and Western religions, is Ananda K. Coomaraswamy, *Time and Eternity* (New Delhi: IGNCA, 1990). For temporal implications of interlocking narrative frames in the Mahabharata and the Ramayana, see David D. Shulman, "Toward a Historical Poetics of the Sanskrit Epics," in *The Wisdom of Poets: Studies in Tamil, Telugu, and Sanskrit* (Oxford: Oxford University Press, 2001). Lewis E. Rowell discusses various temporal frameworks permeating Indian musical traditions in *Music and Musical Thought in Early India* (Chicago: University of Chicago Press, 1992).

3. Leela Prasad, *Poetics of Conduct: Oral Narrative and Moral Being in a South Indian Town* (New York: Columbia University Press, 2007).

4. According to the 2001 census Sringeri is a small town of about four thousand people (Karnataka 2001 census data, http://www.bangaloreit.com/html/govtinformation/censuspaper2/Paper-2%20Chapter-9.pdf [accessed June 10, 2009]). The immediate area around the *maṭha* is populated mostly by *smārta* brahmans, who are so identified because they conventionally follow the *smṛti* ("remembered") tradition, which significantly includes the *Dharmaśāstras,* the treatises most relevant to conduct. Though some brahmans work in the monastery as administrators, priests, or cooks, and older families in Sringeri have ties to the *maṭha* going back centuries, many families are independent of the *maṭha* for their livelihood; they cultivate arecanut, paddy, cardamom, and coffee; teach in schools and colleges; or run stores and lodges. Vokkaligas and Bunts are the other Hindus in town, and the minority communities of Jains and Muslims also live in and outside Sringeri. See B. K. Das, ed., *Census of India, 1981: District Census Handbook, Chikmagalur District, Karnataka* (Bangalore: Government Central Press, 1984).

5. Prasad, *Poetics of Conduct* (2007).

6. For how this imaginative agency reconstitutes the concept of *śāstra* (code, injunction, rule, treatise) in lived experience amid myriad possibilities, and how ethical practices embody "imagined texts" (as distinct from oral, written, or performed texts), see Leela Prasad, "Text, Tradition, and Imagination: Evoking the Normative in Everyday Hindu Life," *Numen* 53, no. 1 (2006): 1–47.

7. I wish to distinguish this "literacy," which can be also more quotidian, flexible, and amenable to improvisation and not singularly dependent on intensity of commitment or repetition of performance that marks the "acquired excellence" which defines "habitus." See Saba Mahmood, *Politics of Piety: The Islamic Revival and the Feminist Subject* (Princeton, N.J.: Princeton University Press, 2005), 136. See Mahmood also for how Egyptian women involved in the mosque movement in Cairo claim and enact their moral and political agency both through various embodied practices and by setting their terms for the cultivation of "piety."

8. Jürgen Habermas, *Moral Consciousness and Communicative Action* (Cambridge, Mass.: MIT Press, 1990), 48.

9. Peter Strawson, *Freedom and Resentment and other Essays* (London: Methuen, 1974).

10. I mention this context in which I heard Dodda Murthy's narration in Prasad, *Poetics of Conduct,* 2007, but do not transcribe it there. It is with Dodda Murthy's permission that I here present and contemplate what it taught me.

11. Diana L. Eck, "India's Tirthas: Crossing in Sacred Geography," *History of Religions* 20, no. 4 (1981): 323–344, quote at 343. For a comprehensive treatment of the subject of pilgrimage and puranic narrative, see Eck, *Banāras: City of Light* (New Delhi: Penguin Books), 1993 [1983].

12. Eck, "India's Tirthas," 331.

13. The Tunga, which originates in the Western ghats, borders the town of Sringeri and winds through many villages in the taluk before joining the Bhadra in Koodli to become the mighty Tungabhadra.

14. In Prasad, *Poetics of Conduct,* I discuss the concept of *aucitya* (dramatic propriety), formulated by Kshemendra in the eleventh century, by analyzing its implications for conceptualizing a moral poetics.

15. Speaking of how time is refigured by history, Ricoeur identifies three "connectors" (calendar time, generation time, and traces) that make historical time a "mixed remembrance." A "trace" can be a physical remnant of the past or a "present thing that stands for an absent past." See Paul Ricoeur, "Narrated Time," in *A Ricoeur Reader: Reflection and Imagination,* ed. Mario J. Valdes (Toronto: University of Toronto Press, 1991), 345. I simply note here, and develop elsewhere, how the Hindu conception of *vāsana* ("the present consciousness of past perceptions," in the words of Monier-Williams) provides a way of yoking "historical" time" and "cosmic time" which Ricoeur laments remain "conceptually unreflected" upon in historical practice. See Prasad, "Estimated Time of Arrival: Time and Diaspora," undated article in progress.

16. "*Samādhi* side": the side of the temple complex across from the river where the present guru resides and where shrines are dedicated to several of the previous gurus.

17. Dipesh Chakrabarty and I exchanged notes on this possibility. My thanks to him for drawing my attention to a news report in *The Telegraph* (dated September 17, 2007) about the callous conduct of some *dōms* (traditional undertakers) in Kolkata when approached by a grieving family seeking to transport a family member's dead body from the hospital to the morgue.

18. For a discussion of how women's roles are imagined in various contexts from Vedic rituals and vrata traditions to life-cycle rites and temple dance traditions, see Julia Leslie, ed., *Roles and Rituals for Hindu Women* (Rutherford, N.J.: Fairleigh Dickinson University Press, 1991).

19. Veena Das, *Life and Words: Violence and the Descent into the Ordinary* (Berkeley: University of California Press, 2006), 97.

20. Ricoeur, "Narrated Time," 338.

21. Gerard Genette, *Narrative Discourse: An Essay in Method,* trans. Jane Lewin (Ithaca, N.Y.: Cornell University Press, 1980).

22. Paul Ricoeur, "Life: A Story in Search of a Narrator," in Valdes, *A Ricoeur Reader,* 425–437, quote at 430.

23. Anandavardhana added a ninth rasa, *śānta rasa* (rasa of peace).

24. A. K. Ramanujan and Edwin Gerow, "Indian Poetics," in Edward C. Dimock, Edwin Gerow, C. M. Naim, A. K. Ramanujan, Godern Roadarmel, and J. A. B. van Buitenen, eds., *The Literatures of India: An Introduction* (Chicago: University of Chicago Press, 1978), 128–143, quote at 128–129.

25. Das, *Life and Words,* 98.

10.

Demoralizing Developments: Ethics, Class, and Student Power in Modern North India

Craig Jeffrey

While carrying out research on student activism in north India, I spent much time with a young man called Jaipal.[1] Jaipal, in his late twenties in 2005, belonged to the middle-ranking Jat caste. He referred to himself as "unemployed" (*berozgār*) after having failed to obtain a government job, but Jaipal was formally enrolled as a full-time student at Chaudhry Charan Singh University (CCSU) in Meerut City. Jaipal was often at the forefront of collective student demonstrations against the CCSU bureaucracy. A typical morning might find him leading protests against the "corruption" (*bhrashtāchār*) of university bigwigs or spearheading an attempt to barricade a neglectful university bureaucrat in his office. But come the evening, Jaipal and his caste peers often went to the homes of university administrators to collude over how to make money from bribery and extortion. It was an open secret in Meerut that many Jat student leaders protested alongside other students *against* "corruption" while also making money through nefarious means.

How can we explain this apparent double-dealing? This essay addresses this question with reference to ethnographic research conducted between September 2004 and April 2005 on student politics in Meerut, Uttar Pradesh (UP). I point to the emergence of collective youth protest founded on anger at corruption and long-term exclusion from secure salaried work. But I also show how class-based networks of Jat accumulation fracture a wider politics of youth unemployment and how Jat student leaders have developed multiple means to justify their apparent "hypocrisy" both to other students and to themselves.

The work of Pierre Bourdieu provides a useful starting point for examining the political and ethical practices of unemployed north Indian youth, and the particular strategies of middle-class sections of this cohort.[2] Bourdieu argued that social inequalities tend to prevent the emergence of collective youth mobilization.[3] He showed how richer sections of the youth population are able to separate themselves from poorer youth by strategically deploying their superior wealth, social capital—instrumentally valuable social bonds—and cultural capital: the range of goods, titles, and forms of demeanor that confer distinction in social settings. Bourdieu was especially interested in the quotidian practices through which class advantage is transmitted and reinforced, and he developed this idea with reference to the notion of "habitus," which, in Bourdieu's work, is usually defined as orientations to action shaping a person's movements, reflexes, and tastes that are both structured by people's experience while also structuring future action. Bourdieu argued that habitus can only be understood with reference to the "fields" of social competition in which people with particular bundles of capital compete for resources.

Consideration of habitus as an emergent product of people's struggles across multiple fields allows us to understand how richer young people's ability to accumulate social contacts becomes internalized in their dispositions. As Bourdieu put it, relatively advantaged social actors often develop a type of *sens de placement,* or "feel for the game," which is crucial in defending social advantage.[4] In his elaboration of habitus, Bourdieu also shows how aspects of people's bodily comportment may allow them to succeed within competitive fields of struggle even where they are not consciously engaged in strategic action.[5] More broadly, Bourdieu's theoretical schema is valuable in drawing attention to how middle-class sections of the youth population are often able to respond positively to situations of economic uncertainty by deepening their investment in social networks, devising new forms of cultural cachet, or emphasizing their moral superiority to working-class peers.

Much of Bourdieu's work suggests, instead, that poorer sections of society are incapable of engaging in critique or effecting meaningful agency. It is therefore useful to set alongside Bourdieu's framework the emphasis of other scholars on the agency and resistance of young people from subordinated sections of society.[6] Drawing on his work with British youth, Paul Willis pays particular attention to how members of the working class sometimes challenge established social forces through forms of cultural production: active and imaginative practices shaped by broader structures and available symbolic resources. More than Bourdieu's, Willis's notion of cultural production draws attention to the creativity of youth and the possibility that young people will form political alliances across class and other social boundaries.

Bourdieu's failure to theorize adequately the meaning of social action also leaves him poorly placed to understand processes of ethical reflection among relatively wealthy sections of society, including richer young men. Foucault's work is important in drawing more explicit attention to the domain of ethics as concrete practices, discourses, and procedures of self-fashioning that assume different forms within particular historical contexts and cannot be reduced to underlying economic or accumulative logics.[7] Three aspects of Foucault's work on ethics are especially salient for my analysis. First, Foucault emphasizes how people consciously scrutinize aspects of their behavior that pertain to questions of morality. Second, Foucault's work encourages enquiry into the plural institutional and narrative structures—or "modes of subjection"—that shape people's ideas of moral action. The state and powerful institutions incite people to assume particular moral stances with respect to everyday aspects of their behavior. Third, Foucault explicitly examined the technological apparatus and spatial forms through which dominant institutions encourage people to adopt ethical modes of practice, and he stressed the importance of the body as a mechanism through which an ethical selfhood is achieved.

But Foucault's work cannot fully account for the role of class in shaping people's attitudes to ethics.[8] Bourdieu is right to insist that in many situations people's efforts to cultivate ethical lifestyles arise out of the congruence between the "ethic" concerned and their social and material interests. This is certainly not to suggest that class determines social life.[9] Nor is it to argue that class is some kind of "explanatory key" that will unlock our understanding of ethics.[10] Rather, it is to point to the runnels and reserves of power that have accumulated within western UP society and to expose how these flows and sedimentations "thicken" political and ethical practice in specific ways. For heuristic purposes, I therefore seek in my analysis of the social and political strategies of young men in UP to combine Bourdieu's attention to the power of class to order social practice with the emphasis of much recent Foucauldian work on conscious reflection on morality, multiple modes of subjection, and the embodied creation of ethical selfhood.

The Political Economy of Uttar Pradesh

Young men in Meerut in 2004–2005 were keenly aware of the straitened circumstances within which they sought to accumulate resources and develop a sense of ethical selfhood. UP is the most populous state in India, containing 166 million people in 2000.[11] On most indexes of development UP ranks among the two or three most impoverished states.[12] The liberalization of the Indian economy from the mid-1980s on has further marginalized UP in comparison with most other Indian states, as evident in the sphere of the employment generation.[13] Outside metropolitan areas, economic reforms have reduced opportunities for government employment. UP's long-established industrial base has almost completely collapsed, and, aside from two state districts, UP has played a relatively minor role so far in the newly emerging information technology (IT), out-sourcing, and other "new industries" for which India has become renowned. In addition, liberalization has often failed to generate private-sector jobs while also reducing the availability of institutional credit and therefore possibilities for entrepreneurialism.[14]

The resulting employment crisis has coincided with the rapid disintegration of the public provision of education. Until the early 1990s the state was expanding its financial support for government schooling. Since that time neoliberal economic reforms have undermined educational provision.[15] With the exception of a small number of elite state colleges, government institutions usually lack teaching aids and equipment, catering facilities, and basic amenities.[16] Numerous nonstate schools and colleges have entered the educational sphere to fill this vacuum, but these institutions are usually poorly regulated, staffed, and funded.[17]

This pattern of state neglect reflects the entrenched nature of caste and class inequalities in UP, the population of which may be roughly divided into three social blocs. Upper castes comprise roughly 20 percent of the population. As substantial landowners, these castes have dominated lucrative salaried employment, local government bureaucracies, and landownership in many parts of UP.[18]

A second bloc of households, including the Jats, belongs to Hindu middle castes and frequently controls access to political and economic power in rural UP. Jats act as local dominant castes in many western parts of the state.[19] Despite comprising just 8 percent of the population of western UP, they monopolize landownership, nonagricultural sources of wealth, and influence within local state institutions.[20] Between the mid-1960s and late 1980s Jats were powerfully represented within the state and central government.[21] This political power allowed rich Jat farmers to benefit from high agricultural support prices and large subsidies on agricultural inputs. Since the death, in 1987, of their political mentor, the Jat politician Chaudhry Charan Singh, Jats have continued to invest profits from agriculture in attempts to join and influence the local state bureaucracy through positioning their sons in government jobs, nurturing networks linking them to the local state, and establishing close connections with district officials.[22] Jats have also participated in high-profile protests aimed at improving the terms of trade between agriculture and industry, and safeguarding farmers' access to subsidized agricultural inputs.[23] In addition, during the late 1990s, Jats successfully pressured the Bharatiya Janata Party (BJP) politician and chief minister of UP, R. K. Gupta, to include Jats in the quota of castes just "above" ex-untouchables in the Indian caste hierarchy but nevertheless suffering from forms of economic and social exclusion, the so-called Other Backward Classes (OBCs).

The remainder of UP's population is mainly comprised of Muslims, poorer castes within the OBC category, and Dalits (a term denoting ex-untouchables; Dalit means broken and oppressed in Hindi). There are elites among Muslims and Dalits in UP, but Muslims, Dalits, and poorer OBCs typically possess few material assets and tend to work in exploitative and insecure conditions. This is especially true of Dalits who have suffered from the stigma associated with being classed as "untouchable."[24]

UP's political economy has also been subject to substantial change since the early 1990s.[25] In particular, the pro-Dalit Bahujan Samaj Party (BSP) held power in UP four times between 1993 and 2003 under the leadership of a Dalit former schoolteacher, Mayawati, and it won a landslide victory in the 2007 state elections. The BSP has vigorously encouraged Dalits to obtain education, often by drawing on the vision of upward mobility based upon schooling and entry into white-collar employment promoted by the Dalit hero, Dr. Bhim Rao Ambedkar.

My research on the relationship between these forms of political change and processes of social reproduction has involved thirty-eight months of ethnographic fieldwork carried out between 1995 and 2007. I conducted doctoral research in the mid-1990s on how rich Jat farmers were co-opting and colonizing the local state in north India. Since 1998 I have focused on the cultural politics of unemployment and the place of education in rural social imaginaries. This paper focuses on the most recent round of my research, which concentrated on the politics of unemployment among students in Meerut.

Meerut is located in a relatively prosperous area of UP, but it remains outside the areas of most significant economic expansion fanning out from Delhi, and there is still little evidence of any IT boom in the city. With a population of about a million in 2001, Meerut has long been a center of government, army operations, and artisanal production. Between the mid-1960s and late 1980s the intensification of cash-crop agriculture encouraged commercial development in the city, and since the early 1990s Meerut has become a major provider of private health care, nonstate education, and financial services.

Students have been important in shaping aspects of Meerut's political history. Meerut College was founded in 1892 and has long been the premier educational institution in the extreme west of UP. Meerut College students were involved in the Indian nationalist struggle, and, after Independence, Chaudhry Charan Singh was aware of the political advantages of mobilizing students. More recently student politics in Meerut has been characterized by the emergence of new student politicians, including Dalits, and by the enormous proliferation of private colleges in the region and associated frustration over the quality of educational provision.

I examined contemporary student politics in Meerut by working mainly in two higher-educational institutions: CCSU and Meerut College. This essay focuses on CCSU, which contained twenty-six hundred students in 2004, roughly a quarter of them upper caste, a third middle-caste Jats or Gujars, and a third Dalit, according to figures obtained from CCSU offices in 2004. The remaining students were mainly from poorer members of the Other Backward Classes. CCSU granted affiliation to several hundred other colleges, most of them privately run and containing roughly one-quarter million students.

Youth Demoralization

Many young men in CCSU grew up believing in a vision of their future progress through school into government employment. This was a moral as well as an economic idea. Students frequently expressed an ardent desire to obtain a government job in order to banish corruption and redirect state resources toward the needs of the poor. This notion of personal and national development reflected the ubiquity of images of progress through education and disinterested government work that are circulated by teachers, in school textbooks, and by the state and development organizations in western UP. It also reflected more caste-specific moral narratives of what constitutes mature adulthood. Jat young men had often grown up with notions of Jats as "loyal servants of the nation," an idea that can be traced back to colonial stereotypes of this caste.[26] The rise of the BSP has been especially important in entrenching a similar model of masculine progress in the minds of Dalit students. The image of a bespectacled Ambedkar with a suitcase and Western-style suit serves as a condensed symbol of young male Dalit aspirations.

At the same time the emergence of large business corporations and nonstate educational institutions in Meerut has resulted in the proliferation of rather different images of successful masculinity, ones based upon individual enterprise and mastery of the market. Students from a wide variety of caste and class backgrounds often referred to a desire to make "*fast money*"[27] through developing a "*business mind-set*" or through acquiring a distinctive package of skills that would allow them to capture jobs in metropolitan India.

To counterpose these models of development is not to imply that only two narrative frameworks shaped young men's ideas about adulthood and ethics. Nor is it to distract from how the two narratives intersect, for example, through their focus on masculine discipline. Rather, it is to argue that for many students in Meerut the models of becoming a government servant or working as some form of entrepreneur were especially salient, and many young men referred explicitly to choosing between these two *lines*.

In practice, students tended to value notions of improvement through entering government service above images of success through business entrepreneurship. This partly reflects the power of the state to inculcate notions of progress through planned development and entry into government jobs in the 1970s and 1980s. Young men's tendency to stress the importance of obtaining a government job also reflects their perception of the risks and rewards associated with different *lines* of work. Students in CCSU and affiliated colleges in the mid-2000s usually lacked opportunities to realize ambitions of becoming successful business entrepreneurs or corporate executives. With rare exceptions, Meerut students did not possess the social contacts required to obtain positions in major businesses in Delhi or well-developed English-language skills necessary for many of these jobs. Moreover, a government position usually offered long-term security, a pension, opportunities to make money on the side, and other perks, and was therefore considered much safer than most private-sector positions.

Very few students in Meerut succeeded in obtaining government work, even among apparently well-connected Jats.[28] The sheer scale of the current employment crisis meant that several thousand applicants often applied for a single government position in Meerut. Demoralization stemmed not only from the students' failure to acquire government posts but also from the manner of their exclusion. Young men spoke of the process of applying for government jobs as dispiriting and burdensome. They cited a need to memorize reams of general-knowledge questions, travel to distant examination centers, and chivy relatives, friends, and social contacts into offering support for their applications. In the wake of these efforts, students often have to wait up to eighteen months to receive news. Because young men can continue to apply for government jobs until they reach their mid-thirties, their experience of repeated failure may be strung out over a period of ten years. In addition, many students spoke of endemic malpractice within the competition for government employment; without bribe money or good social contacts, they claimed, obtaining secure salaried work was impossible. As one respondent put it, in the cut-throat market for government work, everyone now needs *source* (social connections) and *force* (physical strength). In this context, caste-based reservations had become almost irrelevant in the search for a government job.

Young men studying at CCSU were not as well equipped as Jats to respond to their inability to obtain government work.[29] Jats were often able to react to this employment crisis by moving into agriculture, private-sector jobs in the urban informal economy, or politics. Dalits were largely excluded from these opportunities, because they lacked land and the social connections necessary to obtain private-sector employment. Many Dalits, even those with a master's degree, were forced simply to continue their studies and hope that things would change. In their thirties, many Dalits returned to their villages to partake in manual wage labor.

Students' shared experience of exclusion from opportunities to find secure work contributed to a collective sense of frustration, anger, and bewilderment. Appropriating broader narratives of young male aimlessness circulated by parents and the state, these men often characterized themselves as useless, empty, wandering, or unemployed. Young men were not claiming that they were incapable of working or that they lacked employment; many referred to themselves as unemployed while engaged in part-time jobs in the informal economy or while studying at a university. They used these terms, instead, to signal the mismatch between their present occupational status and their educational standing and to signal their own hope that "something better is just around the corner."

There were close connections between young men's sense of moral loss and a feeling of spatial and temporal abandonment rooted in their educational experience. The recent privatization of higher education and the frequency of political actions meant that formal classes were short, infrequent, and disorganized. Institutionalized forms of extracurricular activities and educational facilities on most government college campuses were lacking. Students increasingly obtained most of their knowledge from textbooks written by their professors, which they read in their hostel rooms or in tea stalls, and from private tutorials, which often occurred in the basement of professors' large homes in middle-class parts of the city. Students living in hostels in Meerut usually spent only short periods studying and divided their days between politics, trips to tea stalls, chatting in people's rooms, reading newspapers, and playing games, often badminton, cricket, or cards. Many students argued that these forms of "*timepass*" (passing time) allowed them to counter boredom, but they also referred to their activities with a sense of melancholy borne of an awareness of how the campus had been hollowed out as a space of learning.

Students were aware of a dissonance between the notion of government service leading to moral improvement with which they had grown up and the nefarious competitive networks in which they sought qualifications and jobs. Many students complained that the principles of entrepreneurship and self-interest associated with the business world had infiltrated recruitment to government employment and the educational sector such that "everything has become a market." They expressed particular anger toward government recruitment agents who ask for bribes, university bureaucrats who charge spurious fees, and UP state politicians who look the other way in the face of widespread unemployment. As Karl Mannheim argued long ago, a cohort's common experience of particular social and economic conditions may create lines of shared understanding that cross-cut class and other social divides.[30]

Collective indignation among young men sparked political agitation. During only the first two weeks of my research, students launched demonstrations aimed at reestablishing student union elections at Meerut College, preventing police raids on CCSU hostels, and ending corruption in the process of admission to higher education in Meerut. Distinct from youth protests during the colonial period in Meerut, this mobilization tended to involve students voicing their entitlements *as students* to particular social goods, and the demonstrations included Dalits, young women, and Muslim students. Moreover, whereas student leaders in the past often left campus to organize workshops and protests in rural areas or on the fringes of the city, contemporary student protests were more tightly organized around reshaping the physical space of the campus. Student protests frequently involved blocking major campus roads, barricading university officials in their offices, or closing down the university altogether.

But these protests were sporadic and short, and they focused on immediate issues arising in the life of the university. Caste, class, and gender divisions militated against the emergence of durable civil society organizations within student society. In particular, a group of charismatic Jat students from relatively prosperous backgrounds undermined a broader student movement.

Jat Student Leaders

The example of Habir[31] offers insights into the practices of Jat politicians, who typically came from relatively wealthy rural backgrounds and often referred to themselves as "*middle class.*" Born into a prosperous farming family on the edge of Meerut, Habir was led to expect that he would enter government work. He obtained relatively good schooling at a private institution in a market town and then enrolled in a degree college. In 2000 he arrived at CCSU for postgraduate study. But after repeated failure in government employment examinations he devoted his energies to developing a political profile on campus. In 2001 and 2002 he organized political agitations relating to a range of student issues. These included protests aimed at lowering students' fees in CCSU, establishing a career guidance center for students on campus, ensuring transparency in the admissions process to the university, and reducing corruption within the university bureaucracy. Habir imagined himself as a new type of politician dedicated to the social improvement of the ordinary student.

Habir has never wholly abandoned this interest in spearheading youth protests targeted against the university administration. But in 2003 he used his reputation for representing students to obtain a position on the CCSU student union, and he increasingly combined collective protest with more self-interested forms of political activity. In this new role Habir worked to develop collusive relationships inside the CCSU bureaucracy. He made large sums by using his student union position as leverage in efforts to take a cut of university officials' side incomes.

Habir's case offers wider insights into the strategies of Jat student leaders.[32] Jats have successfully dominated the CCSU student union; of the thirty men who held one of the top two positions in the CCSU student union between 1991 and 2004, twenty-four were either Jats or Gujars. Jats captured these posts partly by developing a reputation for articulating the moral indignation of students as a whole. Aspiring political leaders launched protests against corruption within university and government offices, and these were reported in favorable terms by friends within local newspapers and television stations. These efforts at developing a reputation for ethics drew heavily on national-level political styles and histories of anticolonial struggle. To loud cheers at public gatherings, Jats frequently referred to their readiness to "go to jail for students" or "die in the cause of a just politics."

Some Jats continued to work in the interest of students in general once they obtained a position on the student union. But most leaders downplayed efforts to assist the ordinary student. Instead, like Habir, they concentrated on building social networks that would provide rapid economic profits for their own families and their caste peers. Jat student leaders made money through arranging backdoor admission to colleges affiliated to CCSU. They also acted as intermediaries between the CCSU administration and private educational entrepreneurs, and between university bigwigs and the contractors charged with constructing new educational institutions.[33] Within these networks, Jat student leaders traded on their knowledge of how corruption works and controlling the means of violence, especially Jat youth gangs. Individual Jat student leaders on the CCSU student union could earn between Rs. 800,000 and Rs. 1,000,000 from their posts in the early and mid-2000s. After leaving their student union post, Jat politicians often used their social contacts to obtain permanent employment as university professors or advocates, jobs they could combine with political work.

The power of Jat student leaders rested on their economic capital, social networking resources, and cultural capital. In a manner that recalls Bourdieu's emphasis on habitus and *sens de placement,* student leaders claimed to have become so practiced in the art of politicking that, in many political situations, they experienced "a strange feeling of power welling up from within," which allowed them to forge connections effectively and impress caste peers. Jats' power was also founded on their control over the use of force. Student leaders often had better access to the police than Dalits or even upper castes on campus, largely because Jats could draw upon social contacts established by rural senior kin and exploit affinities of habitus between themselves and middle-caste police officers.

Three sets of students sought to challenge Jat power. First, the rise of the BSP in UP politics had encouraged Dalit young men to contest the dominance of the Jats. In particular, the BSP's emphasis on social mobility through education and service to the nation had encouraged many Dalit leaders to expand their social networks in order to assist other members of their caste and critique the "corruption" of dominant Jats. Dalit leaders often pursued this goal by volunteering to conduct paperwork in government offices. They also tried to ingratiate themselves with government and university officials through developing an air of civilized comportment. Letter writing was an important feature of these strategies. Dalit leaders spent long periods in their hostel rooms drafting letters to senior government officials and politicians which outlined in a rich language of moral vituperation the extent and nature of "corruption." But Dalits' attempts to improve low castes' access to resources and political power moderated rather than transformed processes of class and caste social reproduction within CCSU. Middle castes, particularly the Jats, continued to dominate formal student associations and access to the university administration, as they did in most other higher-educational institutions in Meerut.

A second group of students from diverse caste backgrounds were involved in developing forms of left-wing critique and action within Meerut colleges and universities. Many of these students had part-time jobs on local newspapers where they were often locked in bitter struggles with editors to publish articles critical of the state.

A third group, comprised of un- and underemployed young women in Meerut from upper- or middle-caste backgrounds, was attempting to undermine the strategies of Jat student leaders by cultivating social links within the state. Unemployment among the educated has also affected young women's lives in Meerut: directly, because parents within the urban middle class are increasingly allowing their daughters and daughters-in-law to pursue paid employment outside the home; and, indirectly, because the failure of young men to move rapidly into employment has contributed to increasing the age of marriage. These young women did not usually participate in collective student protests on campus or student union elections. Yet they were often able to make direct and rapid contact with the most senior district-level government officials and thereby exert some influence over politics in the city and in higher education.

The activities of Dalits, left-wing students, and young women were poorly coordinated, but they shared a central interest in critiquing Jat student leaders, whom they depicted as having abandoned the common cause in favor of a selfish consumerist ethic of personal or class-based accumulation. At rallies, via posters, through newspapers, and in everyday discussion they accused Jats of betraying other students through their selfishness.

Jat student leaders engaged in four interlinked strategies to counter these charges. First, they circulated moral discourses in which they stated their opposition to all forms of corrupt practice and referred to their activities euphemistically as "*work,*" "*business,*" or a game (*khel*). Jats referred most commonly to the idea of being engaged in a game of life (*jīvan kā khel*) with distinct rules (*nīyam*) and players (*khelhārī*). Second, Jat leaders attempted to obscure their dealings by issuing denials. Some of the most notoriously "corrupt" student leaders often made bold challenges at large public gatherings. "You tell me one instance when I have been corrupt!" When students started listing examples, the student leader would dismiss their arguments as self-interested and false or accuse them of failing to appreciate "true corruption" (*sahī bhrashtāchār*). Third, student union leaders referred to the necessity of colluding with the state, often with reference to the notion of being caught within a wider network. In this narrative the Jat student leader depicted himself as a pawn within a broader "system" or "game." Fourth, Jat student leaders distinguished between their own "corruption" (*bhrashtāchār*), understood as routine deviations from formal procedures, and "*fraud*," actions that contravened the moral codes embedded within everyday corruption. For example, student leaders said that they regularly colluded with the university registrar to raise students' grades in examinations, a form of corruption which they felt they could justify. But student politicians were livid when it emerged in the summer of 2006 that the CCSU registrar had been lining his pockets by having school students as young as eight years old grade master's theses, an act of "*fraud*" which led many students to burn their degrees.

Young men often reflected on these tactics of euphemism, denial, pragmatism, and relative moral outrage as "spoken performances" (*bolnīwalī bāten*) aimed at shoring up their reputation in the face of moral attack. Jats knew that most students would not be convinced by their rhetoric. But they were equally aware of a need to win over new students at CCSU, many of whom had little idea about who could claim to be genuinely against corruption.

Ethical Reflection

In private settings, however, Jat young men often evaluated their involvement in colluding with university and government officials in ways that differed from the tone of their public performances. For some young men conversations in private hostel rooms offered an opportunity to admit that, behind the public facade, they rather enjoyed being involved in corruption. Colluding with university officials, watching out for opportunities for profit, and negotiating with multiple "*seniors*" to get a cut of corrupt incomes offered a release from the boredom and anxiety of unemployment and a basis for constructing what Michael Herzfeld terms "intimate cultures."[34] As one student leader put it, "We struggle to obtain a good reputation within politics and then, when we win a position . . . Hah! It is like a vacation!" This sense of being "on vacation" was strengthened by young men's appreciation of the daily perks associated with being a student leader in Meerut: receiving free tea in restaurants outside the university, appearing in newspaper photos regularly, and earning the respect of government officials.

Many Jat student leaders also appeared to use the time after winning a student union post to engage in what Foucault called "ethical work" (*travail éthique* or *pratique de soi*).[35] Freed of the immediate compulsion to apply for government employment, petition their parents for financial support, and ingratiate themselves with freshmen, these young men frequently spent time in forms of cultural production that would cast their practices as "ethical." This largely private drive to develop an ethic around their practice differed from their public efforts to justify making money from their union posts, because, in the safety of their own rooms and small friendship groups, Jats made no attempt to deny the scale and nature of their activity—indeed, in some cases they exaggerated it.

Student leaders often elaborated on the idea that their practices were ethical through reference to the Hindi word "*jugār*," which literally means "provisioning" but in the Meerut context more commonly signals a capacity to improvise effectively within particular social situations by bringing together diverse practices or technologies. Jat young men commonly argued that the idea of *jugār* is encapsulated in the image of a rural bullock cart that has been fitted with a modern engine (*jugārī gārī*). On other occasions they explained *jugār* by referring to a person who, on waking in the morning, slips on one smart leather shoe and one plastic sandal, because these two pieces of footwear just happened to be under his bed. As both these examples suggest, *jugār* entailed combining unlike elements in a pragmatic fashion in order to create a workable solution to some "problem." Within the realm of politics, Jats stressed the manner in which their capacity to do *jugār* sensitized them to multiple opportunities to arrive at solutions. One Jat student leader told me:

> *We go into the vice chancellor's office. We don't know what we will get. We try persuasion. We go for blackmail. Then we just try physical threat.* By hook or by crook *we get our work done. This is* jugār.

Jugār was ethical in the Foucauldian sense that it announced a distinctive ethos founded on the manipulation of spatial forms and the self-conscious management of one's emotions, desires, and pleasures. But Jats' vision of entrepreneurial practice was also "ethical" in a second, more specific sense of being based on an idea of moral superiority. Jats emphasized that *jugār* entailed making shrewd use of available resources. In fact, one student leader explicitly linked *jugār* to visions of environmental conservation. This young man combined his efforts to extract money from private educational entrepreneurs with a program to encourage rainwater harvesting in Meerut. He said that he considered these political projects to be united in their commitment to *jugār*. Jats also argued that *jugār* signaled a type of bravery rooted in a capacity to improvise and a refusal to be deterred by convention. This notion was also strongly gendered. Jat student leaders argued that they have the masculine strength to overcome old-fashioned doubts over the morality of liaising with government officials in order to craft a desired outcome.

A small number of Dalit leaders, especially those from comparatively prosperous backgrounds, responded to their failure to undermine student leaders' power by joining Jats in efforts to acquire student union posts and make money from their political clout. Some of these men also laid claim to *jugār*. These Dalits stressed that, as people from relatively poor backgrounds, they are especially attuned to the necessity of judicious opportunism and to possibilities to combine "modern" and "traditional" resources to telling effect. Dalits also contrasted their *jugār* with the allegedly leaden-footed, unimaginative practices of higher castes, "who were born with silver spoons in their mouths."

The rapid commercialization of the Meerut district and the associated rise of private companies and nonstate educational institutions undoubtedly contributed to this private celebration of a particular vision of entrepreneurship among Jats and Dalits. The idea of creatively combining unlike technologies, making bold but difficult decisions, and resolving difficulties through individual enterprise were common tropes of television advertisements, signboards, and leaflets distributed by major firms and private universities. But Jat and Dalit young men regarded the notion of *jugār* as rather embarrassing, partly because the word carried with it the association of not doing things "straight" (*sīdha*) or "right" (*thīk se*). Indeed, some Jat student leaders, including those involved in making money from their positions, chastised their friends for celebrating *jugār*. These Jats regarded having to collude with university and government officials as demeaning and said that they would much prefer to be operating in a system in which such activity was unnecessary. Images of success through individual entrepreneurialism associated with the commercialization of Meerut have encouraged Jats to embrace notions of *jugār*. But many continued to value an ethic of fairness, public service, and disinterested government that they had encountered while growing up in rural areas and through government textbooks within schools. Moreover, collective youth protests and critiques circulated by Dalits, left-wing students, and young women left a kind of moral residue in the minds of many Jats: distaste for the very practices that they felt compelled to engage in. Many Jats negotiated the resulting ethical dilemmas by referring to alternative time horizons. Several Jats pointed out that, although they have a short-term interest in profiting from their position, their long-term goal is to build cross-caste and cross-class alliances in order to protest endemic malpractice within the university. It is also worthwhile recalling that, before experiencing a catalogue of disappointments in their search for salaried employment, many of these Jat young men spoke proudly of their desire to become part of the Indian state and, once in their post, to uphold norms of liberal good governance.

Foucault's work on ethics is therefore important in directing attention toward the significance of morality in young men's lives, youth efforts to develop an "ethics" of practice, and the varied narratives that shape young men's sense of ethical conduct. But the efforts of many Jat student leaders and a few Dalits to develop an image of ethical entrepreneurship also related closely to the accumulative interests of these young people. The discourse and practice of *jugār* emerges as *both* an ambivalent attempt to develop an ethic of practice, as Foucault might have it, *and* as a way for relatively rich young men among the un- and underemployed to mark, bolster, and reproduce their power, as Bourdieu might stress.

Concluding Thoughts

Widespread unemployment among students in Meerut, UP, has led to the emergence of two rather different forms of ethico-political action. On the one hand, a broad range of students have launched critiques of state corruption and educational privatization. On the other hand, relatively rich Jat students have nurtured networks of collaborative praxis that sustain corruption and educational commercialization. Jat student leaders counteract accusations of double-dealing through a range of tactics, including euphemism, denial, and pragmatism. These strategies, and a tendency for Jats to sometimes privately celebrate their corruption, tie in with Bourdieu's argument that people's practices tend to reflect their class habitus and quest for social gain. But in private some Jats reflect critically on their actions, a point that suggests the value of a more Foucauldian engagement with morality as a human goal and the multiple narrative frameworks that shape young men's ethical projects. The broader relevance of these arguments for this book as a whole is to highlight the importance of grounding discussions of ethics with reference to the political economy of regional change, durable class inequalities, and ethnographic reflection on people's own cultural productions.

These conclusions raise the vexing question of the relationship between ethics on the ground—people's sense of themselves as "ethical" beings—and how we as scholars might imagine ethical forms of politics in contemporary UP. At first blush, Jat practices appear to reinforce pernicious inequalities. But it is crucial not to assume a moralizing tone in reflecting on Jat actions. Jat young men's strategies emerged out of an experience of marginalization. Moreover, Jats had contradictory ethical goals, and many hoped in the long term to address problems of social inequity. To posit a contrast between Jat ethics and our own ethical position is also to obscure the extent to which radical political action always involves compromise. As one Jat student leader put it, "I am just doing ordinary politics."

Notes

1. All names are pseudonyms.

2. See Craig Jeffrey, "A Fist Is Stronger Than Five Fingers: Caste and Dominance in Rural North India," *Transactions of the Institute of British Geographers* 25, no. 2 (2001): 1–30.

3. Pierre Bourdieu, *Distinction: A Social Critique of the Judgement of Taste* (London: Routledge and Kegan Paul, 1984).

4. Craig Jeffrey, Roger Jeffery, and Patricia Jeffery, *Degrees Without Freedom? Education, Masculinities, and Unemployment in North India* (Stanford, Calif.: Stanford University Press, 2008).

5. Pierre Bourdieu, *Masculine Domination* (Stanford, Calif.: Stanford University Press, 1999).

6. See, esp., Antonio Gramsci, *Selections from the Prison Notebooks,* ed. and trans. Q. Hoare and G. Nowell-Smith (London: Lawrence and Wishart, 1971); Stuart Hall, "Signification, Representation, Ideology: Althusser and the Poststructuralist Debates," *Critical Studies in Mass Communication* 2 (1985): 91–114; Judith Butler, *The Physic Life of Power: Theories in Subjection* (Stanford, Calif.: Stanford University Press, 1997); Paul Willis, "Cultural Production and Theories of Reproduction," in *Race, Class and Education,* ed. L. Barton and S. Walker (London: Croome Helm, 1982), 112–142.

7. Michel Foucault, *The Use of Pleasure,* trans. R. Hurly (New York: Vintage Books, 1990). See also Charles Hirschkind, "The Ethics of Listening: Cassette-Sermon Audition in Contemporary Egypt," *American Ethnologist* 28, no. 3 (2001): 623–649; Mahmood Saba, *Politics of Piety: The Islamic Revival and the Feminist Subject* (Princeton, N.J.: Princeton University Press, 2005), esp. 25–27.

8. See also Edward Said, *The World, the Text, and the Critic* (Cambridge, Mass.: Harvard University Press, 1983).

9. See Mike Savage, "A New Class Paradigm?" *British Journal of Sociology of Education* 24, no. 4 (2003): 535–541.

10. Dipesh Chakrabarty, *Habitations of Modernity: Essays in the Wake of Subaltern Studies* (Chicago: University of Chicago Press, 2002).

11. Registrar General and Census Commissioner of India, Population in the Age Group 0–6 and Literates by Residence and Sex—India and States/Union Territories (Delhi: Ministry of Home Affairs, 2002).

12. World Bank, *World Development Indicators* (Washington, D.C.: World Bank, 2002).

13. C. P. Chandrashekhar and Jayati Ghosh, *The Market That Failed: A Decade of Neoliberal Economic Reforms in India* (Delhi: Manohar, 2002).

14. Montek S. Ahluwalia, "State Level Performance under Economic Reforms in India," Working Paper No. 96, Center for Research on Economic Development and Policy Reform, Stanford University, 2001; V. K. Ramachandran and M. Swaminathan, *Financial Liberalization and Rural Credit in India* (Delhi: Tukila, 2005).

15. J. Mooij and S. M. Dev, "Social Sector Priorities: An Analysis of Budgets and Expenditures," Institute of Development Studies, IDS Working Paper 164 (University of Sussex, Brighton, U.K., 2002).

16. Geeta Kingdon and Mohammad Muzammil, *The Political Economy of Education in India: Teacher Politics in Uttar Pradesh* (Oxford: Oxford University Press, 2003).

17. Roger Jeffery, Patricia Jeffery, and Craig Jeffrey, "Social Inequality and the Privatisation of Secondary Schooling in North India," in *Educational Regimes in India,* ed. Radhika Chopra and Patricia Jeffery (Delhi: Sage, 2005), 41–61.

18. Zoya Hasan, *Quest for Power: Oppositional Movements and Post-Congress Politics in Uttar Pradesh* (Delhi: Oxford University Press, 1998).

19. M. N. Srinivas, "The Social System of a Mysore Village," in *Village India,* ed. McKim Marriott (Chicago: University of Chicago Press, 1955).

20. Jens Lerche, "Politics of the Poor: Agricultural Labourers and Political Transformations in Uttar Pradesh," in *Rural Labour Relations in India,* ed. Terence J. Byres, Karin Kapadia, and Jens Lerche (London: Frank Cass, 1999), 182–243.

21. Hasan, *Quest for Power,* 1998.

22. Craig Jeffrey, "Democratisation without Representation? The Power and Political Strategies of a Rural Elite in North India," *Political Geography* 19 (2000): 1013–1036; Jeffrey, "Caste, Class and Clientelism: A Political Economy of Everyday Corruption in Rural North India," *Economic Geography* 78, no. 1 (2002): 21–42.

23. Jim Bentall and Stuart, E. Corbridge, "Urban-Rural Relations, Demand Politics, and the 'New Agrarianism' in NW India: The Bharatiya Kisan Union," *Transactions of the Institute of British Geographers,* n.s. 2, no. 1 (1996): 27–48.

24. David G. Mandelbaum, *Society in India,* 2 vols. (Berkeley: University of California Press, 1970); Oliver Mendelsohn and Marieke Vicziany, *The Untouchables: Subordination, Poverty, and the State in Modern India* (Cambridge: Cambridge University Press, 1998).

25. Christophe Jaffrelot, *India's Silent Revolution: The Rise of the Low Castes in North Indian Politics* (Delhi: Permanent Black, 2003).

26. Eric Stokes, *The Peasant Armed: The Indian Revolt of 1857* (Oxford: Clarendon, 1986).

27. Where English words are italicized and in quotation marks, this indicates that my respondents used the English word; it is not a translation from Hindi.

28. See Jeffrey, "A Fist Is Stronger Than Five Fingers"; and Jeffrey, Jeffery, and Jeffery, *Degrees Without Freedom?*

29. For a detailed examination of social differentiation among unemployed young men in UP, see Jeffrey, Jeffery, and Jeffery, *Degrees Without Freedom?*

30. K. Mannheim, "The Problem of Generations," in *The New Pilgrims: Youth Protest in Transition,* ed. Philip Altbach and R. Laufer (New York: David McKay, 1972 [1936]), 101–138.

31. Certain details of Habir's career have been altered to protect his anonymity.

32. For more details of middle-class political strategies and Dalits' reactions to Jat power, see Craig Jeffrey, "Kicking Away the Ladder: Student Politics and the Making of an Indian Middle Class," *Environment and Planning D: Society and Space* 26, no. 3 (2008): 517–536; Craig Jeffrey, "Fixing Futures: Educated Unemployment through a North Indian Lens," *Comparative Studies in Society and History* 51, no. 1 (2009): 182–211; and Jeffrey, *Timepass.* This section summarizes material presented in Jeffrey, Jeffery, and Jeffery, *Degrees Without Freedom?* and Jeffrey, "Fixing Futures."

33. Jeffrey, "Fixing Futures."

34. Michael Herzfeld, *Cultural Intimacy: Social Poetics in the Nation-State* (New York: Routledge, 2005).

35. Foucault, *The Use of Pleasure.*

Part 4.

Ethical Lives of Others

11.

Living by Dying: Gandhi, *Satyagraha,* and the Warrior

Ajay Skaria

> It is not at all true to say that, to be able to fight, it is essential to acquire the ability to use arms; the moment, therefore, a man wakes up to the power of the soul, that very moment he comes to know the strength he has for fighting. That is why I believe that he is the true warrior who does not die killing but who has mastered the *mantra* of living by dying. The sages who discovered the never-failing law of non-violence were themselves great warriors.
>
> —Gandhi

> I claim to be one of the greatest Kshatriyas of India.
>
> —Gandhi

> I have not got rid of the fear of death, despite much thinking.
>
> —Gandhi

Writing in 1921 Gandhi remarks: "I have been collecting descriptions of *swaraj.* One of these would be: swaraj is the abandonment of the fear of death [*maranbhayno tyaag*]. A nation which allows itself to be influenced by the fear of death cannot attain swaraj, and cannot retain it if somehow attained."[1] And a few years earlier, when his attempts in Kheda district to recruit farmers for the British Army met with little success, he wrote to C. F. Andrews: "I find great difficulties in recruiting but do you know that not one man has yet objected because he would not kill. They object because they fear to die. This unnatural fear of death is ruining the nation."[2]

Repeatedly in his writings and speeches Gandhi returns to the question of death. Consider the argument, in chapter 16 of *Hind Swaraj,* between the Editor (the figure who voices Gandhi's arguments) and the Reader (the figure who voices mainstream nationalist arguments). The Reader suggests that violence is justified in some situations: "You will not find fault with a continuance of force to prevent a child from thrusting its foot into fire? Somehow or other we have to gain our end." But the Editor responds:

> Now we shall take your last illustration, that of the child thrusting its foot into fire. . . . Supposing that it can exert so much physical force that it renders you powerless and rushes into fire, then you cannot prevent it. There are only two remedies open to you—either you must kill it in order to prevent it from perishing in the flames, or you must give your own life because you do not wish to see it perish before your very eyes. You will not kill it. If your heart is not quite full of pity [unless your *dayabal* (power of compassion) is total], it is possible that you will not surrender yourself by preceding the child and going into the fire yourself. You, therefore, helplessly allow it to go into the flames. Thus, at any rate, you are not using physical force. I hope you will not consider that it is still physical force, though of a low order, when you would forcibly prevent the child from rushing towards the fire if you could. That force is of a different order and we have to understand what it is.[3]

Note the distinctive way in which the thought of dayabal organizes death and life in this passage. Only if there is total dayabal is the Editor's interlocutor likely to give up his life in the futile attempt to save the child. Dayabal thus leads to the giving up of one's life. And dayabal is not just any sentiment for the Editor. The Editor remarks of *daya,* or compassion: "Tulsi says do not leave daya, as long as the *body* has life." Furthermore, the Editor uses dayabal also as a synonym for *satyagraha,* or passive resistance.

Thus a paradox is involved in the practice of daya and satyagraha: while daya cannot be abandoned as long as the body has life, the exercise of daya, or satyagraha itself, requires the giving up of life or a giving of oneself to death. Perhaps it is this paradoxical relation that Gandhi struggles to conceptualize when he remarks elsewhere that the satyagrahi is the one who has mastered the mantra of "living by dying." Perhaps it is also this paradoxical relation that he struggles to conceptualize in a later chapter of *Hind Swaraj,* where the Editor says that the satyagrahi is one who has death as a "bosom friend."

As the stress on living suggests, the satyagrahi is not simply someone who dies for a cause. Rather, in suggesting that the satyagrahi has death as a "bosom friend," what is envisioned here is not the proper death but the proper life. Abandoning the fear of death, therefore, is not about dying but about living the life proper to swaraj—a word that can be glossed as "freedom," "independence," or the "rule of the proper." Indeed, through his concept of swaraj, Gandhi ventures a concept of the human—and of the life proper to swaraj, or the rule of the swa—which questions and departs from the humanist concept of life.

Finitude

This other concept of the human is centrally organized around immeasurable equality. Now, within the terms of humanism, immeasurable equality is invisible, or incoherent where visible. In the humanist concept of the human, humans are immeasurable in the sense that they are masters of measure: they measure and yet do not ideally submit to measure. It turns out, however, that precisely in order to maintain their immeasurability, they not only have to exercise but also submit to measure. For, to rehearse a well-worn theme in humanist thought (especially in its modern liberal iteration), the emphasis on freedom immediately encounters the fact of the freedom of other rational humans. It is this simultaneous freedom of rational humans that mainstream liberal thought has conventionally conceptualized as equality. Such equality, it finds, can be realized or made real by insisting that all humans are equal in terms of some abstract measure. Thus equality takes the form of measurably equal rights enshrined in law, whether these rights are positive or negative. This fantasy of a world where humans are originally masters of measure and only secondarily submit to measure organizes both the utopias and dystopias of the "state of nature" that were at one time so rife, and that still silently mark the conceptual limits of the liberal political imagination. In other words, liberalism thinks of its practice of measurable equality precisely as a faithful rendering of the immeasurability that for it is constitutive of the human. This emphasis on measurable equality is constitutive of our modern concepts of citizenship, democracy, justice—indeed of our modernity. Within these humanist terms, the phrase "immeasurable equality" does not make sense. For the very implementation of the immeasurability of humans requires a measurable equality.

Nor does Gandhi's affirmation of death usually make sense from within a humanist framework. In humanist traditions, while the human body is finite (and death is a particularly dramatic marker of this finitude), what makes for the humanity of humans is their infinitude. Here finitude is the mark of the thing or the animal, the mark of that which has only limited force. And infinitude is the mark of humans; it is because humans are capable of infinitude that they are, uniquely, free. Thus humanity is centrally about affirming the infinitude of humans, about overcoming the finitude that marks their bodies. And in such an understanding of the infinitude and immeasurability of the human, death is usually a finitude in a privative sense, an empty nullity, immeasurable only because it takes away the bodily life that is necessary to measure, to remain immeasurable and infinite. Here death is what must be constantly transcended, overcome, and fought against. Indeed, there can be no staying with death; death can only be feared. To claim a friendship with death, as the Gandhian satyagrahi does, is indefensibly morbid in humanist terms.

Many nationalists in India (including the Gandhi before *Hind Swaraj*) accepted this rich, deeply nuanced, and often empowering ethical tradition of thinking about the human. For this tradition provided the resources to question colonialism by claiming, in an anticolonial spirit, humanity for the colonized. But by the time of *Hind Swaraj,* Gandhi cannot affirm this tradition even in an anticolonial spirit. By this time, for him the tradition is based on one founding assumption that he cannot accept—its insistence on the infinitude of humans. For Gandhi, the mastery of finitude on which such infinitude is founded already involves a fundamental and unacceptable violence, a violence toward that which is transcended because it is finite. As he was acutely aware, this line between the human and the animal or object always passed between humans, and sustained a hierarchy among them. Perhaps one way to describe the overall stakes of Gandhi's intellectual, ethical, and political interventions, then, is to say that they struggled to conceptualize the human differently, in a way that would not be marked by such a profound domination of the animal and the thing.

The point of departure for Gandhi's interventions was the insistence that the human is marked by a constitutive finitude, and, by staying with and in this finitude, a relation that properly allows for the otherness of the other is possible. This emphasis on finitude occurs repeatedly in Gandhi's writings. In chapter 13 of *Hind Swaraj,* for instance, the Editor, speaking for Gandhi, argues that "true civilization" is "that mode of conduct which points out to man the path of duty [*potani farj,* his own obligation]." This duty requires following "morality [*niti,* ethics]," and morality requires that we "obtain mastery over our mind and our passions. So doing, we know ourselves." He goes on to argue that "the mind is a restless bird; the more it gets the more it wants, and still it remains unsatisfied. The more we indulge our passions, the more unbridled they become. Our ancestors, therefore, set a limit to our indulgences." Thus it was that Indians continued for thousands of years with "the same kind of plough," "the same kind of cottages":

> It was not that we did not know how to invent machinery [*sancha*], but our forefathers knew that, if we set our hearts after such things, we would become slaves and lose our moral fibre. They, therefore, after due deliberation decided that we should only do what we could with our hands and feet. . . . This nation had courts, lawyers and doctors, but they were all within bounds.

But what is at stake in this finitude, or in death as its most dramatic marker, is by no means readily available to us.[4] Precisely because his thinking involved a relatively unprecedented way of questioning humanism, Gandhi struggled to conceptualize the other human that he affirmed, and his thinking of the other human is not readily available to us. It must be comprehended by attending closely to the hesitations and forks that mark his arguments, to the gap between his Gujarati and English writings.

In this essay I track Gandhi's fractured thinking of finitude by attending to his concern with death. In the next section, I focus on how his emphasis on "living by dying" may be too easily understood in relatively familiar terms—that is, as enabling sublation through practices such as *brahmacharya* (celibacy) to a larger phenomenon such as the nation or *moksha* (salvation). I suggest, however, that these terms are insufficient. The remainder of the essay is organized under the sign of immeasurable equality, a phrase I use axiomatically to indicate the most important and most obscured stake of Gandhi's interventions. It is the most obscured precisely because it is quite inaccessible within the humanist traditions that continue to dominate our categories, perhaps never more insidiously than when we proclaim that we have broken from humanism. What makes it the most important is that it entails another way of thinking of the human—that is, another way of thinking about, among other things, politics, religion, ethics, sociality, and the animal. Where humans are immeasurably equal, measure is always violent. And yet a politics of immeasurable equality opposes this violence not in the name of nonviolence but rather in the name of a force greater than violence, the force that Gandhi occasionally described as *satyagraha* (passive resistance), *atmabal* (soul force), or *daya* (compassion).

Obviously Gandhi's arguments about immeasurable equality are too complex even to be systematically intimated within this brief essay. So I set myself a more limited task. The entire essay, after the first section, focuses on the one initial question that must be encountered when thinking about immeasurable equality: What can equality mean in the absence of measure? I argue that Gandhi's emphasis on finitude and death, by proceeding through the figure of the warrior, provided a distinctive way to think about equality. The warrior was the figure who was equal to his own death. The warrior encounters death, I suggest, not as a portal to life eternal but as a finitude in a productive sense, as that to which the warrior seeks to be equal. And this equality with and to death in its immeasurability is necessarily accompanied by an intimation of the immeasurable equality of the other—the warrior's antagonist. This intimation of the immeasurable equality of both self and other is, for Gandhi, central to the concept of the warrior. And yet the warrior must cleave away from it despite his encounter with it. If Gandhi calls the satyagrahi the "warrior," I suggest, it is because the satyagrahi seeks to abide instead by immeasurable equality.

In the future I hope to explore the questions that follow from the formulations I end with here. For what is still not thought through in either of these formulations—neither in the Socratic brahmachari nor the warrior—is precisely what would be involved in the living by dying practiced by the satyagrahi, which proceeds through a friendship with death. A friend always gives only him- or herself. Thus the thought of satyagraha leads to a twofold question. First, with what kind of death is a friendship possible, the death, in satyagraha or dayabal, that becomes a "bosom friend"? And, second, exactly what would be involved in a friendship with death? The answers to these questions would clarify how satyagraha is living by dying, and though not addressed here, my goal in this essay is to prepare for these answers.

Sublation

Consider, for a start, Gandhi's fascinating rendering, in 1908, of Plato's *Apology* from English into Gujarati under the title *Ek Satyavirni katha* [Story of a warrior for truth]. The introduction to the rendering describes Socrates as a satyagrahi who "adopted satyagraha against his own people." And though Gandhi abbreviates several themes from the *Apology,* he foregrounds, quite consistently, perhaps even more than in the English version, Socrates' insistence that he had no "fear of death." The reason for this, to quote from Gandhi's translation, is that "to fear death is equal to [*barobar*] claiming the pomp of knowledge [*gyaan*]. For who has discovered for certain that death is a thing to be afraid of? Why should we not believe that death is the greatest good that can happen to men [*manas*]? . . . If I have any wisdom [*dahapan*], it is this: I claim to know nothing about death."

Socrates' absence of a fear of death follows from his questioning. This questioning, this principle of the question, is the wisdom that sets him apart from everyone else. When the question becomes a principle in this manner, then the question is not driven simply by the desire for answers—the desire to establish a positive knowledge that dispels ignorance. Rather than seeking the truth, here the question itself is the truth, always questioning and dispelling the "pomp of knowledge." If Socrates does not fear the nonbeing that death usually symbolizes, this is because the being of the question questions even the apparent nonbeing of death. The nonbeing of death itself is here sublated into the being of the question.

If Gandhi found Socrates' fearlessness so attractive, this may have been because he, too, often practiced a similar fearlessness, denying the nonbeing of death. In a speech he gave on the death of the Indian nationalist "Deshbandhu" C. R. Das, for instance, he remarked:

> But what I want to do is to explain to you the meaning of death [*mrityuna rahasya*]. If you believe with me that the *Gita* is an allegory [*rupak*],

you will also be able to understand the meaning of death as explained in it:

> What is non-Being is never known to have been, and what is Being [*sat*] is never known not to have been. Of both these the secret has been seen by the seers of the truth.

> This verse contains the whole meaning. Verse after verse states that the body is *asat* [untruth]. . . . But there are probably no other people who fear death and cry and grieve over it as much as we do. In the *Mahabharata,* in fact, it is stated that lamentation after someone's death gives pain to the departed soul, and the *Gita,* too, was composed to remove the fear of death. . . . The more I think about the ceaselessly active life of Deshbandhu, the more I feel that he is alive today. While he lived in the body, he was not fully alive, but he is so today. In our selfishness, we believed that his body was all that mattered, whereas the *Gita* teaches—and I understand the truth of this more clearly as days pass—that all worry about a perishable thing is meaningless, is so much waste of time.

> Non-Being simply does not exist, and Being never ceases to exist.[5]

Both arguments reject the commonsensical contention that associates death with nonbeing, prompting a fear of death. Both arguments also respond by insisting that being persists even beyond death; both share an emphasis, organized quite differently, of course, on the transcending of finite life by the infinitude proper to the human. Within this problematic, "living by dying" means that even as one dies, this death allows another life to live all the more intensely. Within this problematic, if swaraj is the abandonment of the fear of death, this is so only because by such dying can a transcendent and infinitely finite entity like the nation live; here the nationalist dies into the nation.

Such living by dying need not even imply sacrificing one's own life. Disagreeing with a correspondent who had attributed cowardice to the Indian nationalists who espoused violence, Gandhi wrote: "The writer pays poor compliment to the party of violence or by whatever name it may be called, when he imputes to them fear of death. They forfeited their lives when they dedicated themselves to their creed. That they keep themselves in hiding does not mean that they fear death, but it means that they want to hang on to life as long as possible so as to carry out their project."[6] In other words, the heroic nationalists who gave their life to the nation also practiced a certain living by dying, where they gave themselves to their very death for a cause. This very giving of themselves to their death authorized a living on and an evading of death so that their cause, the nation, could be better pursued.

Gandhi never explicitly abandoned this sublative way of thinking about death. Symptomatic of it was his insistence throughout his life that he was only concerned with politics because, in the current age, it was the best way to attain *moksha* (a word he translated quite conventionally as "salvation"). Also indicative of this thinking was his usual presentation of the vow of brahmacharya, or "celibacy," which Gandhi repeatedly claimed was the first vow that should follow the twinned vows of *satya* and *ahimsa* observed by satyagrahis. His understanding of brahamacharya emerges in his remarks in *Mangalprabhat:* "Let us remember the root meaning [*mool arth*] of 'brahmacharya.'" *Charya* means "course of conduct"; *brahmacharya,* "conduct adapted to the search of Brahman, that is, Truth [*brahmani—satyani*]." From this root meaning arises another special meaning, namely, "control of all the senses" [*sarvendriyasaiyam*]. The incomplete definition, which restricts itself only to the sexual aspect of the term, must be entirely forgotten.[7]

When brahmacharya is thought of in this way (an interpretation that is sanctioned by many texts associated with canonical Hinduism), its ascesis is entirely compatible to the infinitization of being beyond death practiced by Gandhi's Socrates or the Gandhi of the funeral speech quoted above. The brahmachari does not fear death because he gives himself to Brahman, so that death, for him, is only a "portal to life eternal." Thought of in this way, the finitude of the brahmachari's life is necessary so that proper subsumption into moksha can take place.

Thought of in terms of brahmacharya, satyagraha is primarily a radicalization of the terrorists' living by dying. The extremists give their lives for a cause and at the same time kill for that cause. But though satyagrahis also die and achieve infinitude, they refuse to kill for it. Thus it can be said that the satyagraha requires an even more fearless relationship with death than that of the nationalists.

Liberal traditions find it easy to understand and even admire such satyagraha. For here satyagraha is primarily a radicalization of those influential liberal traditions that recognize the state as the only legitimate entity, the only entity that one can die or kill for. By dying without taking another's life, satyagrahis seem to respect, undeniably, the state's injunction against violence by any actor other than the state. They submit to the state's violence against them with nonviolent resistance, and refuse to allow for any state of exception in which to practice a founding violence that might produce another state order. Understood in this way, satyagraha becomes an extremely radical liberalism toward which mainstream liberalism expresses the deepest respect and at the same time the deepest skepticism (for here satyagraha is utopian again in the sense that it does not allow for the exception that would allow for the constitution of a state).

Warrior

But although Gandhi never quite abandons the sublative way of thinking of death, by the time of *Hind Swaraj* that thinking is ruptured by a consideration of "living by dying" that is organized around the figure of the warrior. The warrior already occurs in Gandhi's titling of his earlier translation of Plato's *Apology* as *Ek Satyavirni katha,* meaning "Story of a Warrior for Truth". He is even more pronounced in the title of Gandhi's English translation "The Story of a True Warrior."[8] In this English translation (less conventional than another that occurs in Gandhi's *Collected Works*—"The Story of a Soldier of Truth"),[9] we recognize the consolidation of a new concept. Whereas in the Gujarati title the warrior fights for truth, in the English title satyagraha is the truth of the concept of the warrior. But neither the English nor the Gujarati texts do much more with the figure of the warrior.

Yet within two years, by the time of *Hind Swaraj* (the text marking the break between the young and the mature Gandhi), this figure becomes more prominent. In chapter 17 the Editor responds to the Reader's assertion that "passive resistance is a splendid weapon of the weak" by asking: "Is he the warrior who himself [*potey*] carries his death on his head, or he who keeps the death of the other in his own [*potana*] hands? [*Potey maathey maut lai farey tey ranvir ke beejana maut potana haath ma raakhey che te?*]." The English translation adds the adjective "true." "Who is the true warrior—he who keeps death always as a bosom-friend [cannot delete: in original quote] or he who controls the death of others?" Furthermore, whereas in the Gujarati text the satyagrahi carries his own death while the conventional warrior controls the death of others, the English text modifies the argument significantly by insisting that the satyagrahi has a further relation with death, namely, that the satyagrahi has death as a "bosom friend."

In this invocation of the "true warrior," there is clearly a concept of the warrior at work. In Gandhi's explicit formulations, this concept is founded on the sublative notion of the brahmachari. Thus the Editor remarks in chapter 17 (to translate for ourselves from the Gujarati: "To become a *ranvir* [warrior]—it is not as though everybody can do so as soon as he wishes to. A warrior [*ladvaiya*] will have to observe brahmacharya."[10] Indian classical traditions certainly testify to this argument. It may even resonate etymologically. The Editor uses the word *vir* independently to refer to the warrior but also as a suffix in the words *satyavir* and *ranvir.* And the brahmachari is one who retains his *virya* (semen). As is well known, many classical Hindu texts insist that the production of semen requires enormous male energy and that to expend it is to lose that energy and power, that is, to "lose stamina"—Gandhi's translation of the word *avirya.* Thus, to be a brahmachari in such accounts, is simply the essential and unavoidable foundation for becoming a warrior; there can be no warrior who does not practice the sublative ascesis of brahmacharya.

But in the divergence between the Gujarati and English versions of the sentence given above, the concept of the "warrior" is also thought of entirely differently from this sublative ascesis. This other concept of the warrior is, without doubt, as profoundly gendered and violent as the classical concept of the brahmachari-warrior which it displaces. Nevertheless a conceptual segue takes place here. Now what becomes crucial is the warrior's encounter with death.

Perhaps the prefix *ran* in the word *ranvir* is symptomatic of this break. *Ran* usually refers to a battle or battlefield. *Ranvir* thus appears to be somewhat redundant —the brave warrior in battle or in the battlefield. This redundancy, however, does foreground the centrality of battle and the battlefield. The metaphor of battle and the battlefield (and especially the battlefield of Kurukshetra, where the war described in the *Mahabharata* took place) is central to Gandhi's arguments. As we know, he describes the *Bhagavad Gita* (the discourse delivered by Krishna to Arjuna at Kurukshetra, or the battlefield of Kuru) as the single greatest inspiration for his satyagraha. He also sometimes describes the human body as a "little Kurukshetra," and the metaphor of battle and the battlefield governs many of his descriptions of the confrontations involved in satyagraha. Indeed, he also refers repeatedly to satyagraha against the British as a *dharmayudh.* The word is rendered into English in various ways, though perhaps the most common translation (and the correct one in view of the usual translation of *dharma* as religion and *yudh* as battle) is "religious battle." Thus an inversion of the explicit terms of Gandhi's argument occurs in his texts. Rather than brahmacharya being a way to think of the warrior, the warrior becomes the way to rethink the sublative concept of brahmacharya.

Thus we have arrived at a place quite different from the one where we began. Initially the word *brahmachari* took us to the word *ranvir* which in turn led us to the discomforting word *dharmayudh.* A word such as this, within a liberal problematic, can only be misunderstood (as indeed has its equivalent, *jihad*) to mean the pursuit of a goal or values or ethics that are authorized through religion (that is, by a force not amenable to reason) and that are therefore to be pursued religiously (namely, by any means possible). This misunderstanding is not merely an error. It occurs because liberalism encounters a strangeness it cannot fathom when contemplating *dharmayudh,* and therefore the term is necessarily misunderstood because it is evaluated in liberalism's own terms of rule-bound means and rationally defensible ends.

Equal

So what is strange about Gandhi's concept of religious war or of the brahmachari warrior who fights a dharmayudh? The word *dharmayudh* is most commonly associated with the *Mahabharata* (which Gandhi often referred to) and the battle at Kurukshetra. That battle was a dharmayudh because it was governed by rules of conduct followed by both parties. Gandhi's understanding of the rules of conduct involved in a dharmayudh emerges when he compares two alternative translations of an article title, "*Nidaan dharmayudh karo.*" He suggests that the translation "Fight Square If You Must" is superior to "At Least Fight a Religious War."

The basic rule of conduct of a dharmayudh, then, is to "fight square." But how does a warrior do this? In the opening passages of the *Bhishma Parva,* or the sixth book of the *Mahabharata,* before the battle begins, the commanders meet and agree on several battle codes. These provide the necessary equality required of combatants, stating that those engaged in combat will only fight their equals and will never engage in combat against unequal opponents. Though violating these rules of conduct marks even the most virtuous—for example, Yudhistir, who, as Gandhi noted, tells a lie to win a crucial battle)[11]—nevertheless it is this theme of equality that is central to Gandhi's concept of *dharmayudh.*

But what can equality among warriors mean here, when there is no common measure?

Speaking in 1921 to a group of Kathi Rajputs, Gandhi said that they should, for the sake of Hindustan,

> abandon the thought of killing, prepare to die, and become pure [*shudh,* "true"] Kshatriyas. Killing is not a Kshatriya's dharma. The Kshatriya who kills someone weaker than himself is not a Kshatriya but a murderer. He who, in order to rescue the weak [*durbal*], fights with a strong man and kills him is forgiven, but the one who dies when rescuing the weak, without killing even the stronger opponent, is a complete [*pooro,* "true"] Kshatriya. To die—to not run away—this is his dharma. It is not his dharma to create the fear of death in the other [*beeja*]. Rather, his dharma is to abandon the fear of death.[12]

Three arguments emerge from this and related passages. First, the warrior seeks above all to be equal with his own death, rather than to be fearless in the face of death because death sublates the warrior into a being beyond death—that is, nation, moksha, and so on. The warrior seeks to kill only those who are equal. To fight those who are equal, however, and to fight in a way that allows them to remain equal, involves making one's own death a constant prospect. In other words, though it is empirically correct to argue that the warrior seeks to survive the battle, and in this sense embraces not death but the last chance before death, this statement does not at all understand the concept of the warrior. For the warrior's distinctiveness is not only in killing and surviving, in seizing the last chance. To think in this way is to think of death as a commonsensical problematic, where death is considered to be privative or sublative (as that finitude that takes away life or as that which must be transcended for one to become a being beyond death).

By contrast, the very dharma of the warrior is to give himself to his own death. The warrior does not die for some cause that transcends or is beyond his death. (I do not speak here in an anthropological or sociological spirit. Were that the case, it would be easy enough to multiply examples of South Asian warrior cultures that believe in a transcendental afterlife.) Rather, the warrior seeks to live only after having given himself to his own death; the warrior himself has received himself back from his own death. Here it is his own death that gives life to the warrior. As such, what is understood here is not only the proper death but, more important, a distinctive life.

What is meant by the warrior receiving a life equal to its own death? The warrior has received himself back from death, but death here is a peculiar limit. Given his death, which is always his own, the warrior no longer "is." Something significant is revealed here: that this is a life where perseverance in being is no longer dominant. Being a warrior is no longer about being and, above all, is not about the mastery of death that allows a being to exist beyond death. The warrior has been separated from his being in the most radical manner possible—by giving himself to his nonbeing. Of this radical separation there can be no measure, for there no longer "is" something substantive to be measured. (Hence the centrality of finitude, for only in finitude can this separation be suffered: that which is infinite must necessarily seek to transcend this separation.) This is the equality the warrior establishes with his own death, which he has never transcended and from which he is both separated and also received his life. In this life the distinctive immeasurability of the warrior is apparent; that is, the warrior is immeasurable not because his life is infinite or an end in itself but rather because he receives his life from and through a refusal to persist in being, through an equality with death.

Gift

The second argument that can be gleaned from Gandhi's talk to the Kathi Rajputs in 1921 is that equality with death always intimates an immeasurable equality with the other. This intimation of equality with the other sets the life and death of the warrior apart from all privative or sublative forms of dying. In *Hind Swaraj,* the Editor is highly critical of the extremists who call for the assassination of key Englishmen as a way to secure swaraj. Speaking of Madan Lal Dhingra, the extremist who, in 1909, shot and killed a British official, the Editor says: "It is a big mistake [*bhool*] to believe that the murders committed by Dhingra in Hindustan will reap any benefit I do consider Dhingra a patriot [*swadeshabhimani*], but his love [*priti*] was blind [*gheli*]. He sacrificed [*bhog,* "gave"] his own body in the wrong way [*ku-margey*]. And therefore only a loss of benefit [*ger-fayado*] can result."

Precisely how did Dhingra give his body in the "wrong way"? Strikingly, Gandhi argues, Dhingra's violence was not demonstrated so much by his use of arms but rather by his violation of hospitality codes and, in turn, his refusal to bestow equality on his opponents. In an essay written in London immediately after the assassination, Gandhi argued:

> If I kill someone in my own house without a warning—one who has done me no harm—I can only be called a coward. An ancient custom [*asli rivaj*] among the Arabs is that they would not kill anyone in their own house, even if the person was their enemy. They would kill him only after he had left the house and after he had had time to arm himself. Those who believe in violence ["that violence will lead to good"] are brave men [*bahadur*] only if they observe these rules when killing someone. Otherwise they must be looked upon as cowards [*beekan*]. It may be said that what Mr. Dhingra did, publicly and knowing full well that he himself would have to die, attests in no small way to his courage. But, as I have pointed out above, in a state of intoxication [*nasha*] men can act in these ways and also banish the fear of death. Whatever courage is expressed here is the result of intoxication and not a quality of the man himself. A man's own courage consists in suffering deeply and over a long period. Only when an act is preceded by careful reflection [*samajhpurvak*] does that act become a brave one.[13]

Two related points are important to consider here. First, there is the familiar one: "In this the courage is that of the intoxication, not of the man." Gandhi's warrior seeks a death quite distinct from the death of the one who dies fearlessly in the name of a cause. In the latter case, the fearlessness belongs to the intoxication, not to the man. "A man's own courage" emerges only in the finitude that comes when one resists intoxication and sublation, when, in other words, one is equal to one's own death.

Second, the passage does not attack violence per se but rather violence directed at an unequal, for example, one who is unarmed. Similarly, in the earlier passage, the injunction on the Kshatriya is not so much against killing as against killing those weaker than oneself. But what does equality with the other mean here? We are often tempted to interpret this equality in terms of common measure, where an equal warrior would be one with equal power. This, for instance, is what most evidently happens in the *Bhishma Parva,* where, when warriors agree to fight with their equals, their equals are understood as those with the same weapons and equipment.

But the passages we have read suggest that equality, where there is no such common measure, can only mean equality with reference to a death that is always their own, even as it provides a relation between the two. In being equally given to their own deaths—which can never be a shared and substantive measure—the warrior and the other sustain their equality. It is in this sense that the warrior always practices an immeasurable equality with the other. This equality is especially evident when the warrior fights with the knowledge from the beginning that he will lose. In still wagering his death in the battle, he refuses to accept subordination to the other and so he is equal to his enemy. Even where the warrior secures domination over the other, he does so only by means of his own hands and feet, refusing to seek infinity by acquiring or deploying whatever weapons may be necessary to win. In this sense, even if the remark in the Gujarati text is inadvertent in describing the warrior as "he who keeps the death of the other in his own [*potana*] hands," that remark is congruent with Gandhi's understanding of the warrior who kills his equals. Such a warrior keeps the death of the other in his own hands, which is also to say that he always faces the prospect of death at the hands of the other.

Furthermore, this equal relation between the combatants makes the battlefield a site that refuses every totalization that cannot be subsumed or turned into a narrative about either the victory or defeat of one of the actors. As such, this violence, however immense and epic, is nevertheless finite and travels by analogy and metaphor rather than by causality and the mastery causality involves. The warrior does not give his life for a larger or transcendent cause. Rather, he gives up his life because that is what constitutes a warrior. And the giving up of his life is, paradoxically, not a gift to a transcendent entity or even to those whom he protects; perhaps, above all, it is a gift to the one he battles against. This emphasis on being and finding a worthy opponent occurs repeatedly in Gandhi's writings. Consider the remarks he made in a speech in Dakor:

> Though I criticize the British Empire [English Sultanate], I also call it fearless [*bahadur*]. The British love their country. It is their evil [*rakshashi*, demonic] tendencies which are to be shunned. I would even admire Ravana's courage. Tulsidas has said that, if one must have an enemy, let him be like Ravana. To fight against Lakshmana, one must be an Indrajit.[14]

The gift that a worthy opponent gives to the warrior by engaging him—whether in battle or peace—is equality to the warrior's own death. This equality is not a constative equality that the warrior already has, as is the case with the formal equality of measure. Rather, this immeasurable equality must be performed, and it is always performed by being received from the other as a gift. Without receiving it from the other, even where the other seeks to kill him, the warrior cannot claim an immeasurable equality with the other. In the *Bhishma Parva,* which so fascinates Gandhi, perhaps this is why Bhishma seeks to goad Krishna into taking his life. Losing his life to a godly figure like Krishna would have allowed Bhishma to achieve an illustrious equality to his own death.

Thus we arrive at a curious insight, one that is foreign to Gandhi's explicit formulations and yet in another way faithful to them. Through the figure of the brahmachari, Gandhi struggles to think an immeasurable equality with the other, an equality that he articulates most forcefully through the figure of the warrior. The warrior is not only equal to his own death, but he can receive this equality only from the other. At the same time the warrior's dharmayudh is not so much a battle that follows codes of ethical conduct as it is a battle that is fought in equality with death.

The distinctiveness of this immeasurable equality with the other can be elicited by contrasting it with the equality practiced in modern warfare. The modern general must, in principle, respect the enemy combatant's human rights; these rights are laid down in protocols such as the Geneva Convention. Yet these protocols institute only a measurable and abstract equality. Here, in contrast, equality is a rudimentary baseline that must be respected under all circumstances. This way of thinking about equality and rights is intrinsic to our usual liberal distinctions between positive and negative rights and freedoms. Beyond this rudimentary and abstract equality, modern generals must measure so perfectly that they master the enemy without bringing their own deaths into play, without making their opponents into equal combatants. Indeed, it is precisely equality in the immeasurable sense that the modern general must deny to his enemy. Even where modern soldiers are out-measured and have to become heroic, wagering their own lives, their claim is not to that immeasurable equality with death and with the other. Instead, they give their lives to an infinitude—the nation, for example—which is greater than either they or the enemy. As such, modern soldiers can never give the intimation of an immeasurable equality either to themselves or their others: even when modern warfare involves "dying for," such dying occurs for and toward an infinitude. In Gandhi's terms, the modern soldier-hero must, like Dhingra, always "give his body wrongly." From Gandhi's perspective, this kind of modern warfare is cowardly precisely because the purposes of the calculation and measure precludes the soldiers' equality to their own death, and therefore also their equality to their enemy.

In contrast, the warrior's protocols of immeasurable equality sustain a relationship of respect between opponents. This respect between combatants organizes, for example, the suspension of the battle in the *Bhishma Parva* while Bhishma lies dying. This respect recognizes the equality that prevails between the warrior and his enemy, because both put their own deaths into play. Where such equality exists, even when the warrior seeks to kill his enemy, the latter cannot be thought of as evil. Instead, another relation with the enemy is always possible, perhaps one of love and respect. This may be why Gandhi insisted, on several occasions, that even if Indians lacked the courage to practice satyagraha, they should try to develop the courage to act as warriors.

Pre-

These two insights regarding the warrior's immeasurable equality to his own death and to his enemy can prepare us to understand the third argument that emerges from Gandhi's talk to the Kathi Rajputs in 1921. On one occasion, referring to Lakshman and Indrajit, two key figures from the *Ramayana,* he remarks in a letter to his nephew, Maganlal Gandhi:

> Lakshman and Indrajit were both celebates (*brahmacharis*) and had conquered sleep and were therefore equally valorous [*parakrami*]. But the valour of the former was divine, while that of the latter ungodly [*asuri,* "demonic"]. This means that the vow of brahmacharya and other vows are holy and bring happiness only when they are taken as a spiritual discipline [*atmathey*]. If resorted to by a demon, they only add misery. This is a very serious statement to make, but, all the same, it is no doubt true [*yatharth*]. [Missing in the English translation: *Ema shanka jaraye nathi* ("There can be no doubt in this matter").] Lord Patanjali has shown this very well in his *Yogadarshan.* This is the thing our religion teaches us.[15]

Recognizing and perhaps recoiling from the radicalism of his words, Gandhi describes his pronouncement as a "very serious statement to make" but adds that it is nevertheless "the thing our religion teaches us." Here an inversion occurs, and the concept of the warrior is now central to that of brahmacharya. No longer is brahmacharya a way to Brahman or Being (*sat*), and even less is it a way to realize ahimsa, or nonviolence. Rather, it is equally the greatest violence and the greatest nonviolence, equally demonic and godly; in fact it is intrinsic to the very conception of violence. Indeed, it is a moment one might call pre-ethical—a moment necessary to both ethics and the violation of ethics. Moreover, given that the brahmachari is now conceived of through the figure of the warrior, a further implication of Gandhi's argument is that the warrior's immeasurable equality is itself pre-ethical.

We should not think of this pre-ethicality technologically, where the warrior has, through his austerity and discipline, acquired a great force that can be used for either good or bad ends and, in this sense, is a means to an end. It is true enough that Gandhi himself sometimes writes in a way that is congruent with such a technological understanding of brahmacharya. Yet it is precisely a technological and measurable understanding that Gandhi wants to question, and this should caution us against such an understanding of pre-ethicality.

What does it mean, then, to call immeasurable equality pre-ethical? Staying with the example of the warrior, it appears that his immeasurable equality is necessarily accompanied by an immeasurable inequality. There are, first, those who cannot be granted any equality. Perhaps exemplary of this is the account in the *Bhishma Parva* of Bhishma's death, which Gandhi never alludes to but which he would doubtless have been aware of given his fondness for the text. As is well known, Bhishma dies following a battle with Shikhandi, whom he chooses not to fight against. As a woman in a previous birth, Shikhandi is immeasurably unequal to Bhishma, and this inequality cannot be overcome by Shikhandi's skill in weapons, however great. Such immeasurable inequality is central to the concept of the warrior, and prevails not only between men and women but between various groups and between castes—as most famously illustrated in the demand made by the teacher of the *Pandavas,* Dronacharya, for the bowstring thumb of his low-caste disciple, Eklavya. This immeasurable inequality is not a secondary aspect but a necessary condition of the warrior's immeasurable equality.

Second, even with his enemy, the figure with whom he acknowledges an immeasurable equality, the practices of the warrior must necessarily obscure that very equality. The warrior practices equality with the enemy only momentarily. Even though the warrior must fight only against enemies who are his equals, he nevertheless wagers his death—that is, he fights to win or to dominate. (In this limited sense, it is certainly correct to say that the warrior seizes the last chance before his own death.) In this wager the warrior seeks to secure an immeasurable domination over the other. Such domination is very different from the violence and domination characteristic of "modern civilization," which is marked by abstraction and measure. (With the warrior, as I argue at length elsewhere, we glimpse another concept of violence itself, a violence that no longer belongs to the concept of measure and abstraction.)

This, then, is the paradox of the warrior: he exemplifies and is impossible without an immeasurable equality, and yet that immeasurable equality is constituted by immeasurable domination and immeasurable inequality. As such, for Gandhi, the warrior is exemplary not only of immeasurable equality but of the way such equality always comes into the world: always as an obscuring of immeasurable equality, as immeasurability (or a domination, subordination, and equality that does not belong to measure).[16] In other words, with Gandhi's thinking of the warrior, it is not at all the case that first there is a concept of immeasurability which can then be separated into immeasurable equality and immeasurable inequality. Rather, immeasurable inequality inevitably comes in the wake of immeasurable equality, and yet both constitute and obscure the latter. When we are not attentive to this constitutive obscuring, then it seems to us as though immeasurability is a general category of which equality and inequality are merely forms.

It is immeasurability in this pre-ethical sense that the Editor struggles to consider when he insists that *sadhan* ("means") and *sadhya* ("ends") belong together. In the years after *Hind Swaraj,* he sometimes names this belonging together of *sadhan* and *sadhya* as *sadhana.* The word *sadhana* possibly entered Gandhi's conceptual vocabulary in 1922, after he read the English translation of Tagore's book *Sadhana,* which Gandhi once described along with *Gitanjali* as "a world apart." That word, again derived from *sadh* and again a recurring concern of Indian philosophical traditions, is usually glossed as "spiritual discipline geared toward self-realization."

But this is not Gandhi's usage. In his vocabulary *sadhana* came to refer to being given to a task at hand in such a way that one was no longer either a means to an end or even autonomous in relation to that task. For Gandhi, this surrender of autonomy was the mark not only of satyagraha but even of all instrumental action once it came to be assiduously pursued. Thus he does not only talk of his own *sadhana* of *ahimsa* and spinning but also of Hitler's *sadhana* of war:

> We have to be up and doing every moment of our lives and go forward in our *sadhana*. We have to live and move and have our being in *ahimsa,* even as Hitler does in *himsa.* It is the faith and perseverance and single-mindedness with which he has perfected his weapons of destruction that commands my admiration. That he uses them as a monster is immaterial for our purpose. We have to bring to bear the same single-mindedness and perseverance in evolving our *ahimsa.* Hitler is awake all the 24 hours of the day in perfecting his *sadhana.*[17]

As this dizzying passage suggests, even something as overwhelmingly defined by instrumentality and means-end relations as the Nazi war machine can for that very reason not be treated as only instrumental. The more aggressive the pursuit of instrumentality and means-end relations, the more immeasurably it is given to this pursuit, the more it is in an immeasurable relation to the very measure it pursues. In such a formulation, Hitler's war is no longer defined by its instrumentality but by Hitler being given over to it, by his immeasurable relation with it. Of the immeasurable equality of the warrior, Hitler, too, may be an example for Gandhi.

Perhaps because of this immense violence of the warrior's immeasurable equality, Gandhi breaks with it and struggles to think of the satyagrahi as a true warrior. In conceptualizing the true warrior, Gandhi seeks to transform this immeasurable equality by moving it from its pre-ethicality to an ethical commitment. An exploration of the ambiguities of that other direction intimated in Gandhi's intriguing suggestion that the satyagrahi has death as a 'bosom friend,' and that it is in such friendship that the satyagrahi practices living by dying—will have to await another occasion.

For now, in conclusion, I wish only to stress how the arguments made in this essay have pointed to the inadequacy of understanding Gandhi only in terms of his most explicit arguments (which is how we have largely understood him). Understood in this way, Gandhi, analyzed too quickly, comes across as a romantic, and when more rigorously analyzed, as a figure committed to substantive virtues. By this latter understanding, Gandhi is a critical traditionalist; he could even be conceived of as a figure situated outside the thematic of post-Enlightenment thought, adopting the perspective of the traditional intelligensia. If we think in this way, it is tempting to see substantive virtues embodied in the way that the unspecific vows of satya and ahimsa lead on to very concrete vows—celibacy, control of palate, non-stealing, fearlessness, equality of religions, removal of untouchability, and so on.

What I have suggested instead is that yet another argument is also involved in Gandhi's writings, one that he might recoil from but one that is nevertheless faithful to the tensions and fissures of his writings. In this other argument Gandhi's emphasis on vows and virtues initiates a profoundly modern response to the humanist tradition, and its necessary colonialism. This response receives from the humanist tradition the emphasis on equality, but it refigures the latter's abstract equality into an immeasurable equality. In the process this response also refigures the tradition of vows and virtues that it inherits. Vows and virtues no longer establish substantive qualities; rather, they always produce a distinctive relation with the other. In this broaching of another kind of equality and of the politics proper to it, we discern the stakes of Gandhi's emphasis on *niti*—the word he translated as "morality" and that we now more usually translate as "ethics."

Notes

The first epigraph is from "Doctrine of the Sword," in *The Collected Works of Mahatma Gandhi* (hereafter, *CWMG*), 100 vols. (New Delhi, Government of India), August 15, 1920, 21:160. The second epigraph is from "Speech at General Meeting, Dakor," October 27, 1920, in *CWMG,* 21:401. The third epigraph is from a letter to Raojibhai Patel, March 7, 1914, in *CWMG,* 14:103.

1. "Maranbhay," *Navjivan,* August 14, 1921, in *Akshardeha,* 20:471; in *CWMG,* 24:85.

2. Letter to C. F. Andrews, July 18, 1918, in *CWMG,* 17:157.

3. Gandhi wrote *Hind Swaraj* in Gujarati and later translated it into English. I discuss the significant differences between these versions in my forthcoming book, *Immeasurable Equality.* Here, suffice it to say that while I adhere to the official trans-

lation as much as possible, I have also made changes where necessary. On occasion, I have provided Gandhi's Gujarati words in brackets. In the footnotes I first cite the reference in the language that it seems to have been written in originally.

What will also be evident to readers is my immense debt to many thinkers—among them Agamben, Benjamin, Chakrabarty, Chatterjee, Derrida, Heidegger, Kant, Nandy, and Schmitt. I have refrained from providing explicit references to them, because a responsible engagement with these thinkers would have required the kind of careful reading I attempt here of Gandhi. Nevertheless, I have also refrained from erasing phrases or themes that recall these thinkers, because I worry that such an erasure would involve another kind of irresponsibility.

4. In this essay I do not dwell on teasing out what legions of scholars have identified (revealing more about their manner of analysis than about Gandhi's texts) as his romanticism or utopianism, a discourse of intimacy where the two entities are so inseparable that there is no need or possibility for a means-end relation or a relation of measure between them. With an immediate neighbor understood in this sense, conflict needs to be addressed not by resorting to the measure of the judge but by deepening this immediacy, to the extent even of giving oneself over to one's death to those with whom one is intimate. Here the emphasis on immediacy and the renunciation of means and ends impart a changeless and eternal character to "true civilization." This is certainly a defensible interpretation of the Editor's claim that plows, huts, occupations, and education remain the same over thousands of years.

But it is also the least productive of Gandhi's efforts to think satyagraha. Here measure is refused by insisting on a union with the other. In such a union it is impossible to think the separation from the other that is necessary to formulate the question of what might be involved in equality with the other.

If space allowed it would be possible to show that, despite Gandhi's explicit affirmations of this romanticism, it is a conceptually marginal moment in his writing, and one he consistently abandons.

5. "Speech on Deshbandhu's Shraadh Day," *Navjivan,* December 7, 1925, in *Akshardeha,* 27:282; *CWMG,* 32:73.

6. "Confusion of Thought," *Young India,* February 6, 1930, in *CWMG,* 48:299.

7. Letter to Narandas Gandhi, August 3/5, 1930, in *Akshardeha,* 44:70; *CWMG,* 49:422.

8. This is his 1910 translation. See "Our Publications," *Indian Opinion,* May 7, 1910, in *CWMG,* 11:35.

9. See, for instance, the titles of the translation of *Ek Satyavirna Katha,* in *CWMG,* 8:246ff.

10. *Hind Swaraj,* chap. 17; *Akshardeha,* 10:55.

11. Letter to Jamnadas Gandhi, approx. May 30, 1913, in *Akshardeha,* 12:77; *CWMG,* 13:154.

12. "Understanding vs. Literacy," *Navjivan,* October 30, 1921, *Akhshardeha,* Vol. 21, p. 328; *CWMG,* Vol. 25, p. 28.

13. "London," *Indian Opinion,* August 14, 1909, in *Akshardeha,* 9:361.

14. "Speech at General Meeting, Dakor," October 27, 1920, *Navjivan,* November 3, 1920; in *Akshardeha,* 18:361; *CWMG,* 21:401.

15. Letter to Maganlal Gandhi, December 28, 1908, in *Akshardeha,* 9:118; *CWMG,* 9:222.

16. One could argue that even equality with death is similarly obscured in the *Mahabharata.* Perhaps this obfuscation is distinctively marked by the figure of Bhishma, arguably the most famous brahmachari, who acquires his name because of his vow of celibacy. Having taken this vow, he is granted the power to choose the time of his own death. Thus he has mastered both death and the other in a very precise manner: though he is not immortal he can die only when he decides to, and though he is not unconquerable he can only be conquered when he decides to be. Bhishma is equal to death, for though he cannot dominate death, neither can death dominate him. This immeasurable economy organizes both his defeat and his death in the *Mahabharata.*

17. Speech at the Meeting of Gandhi Seva Sangh and Charkha Sangh, *Harijan,* July 21, 1940, in *CWMG,* 78:349 [original English?].

12.

Moral and Spiritual Striving in the Everyday: To Be a Muslim in Contemporary India

Veena Das

When, in 1947, India split into two countries—India and Pakistan—the question might have arisen in the minds of many Hindus and Muslims as to what it would mean from now on to "belong" to this country.[1] My aim in this essay is not to tell the story of Indian secularism and its implications for thinking about the cultivation of political virtues; rather my goal is to reflect on how India figured as a theological space for Indian Muslims in their everyday life, given their proximity to Hindus along with their sense of an Islamic project of "becoming" that the birth of Pakistan represented for them.[2] The question might also be posed as follows: Are there different ways of relating to territory than are catalogued in modernist discourses of nationhood that might have been brought into play in considering what it is to cultivate oneself as a moral person in this "new" land?[3] The same question can be asked of Hindus. For my purposes here, however, I will simply state that the story of Hindu "becoming" outside of Hindu nationalist projects is not symmetrical to that of Muslims—which is why it cannot be told through analogies or polarities.

Moral Perfectionism as a Dimension of Life

> The Principle that the existing subjective thinker is constantly occupied in striving, does not mean that he has, in the finite sense, a goal towards which he strives, and that he would be finished when he reached this goal.
>
> —James Conant commenting on Kierkegaard

There are many ways of thinking about what it is to "be" in a place. In his recent commentary on Emersonian perfectionism and Cavell's reflections on whether America has been able to express itself philosophically, James Conant draws our attention to what he calls the "impossible combination of categories" in that the concept "America" combines what Kierkegaard regarded as both objective and subjective categories.[4] "*At one and the same time,*" Conant says, "'America' names a certain place at a certain time with a certain history and signifies what might happen in that place if certain moral and political ideas could be realized." I note that for Cavell the realization of these moral and political ideas, or what he calls the picture of Emersonian perfectionism, is not premised on an objectively agreed upon idea of the common good toward which we might constantly orient ourselves, but cast rather as a moral striving that, in its uncertainty and its attention to the concrete specificity of the other, is simply a dimension of everyday life. In this picture of spiritual becoming, what one seeks is not an ascent to some higher ideal but giving birth to what sometimes Cavell is moved to call an "adjacent self"—a striving in which the eventual everyday emerges as in a relation of nextness to the actual everyday.[5] The risk in this picture of the moral is not the temptation to break rules but what Steven Mulhall calls the "risk of narcissism."[6] If the kind of picture of moral perfectionism that I am trying to work with in this paper has merit,[7] than the pressing issue becomes not what kind of virtues can be named and how they relate to an Islamic teleology, but rather how do I relate, in this time and in this place, to those who are in my vicinity and with regard to whom I might never be in some kind of "ideal " position of having clear-cut guidelines in terms of rules and regulations from my own religious tradition? Or, even worse, how do I cultivate morality as a dimension of everyday life, when certain forms of knowing (e.g., that Hindus are characterized as *kafirs,* as nonbelievers) somehow contradict my feelings that there are forms of being together that I can come to experience as part of my ordinary mode of life, that I wish to acknowledge but for which I should not be required to give justifications.[8]

I do not mean to suggest that the "we" that came into being in India was at every moment being created out of large ideological projects. Working in low-income neighborhoods in Delhi, I found that a world of shared banalities can also be the basis of a sociality—as when a girl coming home from school complains that some "shadow" or "influence" has fallen on her (often it turns out to be an unnamed Hindu spirit) and she cannot go to school tomorrow. Her mother, as it happens, can produce an immediate remedy because by watching Q TV (an Islamic religious channel) she has learned that reading a particular *ayat* (verse) from the holy Quran over a glass of water removes such influences. With the help of this ritual act the mother might have successfully averted a terrible looming threat from the occult world, or perhaps the child's ruse to miss school simply did not work. Thus there is a braiding together of the most ordinary of events and the most extraordinary of experiences through which the cohabitation of Hindus and Muslims comes to define the everyday.

Or consider the autos and trucks zooming through the city that seem to "talk" to each other through bumper stickers, leaving traces of affects that mark space and time—"Ok Tata"; "*Papa jaldi ghar ana* / Papa come home early"; "*Khuda khair kare* / May god keep everyone safe"; "Hindu Muslim *bhai bhai* / Hindus and Muslims are brothers"; and the ominous gathering clouds of "*Mandir bana ke rahenge* / Eventually we will make the temple"—showing that somewhere, in certain shops, certain homes, the controversy is still alive over the demolition of the Babri Mosque and the making of the Ram Temple that has poisoned the political environment since 1992.[9]

Pakistan: The Destiny of Modern Muslims?

> I have never supported Pakistan.
>
> —Mohammad, a resident of Dharavi in conversation with Deepak Mehta, 2000

In their extraordinary book, *Living with Violence,* Roma Chatterji and Deepak Mehta track the circulation of effects in the aftermath of the riots in Dharavi in 1992–93, following the demolition of the Babri Mosque. Below is an extract from a conversation the authors cite:

> Mamu: I know that the (Babri) Masjid fell and I left for home. Nothing else. In 1947 there were only two people, Jinnah and *As-Salaam* Abdul Ghaffar Khan,[10] not even Gandhi or Maulana Azad. There were four brothers in our family. One was dark and blind in one eye. All of us voted for the Congress because Ghaffar Khan of the red cap asked us to do so. The dark one voted for the Muslim League. We were all born in UP [Uttar Pradesh]. How could we vote for anything other than India? The Shiv Sena may not want us here. But can they deny my corpse its plot of land? Can they bury me in Pakistan?[11]

It is evident that the words Mamu speaks have a mythic theological register as in his reference to one brother "being dark and one eyed" (like the villain of a folk tale) and to the plot of land where one will be buried because one's ancestors are buried in Uttar Pradesh. Here the condensation of several registers of speech gives a far greater density to the notion of India as a space for Muslims than the purely secular notions of minorities and their constitutional rights.

Questions about how to be a Muslim in India surfaced in other contexts. In 2007 I was engaged in reading a collection of *fatawas* (authoritative pronouncements on specific topics issued by religious law specialists) put forth by the Darul Uloom, Deoband, the religious seminary that emerged as an important center for Muslim reform in the nineteenth century.[12] Barbara Metcalf and Mushirul Hasan have both correctly argued that the majority of fatawas issued from this seminary pertained primarily to questions of faith (such as correct forms of prayer).[13] Still I was surprised that questions about religious obligations were often framed with reference to a Hindu presence and to Muslim migration to Pakistan. For instance, there were questions about whether a *dua* (prayer) should be said for the *hakim* (ruler) at the conclusion of the Friday prayer in the mosque since India was not an Islamic state and hence the political leader was not presiding over an Islamic polity. There were also questions as to whether Muslims were obligated to migrate to Pakistan following the tradition of the migration of the Prophet to more holy places. In most cases the answer was mixed. No, a dua on Friday should not be said for the hakim of India because India was not an Islamic state, and, equally, Muslims were under no obligation to migrate from India because, though Muslims were not living in an Islamic state, they had freedom to practice Islam in India. Further, power was shared between Hindus and Muslims as shown by the fact that government officials and even some "rulers" of India, such as ministers and judges, included Muslims.[14]

Within this kind of ambiguity hovering over what is the theological space called India, how do ideas of proximity with a Hindu other shape notions of moral perfectionism as a dimension of everyday life among Muslims?

Scenes of Moral Disputations

> Biradran Islam! Allah Tala ka irshad hai ke ai iman lane walo Allah tala se daro! . . . Allah ke us aihsan ko yaad karo jo allah ne tum par kiya hai . . . tum ek dusre ke dushman the . . . us ne tumhare dil jod diye.
>
> [Oh Brothers in Islam! It is the declaration of Allah, the gracious one, that you who brought the true faith into the world fear Allah. Recall the grace bestowed on you . . . you were enemies of each other . . . he joined your hearts.]
>
> —Extract from a collection of Friday sermons in Urdu, 2005

Islam and the particular moral dilemmas that Muslims face are the subjects of much discussion and debate among Muslims in the urban low-income neighborhoods in Delhi where I have worked on urban transformation for several years. This section examines discussions that occur in the Maulana Azad Colony which has a sprinkling of Syed, Pathan, and Mughal families, along with families belonging in the lower social rungs. Despite the Muslim name, it is a mixed Hindu-Muslim *mohalla* (neighborhood, locality); most of the Muslim families were relocated here from parts of Old Delhi during the national Emergency in 1976 as part of the beautification drive in the city.

People in this neighborhood sometimes explained the nature of the present time to me as the time of *fitna* and *fasad,* both terms referring to disorder, disaffection between communities, chaos, and a refusal to submit to the will of Allah. One resident, whom I shall call Iqbal Mian, explicitly compared the time of fitna to that of *kaliyuga*—"as it is written in the book of the Hindus." This reference to "kaliyuga"—or the fourth age in the Hindu cycle, which in the simplest sense is used to refer to a period of moral decline—might have been a concession to my being a Hindu, but more is at stake as I hope to show later.

In the classical sources on Sunni theology, the idea of fitna evokes the bitter recollection of the great rift in the community shortly after the Prophet Mohammad's death.[15] Dubbed as the great fitna or the first fitna, this conflict pitted some of the closest companions of the Prophet against one another over the battle of succession. Thus it came to denote conflict internal to the Muslim community as opposed to *jihad,* or war waged against the enemies of Islam.[16] However, fitna was double-sided in that it referred to disorder and sin but also to trials and tribulations through which one is purified—the etymological meaning in Arabic refers to the purification of metal by being placed in fire.

Historians of South Asia have described fitna as a political strategy for sowing dissension in precolonial political formations.[17] Others have noted that it can move between the political and the domestic context, when specifically referring to the dangers and temptations that women pose to the orderly Islamic world.[18] I, too, found that the sources from which people derived the meanings of the term as well as the contexts in which it was used were extremely varied. I already mentioned the reference to kaliyuga. The other sources of the term were likely the tracts on Islam that circulate in the neighborhood. Many of these now originate from the Ministry of Religious Affairs in Saudi Arabia and are translated into Urdu. For example, one such book was *Fitna se Nijat* and concerned the Gulf War and the obligations of all Muslims to support the Saudi regime as the exemplar of Islamic values. The referent of the terms "we" and "ours" was now always shifting and encoded important tensions within the community.[19]

Thus there are multiple sources and contending fields from which Muslims in these localities derive their ideas about what being a Muslim entails. Children in the area go to government schools or schools run by Sikh religious organizations (e.g., the Khalsa School) and in some cases by the Hindu reform groups such as the Arya Samaj (e.g., the Dayanand Anglo Vedic School, or the DAV School). Since there is a uniform syllabus and textbooks are prescribed by the government, the textbooks in Hindi language and literature have many references to Hindu mythology that children learn and that seep into the everyday vocabulary of the community. Most children, especially boys, also attend the local madrassa, where they take lessons on the Quran, learn Urdu, and learn the Arabic *qaydah* (alphabet). Competing with the popular books on Islam published with the support of Saudi Arabia are other books originating from various publishers, including books published by the Deoband seminary. These works include collections of fatawas; collections of *khutbas*, or sermons given by prominent Muslim clerics from India and Pakistan; and general books about reform of conduct. There are also many small presses in Deoband, Lucknow, Hyderabad, Karachi, and Lahore that publish tracts on magical healing, stories of *jinns* (beings made of smoke who are mentioned in the Quran) and the *shaitan* (the devil), and books on the reform of practices of women. Finally, sermons given during the Friday prayers, telecasts from Islamic channels, and recorded cassettes of sermons and Sufi music all circulate in the mosque and in people's homes, and are specially telecast on significant occasions such as during the month of Ramadan.

This is not to say, however, that there is a huge market for books in the neighborhood. Rarely would one find more than five or six books in any household. But discussions around what someone might have read or heard are frequent, and hence the "reading public" is larger than the public that buys books.

Iqbal Mian, mentioned above, is an avid consumer of popular books on Islam, but he is hesitant to identify himself with Deobandis, Barelwis, or members of the Ehl-i-Hadith. Instead, he says, he believes in "fundamentals." I am a "*kattar* Muslim" (literally, uncompromising Muslim). Heeding what he might mean by "uncompromising" and locating his sense of what the "compromises" are may help us understand what it means for him to be living in a country that is predominantly Hindu in composition but that has a secular constitution. Above all, what does it entail for him to live in the world with his Hindu neighbors today? How is the question of virtue posed for him as a Muslim but also, as he says, as a person trying to be a "good human being"? In focusing on this one man I am not claiming that he is an exemplar of the concerns of the community but rather that, in his singularity,[20] he provides a window to the kinds of questions about virtue, tradition, and moral perfectionism as a dimension of everyday life with which I began this essay.

Iqbal Mian referred to fitna and fasad in many contexts, but two are most important. First, he claimed that everyone was trying to convert everyone else. The Tabliqis, he said, in trying to confront the "winds of modernity," want to convert those who have come within the sway of "the new light" (*nai roshni ki chapet mein*) by making them return to Islam. The Jamait-e-Islami and the Deobandis, he contended, were concerned with the practices of *kufr* (disbelief) and *shirk* (associating another with God) such as worshiping at a *mazar* (the grave of a saint), to which the uneducated and the *jahil* (ignorant, unenlightened) were particularly susceptible. And the Ehl-i-Hadith were busy converting the elite Muslims to a form of Islam that made any form of adoration, even of the Prophet, suspect. The result, Iqbal Mian said, was that Muslims had become completely confused as to how to follow Islam. Most Muslims were impelled toward becoming what he called "*kanuni* Muslamans"—Muslims by law but without understanding the meaning of Islam: "While they pray and keep the fasts, and offer sacrifice, their hearts are now made of stone. I can tell you that earlier while 40 percent of Muslims were indeed Muslims in the sense of accepting Islam, now only 5 percent are Muslims."

Iqbal Mian, though extremely critical of the forms Islam was now taking, was not driven by some kind of liberal, secular impulse that would assume all religions to be equal. In fact, he was firmly convinced that Islam was the most superior religion among all known religions. Yet he claimed that it posed no threat to any other religion in the world. Iqbal Mian would often say that Islam was not a new religion—in fact, according to him, it was simply an amendment of all earlier religions.

> *IQBAL: I can assure you that you cannot tell me anything from any religion, from science or anything else, that is not found in Islam.*
>
> *VD: So then, with the coming of Islam, does it become wrong to believe in any other religion?*
>
> *IQBAL: Not wrong, but it does not make any logical sense.*
>
> *VD: But suppose I do not want to give up my religion—what then?*
>
> *IQBAL: Well, there are some who believe that Islam does not forbid the practice of other religions but it certainly dims them, makes them less luminous, just as when the moon comes out, the stars are still there but their luster is reduced.*
>
> *VD: Do you agree with that interpretation?*
>
> *IQBAL: See, even your own scriptures say that the rise of the Prophet Mohmamad, peace be upon him, was anticipated and the prophecy was made that he would be the savior of the kaliyuga.*

Here Iqbal Mian was referring to the third section (titled *Pratisarga*) of the *Bhavishya Purana* (History/legends of the future), which purports to give the history of the kaliyuga.[21] References are made to the rise of "Mahmad" as someone who wears a beard, issues the prayer call, and has followers who eat all kinds of animals except swine. The text does not completely endorse the Prophet; instead it assimilates him, along with the English, into the category of the *mlecchas* (barbarians, untouchables), but asserts that, among the mlecchas, he was indeed an *uttam purusha* (exemplary man)—a category normally used to describe Rama. He is also described as an incarnation of a powerful demon, and the religion established by him is considered to be in the category of *paishachya dharma,* or the code of conduct suitable for those in the lowest rungs of life. Though I cannot give a detailed interpretation of these formulations, it is well to remember that these characterizations are to be read in the context of the fact that many social forms are permitted in the kaliyuga and do not carry the moral opprobrium one would attach to practices if seen from some idealist perspective, independent of their location in time.

It is well known among Indologists that the *Bhavishya Purana* is an amalgam of some of the most ancient texts along with accretions that probably ended only after the printed version that appeared in the 1860s. As A. K. Ramanujan stated, despite efforts to impose schema on the *Puranas,* these texts had a very open character which allowed this textual tradition to develop and incorporate commentaries on contemporary events.[22] I was nevertheless intrigued that the stories of the *Bhavishya Purana* should be available for thought among the Muslim communities. Elsewhere I hope to show how these stories are reworked and circulate within these locally embedded publics creating connections that find no authorization in the expert discourses of either Islam or Hinduism.

Iqbal Mian's theory that Islam was basically an amendment of all earlier religions and hence incorporated elements of Hinduism within itself presented an intriguing theory of how to conceptualize tradition in a manner that incorporates, rather than excludes, the other. Of course, the idea of a religious figure being presaged in an earlier one is familiar from certain strands of Christian theology that regard Christ as the second Adam or the sacrifice of the lamb as prefiguring the sacrifice of Christ. In the Hindu notions of time, the idea of a *bija,* or seed that contains all later developments, is widely used in literary texts and in ordinary life. The second direction we could take is that of the ethnographic examples of "foreign" deities or spirits incorporated within a religion but retaining a sense of their troublesome character, as in the case of the fetishes that came into being in Africa or the Caribbean as a result of contact with European rulers or settlers. We shall see that both interpretations are possible and are evoked with different intensities as the context changes and as different affective intensities are evoked in relation to the changing contexts and frames.[23]

The Conversational Nexus

> An entire mythology is stored within our language.
> —Ludwig Wittgenstein, *Remarks on Frazer's Golden Bough*

Iqbal Mian's rendering of fitna as kaliyuga and his evocation of the *Puranas* as authorizing the place of the Prophet, even for Hindus, could be regarded as "small talk" for some purposes. I would argue that such statements need to be understood not as expressions of "belief" but as words that are at hand and thus can be used for getting ahead with one another in contexts other than those in which "expression of belief" is required. Here I elaborate this with the help of a cryptic remark by Wittgenstein in his *Remarks on Frazer's Golden Bough:*

> I should like to say: nothing shows our kinship to those savages better than the fact that Frazer has on hand a word as familiar to himself and to us as "ghost" or "shade" in order to describe the views of these people.
>
> (That is certainly different than were he to describe, for example, the savages as imagining that their heads will fall off when they have killed an enemy. Here our description would contain nothing superstitious or magical in itself.)
>
> Indeed, this peculiarity relates not only to the expressions "ghost" and "shade" and much too little is made of the fact that we count the words "soul" and "spirit" as part of our educated vocabulary. Compared with this the fact that we do not believe that our soul eats and drinks is a trifling matter.
>
> *An entire mythology is stored within our language.*[24]

The thought here is that Frazer, in considering the "savages" as having pre-logical thought, pays too little attention to the fact that a certain kind of invented natural history of humankind is embedded in their practices that allows Frazer and those for whom he writes to "understand" the practices implied by references to ghosts and shades. Had he, instead, described the "savages" as imagining that their heads would fall off after they had killed their enemies, there would be nothing in our language or experience that could provide any ground for understanding.

I suggest, similarly, that the terms at hand such as *kaliyuga, rabb puja, ibadat, bhagwan,* and *khuda,*[25] which travel easily in the speech of Hindus and Muslims and are deployed in both formal and informal contexts, make it possible to imagine the practices of the other and to get on with the daily commerce of living together. Further, the thought that Wittgenstein speaks of a whole mythology being buried in our language should be understood to include the history of concepts, words, and gestures not only as rooted within a tradition but also in the manner in which they travel and become nomadic. For instance, Iqbal Mian prides himself as one who uses *aql,* or reasoning, and thus tells me often that it is his obligation as a Muslim to understand other religions. According to one *hadith* (a saying of the Prophet) he has heard, a Muslim must tell others about the glories of Islam, but he cannot do that without understanding what others hold dear in their own religion. Others in the same neighborhood, whose ideas of Islam have been strongly influenced by the devotional practices at mazars, can quote verses from Qawalis or *dohas* (typically two rhyming lines) from the medieval devotional poetry in which Hindu concepts were freely used. Thus, for instance, Sikandar Mian, who is a great devotee of Nizamuddin Aulia and goes to the mazar every Thursday, often peppered his speech with verses such as "*Kaljug aisi aag Farida*" (Kaliyuga is such a fire, oh Farid). Many scholars of Indian Islam would point to these forms of speech as evidence of "syncretism."[26] I argue, however, that the issue at stake is not that of "belief" at all but of the mythology that lies buried in the languages of ordinary men and women and that surfaces naturally in the contexts in which Hindus and Muslims are already committed to some kind of a common life, whether in engaging neighborliness or in forging political actions to ward off the violence that is always present as a possibility.[27]

A final comment on this point is in order before considering the contexts when these very same practices come under serious scrutiny and acquire a very different affective force. In the predominantly Hindu localities, too, references to kaliyuga, or its more colloquial form *kaljug,* were frequently made. However, although the context was always that of some reference to moral decline, whether as commentary on the behavior of politicians or as gossip about neighbors, people took it as a description of what is possible under the present circumstances and the futility of holding up the moral virtues of the epic characters that lived in the earlier ages of the Hindu cycle of time. Elsewhere I have described how the theory of *kalivarjya,* propounded in *Manu* as well as in the *Puranas,* invents forms of devotion and rules of behavior particularly suited to kaliyuga, which considers the moral decline of men and women a natural fact and thus prescribes standards of behavior that depart from the more stringent standards applied to earlier ages.[28]

Thus, when Hindu men complain that it is indeed kaliyuga and that is why no one can undertake the serious practices of *tapas* (penance) or that it is hard to find women who can approximate the purity of Sita, they nevertheless say that God is pleased even with small acts of devotion given that it is kaliyuga. In contrast, when Muslims speak of fitna and fasad having made the Muslim community weak, the talk is imbued with a sense of moral failure. I referred earlier to the fact that very few women in the neighborhoods observe *purdah,* the practice of preventing women from being seen by men, but if they visit family or friends in Old Delhi where purdah is more stringently observed, they will wear a *burqa* (enveloping outer garment). Sikandar Mian once explained to me the importance of women covering "from head to toenails including the arms." His wife, Bano Begum, was sitting on the bed nearby. When I asked if she agreed, she nodded in the affirmative. So, do you observe purdah? I asked. And she answered:

> Who can observe purdah here—the apartments are next to each other, almost as if they were squashed into each other. The vegetable vendor comes and I have to run down to get vegetables; I must help the children cross the street so that they can safely go with others to school. The house is so tiny that if any repair has to be done, I would literally have to crouch in the kitchen behind a closed door if I were to observe purdah from the workmen. If God asks me on judgment day, why did you not observe purdah, I will tell Him, did you give me the kinds of conditions in which I could have observed purdah? What about your responsibility towards those who believed in you?

In response, Sikandar Mian shook his head and said, "You see the fitna of women—that is why Allah did not give me a daughter—so that I don't fail in my responsibilities as a father." His wife smiled and said, "What happens on the day of *kayamat* (Judgment Day)—we shall see to it that day—there is still a long time for that day to come."

Both Hindu and Muslim women commonly spoke in ways that were seen as evasive, using circumlocutions to avoid confronting men directly. Here it is important to note that the concepts of kaliyuga and fitna exerted pressure differently because each concept, for Hindus and Muslims, was located differently within the larger questions of tradition and authority. When Hindu women explained why they did not keep the stringent fasts in emulation of famous mythological figures, their affect was not that of a moral burden but of a kind of natural history of morality embedded in the nature of time itself. In Muslim conceptions, the sense that the time of fitna was their own creation imbued their actions with a greater sense of moral disquiet, if not failure. However, one can sense the difference in affect in the rendering by Bano Begum, which is somewhat closer to that of throwing up one's hands because morality is the creature of time, versus that of Sikander Mian, who relies on God not to give him daughters so that he does not have to face the fitna of women.

Dangers of the Home

> Beware of woman, for she is made of the crooked rib of Adam.
>
> —From a conversation with a Muslim man in Abdul Azad Colony

Historians of nationalism have emphasized the contrast between the home and the world, contending that, in the colonial context in India, the home was seen as the space untouched by colonialism where tradition could continue to flourish.[29] I have argued in my recent book, *Life and Words,* that the relation between home and world was actually much more complex, especially when we consider how the social contract and the sexual contract were mapped on Hindu-Muslim relations.[30] Charu Gupta has analyzed the popular tracts from the nineteenth century that detail the dangers posed to the Hindu home by the propensity of Hindu women to worship Muslim *pirs* (saints),[31] but similar dangers were imagined for Muslim women in relation to Hindu religious or customary practices.[32] Anxieties surrounding the dangers to the purity of the Muslim home were palpable in the pamphlets and short tracts that circulated in the neighborhoods.

A recent tract published by the Saudi Ministry of Religious Affairs and supplied at no cost for distribution at the local mosque, titled "*Khawteen aur unke Missale*" (Women and their issues) offers not only a general view of women's status in Islam (held to be superior to that of other religions) but also addresses specific quotidian questions. Thus it provides guidance as to whether women may wear short hair; use perfume, paint their nails, or dye their hair; or be required to veil in the presence of other women even when no male is present. The answers are noteworthy not only for the actual rules and prescriptions provided but also for the reasoning given to support them. For instance, women are not permitted to cut their hair short because Muslim women are enjoined to maintain a distinction from *firangi* (Western) and *kafir* (infidel) customs. The text cites a hadith attributed to Imam Abu Duwad stating that "whoever imitates a group is among them," and thus women who cut their hair short became part of the firnagi or kafir communities. The women in whose house I found this book were somewhat embarrassed by the reference to kafirs and said that the term does not apply to Hindus because it refers to those who deny God in any religion or form. In any case, she said, Hindu families were equally particular about the modesty of their women. As evidence she pointed out that, whether Hindu or Muslim, there were only two women in this neighborhood who had short hair.

The concern with regulating difference was also apparent in prohibiting other practices that were analogous to Hindu customs. For example, some twenty years ago it was easy to find bazaar tracts such as *Das Bibion ki Kahani* that were similar to the Hindu *vrata kathas* (stories recited on the occasion of ceremonial fasting) in structure and in the concluding statements of blessing—for example, whoever hears this text will obtain merit, or Allah is pleased with those who hear these texts. The emphasis in the readings has now shifted to more "Islamic" texts such as those extolling the virtues of pilgrimage. The project to make women "better" Muslims, which commenced in the nineteenth century, has now moved from the middle classes to lower-income groups.

Another such tract is in the nature of a warning to Muslim men to watch over their married women and protect their family from illicit unions.[33] The author argues that although men are watchful of the behavior of unmarried sisters or daughters, they neglect the danger that married women pose to the peace and tranquility of the home. The author attributes this laxity on the part of Muslim men to Hindu influences, because, as he says, Hindus are much more watchful over the sexuality of their unmarried women because they fear they will "lose caste" if they fail to perform *kanyadan,* the gift of a virgin daughter in marriage that is at the heart of the Hindu marriage ceremony. The author goes on to cite from Manu that married Hindu women were free to enter into contractual sexual relations (*niyoga*) with men other than their husbands—so "even their scriptures condone sexual misconduct." This reference to Manu is notable because later texts in both Sanskrit and vernacular from the thirteen century on have maintained that practices such as niyoga are not permissible in the kaliyuga. In this particular context, the reference to the Hindu influence shows how Hindu-Muslim antagonisms are mapped on male-female relations within the domestic realm.

Whereas the kinds of tracts described above used a variety of linguistic forms—illustration, citation, and warning—to guide spiritual perfection through cultivating the body and regulating social and sexual conduct, other texts were more directly prescriptive. The most prominent of these are the fatawas mentioned earlier that are issued from various seminaries, which even when not directly solicited could be the subject of much discussion and speculation.[34] One important feature of the fatwa, as is well known, is that it answers a question that has been posed and need be followed only by the person who sought an opinion. As Barbara Metcalf and others have shown, the growth of seminaries like the Deoband seminary in the nineteenth century was marked by a desire to reform the Muslim community.[35] However, since one could ask for a fatwa by simply sending a letter, the practice also introduced a more distant authority through which one could contest the opinions given by local Islamic scholars, or *muftis,* in personal encounters. If we simply count the type of issues on which fatawas have been issued, very few directly relate to questions of Hindu-Muslim relations. Though most fatawas issued from Deoband clearly are about Islamic practices pertaining to marriage and divorce or correct ways of offering prayer, a fatwa, when inserted within local relations, might also impinge upon Hindu-Muslim relations in significant ways.[36] Consider the following fatwa issued by the Deoband seminary.[37]

> Question: "There is one person who during discussion said that he has an equal respect for Hinduism as for Islam. Is he guilty of *kufr* (disbelief) or has he committed a *gunah* (sin). What is the *shariati* command on this?"
>
> Answer: "To regard the *mazhab* (religion) of Hindus as equally correct as the *mazhab* of Islam is the sin of *kufr*—this is on the authority of Fikh Akbar and it is necessary to object to this. God knows best."[38]

Other such questions concern, for example, whether a man whose wife wears a sari can lead the Friday prayer; whether a dua should be said for the hakim in India since India is not an Islamic state; and whether it is permissible to participate in *holi* (the color festival) for the sake of good community relations if no worship is involved. I know of only one man in the neighborhood who sought a fatwa on the question of whether someone who spends his time in a mazar and believes that his sick mother was saved by the grace of Nizam-ud-din Aulia can be entrusted to lead Friday prayers. The attempt to seek a fatwa in this case was related to a family quarrel between two brothers. The brother who had sought the fatwa had "converted" to the Ehl-i-Hadith way of Islam and was increasingly objecting to his elder brother's allegiance to the Sufi orders (*silsila*s), which implicitly challenged the younger brother's place in the community.

The particular point I want to make regarding such fatawas is that even though it is not incumbent upon anyone who has not sought an opinion on a religious or social matter to follow the advice of the fatwa, such rulings nevertheless put pressure on the community to be watchful that Hindu practices might seep into the community and thus corrupt the Islam that is practiced. Combined with books originating from various parts of the Islamic world, cassettes of khutbas or Friday sermons and televised programs from religious channels, many people felt that their practices were under attack and sometimes from their own kinsmen. How do people in the Abdul Azad Colony relate to such articulations of what is to count as authorized conduct or misconduct?

"Our" Islam

Shaam
Is tarah hai ke har ek ped koi mandar hai
Koi ujda hua benoor purana mandar.

Evening
Is thus that each tree is some temple
Some ruin of an ancient lightless temple.

—Faiz Ahmad Faiz

Faiz's haunting poem on the evening, still and silent, is suffused with Hindu imagery of a forgotten temple as if nature itself kept the memory of old, forgotten connections. Do Hindu concepts, similarly, just seep into conversations without announcing themselves as "religious" concepts?

Once when discussing the role of fatawas with Sikandar Mian, he told me he did not understand how we can give up our pirs—after all, we did not get our Islam straight from the Prophet (peace be upon him). Nor, he continued, were we simply converted by force. It is the piety of the pirs and the *rishi-munis* (Hindu ascetics who are sometimes assimilated to the pirs among Indian Muslims) that made us see that Islam was our religion, too. Sikandar Mian, Farhana Begum, and Mohammad Talib—all residents of this neighborhood and all devout followers of various pirs—were clear that they did not perform *sijda* (the ritual gesture of submission to the one God) and thus the pirs were, for them, intermediaries between God and men.[39] Another point was involved, however, namely their allegiance to poetry, particularly the poetic forms *qawali* and *masnavi,* as a way of knowing the inner (*batini*) meaning of the names of God and of the revelation itself.[40] Sikandar Mian told me that he does not understand how the mazhab of the Hindus can be castigated as kufr. "The Quran itself says that God sent prophets for every age and in every community and that only a small number are mentioned in the Quran. So how do we know that Krishna, for example was not a prophet?" I do not discount here the strong possibility that such statements were made in this form precisely because I am a Hindu woman, but surely something was at stake in being able to derive this formulation from an exegesis of a statement that could be attributed to the Quran. The issue, I suggest, is not that of belief or indeed of pragmatism but of a certain sensibility that, in a face-to-face confrontation, cannot bear to cause hurt to the person one is facing.[41] This sensibility is in accordance with a very complex idea of being human (as opposed to being angels who never err) and of the question of who has the right to judge.

In their houses women often criticized the groups of men who lingered on in the mosque after the Friday prayer to discuss various issues. "Even Allah refuses to judge before Judgment Day," one woman said, "and yet these people know who is a good Muslim and who is a bad Muslim. They just sit in the mosque and say, so-and-so drinks alcohol, so-and-so associates with Hindus, so-and-so's sister is having an affair with a Hindu. We say, be fearful of Allah—if he has chosen not to make public their transgressions, who are you to announce your suspicions to the world?" On another occasion Farhana Begum told me that the poet-saint Baba Farid dreamed one night that he had seen Lord Krishna standing in a line of prophets, and this is why his poetry, she said, makes so many references to the "dark one" (*samwra, kala*).

One may recall here that Islamic mystic poetry of the medieval period used both Hindu figures and Hindu imagery in constructing the romantic tales that were seen as allegorical of one's love for God. Famous romances such as *Padmavat* were written in Awadhi and many of the poems of Amir Khusro, Kabir, Rahim, and other poets were in Hindavi.[42] Although Muslims in these neighborhoods were not particularly knowledgeable about this literature, fragments of dohas or new renderings of the Heer Ranjha story surfaced on different occasions. For instance, I noted that wedding invitations often included a couplet in honor of guests that, ideally, were to be composed by family members. These often turned out to be improvisations on known poems, sometimes recycled through film songs.

The question of who speaks in poetry is a complex one.[43] People in the locality often reveled in the fact that the Quran was considered a text of sublime beauty. However, though most people could read the Quran, their ability was limited to reciting a part they had committed to memory. People were firmly convinced that not a single *nuqta* (alphabetic dot) of the Quran had been altered since its inception, and so they viewed any improvisation as blasphemous. However, where poetry was concerned, improvisation was the order of the day. I have heard couplets recited in Hindi, Urdu, or Hindavi. Some people were inclined to settle a point by reciting a poem or a portion of it. Instead of engaging in long arguments, as my friend Iqbal Mian was prone to do, they would recite something that would condense the discussion in a manner that nothing more remained to be said.[44]

I realized the full affective force of their references to "our Islam" and their sense of being Muslims here and now—in this country and at this time—when, in subtle and not so subtle ways in the media and in political speeches, Hindu leaders were demanding that Muslims prove their allegiance to the country following one of a series of bomb blasts in Delhi in 2004.

Soon after this bombing incident, while discussing with friends how Muslims were constantly being asked to prove their allegiance, one of the men recited the following verse:

Tere ishk mein ji-jaan ko lutaya ham ne
Teri zameen pe ghar apna basaya hum ne
Phir bhi gila hai ke wafadar nahin
Hum wafadar nahin tu bhi to didldar nahin.

For your love we squandered life and heart.
On your earth we made our home.
Yet the complaint that we are not faithful
If (you say) we are not faithful, then you, too, are without love.

I realized that this was an improvisation of one of the verses of the poet Iqbal from his famous poem "Shikwa" (Complaint) but also that the last two lines had been recycled and were now embedded in Qawalis and popular songs. Yet the manner in which he recited the poem brought the discussion to a point where there was nothing left to say. His improvisation had made two points clear: that he claimed India as his country, and that if Muslims could not be fully faithful from some points of view, then India too was unable to welcome them with a full heart. This combination of belonging and alienation, of acknowledging that there was a larger Islamic community spread throughout the world to which Muslims belonged and yet that their particular Islam authorized them to claim India as their own—to me this summed up the combination of antagonism and agony through which Hindu-Muslim relations are expressed within specific local worlds.

Concluding Observations

In the streets of these low-income neighborhoods, forms of Islam and Hinduism are being brought into play in which different regions of tradition are articulated. Some of these forms might be described as spiritual exercises in the sense of a therapy of passions in the conduct of everyday life with the help of appropriate texts such as the hadith or the cultivation of appropriate bodily dispositions.[45] But there is a dimension of everyday life that cannot be derived from a reflection on well-honed concepts but combines different fragments from the past, improvisations on concepts that are simply "at hand," in Wittgenstein's terms. This is neither a story of secularism nor of syncretism but rather one in which the heterogeneity of everyday life allows Hindus and Muslims to receive the claims of each other that have arisen by the sheer fact of proximity, face-to-face relations, and the privileging of aesthetic immediacy of emotions even over the prohibitions emanating from various authoritative discourses of Islam and Hinduism. That we could consider this kind of relational life a form of moral perfectionism in its insistence on the ordinariness of life and in the willingness to be educated by each other—that is what is at stake in this essay.

Acknowledgments

I am grateful to all participants in the seminar "Genealogies of Virtue" and to the members of the anthropology colloquium at Harvard for their perceptive comments on earlier versions of this chapter. I am grateful, as ever, to Talal Asad for continuing discussions on this and other themes; to Anand Pandian for his acute comments; and to Naveeda Khan, Deepak Mehta, Steven Caton, Arthur Kleinman, and Bhrigupati Singh for all kinds of help in thinking about issues raised in this chapter. To the persons identified in the essay as Iqbal Mian, Sikandar Mian, and Bano Begum, my grateful thanks at the delight they take in our friendship.

Notes

1. For a sense of the debates around secularism in the Indian context, see Rajeev Bhargava, ed., *Secularism and Its Critics* (New Delhi: Oxford University Press, 2005).

2. My argument is not that the idea of Pakistan as an Islamic state was given at the outset but that, for Muslims who chose to remain in India, the claims of Muslim

aspiration with regard to Pakistan put a new pressure on what it meant for them to belong to India. The rich literature on the theme of the emergence of Pakistan makes it clear that there were conflicting interpretations of the demand for Pakistan. See for instance, Ayesha Jalal, *The Sole Spokesman: Jinnah, the Muslim League, and the Demand for Pakistan* (Cambridge: Cambridge University Press, 1985).

3. The idea of cultivation as working on the self that is deeply embedded within an agrarian form of life is richly explored in Anand Pandian's book *Crooked Stalks: On the Virtues of Development in South India,* (Durham, N.C: Duke University Press, 2009). My interest, on the other hand, is to render ideas of goodness beyond what can be named.

4. James Conant, "Cavell and the Concept of America," in *Contending with Stanley Cavell,* ed. Russsell B Goodman (London: Oxford University Press, 2005), 55–82.

5. See, especially, Cavell's essay of sublime beauty, "Thoreau thinks of ponds, Heidegger of rivers," in his *Philosophy the Day after Tomorrow* (Cambridge, Mass.: Harvard University Press, 2005), 111–132.

6. Steven Mulhall, *The Conversations of Humanity* (Charlottesville: University of Virginia Press, 2007).

7. I put this as a conditional because in my work with the urban poor I find that there is no contradiction in the hopes they entertain for a better material life and a striving for a moral life that includes, but is not exhausted by, what is officially prescribed.

8. It has been suggested to me by an anonymous reader that, historically, the term *kafir* was used in a neutral way. For an account, however, of the manner in which the terms *iman* and *kufr* evolved in the Islamic context and the moral opprobrium surrounding the term *kafir,* see Toshihiko Izutsu, *The Concept of Belief in Islamic Theology: A Semantic Analysis of Iman and Islam* (Kaulalampur: The Other Press, 2007).

9. Kathleen Stewart has examined how ordinary affects might be tracked; see *Ordinary Affects* (Durham, N.C.: Duke University Press, 2007).

10. Roma Chatterji and Deepak Mehta, *Living with Violence: An Anthropology of Events and Everyday Life* (New Delhi: Routledge, 2007), 66–67.

11. See Mukulika Banerjee, *The Pathan Unarmed: Opposition and Memory in the North West Frontier* (Oxford: James Curry, 2000).

12. *Fatawi Darul Uloom,* 10 vols. (Deoband: Zakariya Book Depot, n.d.). Each volume is organized around a particular theme such as *nikah* (marriage), *zakat* (obligatory charity), and so on. There is no separate volume on fatawas relating to Muslim-Hindu relations, but these questions are posed in the context of an issue pertaining to Islamic life.

13. Mushirul Hasan, *Moderate or Militant: Imaging India's Muslims* (New Delhi: Oxford University Press, 2008); Barbara D. Metcalf, "The Study of Muslims in South Asia," talk delivered at the University of California, Santa Barbara, December 5, 2005.

14. In the division between *dar-ul-harb* (non-Islamic states in which Muslims are said to be obliged to wage war) and *dar-ul-Islam* (Islamic states), India was considered to be *dar-ul-Aman* (the land of peace). This status, however, was open to contests especially regarding the question of obedience to the ruler within a non-Islamic state.

15. See Abdul Kader Tayub, "An Analytical Survey of al-Jabari's Exegesis of *Fitna,*" in *Approaches to the Quran,* ed. G. R. Hawting and A. K. A. Shareef (London: Routledge, 1993).

16. I am acutely aware that the weight of terms such as *jihad* has shifted historically and that no simple translation suffices.

17. André Wink, *Land and Sovereignty in India: Agrarian Society and Politics under the Eighteenth Century Maratha Svarajya* (Cambridge: Cambridge University Press, 1986), 25–26.

18. Stefania Pandolfo, *Impasse of the Angels: Scenes from a Moroccan Landscape of Memory* (Chicago: University of Chicago Press, 1997).

19. Several *fatawas* I examined from earlier periods had raised questions about the status of certain practices followed by the *Ehl-e-Hadith* such as that of saying *fatiha* behind the Imam.

20. I use the idea of singularity in a technical sense to suggest that Iqbal Midan might be treated not as an exemplar, or for that matter as unique, but rather as articulating a position that allows various new possibilities to emerge.

21. I know of no critical edition of this text. B. K. Chaturvedi, *Bhavishya Purana* (New Delhi: Diamond Book Depot, 2004).

22. A. K. Ramanujan, "Folk Mythologies and Puranas," in *Purana Perennis Reciprocity and Transformation in Hindu and Jaina Texts,* ed. Wendy Doniger (New York: State University of New York Press, 1993).

23. See E. E. Evans-Pritchard, *Nuer Religion* (London: Oxford University Press, 1956).

24. Ludwig Wittgenstein, *Remarks on Frazer's Golden Bough,* ed. Rush Rhees (Atlantic Highlands, N.J.: Humanities, 1979); emphasis added.

25. These are nomadic terms that can be used in inter-communal contexts.

26. See, for instance, Imtiaz Ahmad and Helmut Reifeld, eds., *Lived Islam in South Asia: Adaptation, Accommodation, and Conflict* (New Delhi: Social Science Press, 2004); and Tony K. Stewart, "Alternate Structure of Authority: Satya Pir on the Frontiers of Bengal," in *Beyond Turk and Hindu: Rethinking Religious Identities in Islamic South Asia,* ed. David Gilmartin and Bruce B. Lawrence (Gainesville: University Press of Florida, 2000), 21–55. See also the magisterial work of Muzzafar Alam, *The Languages of Political Islam, 1200–1800* (Chicago: University of Chicago Press, 2004), 105. Occasionally Alam uses the idea of a syncretic impulse, placing the word syncretic in scare quotes (105). My own problem with the notion of syncretic is its weight on the idea that belief leads one to think of pristine religion prior to the syncretism.

27. One of the flash points in all neighborhoods is a Hindu-Muslim marriage or affair.

28. See Veena Das, *Structure and Cognition: Aspects of Hindu Caste and Ritual* (New Delhi: Oxford University Press, 1977).

29. For a classic statement on the issue of gender and colonialism, see Partha Chatterjee, *The Nation and Its Fragments: Colonial and Postcolonial Histories* (Princeton, N.J.: Princeton University Press, 1993).

30. See Veena Das, *Life and Words: Violence and the Descent into the Ordinary* (Berkeley: University of California Press, 2006).

31. Charu Gupta, *Sexuality, Obscenity, Community: Women, Muslims, and the Hindu Public in Colonial India* (Delhi: Permanent Black, 2001).

32. See Faisal F. Devji, "Gender and the Politics of Space: The Movement of Women's Reform in Muslim India, 1857–1900," *South Asia: Journal of South Asian Studies* 14, no. 1 (1991): 141–153.

33. This ten-page tract is titled *Ghar ki Hifazat* (The protection of the house). It is published from Nai Gali, Chandni Chowk, but no author or date is cited.

34. For a general understanding of *fatawas* as providing an important resource for legal development in the Islamic context, see M. K. Masud, B. M. Messick, and D. S. Powers, eds., *Islamic Legal Interpretation: Muftis and their Fatwas* (Cambridge, Mass.: Harvard Center for Middle Eastern Studies, 1996).

35. Barbara D. Metcalf, *Islamic Revival in Deoband, 1860–1920* (Princeton, N.J.: Princeton University Press, 1986). See also Metcalf, *Islamic Contestations: Essays on Muslims in India and Pakistan* (New Delhi: Oxford University Press, 2004).

36. Barbara Metcalf has consistently maintained that most reform initiated by movements such as the Deoband movement concerned issues that were internal to Muslims. See Metcalf, "The Study of Muslims in South Asia," talk given at the University of California, Santa Barbara, December 2, 2005. Available at http://www.columbia.edu (accessed May 12, 2008). However, reform as purification of Islam often, but not invariably, relates to Hindu influence—thus everyday practices involving Hindu-Muslim interactions become suspect.

37. Unfortunately the published volumes of the fatwas indicate the number of the fatwa but not the date, though the time may be roughly constructed through other markers in the text.

38. In order to ascertain if this opinion would continue to hold today, I sought an online fatwa from the seminary and obtained the same response.

39. For the complex relation with pirs in the context of Islamic modernity, see Katherine P. Ewing, *Arguing Sainthood: Modernity, Psychoanalysis, and Islam* (Durham, N.C.: Duke University Press, 1997). See, in addition, the various essays in Pnina Werbner and Helene Basu, eds., *Embodying Charisma: Modernity, Locality, and the Performance of Emotion in Sufi Cults* (London: Routledge, 1998). Whereas Ewing uses the concept of a Lacanian split self, for Sikander Mian the issue was the inheritance of Islam.

40. The relation between poetic speech and divine speech in Islam is extremely complex. Verses 224–227 have been usually taken as injunctions against poets as prone to demonic inspiration, distracting people from contemplating the Quran. However, the Quranic text itself is recognized as possessing a sublime poetic beauty. Iqbal Mian was inclined to be suspicious of others who took frequent recourse to poetry; his argument, however, was that to become mad for poetry and lose control was against the injunction to maintain balance in the pursuit of all pleasures. Others thought that only God could have bestowed poets with the genius they demonstrated. I am grateful to Andrew Joseph Bush for educating me on these issues.

41. This take differs somewhat from that which would oppose textual Islam with lived Islam or render the problem as that of syncretism, since I argue here that there is pressure on the question of the moral from both the desire to be part of a pan-Islamic moral community with attention to controversies happening elsewhere, such as in Saudi Arabia or Pakistan, and also to be responsive to the pressure of the proximate in the form of direct Hindu presence in one's life. The neighbor here is not an abstract other but one whose existence one directly struggles with.

42. For an example of this literature, see the beautiful translation by Aditya Behl and Simon Weightman, *Madumalati: An Indian Sufi Romance* (London: Oxford World Classics, 2000).

43. Pandolfo, in *Impasse of the Angels,* thinks of the poetic subject as caught between the movements of dispossession and recollection, enabling us to see poetry as a scene of exile.

44. Poetry recitation here is different from the scene of competitive compositions in Yemen described in the classic work of Steven Caton, *Peaks of Yemen I Summon: Poetry as Cultural Practice in a North Yemeni Tribe* (Berkeley: University of California Press, 1990); and Lila Abu-Lughod, *Veiled Sentiments: Honor and Poetry in a Bedouin Society* (Berkeley: University of California Press, 1990).

45. See, respectively, Pierre Hadot, *Philosophy as a Way of Life,* trans. Michael Chase (Oxford: Blackwell, 1995); and Saba Mahmood, *Politics of Piety: The Islamic Revival and the Feminist Subject* (Princeton, N.J.: Princeton University Press, 2005).

13.

Ethical Publicity: On Transplant Victims, Wounded Communities, and the Moral Demands of Dreaming

Lawrence Cohen

Instead of combing the archive for the necessary sources of an Indian versus a European practice or theory of ethics, might one eschew the binary machine and approach the specificity of moral worlds and their incitements for autopoiesis in a different way? Here I want to think at the intersection of some of the multiple demands people face under the sign of ethics: the ubiquity and location of audit practices, the invitations of the archive, the imagined distribution of wounds dependent upon one's location and experience, and the centrality for identity of taking offense. The varied modes of engagement each of these sites might suggest are here linked through a provisional concept of an ethical scene. This essay is itself provisional, a working across.

I begin with the modern audit of the relations we might term supplementable. By audit, I refer to proliferating managerial rationalities of institutional accountancy (through both self-report and external scrutiny). The anthropological conversation on so-called audit cultures locates these as an emergent feature of what Peter Pels has termed "the global spread of neo-liberal values" and Marilyn Strathern describes through Nikolas Rose's term "ethico-politics."[1] Many of us are familiar with audit in the sense these authors discuss: thus as a professor I am not only subjectively evaluated on my teaching but increasingly am asked to demonstrate conformity in curriculum design to norms external to my own discipline but amenable to enumeration and accountancy.

By supplementable relations or more generally supplementarity, I refer to the ability of individuals or populations to constitute their longevity through access to the organic forms—complex molecules, tissues, organs, or bodily milieus—of other persons. My research focus has been the promise that a specific expectation of supplementarity—the potential availability of another's kidneys—sets in motion. A kind of second-order auditor myself, I examine the efforts of states, NGOs, clinical enterprises, patient groups, media corporations, and other bodies to audit or otherwise monitor the social worlds this expectation or promise generates. Such bodies variously observe and evaluate the clinical apparatus organizing supplementable relations and whether it sustains or fails to sustain presumptive norms limiting exploitation.

Listen to Me

What I learn seems of interest: reporters come calling. Since 1998, I have been deemed a minor expert. Thus audits bear particular relations to publics, as I discuss here and in more detail further on.

Minor experts are called to speak persuasively about a problem keyed to their skills and authority, and to do so in relation to two intertwined entities: "authority" and "the public." To the extent authorities pay attention to lay publics or in their scale and distribution act as particular publics, scholars seeking the reasonable embrace of expert status write to an assemblage of such publics. Experts are minor for at least two reasons. The problem may be considered of minor interest; or the problem is major but the expert minor. Minor experts fail to render an account of the problem to sustain a public's attention. Academics of my generation, offered positions based in part upon the effective manipulation of the technical language of the human sciences and in part upon the promise of relevance to major problems, find ourselves courting minority to the extent we are trained to resist accounts of problems that promise false clarity.

The problem with which I have become associated, the so-called market or traffic in human organs, is deemed of relatively major concern. I knew this before the journalists came calling. The interest of various friends and kin could not be counted on when I was studying senility, male friendship, or Indian provincial politics. But these relations formed a captive audience once my topic was the giving and selling of kidneys in India.

My minor-expert status is not for the lack of a desire to achieve the apotheosis of the public intellectual able to deliver on the promise of moral clarity. I have coaching in clarity. One of my colleagues, an epochal figure for a series of essays from the sixties that clearly defined anthropology's relevance, helpfully offered the following. No matter the question, give them two clear sentences, with a single point. Give them a simple story.

But stories have expected elements and forms and these precede and shape interest. The story in question, for the predominantly European and North American interlocutors (media corporations, state agencies, and freelance outfits) that have contacted me, has had the following form. Things are wretched in India, where, at least for the poor, life is nasty, brutish, and short. The organs trade is of a piece with this wretchedness, extending it even as globalization produces new Indian wealth. You, expert, have three options: (1) you will tell us that this wretchedness will spread to the West if we adopt a market in human organs; (2) you will suggest that regulating the market would end the wretchedness in India, and that we in the West need move toward the latter option, a regulated market in organs; or (3) you will suggest that in India, where corruption is endemic (and both ethics and rational individualism, according to two old arguments, are absent), regulation based on rational choice does not work. But you will admit that in the West a regulated organs market may yet be an ethical solution. While you expound on (1), (2), or (3), assuming this is video, we will show visuals of wretched-looking women in saris revealing their post-operative scars while mournful Indian-style music plays in the background. Thus we give your problem publicity, that is, a public.

Here I may get into trouble. Because my sense is that the characterization of India versus the West shared by options (1), (2), and (3) is at critical junctures a dubious one, I violate the narrative conditions of my value. This value is to help members of the journalist's presumably non-Indian public understand their own imagined terrain of action and feeling—about medicine, about transplantation, and about organs—in reference to the suffering of an other, here the Indian other as available through a montage of expertise, sentiment, and gendered apparel. More than for some other problems, transplantation's public, like its medicine, appears to require the presence of a particular kind of distanced other body. Few of these interlocutors, for example, see the generation of value in a news story about racially differential access to organs in the United States.

But when I point to the inequitable distribution of other people's organs in "the West" or to the movement of organs among the poor in India as not inevitably involving monetization and sale, I fail to accede to the dominant conditions of my problem's publicity. I do not participate in the distinction between the deserving and the undeserving poor that appears to organize the value of expert analysis for this problem. The more anxiously cosmopolitan of my interviewers apologetically frame the stakes as the limits of American market-based demand for ethical "content." My job is to stick to Indian suffering, but I am free to contextualize it as much as the genre of talking-head interview allows. Should I therefore follow Walter Lippman and damn the public consumption of expertise?[2] There is certainly an argument to be made that what passes for documentation of human rights abuses (or the lack thereof) and material for reasoned moral debate is a recycling of the cliché and spectacle driving mass reportage.

A powerful alternative to mass culture arguments of this sort has been made by Charles Hirschkind, in reference to men in Cairo who spoke to him of the work necessary to be done on oneself in order to be able to listen to religious discourse. Hirschkind troubles the easy recourse of critics to models of passive sensorial "reception."[3] Implicit in this project is an observation that ethical projects (in this case, of Islamic piety) can be discounted through the accusation of mass affect. But to the extent that my own experience of moral sentiment may involve a lack, failure, or limit to such work on the self, I need be careful of extrapolating Hirschkind's work for my own purposes. I do not want to presume a doubly damned subject, both a mass-culture-determined zombie and a lazy failure at the necessary work of self-formation. If the argument I want to make is contrary to any sense that the technological "massification" of moral outrage inevitably disables ethical work in our time, it yet cannot depend upon variably distributed practices of sensorial training and ethical formation such as those Hirschkind delineates in relation to the Egyptian men with whom he spoke. If there is a form of training at work in the story I offer here, it is less delimited to subcultures and counter-publics.

To put it baldly, I am interested in the conditions for ethical life within mass culture. This is an experiment in thinking at some abstraction: despite my focus on other work on the specificity of regional media worlds and the relations and affects they both presume and bring into being, here I want to bracket this specificity and think not in the universal but the general sense. The effort here is to define these conditions for ethical life within mass culture as the ability to turn the consumption of "ethical scenes" into projects of individual and collective engagement in the world. If the journalist needs a recognizable other, to return to the particular kind of audit in which I find myself repeatedly inserted, we might want to ask what conditions of scene-making are necessary for the creation of ethical practice in our time, and underlying the ubiquity of such scenes, how ethics and publics might be interrelated.

Ethical Scenes

I suggest that many of us, in much of the world, come to know or feel ourselves to be moral or ethical subjects in our being addressed as a public.[4] One could reverse the proposition. Constitutive of that address that leads us to be aware of ourselves as publics is what we might term an "ethical scene."

I am not, at the outset, making claims regarding the quality of our participation as ethical publics. But I want to argue the following: that it is often through such moments of address by or in the face of such scenes that we recognize or know ourselves as ethical.

In the first part of this essay I work toward variant conceptions of an ethical scene. One such scene might be framed in terms reminiscent of Emmanuel Lévinas. I come to consider or know myself as ethical in the mediated address of the other's suffering. The "face to face," the sense of obligation to the other that orients the subject, is a mediated scene. A somewhat different scene is organized around the suffering of one's group—for example, one's nation, religious community, or caste. I come to consider or know myself as ethical in the face of the humiliation of my group.

The example I use from the first sort of scene comes not from the archive of terror and extreme violence we may think of in reference to Lévinas but from my work on the transplant operation. The example I use from the second sort of scene is what I term the "circulation of offense in contemporary India": groups reestablishing their relation to the state through a demand for censorship of material deemed hurtful. These two examples will, in their juxtaposition, push us toward what are perhaps too familiar oppositions of self and other. To trouble the ease with which we think about the ethical invitation or demand of a scene and what we mean by the self or other of that scene, I preface my turn toward transplantation with a detour through an old story.

Waking and Returning to Sleep

In some of the tales she engages and retells from the Sanskrit *Yogavasishtha,* Wendy Doniger centers our attention on what we might term a "limit to biography."[5] Characters in the narrative develop—they grow up, encounter problems, achieve in some cases an adult form—but neither the knowledge nor the virtue they may come to in the space and time of that life is the point. At some time over the course of a life, through falling asleep and dreaming or by dying and being reborn, they become somebody else. This somebody else once again moves from childhood into a particular kind of life, only to have the same or some other transforming thing happen in turn. In the tale "The Monk Who Met the People in His Dream," a long line of creatures succeeding one another through dream or death culminates in one of them being reborn as God, in this case as the god Rudra. Being God, Rudra revives or wakes up all the other previously living or awake creatures that came before him, until, one hundred strong, they encounter their common identity: "they all united together and became Rudra, a hundred Rudras in one."

Such a waking-into-truth is not remarkable as a figure, either in the metanarrative conventions of Sanskrit cosmopolitanism or in other performances of ontology, and indeed the tale of the monk will culminate in a final prediction about this chain of creatures once they return from momentary Rudra-hood to their own bodies and lives: "after a while they will wear out their bodies and will unite again back in the world of Rudra."[6] Doniger's analysis of the tale is characteristically subtle, and it troubles dominant European accounts of the monolithically negative orientation of Indian philosophical ethics.

Since one purpose of this essay is to think about the limits to becoming as a figure for the ethical, I can content myself with the familiar and apparent moral of the story: that the achievements of form within the space of a life, or over several lives, amount to a misrecognition. The good that we can speak of in reference to the particular forms of the lives of the monk and his fellow dreamers would thus appear ontologically shaky: there is a world of awakening, the world of Rudra, in which the real and I think the good will bear a relation to a kind of meta-form we can but (sleepily) intuit in the figure of the deity himself. Such a more or less idealist reading of the story has an extended lineage in the history of claims for (and against) a so-called Indian ethics. If our reading stops at this point, associating India as a moment or species of ethical imaginary with what we might provisionally call an ethics of idealism (one situated here in reference to the Yogavasishtha but more commonly through the Upanishads and Vedanta), then all the familiar reprises could follow. One might track the extensive commentarial practices glossing these varied Sanskrit idealisms and their unexpected relevance for European, Indian, and American commitments to the examined life over the nineteenth century, most notably in terms of English and German Romanticism, Bengali Renaissance, and Transcendentalism. In particular, one might rehearse subsequent moral claims for this "Upanisadic" and "Vedantic" India (e.g., Arthur Schopenhauer's *The World as Will and Representation* and the line that leads from Schopenhauer to Paul Deussen and thus to Vivekananda through the recognition of the other as oneself as fundamentally moral) and against it (e.g., Albert Schweitzer's different reading of this line of thinking as unable to move beyond the negation of life to action).[7] At stake in both these claims, for and against, is whether the Upanishads and Vedanta are adequate sources for an ethical life in modernity. Finally, given the reliance of both these claims for and against the adequacy of such a presumptive Indian idealism, one might turn to the familiar moral action of our time, that is, the gloss reducing all such debates on "Indian ethics" to the situation of colonialism, either by rescuing the subject of India from its Orientalist association with the dreamworld or by refusing the colonial-national shibboleth of "India" as a necessary or sufficient frame.

But it is not in the waking from life that I want to begin but rather in the returning to dream it. What interests me in Doniger's telling of the tale is the disruption she offers between the first awakening—when Rudra awakes to himself and calls all the dead and dreaming into their shared trajectory—and the tale's end, in effect the second awakening of the multitudes into their Rudra-hood. Here is the account of this in-between, in Doniger's translation:

> They were all awakened by Rudra, and they all rejoiced and looked upon one another's rebirths, seeing illusion for what it was. Then Rudra said, "Now go back to your own places and enjoy yourselves there with your families for a while, and then come back to me."

Awakening, the initial or past awakening, is not the end of the story: we go back, we live and die again, we return to sleep or, more accurately, to that movement between states of apparent wakefulness and dreaming that constitutes the sense-world, the world as Dream with a capital D. There is a return into time ("for a while"), into community ("with your families"), and into order ("back to your own places"). This return is not sorrowful, for no less than the discovery of all the other Rudras it is a cause (indeed a divine injunction) for pleasure ("enjoy yourselves there"). If awakening from the chain of rebirths is a dominant figure of salvation, gnosis, or release—that is, of moksa—then the storyteller recognizes the duality of both injunction and pleasure: not only in moksa but in its sometime opposite, dharma, the this-worldly moral order.[8]

I linger on the in-between for what it suggests: that human value (purushartha) is not present only in the heroic, namely, the awakening, but in the everyday or economic in the sense the story admits of oikos, of garhasthya—that is, in the cohabitation of the Dream; and, second, that this cohabitation is not only a matter of order (dharma) but of gain (artha) in the sense not only of things but relations and of the enjoyment (kama) of these—in other words, this cohabitation of the dream is dharma in its most capacious sense, not only of role injunction but of the fullness of life in relation to others.

I want to frame the epistemological and ontological provocation of the text's familiar collapse of dharma and the Dream as way to conceive of an ethical scene, here the cohabitation of the everyday in the space and time of the in-between. The tale of the monk who met the people in his dream oscillates between two narratively cogent and sensorially mediated "scenes," that of awakening to one's shared Rudra-hood and that of returning to dream one's relations to others. Each in a distinct way demands of a hearer or reader an engagement wioth his or her possible non-separateness from the other, stressing either identity or relationship.

Awakening into one's Rudra-hood demands a recognition of identity across radical difference: I may conceive of myself as human and as alive and as writing these words (initially) in 2008, but I am none other than that elephant or that bee, than those who are dead, than that which is God, and than that which may be imaginary but is yet imaginable. All of us share the condition of form and—as we move from dreams to the interpretation of dreams—of name. Schopenhauer's hope was that this recognition of the collapse of all distinction into identity, far from numbing the possibility of action, anticipated the possibility of compassion and therefore of engagement. The claim would seem to be that compassion requires not a sense, to invoke Lévinas, that it is the other who suffers but rather that it is the other who is another Rudra and therefore myself who suffers. The pleasure of such an identification, as all the Rudras in the tale rejoice in their simultaneous Rudra-hood, lies in its plural condition. At stake is not just "I, Rudra, am" but "I am as you are." For dualists, such plurality may entangle pure consciousness in energy/matter. But the various non-dualisms may draw on some conception of aporia (neti neti) or, positively, of play or lila in staging this multiplicity of the One.

I think of the scene we are called upon to witness in the Padma Purana of the unworldly love, the alaukik prem, of the gods Shiva and Vishnu. The two gods appear at an ashram where the entanglement of human relations and duties has produced predictable carnage among two groups of sages all of whom die.[9] The great gods' simultaneous presence signals a different order of moral imperative. These sages may have had duties that, given their respective sectarian commitments, necessitated their suicide in the face of an unforgivable assault to their teacher or deity. The two gods offer an alternative conception of identity. Once they revive the dead, the engage in youthful horseplay with each other in a fragrant pool and then together relax as intimate friends. More so than the asymmetric relations, for example, between Lord Krishna and the adoring cowherd girls, this alaukik prem conveys, simultaneously, identity and multiplicity.

Conversely the tale suggests a second such "ethical scene," one in which we return from the unworldly demand of the scene of awakened recognition to the apparently humbler, laukik, or worldly demand of living with others. These others are not those we cannot imagine as being like ourselves. They are, rather, those with whom we have some kind of relatively proximate, relatively intimate relation: the kinsman, the beloved, the neighbor, the rival, or the enemy. Here, we are called upon to the witness the possibilities and limits of an ethical life in relation, of that combination of skill and order that the varied shastras of kama, artha, and dharma would have us undertake.

And here I think of the demands of the melodramatic social film, arguably the dominant genre of Hindi cinema. In the film I return to below, the 1985 *Saaheb,* most of the action takes place in the home of a joint or extended family. The aging father is a widower: his wife is present in several key scenes as a garlanded photograph in the central room of the house. There are four sons; the three eldest are married. Bhabhiji, the most senior of the three daughters-in-law, is different than the other two. We see her least often with her husband, as a couple, and far more often as a support for the more vulnerable members of the family: her father-in-law and her youngest and still unmarried brother-in-law, Saaheb. And there are two daughters: one married who will only appear at the end of the film, and one whose wedding expenses the old man cannot afford and for which his encoupled sons, thinking now of their own children and comforts, are reluctant to contribute. The scene where the father unsuccessfully asks each of his three older sons, whom he has settled into good jobs, to help him with the expenses of their sister's wedding (the fourth son, Saaheb, is a poor student and pins his future hopes on football [soccer] stardom) sets up a series of camera shots. We see the father with his late wife, the father with the sons, the sons alone, the sons and their wives, and the father with Bhabhiji and Saaheb. Each shot foregrounds a relation and situates, through an exchange of looks, the conflicting desires and duties at stake. Each demands of us a judgment of the skill and of the order or rule at stake.

This scene of cohabitation is not simply the family situation as dreamwork. It is not that we dream of the ethical as a situation of relation necessitating order and skill and awake to it as a situation of identity necessitating compassion. It is that we are called—here by God, by Rudra, that is, by ourselves—to dream again. To cohabit an ethical scene is to reinhabit it. Film—like the dream to which all the Rudras return—is to be enjoyed, for a time that cannot be infinite. There is loss, there is the breach, there is forgetting, and there is death. Film may offer a rehearsal of the demands of our reinhabiting the world of relations.

I have taken this detour for numerous reasons. First, I want to keep in mind this tension between (1) a scene that is ethical because I am called to recognize the other as more or less identical to me; and (2) a scene that is ethical because I am allowed to imagine the other as variously related to me, that is, as constituted through specific relations to me.

Second, there are conditions for my reading the Yogavasishtha as relevant to contemporary debates on ethics and the ethical, and vice versa. The condition I hope to foreground is that either practice—of recognizing the other as identical or of imagining the other through relationship—requires that we take note of a form that I am calling a scene. Scenes do not only matter under conditions of mass mediation. They become a way to link practices of address and public engagement that emerge with print capitalism and, subsequently, to earlier and emergent narrative forms that do not bear an obvious relation to media spectacle.

Third, I have so far avoided any explicit copula between "ethics" and "India" in this essay, allowing for the only, at times impossible, question—Is there an Indian ethics?—that haunts the colonial archive. The link between the Sanskrit text and the varieties of contemporary experience at stake in this essay is not the expansive space and duration of culture Doniger may or may not presume. Nor is it a postcolonial alternative in which the split-off pre-capitalist or premodern subject seems as unitary as in the hoariest Orientalism. The challenge is neither to read the present through the text nor the text against the present. To be responsible to the text is to cohabit the present world with it: it is to engage the text as a primer for possible argument, concepts, and forms. Doniger does this, which is what makes her readings compelling.

Fourth, the practice of anthropology argued for here would make its own claims for ethical practice precisely in those qualities of thinking—the working through detours and juxtapositions—that exile this kind of writing outside major circuits of expertise.

Transplant Ethics

I was drawn to the figure of ethical publicity more than a decade ago, when I attempted to account for the spectacular life the surgical transfer of organs had assumed ubiquitously, if differentially, across the scale of rural district, state, nation, and global network. By spectacle, in this case, I include the proliferation of rumors, scandals, and audits surrounding the image, fable, and fact of the vampire economy of poor people's organs. This work—and the primary sites of audit, scandal, and rumor I track—has shuttled between Chennai, Bangalore, and Delhi, and between these cities and multiple globally dispersed centers of media production, clinical expertise, buyer demand, and research funding.

The vast scale of the transplant industry and the transnational organization of demand and publicity produce a species of conversation marked as global and increasingly termed "bioethics." International conferences and professional associations give heft to this conversation. When, in 1998, I along with three colleagues presented our collaborative work on the ethics of contemporary transplantation at one such "global bioethics" conference in Tokyo, I met conferees not only from Europe and its settler societies but, in particular, from across Asia. A concern of some non-Europeans and Europeans in Tokyo was the need for attention to "local" ethical practices and traditions. At such moments of concern I tend to be asked, as the anthropologist in the room, to speak. Once again I betray the invitation to expertise. Most striking at the Tokyo conference was not the play between globalizing European ethics and so-called local alternatives but rather an alternative set of global frames. The most notable of these across the panels I attended was a Christian focus on the cultivation of humility and love in relation to the other. Sometimes the imitatio Christi was overt. At other times, particularly in my conversations with conference attendees from western and southern India, it drew upon a set of pedagogic and disciplinary apparatuses associated with the role of mission schools in colonial and postcolonial India. And on still other occasions it announced itself as a novel synthesis of "East and West," particularly in the single most popular event I attended, a lecture by an American then working in Japan, Daryl Macer, whose *Bioethics Is Love of Life* was ubiquitous among non-Western conferees.

In India, over the late 1990s and early 2000s, I began to attend conferences and workshops on what was often framed as "Indian bioethics." Here, too, a similar mood asserted itself, one more semiotically and affectively Christian (and arguably Protestant) even amid calls for ecumenical religious engagement. The mood was conjoined by a call to reclaim tradition. The narrative behind the framing events of such conferences betrayed a perhaps familiar account of postcolonial lack. One might summarize: "despite our great Hindu, Buddhist, Jain, Muslim, Sikh, and Christian traditions of moral engagement, we have in medicine and science embraced the value-free secularism of the West to our detriment. Paradoxically it is the West that has turned to us in search of alternatives to its own modernity. We must rediscover our traditions, very much alive in India's villages and towns. Let us pray."

Implicit was a sense that we have become less than moral, as physicians (many at such meetings were doctors) if not as a nation, and that Christian love was somehow key to the rediscovery of India. At times this narrative of loss and reclamation traveled close to forms of language and affect that circulate widely in contemporary India under the frame of a renascent Hinduism emerging out from under the yoke of Islamic oppression or decadence. In this context, that I was a Jew (I was usually taken to be a Christian, a presumption that emerged as I was asked several times to offer a reading from the Bible or a hymn) led to conferees coming up to me in the interstices of the formal events to bond over our presumed shared antipathy to Islam. Such moves are not particularly limited to ethics conferences: I note these details to give a sense of how a discipline of Christian love and the urgency of Hindu reassertion constituted bioethical situations over the first decade of the project of an Indian bioethics.

Fellow conferees were surely not wrong to suggest that specific norms and evaluative practices, material for an "Indian ethics," were to be found in villages and towns. Such a project remains attractive to many and globally circulates. I attended a conference in Hawaii, in 2008, where a Belgian graduate student utilized Hindu and Buddhist philosophical texts and religious practices (not, for what it is worth, the Yogavasishtha) to argue for a distinctive conception of the self, the good, the gift, and so forth, grounding how persons might frame the movement of organs between bodies as a problem. Here the ground for a distinctively Indic ethics is to be found not so much in the villages but in their corollary site of authentic tradition for many anthropologists of the 1950s through the 1970s: in Sanskrit and Pali texts.

I have made the point above that my problem with the adequacy of such an approach lies not in its material—surely both "ancient texts" and small-town norms and forms cannot but enrich serious conversation—but in the isomorphism by which all are expected to line up neatly and thus give us "India." Throughout my work on the transplant, I have avoided organizing my questions around the scholarly presumption of a "local" morality or virtue ethics. The alternative to the "local" for me is not the universal. Nor is it necessarily the globally dominant assemblage of neoliberal governance with all that it implies: the accompanying thematics of injury, rights, and the recognition of responsibility; the accompanying evacuation and triage of care; and the intensified mediatization that is at the center of much that I discuss. Rather, it is that I am interested in a form of collective address, participation, and spectatorship—publicness—that constitutes itself as ethical in a way that resists its assimilation to the local as a field either of practice or of code.

In other words, if to be and belong to a public is, after Warner, to recognize that one is addressed (thus the interpellative form: "Hey, Public!") and to orient oneself as the putatively unmarked mass subject of that address, I remain struck that a dominant form of address is as the mass subject of outrage or excitation in the face of particular modalities of wounding.[10] By the formation of a subject in relation to a wound I am not immediately referring, I should clarify, to contemporary forms of Nietzschean critique, as in the well-known work of scholars like Wendy Brown, Lauren Berlant, and Dawne Moon, in which what may be at stake are the limits to a politics of identification with one's own injury. I do return to the question of identification with the wound below in reference to the circulation of offense and the demand for censorship. But the subject of public address to which I refer here emerges in the first instance in relation to the wound of the other.

Kidney scandals sell papers and mobilize politicians in significant measure, I suggest, as they address a public that comes in its very address to know itself as ethical. "Ethics" here is in some sense a floating signifier: we know ourselves and our affects as ethical in the moment of address because we are addressed as such, independent of teleological calculus or deontological procedure or code. And though, as Hirschkind has demonstrated, we need to trouble the presumption of the passive subject's interpellation by demagogues or the culture industry and be attentive to disciplinary practices by which persons may cultivate "an ethically responsive sensorium," here I am interested in an ethics of address that stands outside the binary of the disciplined versus the duped subject of publicity. Ethical publicity in my conception is not ethical because it potentiates or demands that the subject of its address cultivate a particular habitus. We may, under both neoliberalism and its discontents, be steeped in *Bildung,* but I ask that one imagines a becoming-ethical that does not presume an askesis but rather that is the base condition of publicness and publicity.

To the extent that persons come to know themselves as ethical subjects as and through public address, what questions might organize meta-ethical engagement?

The Audit and Spectacle of Rights

The first "way in" might look more carefully at audit. Audits, in the emerging anthropological literature, invoke a public, for this literature, in at least two ways. First the audit, Cris Shore and Susan Wright argue, is a "visible instrument of political rule." The audit would establish a relation of trust between a government and its public by enunciating a common distrust of various institutions and demanding a public hearing as the condition for the restoration of trust. The public, in this sense, in being addressed by the audit, is asked to locate ethics as a form of accounting distinct from political action. Trust and distrust comprise the affective terrain, and one cannot really speak of an ethical public as much as of a public schooled in the demand for ethics as a managerial technique to be given by the state. As this gift is "visible" or (literally) "audible," ethics is as much a performance or ritual as a technique of trust.

However, Shore and Wright also describe the audit as "a public inspection"; here one gets the sense of a public identifying with and acting as the auditor in the consumption of such transacted ethical scenes. Such a public is ethical to the extent it is committed to the neoliberal state's collapse of ethics and audit, and to the extent that it accedes to its address not only as the beneficiary of audit but as the auditing public itself. Here the actuarial and the spectacular collapse into a form of ethical publicity.[11]

Pels in my reading seems to posit the audit as a globally distributed emergent form. But the relation between accountancy and spectacle and the moment of their collapse cannot be easily generalized: ethical publicity confronts a recurring hermeneutic of absence in the Indian postcolony. By way of contemporary example, N. Arumugam, a cardiologist and the Malaysian Tamil president of the World Medical Association, gave a press conference in Chennai in 2007. The Hindu newspaper reported on his appeal, offered to both organized medicine and the government of India:

> Doctors must not indulge in unethical practices. This is the mandate of the World Medical Association, which was constituted after the Second World War during which flagrant violations of ethics were common. . . . Our main role is to lobby with governments and nations about the necessity of ethics.

Ethics, for the World Medical Association, are to be understood as a distributive problem. The newspaper summarized the doctor's reasons for coming to India: "the position in developing nations is far worse than in developed countries where [Arumugam] noticed that rules and regulations are implemented strictly."[12]

If this distributive account of ethical difference appears overdetermined as a postcolonial rhetorical form, we might note that the reporter picks up on the scopic quality of ethical audit: Arumugam as Association president travels around the globe where he "notices" ethics as two distinct and totalizing scenes mapped onto the nation, on the one hand a scene of rule-implementation and, on the other, what we might in contrast term a "scene of rule-exception." If the president's travels comprise a species of second-order audit, to paraphrase Nikolas Luhmann—that is, the World Medical Association auditing the presence or absence of effective audit practices in the promotion of worldwide medical accountability—the judgment of audit is restricted to national-bureaucratic milieus assessed independently from one another. Thus, though two staples of media and expert attention to problems of medical accountability—the so-called traffic in organs and, increasingly, the conduct of clinical drugs trials—usually involve asymmetric relations of supplementarity between regions and nations graded along axes of wealth, the scopic form of the second-order audit restricts the problem to the rule-exceptional environment of the poorer partner.

Arumugam's appearance in Chennai comes just after the latest south Indian kidney scandal: the so-called racket in Tsunami Nagar, the suburban Madras village of Eranavoor, "exposed" by police this past January. But for the details of the tsunami, the story is a familiar one: these scandals cycle. A neighborhood loses its dominant form of male labor, in this case fishing, when the boats are destroyed. The result is that income declines and men's absenteeism and drinking increase. Recruitment is of women for the most part and follows one of two scenarios: either an entrepreneurial nephrologist sends one of his agents, a former kidney seller for whom the money has run out, to follow up a local kin connection in the village, or one of the villagers follows up with a relation elsewhere, in one of the many kidney vakkams (or kidney slums) now dotting the urban area. Donors receive about forty to forty-five thousand rupees, the equivalent of about a thousand dollars in either of the two North American currencies. The money disappears quickly: donors cite fees to brokers, preexisting debts, and the demands of husbands. Moreover, donors repeatedly claim that they are no longer fit for labor. In the words of a thirty-year-old women named Thilakavathy, according to several newspapers and wire services, "I used to earn some money selling fish, but now [after the surgery] stomach cramps prevent me from going to work."[13]

The Tsunami Nagar women all attended a particular clinic, allegedly staffed by one of the most famous physicians worldwide arguing for a regulated market in kidneys. The forensic, journalistic, and academic response tends to follow the police to the slum, soliciting narratives along three themes: (1) contingency and necessity: the factory closure, the tsunami, and the collapse of cotton prices deprived us of income, and thus we had no choice; (2) standardization: we received forty to fifty thousand rupees, the expected amount; and (3) failure: family, money-lender, husband, and fate ate the money, and now I cannot even work as I did before.

Experts on transplant ethics now abound: we staff blue-ribbon panels, speak weekly to globally distributed media, and exhort governments. Major experts become a routine feature of any entrepreneurial clinical landscape under privatization, such as the high-profit maximization of transplant supplementarity. Their ongoing presence leads the state, here the government of Tamil

Nadu as well as the central government, to set up committees of audit to regulate medicine; as these authorization committees are quickly suborned by the transplant industry, they become second-order auditors but in an extra-governmental position.

We might term this position that of the "ethical audit." Though the phrase threatens redundancy to the extent that auditing and ethics collapse, as Pels and collaborators can be taken to argue, I refer by it to a species of accountability review found most intensively in universities and rights-based NGOs. Such an audit takes as its currency violation, as its method publicity, and as its object professional or governmental institutions to which it has no formal relation or responsibility. The resulting publicity of violation renders different institutional forms and problems commensurable; the sustainability of institutions of ethical audit depends on their ability to secure a steady flow of such violation. Both these effects, of commensuration and institutional security, offer incentives for entrepreneurship: we need to speak not only of ethical auditors but of ethical entrepreneurs or brokers.

The tsunami enters into the public narrative of contingency and necessity in what may mark a shift. Some residents of Chennai fishing villages as well as inland slums had turned to the fungibility of organs long before the tsunami. But under the assemblage, emergent in the 1980s and 1990s, of immune suppression technology, privatization of medicine and economic liberalization, factory closures, and the emergence of recruitment networks, the publicity of the event and of the political promises that gathered in its wake allowed for the mobilization of a far broader second-order audit: not only the clinics and medical associations in question, not only the authorization committees, but also the assembled members of the Legislative Assembly, party presidents, the chief minister, and the prime minister, all of whom visited the village and promised restitution. The story—Indian tsunami victims sell their kidneys to survive—quickly went global, its ironic trope confirming the ethical maldistribution that the World Medical Council had noticed, and in its consumption allowing for the ethical scene of contemporary cosmopolitanism: I participate in your wound. The scale of the ethical public—the imaginable global ecumene participating in the failure of the Indian state and shaming the nation—constituted a palpable political risk. The degree of publicity, and of shame and risk, was such that nephrologists were able to promote an argument they had been long made but that had heretofore failed to engender its own ethical public: that the state would never succeed at regulating the trade because the need both of patients and the poor was too great, and that an ethical response to the tsunami audit involved recognizing this persistent failure and regulating rather than banning the market. At this juncture it remains an open question as to what kind of public will solidify around this argument of the persistent failure of audit.

The Other's Wound Is Mine

In much of the world, participation in the ethical public of the second-order transplant audit involves not just the participation in the other's wound but also the imaginative identification of one's own partial lack of a horizon with that wound. I came to this project initially because of conversations with friends in Banaras who began, in the early 1990s, to speak of selling a kidney to address their inability to properly care for their children or settle their siblings. There were many sources for this wish—and I call it a "wish," for unlike the mostly women in Chennai with whom I have been working, none of these mostly men were actually planning to sell—but two sources were primary: (1) reading or discussing news stories of "kidney rackets" elsewhere in the country; and (2) the 1985 Hindi film *Saaheb,* mentioned above, in which, after his older sons fail him, the elderly father and his youngest son, Saaheb, try to sell a kidney to arrange for the marriage of their respective daughter and sister. Saaheb succeeds, sacrificing his future career as a football star by having the operation. That the operation is a sacrifice is underscored by the repeated match cuts in the film, the scene shifting back and forth between the sacrificial oblations dripping into the fire during the sister's wedding and Saaheb's blood dripping within the transfusion apparatus during his simultaneous operation.

Participation in the wound of the other, in these cases, did not involve a discourse of rights, the formation of oneself as ethical subject in relation to the other's suffering in the absence of rights, as how for example many North Americans may orient themselves to the public address of the transplant scandal, to wit: I am that ethical being who participates in outrage or concern in the face of the image of these ghastly events. The friends I speak of were aware from both news coverage and popular culture that the transplant sale carried a double violence—money that would not last and a body whose future would be curtailed. But acceding to public address, participation in the scene of this violence allowed, precisely in the distance between that body and one's own, the formation of a wish—maybe I will sell my kidney—and the imaginative restitution of a lost biomorality for these men: I can care for my children; I can settle my sisters and brothers.

Here the distinction I draw from my reading of the tale of the monk may be helpful. The ethical scene here is not primarily that of the wounding of the Chennai slum seller witnessed on television or of the football player in the film Saaheb, each an enactment of the human with which the wound's public can identify and in so identifying discover their own humanity. The ethical scene is that of the failure of a moral form (the extended family in Westernized modernity) and its distributed burden: on Saaheb's unmarried sister; on his father, confronted by failure; on his sister-in-law Bhabhiji, unable to translate her virtue into a solution; and on the football player, Saaheb himself, unable to get a job without the help of his family. The scene the film reveals is that of the wounding of a relational form within which its public is encouraged to locate him or herself: what it rehearses is the possibility of one's sacrificial commitment, restoring these to a proper ethical form.

I am not arguing for an inevitable binary in how publics are constituted between the two cities where my conversations on wounding took place: San Francisco versus Banaras. Many conversations I had in Banaras over media reports of "kidney scandals" in which persons were allegedly duped into giving up an organ involved a sense of identification through a figure I would call the human. But the human was not the only, nor necessarily the primary, form in which scenes of the other's wound were encountered. If a Banaras acquaintance rehearses the possibility of his selling his own kidney, he is participating in the ubiquitous scene of the poor selling their kidneys in a particular way. This participation is not that of awakening to the harsh reality that kidneys are being sold (or, conversely, the harsh reality that people are dying on waiting lists while kidneys are "wasted") and identifying with the suffering of another in a way that generates recognition of one's moral outrage. Rather, the participation is that of the mingled pleasure and pain of a continual return to a form of relationship in which outrages happen (such as the sons and daughters-in-law refusing to help their sister to get married, leading decent fathers and sons to try to sell their organs). If one is drawn to the publicity of the other's suffering here, it is not only under the sign of enlightenment or moksha—an awakening to the shock of the suffering other through which one recognizes one's own human capacity to act—but under the sign of relationship or of dharma, as a reimmersion in the forms through which persons relate to one another and a discovery of the capacity for sacrifice within and for the sake of these forms.

The Sovereign Gift of Censorship

These modes of ethical publicity—identification and relationship—are not exclusive to one another. I turn to my final example.

We are accustomed to thinking of the escalating banning of books deemed offensive to particular "communities," in India as perhaps elsewhere, in terms of state recognition of the wound to the community's own body, its moral fabric, and its self-respect, within a sociology of vote banks or a technical rationality of security. Community in this context usually implies Hindus, Muslims, Sikhs, or Christians, though it can also refer to different caste groups or sectarian identities. From Salman Rushdie's novel *The Satanic Verses* to the Hollywood film *The Da Vinci Code,* numerous works deemed offensive by the courts to the sentiments of these various communities have been withdrawn from the Indian market. To presume that the bloc in power censors to cultivate a vote bank is an accusation of bad faith. To presume that censorship is a necessary biopolitical maneuver to safeguard populations against predictable riots reflects a more ambivalent or even positive account of the state as moral actor.

Censorship, I contend, is both a condition of and response to the identity of ethics and publicity in the time of the scene of audit, through which a government establishes itself as an ethical participant in the wounding of the other. I am not offering a totalizing sociology of censorship or of offense here but trying to frame a question about the state as itself an ethical subject of public address.

By now a commonplace is the idea that such censorship presumes a divided population: the easily inflamed "masses" and the more deliberative elite. Media, to serve its presumed double role of governing and controlling masses and providing necessary information to the elite, must provide content that conveys what is understood as the actual event enabling the elite to make an effective assessment and response while doing so in a coded language that avoids inflaming the masses further. In reporting events that become axiomatically available as communal riots, to use the most prominent example, media may report on actions precipitated by communities without specifying whether these are Muslim, Hindu, or Sikh. The exclusion of the name of the community does not presume that mass readers will therefore not learn whether a Hindu, Muslim, or Sikh individual or group was associated with what is marked as the initial violent or defamatory gesture: it presumes, rather, that counterviolence can and must be contained through this exclusion, by not legitimating the widely circulating rumors naming the offensive community.

From the time of the Rushdie affair and increasing during the subsequent decades, the relation of the figure of "the community" to censorship moves beyond the question of inflammatory reportage and elite control of mass affect. At stake is the existence of an utterance or gesture—within a scholarly or artistic work or as performed by a given individual—that wounds what is described as the sentiments of a community. Examples of claims of communal wounding have become a dominant feature of the political and cultural landscape. Wounding agents are legion and include

Salman Rushdie in the novel *The Satanic Verses* wounding Muslim sentiment
Deepa Mehta in the film *Fire* wounding Hindu sentiment
Deepa Mehta in the film *Water* wounding Hindu sentiment
James Laine in the scholarly work *Shivaji* wounding Maratha sentiment
the film *The Da Vinci Code* wounding Christian sentiment
the film *Dasavatharam* wounding Vaishnava sentiment

the film *Aaja Nachle* wounding Dalit sentiment
the film *Jodha Akbar* wounding Rajput sentiment
the painter M. F. Husain wounding Hindu sentiment
the actress Manisha Koirala wounding Muslim sentiment
the actress Mallika Sherawat wounding Hindu sentiment
the actress Shreya Saran wounding Hindu sentiment
the religious leader Gurmit Ram Rahim wounding Sikh sentiment
the legal scholar R. K. Bais wounding Marwari sentiment
the state government of Haryana wounding Jat sentiment
the state government of Haryana wounding Sikh sentiment
the actor Aamir Khan wounding Gujarati sentiment
the actor Rajnikanth wounding Kannadiga sentiment
the actor Shah Rukh Khan wounding both Hindu and Muslim sentiment
the Bombay restaurant *Hitler's Cross* wounding Jewish sentiment
the novelist Tasleema Nasreen wounding Muslim sentiment
the newspaper *Mumbai Mirror Buzz* wounding Muslim sentiment
the columnist Soli Sorabjee wounding Jain sentiment
the newspaper *Makkal Osai* wounding Christian sentiment

And many hundreds of other recent examples exist. What merits attention is not only that these are claims for the collective experience of one's own wound. The critical subject participating in the consumption of these scenes is neither the wounded community nor its other but the agency of the state itself. Both the demand for censorship by spokespersons for a community and the state's preemptive censoring of an utterance to limit such offense presume that the state is the ethical subject witnessing the scene of the community's wounding and responding through the gift of censorship.

Obviously discussions of offense as a contemporary problem are not limited to India. But the contemporary Indian state has been particularly prominent as a subject of ethical publicity. Its acts of censorship often preempt the formation of an offended public, as in the case of Rushdie. In other words, the state establishes itself as experiencing the hurt of the community, here Islam, before a mass subject of offense could emerge. That the state in the moment of ethical address stands in relation to an other is, I think, critical here and is important in making sense of those moments when government can, and cannot, imagine the Hindu as wounded. I am using state and government interchangeably here, as in a given instance it is not always clear in a given instance whether the bureaucratic apparatus or ruling party, the court or the secretariat, constitutes the ethical subject of a censorship.

The constitution of the government as ethical raises the question of the gift and the sovereign relation that a particular mode of exchange may demand.

The state may participate in the wound of the other preemptively, but just as often the aggrieved public will in the moment of its emergence make an appeal to the state. The state both preserves order and recognizes communities within such a landscape of interpellation by widely and ecumenically distributing the act of censorship. We might frame this distribution as a gift that maintains or renews the state's sovereign position as the dispenser of life-affirming value that, in the language of Gloria Raheja and McKim Marriott, constitutes its centrality.[14] The state affirms the promise of the universal capacity of the nation to protect all its citizens by granting to each community the recognition of offense through censorship as a sovereign gift. Censorship renders sovereignty ethical. This is a biomoral engagement, in Marriott's post-Schneiderian terminology: the modern state achieves ethical sovereignty in participating in the wound of the other. This participation constitutes the state as central in that it encompasses all potentially wounded communities, linked through their common participation in a kind of revolving traumatology.

The community thus belongs to the nation to the extent that it can claim the protection of a sovereign state that recognizes it as an entity wounded by a past or future insult. Sovereignty in turn is the capacity to engage the wound of the set of all others that can be constituted as belonging. The question remains whether such engagement might be characterized in terms of either identification or relationship.

One might note elements of both modes of participation in the ethical scene. As in the case of identification, state censorship involves the identity of the wounded community with another. But this identity is not with the state itself—the binary of the elite state's reason versus the mass population's affect haunts censorship still—but with the set of all other communities that can be taken to constitute the nation. As in the case of relationship, censorship allows for the reinhabitation of a moral order of relations, here a just and skillful transactional polity with the state at its center as a donor to all legitimate parties.

Toward an Ethics of Waking and Sleep

It has been my claim in this essay that the capacity for recognizing the wound of the other may constitute and be constituted by myriad practices and material conditions of public address in which one variously comes to find oneself within an ethical scene, whether one is sovereign or merely subject. The effects and intensities of such recognition are various. Ethical scenes are not the only or necessarily the primary vehicle by which persons engage or remake the world. But imagining and tracking the efforts of persons to comprehend situations and to struggle to be adequate to them might do well to consider the range of such scenes in which they find themselves enjoined to feel or to act.

I have used a distinction between waking to truth and an imperative to act versus returning to the demands and imperatives of a dreamworld as a means to differentiate kinds of scenes and their distribution in relation to culture and history. In closing, I would use the distinction in a different way. Attention in anthropology and other fields to the challenge of self-formation may open us in more careful ways to practices of awakening to situations. But there is more to sleep then the "not yet" of the ethical. I offer the conception of an ethical scene as a way to think about life and human potential in relation to the other pole of what Rudra demands of us, of our ethical lives as (also) a necessary and continual reinhabitation of the dreamworld: and thus of the ethical scene in all of its mediate and in many cases foreclosed possibility as nonetheless the stuff of our dreams and the material for any new stories.

Acknowledgments

Thanks to Daud Ali, Anand Pandian, and the University of British Columbia for the invitation to think about the ethical in a different way, and to Anand for the gift of his own reflection over many years; to all conference attendees and guests for their comments; to Veena Das for her rigorous work on the question of reinhabiting the world; to the South Asia seminar at the University of Pennsylvania and, in particular, to Lisa Mitchell; and to my colleagues and students at Berkeley and, in particular, Katherine Lemons and Alex Belieav.

Notes

1. For these discussions and others see Marilyn Strathern, ed., *Audit Cultures: Anthropological Studies in Accountability, Ethics, and the Academy* (New York: Routledge, 2000).

2. Walter Lippman, *Public Opinion* (New York: Harcourt, Brace, and Co., 1922).

3. Charles Hirschkind, "The Ethics of Listening: Cassette-sermon Audition in Contemporary Egypt," *American Ethnologist* 28 (2001): 623–649.

4. I do not make a sharp distinction in this essay between the moral and the ethical. The distinction is not made by many persons with whom I have been in conversation, it does not easily translate into the distinctions of other languages, and it at times forecloses an openness to what any such language may index. On a public is an entity that comes into being through an acknowledgment of its being addressed, see Michael Warner, *Publics and Counterpublics* (New York: Zone, 2002).

5. Wendy Doniger, *Dreams, Illusions, and Other Realities* (Chicago: University of Chicago Press, 1984), 127–259. See also Doniger, *The Hindus: An Alternative History* (New York: Penguin, 2009), 518–519.

6. Doniger, *Dreams, Illusions, and Other Realities,* 206–209.

7. See Paul Hacker, *Philology and Confrontation: Paul Hacker on Traditional and Modern Vedanta,* ed. William Halbfass (Albany: State University of New York Press, 1995), 273–336 and Albert Schweitzer, *Indian Thought and Its Development* (New York: Henry Holt, 1936).

8. The literature on "dharma versus moksa" is voluminous to the point of cliché: a familiar way in might start with J. A. B. van Buitenen, "Dharma and Moksa," *Philosophy East and West* 7 (1957): 33–40;, and D. A. Ingalls, "Dharma and Moksa," *Philosophy East and West* 7 (1957): 41–48.

9. The version of the text I have read is the Hindi translation and abridgment in the Hindu devotional publication Kalyan, produced in Gorakhpur and available in Banaras and its hinterland.

10. Warner, *Publics and Counterpublics,* p. 89.

11. Peter Pels, "Ethics and the Technologies of the Anthropological Self" and Cris Shore and Susan Wright, "Coercive Accountability: The Rise of Audit Culture in Higher Education," both in *Audit Cultures: Anthropological Studies in Accountability, Ethics, and the Academy;* and Nikolas Rose, *Powers of Freedom: Reframing Political Thought* (Cambridge: Cambridge University Press, 1999).

12. Ramya Kannan, "Medical Professionals Must Not Indulge in Unethical Practices." *Hindu* (September 2, 2007), downloaded from http://www.thehindu.com/2007/09/02/stories/2007090260560900.htm on February 9, 2010.

13. R. Bhagwan Singh, "Indian Police Probe Kidney Sales by Tsunami Victims." *Reuters* (January 16, 2007), U.S. edition, downloaded from http://www.reuters.com/article/idUSDEL21432720070116 on February 9, 2010.

14. See Gloria Raheja, "Centrality, Mutuality, and Hierarchy: Shifting Aspects of Inter-Caste Relationships in North India," in *India through Hindu Categories,* ed. McKim Marriott (Delhi: Sage, 1990).

Contributors

Daud Ali is Associate Professor and Chair of South Asia Studies, University of Pennsylvania. He is author of *Courtly Culture and Political Life in Early Medieval India,* co-author of *Querying the Medieval: Texts and the History of Practice in South Asia,* and editor of *Invoking the Past: The Uses of History in South Asia.*

Bernard Bate is Associate Professor of Anthropology, Yale University. He is author of *Tamil Oratory and the Dravdian Aesthetic: Democratic Practice in South India.*

Ritu Birla is Associate Professor of History, University of Toronto. She is author of *Stages of Capital: Law, Culture, and Market Governance in Late Colonial India.*

Dipesh Chakrabarty is Lawrence A. Kimpton Distinguished Service Professor in History, South Asian Languages and Civilizations, and the College, University of Chicago. His authored books include *Rethinking Working-Class History: Bengal 1890–1940; Provincializing Europe: Postcolonial Thought and Historical Difference;* and *Habitations of Modernity: Essays in the Wake of Subaltern Studies.* His co-edited books include *From the Colonial to the Postcolonial: India and Pakistan in Transition; Cosmopolitanism;* and *Subaltern Studies IX.*

Lawrence Cohen is Professor of Anthropology and of South and Southeast Asian Studies at the University of California, Berkeley. He is author of *No Aging in India: Alzheimer's, the Bad Family, and Other Modern Things* and editor (with Annette Leibing) of *Thinking about Dementia: Culture, Loss, and the Anthropology of Senility.*

Veena Das is Krieger-Eisenhower Professor of Anthropology, Johns Hopkins University. Her authored books include *Life and Words: Violence and the Descent into the Ordinary* and *Critical Events: An Anthropological Perspective on Contemporary India.* Her edited and co-edited books include *Mirrors of Violence: Communities, Riots, and Survivors in South Asia; Social Suffering;* and *Violence and Subjectivity.*

Emma Flatt is Assistant Professor of History, Nanyang Technological University. She is co-editor of the forthcoming *Fragrance, Symmetry, and Light: Gardens and Garden Culture in the Medieval Deccan.*

Charles Hallisey is Senior Lecturer on Buddhist Studies in the Faculty of Divinity, Harvard University. He is author of the forthcoming *Flowers on the Tree of Poetry: The Moral Economy of Literature in Buddhist Sri Lanka.*

Craig Jeffrey is University Lecturer of Geography, University of Oxford, and Fellow of St. John's College, Oxford. He is author of *Timepass: Waiting, Micropolitics, and the Indian Middle Classes;* co-author of *Degrees Without Freedom? Education, Masculinities, and Unemployment in North India;* and co-editor of *Telling Young Lives: Portraits in Global Youth.*

James Laidlaw is University Lecturer of Social Anthropology, University of Cambridge, and Fellow of King's College, Cambridge. His authored, co-authored, and co-edited books include *Religion, Anthropology, and Cognitive Science; Ritual and Memory: Toward a Comparative Anthropology of Religion; The Essential Edmund Leach* (2 vols.); *Riches and Renunciation: Religion, Economy, and Society among the Jains;* and *The Archetypal Actions of Ritual.*

Anand Pandian is Assistant Professor of Anthropology, Johns Hopkins University. He is author of *Crooked Stalks: Cultivating Virtue in South India* and co-editor of *Race, Nature, and the Politics of Difference.*

Leela Prasad is Associate Professor of Ethics and Indian Religions, Duke University. She is author of *Poetics of Conduct: Narrative and Moral Being in a South Indian Town;* editor of *Live Like the Banyan Tree: Images of the Indian American Experience;* and co-editor of *Gender and Story in South India.*

Bhavani Raman is Assistant Professor of History, Princeton University. She is author of the forthcoming *Document Raj: Scribes and Writing in Company Rule Madras, 1780–1860.*

Ajay Skaria is Associate Professor of History, University of Minnesota. He is author of *Hybrid Histories: Forests, Frontiers, and Wilderness in Western India* and the forthcoming *Immeasurable Equality: Democracy, Religion, and Gandhi's Politics,* and co-editor of *Subaltern Studies XII.*

Index

Aquinas, 65–66
*aṟam (*also *aṟam),* 9, 43–45, 47, 52, 54, 56
Aristotle, 4, 66, 146, 155
artha, 8, 102, 105, 259–260. *See also trivarga*
Arthaśastra, 27–28
Arya Samaj, 236
Asad, Talal, 5–6, 58n10, 65
ashur k̲h̲āna 169n1
aṭi (lines), 53
atikāram (power), 45
Ātticuṭi (ethical poem), 11, 44–45, 47, 51, 53–55, 60. *See also* Auvaiyār
audārya (magnanimity), 24
Aulia, Nizamuddin, 241, 245
Auvaiyār (Tamil poet): 43–44, 46–47, 49, 51, 54–57; *Mūturai,* 49, 53, 55–57
ayat (verse), 233
Azad, Maulana Abdul Kalam, 130

Baba Farid (poet-saint), 246
Babri Mosque, 234
Bahmani Kingdom: 11, 153–154, 161–162, 164, 169, 171n40
Bahujan Samaj Party, 196–197, 201. *See also* Dalits; Uttar Pradesh
baiṭhak (squats), 158
Bāṇa (poet), 27–28
Banaras, 11, 268–269
Banerjee, Sumanta, 115n20
Banks, Marcus, 78n2
Barani, Zia al-Din, 168
The Bazaar Book or Vernacular Preacher's Companion, 102–105, 107–108, 110, 113
Bellary, 48
Bengal Renaissance, 258
Benjamin, Walter, 133
Berlant, Lauren, 262
Berlin, Sir Isaiah, 119
Bhagavad Gita (also *Gīta*), 83, 182, 216–217, 220
Bhandarkar, Sir R.G., 125, 127
Bhartṛhari, 25, 27, 31
Bharatiya Janata Party, 195
Bhavishya Purana, 238–239
Bhishma Parva, 221, 223, 225, 227
Bhojaprabandha, 29, 36. *See also* anthology and *subhāṣita*
bhrashtāchār (corruption), 192, 203
Bidar, capital of Bahmani Kingdom, 153–154, 161, 164, 166
bid'at (heresy), 167–168
Bijapur, 161–162, 164–165
birādarīyat (brotherhood), 157
Blackburn, Stuart, 114n13
Bloch, Mark, 117–122, 124, 132–133
bolnīwalī bāten ("spoken performances"), 203
Bombay: High Court, 94; Legislative Council, 126; Native Piece-Goods Merchant's Association, 88. *See also* colonial India
Bourdieu, Pierre, 193–194, 201, 206
brahmacharya (celibacy), 215, 218–220, 226. *See also* Gandhi
Brahmin: and *dharma,* 11; households, 12; sacred cord and Vedas 108–109
brahmodya (disputational assembly), 23
Bṛhaspati (sage), 38n6
Britain: British army, 211; British colonial bureaucracy, 129–130; British empire as a universal political institution, 132; English legal tradition, 65; imperial trade routes, 62; Jain organizations in, 64; loyalty to British empire, 124–125; principle of *mortmain,* 94; satyagraha against British rule, 220; United Kingdom, 63
Brown, Wendy, 264
Bryson, Anna, 17n19
buddhi (will or disposition), 10
Buddha: Buddhahood of, 146; insights of, 146–147; previous lives of, 146
Buddhaghosa, 145
Buddhism: Buddhist courtly gāthās, 23, 31; Buddhist monastery, 22–23; ethics and teachings, 23, 143, 145–147; *Jataka* stories, 146–147, 149
Burkhardt, Jacob, 116
burqa, 241

Cairo, 5, 255
Cambridge History of India, 129

Indian History Congress, 124, 129
Indian Income Tax Act, 91
Indology, 125. *See also* Bhandarkar
Iliad, 118
Iran, 153–159, 161–162
Islamic: *adab,* 45, mysticism, 155, religious warrior, 156

Jacobsen, Knut A., 79n7
jahil (ignorant), 237
Jaffna Peninsula, 44, 101, 104, 109
Jain: animal liberation, 64; asceticism 68–69; compassion (*karuna*), 72; "Declaration of Nature," 63, 73–74; "Eco-Jainism," 66, 69; environmentalism, 64; lay Jains, 61–64, 74, 77; Mahavira, 70–71; non-attachment (*aparigraha*), 61, 77; nonviolence (*ahimsa*), 61, 77; population, 61; quasi renouncers (*samanis*), 63; renouncers, 61–64, 66, 72, 75, 77–78; "Right View" (*samyak darshan*), 68, 72; Svetambar Terapanth, 63; *Thirukkural,* 103–106, 108–112; *tirthankars,* 70; university, 64; Ur-ecology, 64; *vairagya,* 69; vegetarianism, 64; Young Jains, 64
Jamait-e-Islami, 237
James, William, 117
jang-i ḵẖana (domestic quarrels), 167
Jats: *jugār,* 204–206; notions of masculinity, 197, 204; population in Uttar Pradesh, 195; student leaders and politics in Meerut, 200–206. *See also* caste; Dalits; and Uttar Pradesh
Jatakas, 146–147, 149
jati, 48. *See also* caste
javānmard (young man), 157, 170n12
javānmardī (young manliness): 11, 153–169, 170n12, 171nn39,40; *futūwat,* 156–168, 170nn11,15,16,18,19, 171n40, 172n42
Jesus Christ, 109–110
jihad, 157, 220, 236
jinns, 237
jīvan kā khel (game of life), 202
jugār, 11, 204–205
Junagarh, 28

Kabir, 246
kafir (nonbeliever), 233, 243
Kahler, Erich von, 122
kaliyuga (also *kaljug*), 236, 238, 241–242
kālo'tivartate (passing of time), 28
kalvi (learning), 108
Kāmandaki, 39n25
Kandapuranam, 101, 110
kanyadan, 244
karanam literature, 9
kama (also *kāma*) 8, 102, 105, 259–260
Kāmasūtra (also *kamasutra*), 27–28, 105
Kant, Immanuel, 3–4, 86
Kapiñjala, 29
kaṟṟ (learning), 50
Karunanidhi, Mu., 113
Kashani, 'Abd al-Razzaq, 159
Kashifi, Husain Va'iz, 159, 162–164, 166
kathā (story): literature, 31, 33, 36
kāṭu (uncultivated waste or forest), 59nn16, 21
kavigoṣṭhīs, 29. *See also goṣṭhīs*
kāvya (poetry), 23, 28
kayamat (Judgment Day), 242
Keane, Webb, 17n20
Keladi kingdom, 175
khalq (nature), 160
ḵẖānaqa (Sufi hospices), 157
khel (game), 202
khelhāri (players), 202
khutbas (sermons), 237
Kierkegaard, Søren Aabye, 233
Klokke, Marijke J., 41
Knox, T.H., 120
Ko ṟaivēynta, 43–44, 51–53
kotwāl (magistrate), 165
Krishna (Hindu God), 225, 246, 260
Kṣemendra, 30, 34
kshatriya (also ksatriya), 11, 223
kufr (disbelief), 237, 244, 246
kuṇam (character), 55
kushtī-gīr (wrestler), 159
Kusumadeva, 31

Laidlaw, James, 17n24, 18n34
lakṣaṇas (attributes), 26
Larson, Gerald, 17n25